Regulating Religion

REGULATING RELIGION

The Courts and the Free Exercise Clause

Catharine Cookson

OXFORD
UNIVERSITY PRESS

2001

OXFORD
UNIVERSITY PRESS

Oxford   New York
Athens   Auckland   Bangkok   Bogotá   Buenos Aires   Calcutta
Cape Town   Chennai   Dar es Salaam   Delhi   Florence   Hong Kong   Istanbul
Karachi   Kuala Lumpur   Madrid   Melbourne   Mexico City   Mumbai
Nairobi   Paris   São Paulo   Shanghai   Singapore   Taipei   Tokyo   Toronto   Warsaw

and associated companies in
Berlin   Ibadan

Published by Oxford University Press, Inc.,
198 Madison Avenue, New York, New York 10016

Oxford is a registered trademark of Oxford University Press.

Library of Congress Cataloging-in-Publication Data
Cookson, Catharine.
Regulating religion : the courts and the free exercise clause / Catharine Cookson, 1952–
    p.   cm.
Includes index.
ISBN 0-19-512944-X
1. Freedom of religion—United States.   2. Church and state—United States.
3. Religion and politics—United States.   4. Casuistry.   I. Title.
KF4783 .C665 2000
342.73′0852—dc21   00-024873

9 8 7 6 5 4 3 2 1

Printed in the United States of America
on acid-free paper

Preface

I suppose that every author writes with a conversation partner in mind. Rather than leave the reader guessing, I will "come clean" at the outset. My theoretical sparring partners throughout this project on the free exercise clause are three-fold: anarchy, authoritarianism, and emotivism. Anarchy is the tyranny of individuals. It is a distorted view of liberty which denies that the individual for whom freedom is a birthright concomitantly owes a debt of loyalty and responsibility to society, including the responsibility to obey laws with which one disagrees. Authoritarianism is anarchy's opposite: It is a tyranny of principles. Individual rights are overshadowed by the individual's primary duty to obey. Authoritarianism is characterized by a paranoid and disproportionate fear of and overreaction to anarchy. Emotivism is the authoritarian rule of "facts" and "data," the "hard" evidence of measurable outcomes such as productivity and efficiency. Such "hard" evidence is considered the only reliable measure of good/bad. Choices premised upon "soft" considerations such as values and rights, morals and conscience, are unjusticiable because these are all matters of individual taste.

Anarchy is evinced all too regularly in the news reports of late. Militia movements deny the authority of any government but their own self-government.[1] Claims of free speech and free exercise of religion are made as though these individual rights are absolute and must always trump any other competing interest of community welfare.[2] A group called the Fully-Informed Juror's Association (FIJA) campaigns to inform jurors that they do not have to follow the courts' instructions on the law and that they do not have to accept that the law is what the judge tells them it is. FIJA has the backing of folks on the left (spurred by the War on Drugs) as well as on the right (motivated by antigun laws, pro-choice rulings, and tax laws).[3] Accordingly, I do not take the threat of anarchy lightly; however I also refuse to call every principled exception to a rule "anarchical."

An *unthinking* rigorism leads to unprincipled disorder. A rise in authoritarian rigor can trigger a concomitant rise in radical individualistic, anarchical movements. More frequently, laws are being mechanically and unthinkingly applied to situations in which such application defies equity and fairness (e.g., prosecutions for the use of marijuana to alleviate the side effects of chemotherapy). Laws now take away a judge's discretion in sentencing, resulting in harsh penalties despite mitigating circumstances. Such rigorism does not increase respect for law; rather it "will bring the whole authority of law into question, and shaken [*sic*] it to the foundation."[4]

A philosophy of emotivism is often behind judicial proclamations of inability to achieve equity in the unusual, atypical situation. Judges defer slavishly to the democratic political process which produces a law, professing an inability to choose meaningfully between competing values even when faced with a situation which may not fit the paradigm the law at issue was meant to address. This claim of "institutional incompetence" mirrors the emotivist's project. As Alasdair MacIntyre in *After Virtue* notes, at the heart of emotivism is the belief that all discourse on values and principles is premised simply upon personal preference and mere opinion:

> Questions of ends are questions of values, and on values reason is silent; conflict between rival values cannot be rationally settled. Instead, one must simply choose—between parties, classes, nations, causes, ideals. . . . [T]he choice of any one evaluative stance or commitment can be no more rational than that of any other. All faiths and all evaluations are equally non-rational; all are subjective directions given to sentiment and feeling.[5]

"Facts" are deemed to have an objective basis, but "value" judgments do not because they are considered merely subjective. Anyone can pronounce a moral viewpoint, for such judgments are without criteria; they merely depend upon the individual's whim or choice. Managers and experts, in contrast, are perceived to be dealing with specialized facts; their pronouncements and their solutions to disagreements are seen as resting upon their superior objective knowledge and skill.[6] Similarly, laws are deemed objectively neutral and the legislators are imbued with objective expertise because they have the legitimacy of the electorate. The "hard facts" in this instance are the numbers which elected the legislators and the numbers which passed the legislation. Judicial discernment, in contrast, is considered soft, a matter of a judge's individual taste. The problem, here, is not the democratic system or the legislative process. The problem is that, once the legislation is passed, people whose behavior falls outside the letter of the law but remains within the spirit of the law and the good it was meant to accomplish are convicted willy-nilly, regardless of the existence of competing principles and regardless of the fairness of that conviction. Such people in effect are used simply as means to accomplishing what are now unexamined, unreviewable, and unquestionable ends.

Thus, modern society is bifurcated "into a realm of the organizational in which ends are taken to be given and are not available for rational scrutiny and a realm of the personal in which judgment and debate about values are central factors, but in which no rational social resolution is available."[7] The result is a perceived binary opposition between individual freedom and collective necessity. The emotivist perceives the only available choices to be an alignment for the anarchy of individual liberty on the one hand, or an alignment for regulation and order on the other:

> But in fact what is crucial is that on which the contending parties agree, namely that there are only two alternative modes of social life open to us, one in which the free and arbitrary choices of individuals are sovereign and one in which the bureaucracy is sovereign, precisely so that it may limit free and arbitrary choices of individuals.[8]

Justice Antonin Scalia defined the free exercise issue in the 1990 U. S. Supreme Court case of *Employment Div. v. Smith* in much the same terms: either the anarchy of the individual religious conscience would rule, or the government bureaucracy must be left alone to regulate as it deems necessary for (what Justice Scalia assumed to be) society's best interests. There could be no middle course, because judges would then be faced with the impossible task of "weigh[ing] the social importance of all laws against the centrality of all religious beliefs."[9] Political philosopher Henry S. Richardson, writing at about the same time as the *Smith* opinion was being issued, maintained that the essence of the problem is irrationality: "One seems forced to fall back on an intuitive balancing of the clashing norms."[10] Pure balancing, he argues, "affords no claim to rationality, for to that extent its weightings are purely intuitive, and therefore lack discursively expressible justification."[11] And once the *process* of resolving free exercise disputes is labeled intuitive and irrational, the matter then becomes nonjusticiable. The only logical choice left to the court is the choice between regulation and anarchy.

I suspect that emotivism and authoritarianism, rather than the need for logic and rational justification, have been behind the Court's claimed inability to respond when justice and fairness demand consideration of competing goods or principles. The result is a tyranny of principles (including the emotivist's principle of deference to "objective expertise"), as well as a concomitant response in favor of a tyranny of individuals (anarchy). These twin aspects of emotivism are evident, for example, in the rise of efforts, under the rubrics of free speech and free exercise, to place formal Christian prayers sanctioned by school authority back into the public schools.[12] The free exercise right is asserted here in terms of anarchical, radical individual rights: "*my*" individual rights, "*my*" absolute right to free exercise, without regard to the disestablishment principle or to competing interests of the community. Interestingly, where they are able, religious adherents (also or instead) argue the authoritarian side of emotivism: They reject any court's interpretations of the first amendment which recognize civil liberties contrary to their beliefs because these interpretations are based upon nothing more than the justices' personal opinions and subjective feelings.[13] Their majority status and legislative influence are the hard facts which objectively, and thus conclusively, should decide the issue.

The 1997 U. S. Supreme Court case of *City of Boerne v. Flores* reaffirmed the Court's commitment to Justice Scalia's free exercise jurisprudence in the *Smith* case, and it effectively passes the burden of protecting the free exercise of religious duties back onto the fifty states. Many, if not most, will attempt to use some form of the "compelling state interest" test which was in effect prior to the *Smith* case, but the problem of the vagueness of this test remains, and such vagueness can elicit fear of religious anarchy and the authoritarian response provoked by such fear.

This project rejects arguments premised upon anarchy, authoritarianism, and/or emotivism in free exercise discourse and jurisprudence. Instead, as will be argued, this project proposes a return to classic casuistry as a pragmatic and principled "middle way" of resolving free exercise conflicts.

A project this ambitious could not have gotten this far without criticism and encouragement; for both, I express my deepest appreciation to Richard Miller, Dan Conkle, David Smith, and Stephen Stein. I thank Edward Mc-Glynn Gaffney, Jr., for his close critical reading of the manuscript and his detailed comments and helpful suggestions. Whatever strength or clarity the argument has is due to their efforts; the opinions, weaknesses, and errors are mine.

Norfolk, Virginia   C. C.
April 2000

Contents

Regulating Religion

Introduction

Free exercise conflicts occur when religiously compelled behavior (whether action or inaction) comes up against a statute which outlaws or criminalizes
such behavior. This project explores the panoply of theories, self-understandings,
contexts, and societal constructs at play in such free exercise conflicts. In order to
maximize the possibilities for successful conflict resolution, it is proposed that free
exercise issues be treated as a conflict of principles: In every bona fide free exercise
claim, the good of religious freedom to fulfill one's obligations to one's God is in
potential conflict with the good of societal order as represented by the law.

It is axiomatic that politics and government tend to prefer simple rather
than complex analyses and solutions to most social problems. We often react
instinctively to an episode of illegal behavior by resorting to the simple bipolar
paradigm of good versus evil. Behavior which violates legal norms is frequently
perceived as evil, renegade, and "outlaw," and groups which promote or sponsor
such behavior are lawbreakers, guilty of criminal conspiracy. To the extent that
public policy is most comfortable dealing in stark, polar opposites such as anarchy and chaos versus law and order, the notion of a free exercise claim as a
conflict of *goods* thereby goes against our instinctive reactions, adds messy complexity to the matter, and thus may be too quickly and easily dismissed.

The normative criminal model of guilt or innocence focuses upon whether
or not the defendant committed the criminal act.[1] Free exercise conflicts do not
fit the assumptions of this model, for the behavior usually is readily admitted;
the issue is not *if* the law was broken, but *why*. Thus, at the outset, the free exercise case evolves around "defenses" and "excuse"—terms imbued with negative connotations, which can immediately place the religious adherent at a
disadvantage.

To take into account both the natural tendency to a bipolar (good-versus-
evil) analysis and the essential aspect of free exercise conflict as a conflict of principles, my project will use as a descriptive aid a symbol/metaphor: the myth of
wilderness. As explained by Henry Nash Smith in *Virgin Land* and by Roderick

Nash in *Wilderness and the American Mind*,[2] the idea of wilderness resonates within the American psyche in complex and contrary ways: wilderness as a holy place of purification; wilderness as an empty place to cultivate and make bloom; wilderness as a dangerous, uncontrolled place.

Christians settling in colonial as well as frontier America had several images of wilderness upon which to draw as they formed a self-understanding of their activities. As Nash has noted, both the Hebrew Bible and the New Testament contain graphic depictions of wilderness—the more positive being wilderness/desert as a place of freedom from persecution, a place of sanctuary, testing, and purification. One may commune with God in the wilderness. Examples include the Israelites' encounters with God during their exodus into the desert, as well as Jesus' fasting and prayer in the desert for forty days.[3] Nash points out that "Christianity . . . retained the idea that wild country could be a place of refuge and religious purity."[4]

Another relatively positive religious connotation inherent in the concept of wilderness is that of an undeveloped, empty land which Christians have a God-given duty to cultivate. Imagery such as making a garden bloom, and replacing the "howling wilderness" with cultivated fields and orchards, was part of the American story as far back as the Pilgrims who settled the Plymouth Colony.[5] God's command to humanity in Genesis 1:28 to be fruitful and multiply, to fill the earth and subdue it, became a mandate (if not Manifest Destiny) for Christians to bring order to the barrenness of the American wilderness and make it prosper.

There was, however, another equally compelling aspect of wilderness prominent within the American psyche, derived from biblical imagery as well as Christian European folklore. As Nash points out, wilderness was also "a potent symbol applied . . . to the moral chaos of the unregenerate. . . ."[6] "If paradise was man's greatest good, wilderness, as its antipode, was his greatest evil . . . [In wilderness, the environment] was at best indifferent, frequently dangerous, and always beyond control."[7] An Old Testament vision of wilderness made it a place of evil, a place of immorality, the place where the devil lived. The ancient Israelites saw the wilderness as land "sacred 'in the wrong way.' It is the demonic land, . . . the land of confusion and chaos."[8]

The Christian missionary experience in conquering pagan Europe left westerners with a vivid folklore of wilderness beasts and unholy wild people cavorting about, committing atrocities and notably unable to control lustful appetites.[9]

> In early and medieval Christianity, wilderness kept its significance as the earthly realm of the powers of evil that the Church had to overcome. This was literally the case in the missionary efforts to the tribes of northern Europe. Christians judged their work to be successful when they cleared away the wild forests and cut down the sacred groves where the pagans held their rites. [Footnote omitted.] In a more figurative sense, wilderness represented the Christian conception of the situation man faced on earth. It was a compound of his natural inclination to sin, the temptation of the material world, and the temptation of the forces of evil themselves.[10]

This last suspicion, that those who live in the wilderness—that is, those who live outside the boundaries of law—have succumbed to their lower, sinful nature, captures society's instinctive reaction to religious adherents in free exercise cases. Free exercise clashes, by definition, occur when a religious practice is outside the law. To this initial indicia of lawlessness, society often imputes to the religious adherents additional layers of wilderness attributes such as licentiousness and anarchy.

The myth of wilderness is helpful to this project because it enables us to understand how people can approach the same phenomenon with such drastically different assumptions and how the same activity may have different ramifications, meanings, and consequences depending upon the framework in which it is seen. Nondominant religious groups whose religious beliefs compel them to undertake behavior which violates mainstream society's moral norms especially tend to be regarded as living in immoral chaos. Members of society may feel the need to convert the wilderness barbarians into a law-abiding, moral citizenry, or even to move forcefully to contain the breach in the boundaries of civilization in order to protect society.

Yet, the religious group's own framework and self-understandings may be founded in quite opposite perceptions, which are describable in terms of the positive wilderness image of the pure remnant, seeking a wilderness refuge from the unholy, impure mainstream. Such a group does not view its behavior as uncontrolled, but rather as *more* obedient to God's will, and thus *more* virtuous and law abiding than the societal mainstream.

The nonmainstream group's self-perceptions might also be founded in an understanding which can be described in terms of an alternative version of cultivating the wilderness. The religious group perhaps may not see itself as wilderness dwellers who have rejected the mainstream values and norms, but rather as better cultivators of the society's core values. The religious group views itself as *more centered* in the true values of the society than the forces who are opposing it. Thomas Tweed, for example, notes that one of the reasons American Euro-Buddhists (seeming outsiders to Victorian Protestant America) were attracted to Buddhism was that they perceived it to be *more perfectly* reflective of core American cultural commitments to tolerance, rationality, and the scientific method. The Euro-Buddhists believed that these important American values were being betrayed by the Protestantism of the day.[11]

Note, again, that this project intends the wilderness myth simply as a metaphor for paradigmatic free exercise conflicts. The wilderness is not proposed here as a literal explanation of free exercise conflicts.[12] Rather, the wilderness trope is presented as an organizational tool as well as a descriptive means by which to unlock the complexity that lies at the heart of free exercise conflicts. The metaphor "tells us something new about reality" in the sense that it has disclosed another possible way of viewing free exercise conflicts.[13] New meanings may be uncovered and new insights may be gleaned when one embraces the tension produced by contradictory literal interpretations and uses that tension as a means of "play" which can expand the horizon of the matter and mediate possible new ways of questioning and understanding free exercise conflicts.[14]

The Legal Boundary between the Garden and the Wilderness

Legislation or the Free Exercise Clause?

The problem addressed in this project is how to determine the point at which the "people of the wilderness" pose a serious enough threat to society that their need and right to the free exercise of religion must be overridden with legislative coercion. My goal is to develop a suitable, practical process which resolves this problem in a way that eschews the instinctive "us-versus-them" polarization. This process will be grounded in a casuistical model premised upon respecting the competing goods at issue while seeking a practical way to resolve such conflicts fairly.

As a first step toward the development of a casuistical free exercise analytical process, this chapter examines the various standards of review or tests which historically have been used by the U.S. Supreme Court[1] in analyzing and resolving free exercise issues. Particular attention will be paid to the "no exception" test adopted in 1879 in the *Reynolds* case, the "clear and present danger" test of the 1940s, the more recent "balancing of compelling interests" type of approach, and finally the "neutrality" standard announced in the 1990 case of *Employment Division v. Smith.*

A review of the Court cases will show that the underlying analytical process can be as influential to a decision as the abstract "test." I will thus attend to details which help to uncover processes and rationales used to reach a decision. For this purpose, I will highlight cases which have produced starkly differing results under comparable factual circumstances. Furthermore, I will note the presence of aspects of the wilderness myth and perceptions of Otherness[2] in the analysis of these Court opinions. Court portrayals of religious adherents as anarchic and contemptuous of law and order are signals that the justices perceive the religious adherents as lawless people. The lawless are not, as a rule, supported in their efforts to protect the right to free exercise. Where the courts (or individual dissenting justices) favor the free exercise claim, the opinions tend to justify the decision with bridge-building explanations which emphasize positive aspects of the wilderness myth present in the group or its practice, and/or find that the religious adherents are in fact engaging in familiar (and not Other) behavior. We will see that the Court's bridge-building techniques rely upon elements which are central to casuistry: analogy, paradigm, and context.

Reynolds v. United States (1879)

Reynolds v. United States[3] was the first U.S. Supreme Court case to determine the scope and meaning of the free exercise clause. The free exercise issue in this pivotal 1879 case centered upon the Mormon practice of polygamy[4] and whether the guarantees of free exercise under the Constitution protected Mormons from criminal punishment under the federal Morrill Anti-Polygamy Act of 1862 (as amended by the Poland Act of 1874). Although general in its wording, the federal law was enacted specifically to eradicate the Mormon religious practice,[5] which had been allowed under Utah territorial laws.

Reynolds offered extensive proof as to his religious motivations and obligations at trial. The trial court, however, ruled that such evidence was irrelevant to the criminal prosecution, and it refused to give the following jury charge requested by Reynolds: [T]hat if they found he had married in pursuance of and conformity with what he believed at the time to be a religious duty, their verdict should be 'not guilty.'"[6] The trial court judge instead barred the jury from considering the religious context of the practice; the jury had only to determine the limited fact of more than one marriage, a fact freely admitted by Reynolds, in order to convict Reynolds of the crime. Thus, the charge ultimately given to the jury was

> that if he [Reynolds], under the influence of a religious belief that it was right, had "deliberately married a second time, having a first wife living, *the want of consciousness of evil intent*—the want of understanding on his part that he was committing crime—did *not excuse* him, but the law *inexorably*, in such cases, *implies criminal intent.*"[7]

The trial judge made his attitude toward the religious issue quite clear to the jury in another portion of his charge:

> I think it not improper, in the discharge of your duties in this case, that you should consider what are to be the consequences to the innocent victims of this delusion. As this contest goes on, they multiply, and there are pure-minded women and there are innocent children,—innocent in a sense even beyond the degree of the innocence of childhood itself. These are to be the sufferers; and as jurors fail to do their duty, and as these cases come up in the Territory, just so do these victims multiply and spread themselves over the land.[8]

Note that these depictions of Mormons mirror the negative polar aspect of the wilderness myth: barbaric men with religious delusions, living beyond the moral boundaries of civilization and victimizing helpless women and children. The jury convicted Reynolds of the crime. Reynolds's conviction was ultimately upheld[9] by the Utah Supreme Court, whereupon he appealed to the U.S. Supreme Court.

This case raised several issues for the Court: (1) Was polygamy a religious obligation? (2) If it was, how does this impact upon the elements necessary to convict a person of a violation of the antipolygamy laws? (3) What is the meaning of the phrase, "free exercise of religion"? (4) How should the right of free exercise interact with congressional legislative prohibitions on certain conduct? How the Court dealt with these complex matters will be discussed with an eye to language and arguments which reveal the underlying assumptions that the Court brought to this case.

Mirroring the religious orthodoxy of its day, language in the federal Morrill Anti- Polygamy Act specifically had rejected the notion that polygamy was a religious duty. But Chief Justice Morrison Waite, author of the opinion for the Court, noted that Reynolds had proved at trial (1) that the practice of polygamy was a doctrine of the Mormon Church, (2) that the Mormons believed that God had directly commanded them to undertake the practice, and (3) that the Mormons were convinced that one would suffer damnation in the afterlife for failure or refusal to practice polygamous marriage.[10] Accordingly, the Court dismissed the notion that plural marriages were not religiously imposed obligations, and it rejected popular arguments that religion simply was being used as a pretext and subterfuge to feed the lusts of uncivilized men.

The Mormons' practice thus came within the general rubric of the phrase "exercise of religion": In other words, the Mormons had proven that polygamy was a religious obligation. But the Court ultimately held that the free exercise clause of the Constitution did not include the right to freely exercise the religious practice of polygamy; in the view of the Court, it was enough that Congress had prohibited it by criminal statute.

To reach the conclusion that obligations to one's God are automatically secondary to the citizen's duty to obey the laws of the state, the Court focused on formulating a legal definition of the term "religion" as used in the First Amendment, rather than on the ordinary usage and meaning of "free exercise." In this way, the Court was able to sidestep the reality of the situation (i.e., that the Mormons were, indeed, being prohibited by Congress from freely exercising their religious duties). The Court instead deemed that the appropriate course of action was to look "to the history of the times in the midst of which the provision was adopted."[11] The Court's opinion specifically drew upon documents authored by Thomas Jefferson, including a letter he wrote to the Danbury Baptist Association in 1802:

> Believing with you that religion is a matter which lies solely between man and his God; that he owes account to none other for his faith or his worship; that the legislative powers of the Government reach actions only, and not opinions, I contemplate with sovereign reverence that act of the whole American people which declared that their Legislature should "make no law respecting an establishment of religion or prohibiting the free exercise thereof," thus building a wall of separation between Church and State.[12]

Jefferson's letter interjected the notion that a natural right, such as freedom of religion, harmonizes with one's obligations to the societal order: Jefferson was convinced that man "has no natural right in opposition to his social duties."[13] The Court in *Reynolds* interpreted this to mean that the natural right must automatically end where the statute begins. Accordingly, Jefferson's philosophical belief in the harmony between social and moral obligations was turned by the Court into a hard and fast rule that the moral obligation must bow to the social. The Court made no attempt to harmonize the two, but instead declared one subordinate to the other.

Based upon all of the above, the Court ultimately concluded that the federal "free *exercise*" clause was, in actuality, a "freedom of religious *belief*" clause which merely protected religious opinion: "Congress was deprived of all legislative power over mere opinion, but was left free to reach actions which were in violation of social duties or subversive of good order."[14]

Having determined that religious actions were ultimately under the state's jurisdiction, the Court turned to the specific issue of the case: the congressional ban on polygamy. The actual context of the Mormon situation, the facts and effects of its practice of plural marriages, was never explored by the Court, however, and, indeed, not even addressed with respect to the free exercise issue. Nor were the history and context of the legislative ban on polygamy examined in the opinion, in order to test the factual premises (if any) of the Congress. A weakness in factual justification can be indicative of irrational or arbitrary action, based upon passions and prejudices and not upon reason and equity. But the Court did not apply its power of judicial scrutiny to the particular situation before it. Rather, the Court couched its decision with sweeping condemnations reminiscent of the political and religious rhetoric heard in Congress during the lopsided debates over the antipolygamy measures.

In order to appreciate the ramifications of deferring to the legislative wisdom in this area, one must recall the distinction between legislation and adjudication. The legislative process is driven by politics, not evidence. There is no requirement that a wise course of action be taken. Only the most minimal amount of evidence in support of the policy need be offered. Unlike the courtroom situation, nothing need be factually proven or even factually probable before Congress enacts a policy measure or proscribes an activity. Popular opinion, even if uninformed, propels the lawmaking process, and unless the enactment is challenged as unconstitutional, there is no accountability other than back to that same popular consensus. And in the *Reynolds* case, the Court's rationale for supporting the criminal statute over the religious practice was so superficial as to amount to an abdication to Congress's political judgment.

Chief Justice Waite began by describing polygamy in general as being "odious among the Northern and Western Nations of Europe. . . ." Note the glaring absence of the southern and eastern European countries in the Court's discussion. The neglect was not an oversight: Catholicism was prevalent in these unmentioned portions of Europe. The clear message from a unanimous Court during this period of mass Catholic immigration into the United States was that northern and western (i.e., Protestant) European countries represented superior cultures, the epitome of civilization. The Court continued, stating, "and, until the establishment of the Mormon Church, [polygamy] was almost exclusively a feature of the life of Asiatic and African people"[15] (meaning, at that time, the uncivilized, "pagan" areas of the world). Thus, while facially resting its opinion on what was proper for a civilized country, in fact the opinion was based upon what was considered proper for a Protestant country.

Reynolds raised as a defense to his conviction that by his plural marriages he had no intent to commit the crime of polygamy, but was acting under the loftiest spiritual motives as required by his religious beliefs. But the Court rejected Reynolds's argument that religious intent and sacred purpose were relevant to the issue of criminal guilt. Instead, the Court in *Reynolds* firmly established the precedent, which still persists, of legally equating religious intent with criminal intent and its concurrent harms: The Court stated simply that Reynolds made no mistake, that he *intended* to have two wives. The context of the religious action, including the context of the experience of Mormon polygamous families, thus became irrelevant. The harms of criminal polygamy were assumed to be present in the religious practice of polygamy.

As already noted, the Court made no effort to ascertain whether the actual facts of the situation (i.e., family life in Mormon plural marriages) warranted such regulation of the social order so as to prohibit the devout practice of a sincerely held religious belief and imprison the members of pious Mormon families. No inquiries were made in the opinion as to whether the regulation of a practice deemed subversive of good order was, in reality, a regulation fueled by counter-religious passions and prejudices. The practical outcome of the Court's reasoning was that, if the practice disturbed the sensibilities of the (Protestant Christian) majority enough that they petitioned Congress furiously against it, the fact of their furor was subversive enough of good order to ban a practice otherwise carried on peacefully enough by the believers. The need for social uniformity (i.e., the minority conforming to the will of the majority) was held to be paramount over the constitutional protection afforded religious practice:

> [T]he only question which remains is, whether those who make polygamy a part of their religion are excepted from the operation of the statute. If they are, then those who do not make polygamy a part of their religious belief may be found guilty and punished, while those who do must be acquitted and go free. . . .[16]

The focus, here, is upon the isolated action and the seemingly disparate treatment of two individuals who have chosen to engage in that action. If one views the action acontextually and posits the actor as making an unencumbered, free choice to engage in that action, then it seems unfair to punish the one and not the other. But this focus loses sight of the possibility of contextual differences and of the grounding of the free exercise clause within the tradition of religiously compelled behavior not freely chosen.[17]

Accordingly, another way of viewing the "unfairness" of treating differently two persons engaged in the same behavior is to refocus instead upon equality of treatment of religious behavior. If the category of focus is equal treatment of religious obligations, a different sense of unfairness and unequal treatment emerges.

The obligations and prohibitions of dominant forms of Protestantism have been codified into the laws made by that majority. Sunday closing laws, for example, had long enabled Sunday worshipers to fulfill their obligations with the sanction and protection of the government. Sins of Christianity had become crimes against the state: Profanity laws made it a crime to take the Lord's name in vain; the virtue of temperance became the law of prohibition (with built-in exemptions for Christian sacramental wine to accommodate). Religious adherents who do not follow typical mainstream Christian practices and prohibitions suffer a second-class citizenship under some of these laws.[18]

The Court in *Reynolds*, however, broadly declared that a religious practice under *any* circumstances could not serve as a "defense" to a crime. Congress "was left free to reach actions which were in violation of social duties or subversive of good order."[19] The Court reasoned that to permit the disobedience of any law in the name of a higher religious duty was to permit anarchy:

> Can a man excuse his practices to the contrary because of his religious belief? To permit this would be to make the professed doctrines of religious belief superior to the law of the land and in effect permit every citizen to become a law unto himself. Government could exist only in name under such circumstances.[20]

Who decides what is truly essential to the peace and good order of society? The Court deferred completely to Congress's discretion. The Court required no review, no searching inquiry to ascertain the facts and circumstances surrounding either the religious practice or the enactment of the criminal statute. There simply was no room for a middle course of action here.[21]

In subordinating all free exercise claims under the Constitution to the prohibitions contained in criminal statutes, the Court adopted a circular form of reasoning. The constitutional protection afforded a religious practice is limited by the mere existence of a congressional statute prohibiting the practice, the very same statute that the Court should be scrutinizing to determine whether it (the statute) is constitutional. In other words, the standard by which the Court would hereinafter measure the constitutionality of the application of a statute which proscribed a practice that some held to be a sacred duty was the mere existence of the statute itself.

The *Reynolds* standard continued as the law of the land for the next sixty years. One example of its ramifications for nondominant religious groups can be seen in the 1903 Texas state court case of *Sweeney v. Webb*.[22] The statute at issue gave counties the option of prohibiting the sale of alcohol within that county for all uses except medicinal and sacramental. Citing the opinion in the *Reynolds* case, the court noted that religious freedom did not extend to actions which violated the law. The court then interpreted the statutory exemption for "sacramental" uses quite narrowly and literally, holding that the exemption did not include use in the "Jewish mode of worship" because such

> mode of worship knows no sacraments, but the same requires the use of wine on a number of occasions during each week and each year. Such use of wine has no symbolical or mystical meaning, and is in no sense for sacramental purposes, but is used on such occasions as a beverage.[23]

The court furthermore found no discrimination against "Jewish worship" because the wording of the statute did not specifically mention such worship:

> The effect of the statute is to absolutely prohibit the sale of intoxicating liquors as a beverage in the locality where adopted. In this respect it operates upon all persons alike. It is only as medicine, and then upon prescription, or for sacramental purposes, that intoxicants may be lawfully sold. . . . It is contended that its sale for sacramental purposes is a discrimination against Jewish worship. The contention is not sound. There is no discrimination against the use of wine in their mode of worship. The prohibition is against the sale of intoxicating liquors.[24]

This case was decided in 1903, before automobiles were widely available for easy travel to neighboring counties (assuming that these counties were not also "dry"); the case fails to discuss the unequal hardship (or even impossibility) of obtaining wine for Jewish rituals.

Cantwell v. Connecticut (1940)

The Court did not officially deviate[25] from the *Reynolds* free exercise standard until a series of cases in the 1940s involving Jehovah's Witnesses.[26] The first of these was *Cantwell v. Connecticut*,[27] in which a father and two sons were arrested on two charges, one of which included inciting a breach of the peace.[28] The Jehovah's Witnesses had been going from house to house in a predominantly Catholic neighborhood, requesting permission to play one of their recordings which described various books on religious topics. At one point, Jesse Cantwell stopped two men who happened to be Roman Catholic, requested and received their permission to play a recording, and then played one which contained an attack on the Roman Catholic Church. Justice Owen Roberts, author of the Court's opinion, described what happened next:

> Both [Catholic men] were incensed by the contents of the record and were tempted to strike Cantwell unless he went away. On being told to be on his way he left their presence. There was no evidence that he was personally offensive or entered into any argument with those he interviewed.[29]

The state courts had found enough evidence under these facts to support the conviction for inciting a breach of peace. The Court accepted the state's findings "that the petitioner's [Cantwell] conduct constituted the commission of an offense under the State law . . . as binding upon us to that extent."[30]

Convictions for solicitation without a license and for "incitement to breach of peace" are "actions which were in violation of social duties or subversive of good order,"[31] and thus would have been within the proper scope of regulation of behavior (as opposed to religious belief). Under the broad principle of the *Reynolds* case, the fact of conviction under the law thus would have been conclusive. In *Cantwell*, however, the Court did not defer automatically to the state's regulatory power, but instead conducted a searching inquiry into the context of the situation and the societal interests at stake. Note the Court's characterization of the issue as a conflict of important interests:

> Even the exercise of religion may be at some slight inconvenience in order that the state may protect its citizens from injury. . . . Decision as to the lawfulness of the conviction demands the weighing of two conflicting interests. The fundamental law declares the interest of the United States that the free exercise of religion be not prohibited and that freedom to communicate information and opinion be not abridged. The state of Connecticut has an obvious interest in the preservation and protection of peace and good order within her borders. We must determine whether the alleged protection of the State's interest, means to which end would, in the absence of limitation by the federal Constitution, lie wholly within the State's discretion, has been pressed, in this instance, to a point where it has come into fatal collision with the overriding interest protected by the federal compact.[32]

The Court defended this first step away from the deferential rigidity of the *Reynolds* free exercise test by noting that the regulation violated in this case was not a statute reflecting a legislative judgment "narrowly drawn to prevent the supposed evil." No direct or specific incursions into the legislative domain would be involved. Rather, the "incitement to breach" was based upon "a common law of the most general and undefined nature."[33]

The Court found that Cantwell's religiously compelled behavior, although a violation of the common law crime of incitement to a breach of the peace, "raised no such clear and present menace to public peace and order as to render him liable to conviction of the common law offense in question." In reaching this decision, the Court determined that the constitutional guarantees of the free exercise of religion and speech should be given equal consideration with society's interest in good order. Thus, only if a legislature determined that Cantwell's specific behavior was "a clear and present danger to a substantial interest of the State" could his religious freedom be overridden.[34] The Court in the *Cantwell* opinion thus implicitly rejected the bright line espoused by the *Reynolds* standard between action and belief, between a breach of good order and merely holding a religious opinion. The Court instead recognized the free exercise issue as a complex problem of competing principles, and it actively scrutinized the legal and factual contexts of the case in order to achieve a just resolution of the conflict. The focus in free exercise cases thereafter began to shift from a mechanical application of the action/belief standard to a searching consideration of the conflicting goods at stake.

The Court resolved this conflict of goods by using analogies and paradigms. By analogy to another First Amendment guarantee, freedom of speech, the Court reasoned that the standard of review for both types of first amendment claims should be the same: "clear and present danger to a narrowly drawn interest." This analogy to free speech was helpful, for in noting the potential to spark controversy which is inherent in both political speech and religious evangelizing, the Court had described Cantwell's behavior in familiar and recognizable terms; hence, as strange as Jehovah's Witnesses were to the rest of society,

Cantwell still was not deemed to be outside the boundaries of civilization. The Court found a way to relate his behavior to the familiar.

The Court also used paradigms to help bridge the boundary between garden and wilderness. Citing paradigmatic examples of the crime of incitement to a breach of peace, the Court determined that the essence of the violation was behavior which "consisted of profane, indecent, or abusive remarks directed to the person of the hearer." In light of its religious purposes, Cantwell's behavior, while naturally arousing animosity, did not sufficiently fit the paradigm to warrant punishment:

> We find in the instant case no assault or threatening of bodily harm, no truculent bearing, no intentional discourtesy, no personal abuse. On the contrary, we find only an effort to persuade a willing listener to buy a book or to contribute money in the interest of what Cantwell, however misguided others may think him, conceived to be true religion.[35]

The Court acknowledged the necessity that there be "limits to the exercise of these liberties [referring to both freedom of religion and freedom of speech]."[36] The Court also acknowledged that "sharp differences" naturally arise in the realm of religion. Yet, as noted, the Court concluded that "in light of the constitutional guarantees [referring to religious freedom as well as freedom of speech], [Cantwell's conduct] raised no such clear and present menace to public peace and order."[37]

The comparison is stark between the *Reynolds* and *Cantwell* opinions with respect to the Court's attitude toward disturbances of the peace from those opposed to the practice of a nondominant religious group. In *Cantwell*, the adverse reaction of others to the religiously motivated behavior, although such reaction was disturbing to the peace, would not be enough in and of itself to nullify the religious freedom. In *Reynolds*, however, the disruption of the religious sensibilities of the majority over the Mormon's religious practice was conclusive that the practice was violative of good order and public peace.

The "flag salute" cases: *Minersville School District v. Gobitis* (1940) and *West Virginia State Board of Education v. Barnette* (1943) (overruled *Gobitis*)

A scant two weeks after the *Cantwell* opinion was issued, the Court decided another free exercise case, *Minersville School District v. Gobitis*.[38] In *Gobitis*, two children, ten and twelve years old and members of Jehovah's Witnesses, were expelled from public school for refusing to salute the national flag in a pledge of allegiance, as required by the local board of education in Minersville, Pennsylvania. The children refused the flag salute because of their belief that God forbade such an exercise, in accordance with Exodus, chapter 20: "Thou shalt not make unto thee any graven image, or any likeness of any thing. . . . Thou shalt not bow down thyself to them. . . ."[39]

The Court's opinion in this case was written by Justice Felix Frankfurter. While formally insisting that it was following the *Cantwell* standard of review, the opinion disregarded the scope of protection delineated for free exercise in the *Cantwell* case. The difference between the two cases lies in the amount of scrutiny and contextual examination the Court was willing to undertake. By use of analogy and paradigm, the garden and the wilderness had been bridged in *Cantwell*. In *Gobitis*, however, the Court allowed the secular nature and general purpose of the legal requirement to obscure what was directly at issue in the case (punishment of children's peaceable conscientious objection).

Justice Frankfurter characterized the competing claims at issue in *Gobitis* as a conflict between authority and liberty (not "higher duty" or religious obligation). Frankfurter then defined the authority at stake in the school's flag salute requirement as of the utmost importance to the state: the "authority to safeguard the nation's fellowship."[40] Frankfurter's rhetoric emphasized that "the promotion of national cohesion" (as represented by the flag salute requirement) was "an interest inferior to none in the hierarchy of legal values. National unity is the basis of national security."[41] Frankfurter justified his departure from the standard of free exercise analysis established in *Cantwell* by distinguishing the general common law regulation at issue therein, with the specificity of a secular-purposed, legislative enactment such as that of the school board.

At this point in history, the Court was in the midst of a dramatic shift in its doctrine of judicial review of legislation.[42] Frankfurter was clearly concerned that the Court would be interfering with a specific determination by a "legislative body" that the requirement was vital to society. While he appreciated the complexity of "reconcil[ing] two rights" and acknowledged "that no single principle can answer all of life's complexities,"[43] Frankfurter ultimately deferred to the school board because he felt that the Court had no meaningful and principled analytical process by which it could scrutinize legislation that was in conflict with an individual right. Courts "possess no marked and certainly no controlling competence" in this area, and "it is not the *personal notion* of judges of what wise adjustment requires which must prevail."[44]

Underlying this position of deference was a perception that the Court's finding in favor of the religious adherent would be an insult and an affront to the legislature (and thus to "the processes of popular rule"). Such a ruling would "stigmatize legislative judgment" and would be an "exercise [of] censorship."[45] Accordingly, the standard of review was simply the "rational basis" standard for due process.

Justice Stone wrote the lone dissenting opinion in *Gobitis*, emphasizing the importance of both civil liberties guarantees *and* specific government interests. When these demands conflict, there must be "reasonable accommodation" between them; the Court cannot automatically defer to the democratic process.[46] A "searching judicial inquiry into the legislative judgment" is particularly required in situations "where prejudice against discrete and insular minorities" may have negatively affected the minorities' abilities to participate meaningfully in the political process.

> History teaches us that there have been but few infringements of personal lib-
> erty by the state which have not been justified, as they are here, in the name of
> righteousness and the public good, and few which have not been directed, as
> they are now, at politically helpless minorities.[47]

Not only was the Gobitis family without political influence, but also at first had
difficulty obtaining legal representation. No local attorney would handle the
case.[48]

Remarkably, the decision in *Gobitis* was overturned three years later (1943)
in a similar "flag salute" case, *West Virginia State Board of Education v. Barnette*.[49] A hallmark of the Court's opinion in *Barnette* is the analytical method
used to reach its decision. Justice Jackson (author of the Court's opinion) carefully and critically examined the actual *context* of the conflict, refusing to defer
to the government's broad assertions that the matter of saluting the flag involved
"national security" because it inculcated "national unity." Such "oversimplifica-
tion," he noted, is "handy in political debate" but "often lacks the precision necessary to postulates of judicial reasoning."[50]

In answer to the question, "What's going on here?" Justice Jackson found a
situation dramatically different from the asserted "threat to national unity" to
which the Court in *Gobitis* had deferred:

> Children of this faith [Jehovah's Witnesses] have been expelled from school
> and are threatened with exclusion for no other cause [than their refusal to
> salute the flag]. Officials threaten to send them to reformatories maintained for
> criminally inclined juveniles. Parents of such children have been prosecuted
> and are threatened with prosecutions for causing delinquency.[51]

Justice Jackson searchingly analyzed not only the state's declared interests, but
also the impact and ramifications of the state's assertion of power over the school
children and their parents. Jackson defined the issue as that of the "power of the
state to expel a handful of children from school" and found that, at the heart of
the case, "we are dealing with a compulsion of students to declare a belief."[52] He
declared as a matter of broad and general principle that the government cannot
force someone to "utter what is not in his mind," whether or not the individual's
objection is based upon religious, political, or other reasons:

> If there is any fixed star in our constitutional constellation, it is that no official,
> high or petty, can prescribe what shall be orthodox in politics, nationalism, reli-
> gion, or other matters of opinion or force citizens to confess by word or act their
> faith therein.[53]

Accordingly, the action of local officials in this case to compel students to make
the pledge of allegiance "transcends constitutional limitations on their power
and invades the sphere of intellect and spirit which it is the purpose of the First
Amendment to our Constitution to reserve from all official control."[54]

The judicial review in this case was far more searching than that conducted
by Justice Frankfurter in the *Gobitis* opinion. In *Gobitis* the Court refrained
from scrutinizing the context because of a professed lack of competence to decide between the competing interests of the individual and the state, and a per-

ception that the Court owed a legislature deference out of respect for the political process. A religious minority's only remedy, according to Justice Frankfurter, was to persuade the legislature to give an exemption. Justice Jackson, for the majority of the Court in *Barnette*, however, rejected this limited view of the judicial role when individual liberties are infringed:

> Nor does our duty to apply the Bill of Rights to assertions of official authority depend upon our possession of marked competence in the field where the invasion of rights occurs. True, the task of translating the majestic generalities of the Bill of Rights . . . is one to disturb self-confidence. But we act in these matters not by authority of our competence but by force of our commissions.[55]

In one of the most famous passages of any Supreme Court opinion, Justice Jackson criticized the *Gobitis* Court's vision of the political process as the only place where minorities can defend their rights under the First Amendment over against majoritarian incursions:

> The very purpose of a Bill of Rights was to withdraw certain subjects from the vicissitudes of political controversy, to place them beyond the reach of majorities and officials and to establish them as legal principles to be applied by the courts. One's right to life, liberty, and property, to free speech, a free press, freedom of worship and assembly, and other fundamental rights may not be submitted to vote; they depend upon the outcome of no elections.[56]

When such specific, protected, individual rights are in conflict with legislation, the standard of review of such legislation is not, as applied in the *Gobitis* case, a cursory inquiry as to whether there was any "rational basis" for adopting the legislation. Rather, the Court in *Barnette* returned to the test used in the *Cantwell* case, a strict scrutiny, "clear and present danger" standard:

> But freedoms of speech and of press, of assembly, and of worship may not be infringed on such slender grounds [as the "rational basis" test]. They are susceptible of restriction *only to prevent grave and immediate danger to interests which the state may lawfully protect.*[57]

The Court used two key analytical tools: It placed the issue within its context, and it compared the situation at bar with other analogous, paradigmatic situations. In *Cantwell*, the garden and the wilderness were bridged by analogies which served to place the Other's[58] behavior squarely within the realm of the familiar. Here, the refusal to participate in a pledge of national unity made the Jehovah's Witnesses distinct outsiders to the community: Their allegiance to God over the state clearly placed them in wilderness territory. Yet, by acknowledging the individual's freedom of conscience as a basic, founding principle of our society, the Court found that this wilderness was also familiar territory: Our outermost boundaries were intended to *include* vital differences "as to things that touch the heart of the existing order." Dissenters such as Jehovah's Witnesses are yet within the boundaries of society and thus within the protection of the law. Crucial to this analysis and conclusion, however, was the Court's determination that the Others were not chaotic lawless barbarians living in the far reaches of the negative aspect of the wilderness myth. The Court emphasized that the stu-

dents' "insubordination" simply did not fit the usual paradigm of juvenile delin-
quency. They were not disturbing the class: "Nor is there any question in this
case that their behavior is peaceable and orderly." Their behavior did not "interfere with or deny the rights of others." Their only disobedience was premised
upon a conscientious objection due to obedience to a higher law. The children
and their parents were not otherwise lawless or disrespectful of the state's authority in general.

Furthermore, the punishment for conscientious objection simply did not fit
the behavior at issue: incarceration of children in reform schools and criminal
fines and punishment of parents solely because the students engaged in peaceable conscientious objection. It was difficult for the Court to accept that the *silence* of a few students warranted such a harsh response, and that their actions
(or rather, their inaction) constituted a "clear and present danger" to society.
Wherever the outer boundaries of the free exercise clause might be, the children, at least in this case, had not crossed them.

One other aspect of this case was important to the final outcome: the escalation of legal (and extralegal) actions against Jehovah's Witnesses as a result of the
Court's opinion in *Gobitis*. One contemporary law review article noted the increasing use of both legal and mob actions against Jehovah's Witnesses:

> This cult has found it necessary to struggle against a tremendous surge of un-
> friendly local opinion and opposition — opposition aided by local laws designed
> to curtail the Witnesses' functions and activities — opposition aided and abetted
> by zealously antagonistic local law-enforcement authorities. . . . Seemingly,
> liberals as well as conservatives have given the Witnesses "short shrift." From
> Texas to Maine these religious crusaders were subjected to harassment by local
> law enforcement authorities and by mob violence. It was odd that we, Ameri-
> cans, would think it necessary to resort to force to stop this type of movement,
> and that we would actually direct and participate in the use of force against
> men and women members indiscriminately. Yet, details of such occurrences
> are separately recorded in magazines such as *Life, Time, Christian Century*, and
> the *Nation*. The Witnesses have had their "kingdom halls" burned, their auto-
> mobiles destroyed, their persons subjected to brutal beatings and pot-shots.[59]

Rather than Frankfurter's intended signal to mobilize patriotism and build up
national unity for the increasing possibility of a European war effort, the opinion
in the *Gobitis* case was interpreted by the public (albeit most unwittingly) as a
signal of approval of efforts to persecute and criminalize Jehovah's Witnesses.
The Court succeeded mainly in unleashing a mobilization of violence against
such "un-American" outsiders.

The decision in *Gobitis*, as noted, caused a wave of legal efforts against the
Witnesses.[60] In fact, the compulsory flag salute requirement in West Virginia,
which led to the *Barnette* case, itself was adopted as a result of the Court's opinion in the *Gobitis* case. Justice Jackson noted that the West Virginia Board of
Education's resolution which adopted the requirement "contain[ed] recitals
taken largely from the Court's *Gobitis* opinion. . . ."[61] The Board of Education
anticipated religious objections to the flag salute, and indeed received input
from Jehovah's Witnesses indicating their willingness to make a pledge in lieu of

the flag salute.[62] Yet, they felt no need to accommodate conscientious objectors and made this quite clear in their resolution:

> WHEREAS, The West Virginia State Board of Education recognizes that the manifold character of man's relations may bring his conception of religious duty into conflict with the secular interests of his fellowman; that conscientious scruples have not in the course of the long struggle for religious tolerance relieved the individual from obedience to the general law not aimed at the promotion or restriction of the religious beliefs; that the mere possession of convictions which contradict the relevant concerns of political society does not relieve the citizen from the discharge of political responsibility. . . .[63]

Justice Frankfurter's policy of deference to the political process as the proper place to work out accommodation of nonconforming religious principles had removed any impetus for that process to reach such accommodation. The Court in the *Gobitis* case had left the power with the state and would offer no searching judicial review of its use of that power; accordingly, as seen in the board of education's resolution, the state felt its refusal to accommodate conscientious objectors was not simply "rational" but actually *constitutionally* justified. Hence, the circularity of the *Reynolds* standard of constitutional review (deferral to the legislature) becomes compounded: The legislative body in *Barnette* relied upon the Court's constitutional interpretation which had deferred to legislatures. The school board in *Barnette* accordingly felt that under the Constitution it had broad, sweeping legislative power, unfettered by the need to take into consideration the conflicting religious obligations of minority constituents.

Justice Jackson warned of the dangers such broad power posed to the rights of individuals:

> Struggles to coerce uniformity of sentiment in support of some end thought essential to their time and country have been waged by many good as well as by evil men. Nationalism is a relatively recent phenomenon but at other times and places the ends have been racial or territorial security, support of a dynasty or regime, and particular plans for saving souls. As first and moderate methods to attain unity have failed, those bent on its accomplishment must resort to an ever-increasing severity. As governmental pressure toward unity becomes greater, so strife becomes more bitter as to whose unity it shall be. . . . Those who begin coercive elimination of dissent soon find themselves exterminating dissenters. Compulsory unification of opinion achieves only the unanimity of the graveyard. It seems trite but necessary to say that the First Amendment to our Constitution was designed to avoid these ends by avoiding these beginnings.[64]

Justice Jackson cited specifically the ultimate futility of, as well as the brutality caused by, such historical paradigms of coercive governmental effort as "the Roman drive to stamp out Christianity as a disturber of its pagan unity" and "the Inquisition, as a means to religious and dynastic unity. . . ."[65] Here, Justice Jackson acknowledges the strength and power of the duty to conscience and the obligation to one's God as a practical impediment to the ultimate success of governmental efforts to achieve a coercive unity at the expense of such duties. Martyrs, not converts, are the result.

The key lesson of the *Gobitis* and *Barnette* cases is that the Court cannot shirk its responsibility to searchingly review conflicts between religious conscience and governmental mandates. Justice Jackson is not denying completely the state's power to create martyrs; his point, rather, is that the First Amendment freedoms "are susceptible of restriction only to prevent grave and immediate danger" to a state's lawful interests. Such danger must be found to be present before the state, in order to advance and protect governmental interests, may force sincere religious adherents into acts of "martyrdom."

The "peddler" cases: *Jones v. City of Opelika* (I: 1942; II: 1943) and *Murdock v. Pennsylvania* (1943)

Nineteen forty-three was a turbulent, crucial year in free exercise jurisprudence: Not only did the Court in *Barnette* reverse the three-year-old decision in *Gobitis*, but in the case of *Murdock v. Pennsylvania*[66] (which included a rehearing of *Jones v. City of Opelika*) the Court reversed the eleven-month-old precedent in *Jones*.[67] *Jones* and *Murdock* involved prosecutions of Jehovah's Witnesses for violating various local licensing ordinances. Rather than a strict chronological analysis, the discussion of these "peddler" cases will be organized according to sides taken on the issue of free exercise protection, beginning with what was ultimately the "losing" argument written by Justice Reed, who was in favor of the governmental regulation in *Jones I*.

Jones I included appeals from cases in three states involving licensing requirements imposed upon itinerant door-to-door sellers and transient street merchants for the privilege of plying their wares. In each case Jehovah's Witnesses were convicted for selling their religious literature without a license. The facts showed that each Jehovah's Witness defendant was a minister engaged in preaching the "gospel of the kingdom" and distributing books explaining the religious beliefs. A fixed donation was requested for each book, but sometimes the books were given for free. This activity was carried on door to door, and also in the public streets, for the Witnesses claimed the streets as their place of worship and religious exercise: In conformance with the gospel commands in Matt. 10:11–14 and 24:14 they went "from city to city, from village to village, and house to house, to proclaim [religious doctrines]."[68]

The licensing requirements varied with each case. The city of Opelika, Alabama, required a $10.00 license fee per year for book agents ("Bibles excepted") and a $5.00 fee for transient booksellers. Fort Smith, Arkansas, required a license for each person "peddling" goods, including books, at a fee of $25.00 per month, $10.00 per week, or $2.50 per day. Casa Grande, Arizona, imposed a quarterly license fee of $25.00 (payable in advance) on "transient merchants, peddlers, and street vendors." Jeannette, Pennsylvania, required that all "persons canvassing" purchase a license for a fee of $1.50 per day, $7.00 per week, $12.00 for two weeks, and $20.00 for three weeks. The cost of the licenses was extravagant compared to the amount of money likely to be raised by a Witness from the sale of books and pamphlets. Individual Witnesses paid three cents each for the pamphlets, which were offered for purchase at five cents each. The books were purchased by part-time workers for twenty cents; full-time evangelists paid only five cents each. Furthermore, there "was evidence that some of the petitioners paid the difference between the sales price and the cost of the books to their local congregations. . . ."[69] The religious publishing house of the Jehovah's Witnesses is the Watch Tower Bible & Tract Society, a nonprofit organization.

The Court in *Jones I* framed the constitutional issue as follows:

> The sole constitutional question considered is whether a non-discriminatory license fee, presumably appropriate in amount, may be imposed upon these activities.[70]

Justice Reed argued that all itinerant vendors, not just Jehovah's Witnesses, were subject to the same fee. This was not a discriminatory tax which targeted religious groups, and thus the licensing requirement did not infringe impermissibly on the religious exercise of Jehovah's Witnesses.

> Nothing more is asked from one group than from another which uses similar methods of propagation.[71]

The Court dismissed the notion that local licensing fee requirements as applied to the Jehovah's Witnesses were per se unconstitutional as a prior restraint on their activity, and it indicated that "reasonableness" of fees would be determined on a case-by-case basis, with the religious adherents having to prove that "the burden of the tax was a substantial clog upon [their] activities."[72] The Court otherwise found nothing on the record to indicate that such a burden was present.

As in the *Gobitis* decision, the Court emphasized the need "to ensure orderly living"[73] and the need for "necessary accommodation to the competing needs of his fellows."[74]

> The determination of what limitations may be permitted under such an abstract test rests with the legislative bodies, the courts, the executive and the people themselves guided by the experiences of the past, the needs of revenue for law enforcement, the requirements and capacities of police protection, the dangers of disorder and other pertinent factors.[75]

But there was no listing of what, if anything, the localities had offered in the way of proof as to past "experiences" which would justify the licensing requirement. The Court conducted no searching inquiry into this aspect of the case.

According to the Court, the license requirement was not a regulation of *religion*, but only of "operations which are incidental to the exercise of religion."[76] To require licenses of itinerant preachers, it was "enough" for the justices "that money is earned by the sale of articles."[77]

> When proponents of religious or social theories use the ordinary commercial methods of sales of articles to raise propaganda funds, it is a natural and proper exercise of the power of the state to charge reasonable fees for the privilege of canvassing. . . . If we were to assume, as is here argued, that the licensed activities involve religious rites, a different question would be presented. These are not taxes on free will offerings. But it is because we view these sales as par-

taking more of commercial than religious or educational transactions that we find the ordinances, as presented here, valid.[78]

The activity of the Jehovah's Witnesses did not fit the paradigm of mainstream U.S. Protestantism, but instead seemed to the majority of justices to be itinerant street peddling. Because their activity was thus "commercial," the Witnesses had to contribute, like all other commercial vendors, something "for the privilege of using the streets and conveniences of the municipality."[79]

In summary, the Court in *Jones I* based its decision to uphold prior licensing requirements for Jehovah's Witnesses who preached and carried religious litera-ture in the streets and door to door, upon (1) a distinction they drew between the paradigmatic religious activity of "preaching and instructing" and the paradig-matic commercial activity of street peddling; (2) characterizations of a prior li-censing fee as analogous to regulations of time, place, and manner of speech, and as neither a total prohibition nor a prior restraint; and (3) a total deference to local wisdom that such a licensing tax was necessary for good order.

Justices Reed and Frankfurter delivered vigorous dissents eleven months later in *Jones II*, when the Court reversed its decision in *Jones I*. Justice Reed again emphasized the difference between a privilege tax on soliciting free-will contributions and a "sale" of religious literature. He compared this sale (made as an incident to proselytizing, and consisting of religious tracts) to the secular money-raising ventures of other churches, such as bazaars and church suppers. Justice Reed felt bound by the state court's characterization of the Jehovah's Wit-nesses' "transactions" as sales for the purposes of the local licensing ordinances, and he would not reexamine their conclusions in light of the purposes and pro-tections of the free exercise protection.[80]

Justice Reed in his dissent in *Jones II* also stated explicitly what had been im-plicit in *Jones I*: The activity of the Witnesses simply did not fit his paradigmatic image of "religious exercise."

> Nor do we think it can be said, properly, that these sales of religious books are religious exercises. . . . Certainly, there can be no dissent from the statement that selling religious books is an age-old practice or that it is evangelism in the sense that distributors hope the readers will be spiritually benefitted. That does not carry us to the conviction, however, that when distribution of religious books is made at a price, the itinerant colporteur is performing a religious rite, is worshipping his creator in his way. . . . These are, of course, in a sense, re-ligious practices but hardly such examples of religious rites as are encompassed by the prohibition against [sic] the free exercise of religion.[81]

Justice Reed further analogized the taxation of the Witnesses' activity to the taxa-tion of commercial newspapers: Simply because the content—the freedom of speech, ideas, etc.—is protected does not mean that the state cannot tax the sale of the ideas in newspapers. General taxation does not violate the free press guar-antee because such taxation is not a "prior restraint upon publication." Textu-ally, "free" does not mean "without cost." Rather, the words "free" in the First Amendment mean "a privilege to print *or pray* without permission and without accounting to authority for one's actions."[82]

Note, here, that the Court equates "religious exercise" with "prayer." Justice Reed limited the scope of protection of religious activities under the free exercise clause to such spiritual rites, untainted by "price":

> And even if the distribution of religious books was a religious practice protected from regulation by the First Amendment, certainly the affixation of a price for the articles would *destroy the sacred character of the transaction.* The evangelist becomes also a book agent. . . . The rites which are protected by the First Amendment are in essence spiritual—prayer, mass, sermons, sacrament—not sales of religious goods.[83]

The Jehovah's Witnesses violated the "boundary" between peddler and evangelist when they asked for payment in return for the religious literature. They were no longer engaged in a truly religious activity when they failed to distribute their religious literature for free as a matter of course.

Justice Frankfurter in his dissent in *Jones II* emphasized a different boundary infraction: Jehovah's Witnesses were outsiders because they refused to contribute to the costs of government by paying the licensing tax:

> [H]as the state given something for which it can ask a return? There can be no doubt that these petitioners, like all who use the streets, have received the benefits of government. Peace is maintained, traffic is regulated, health is safeguarded—these are only some of the many incidents of municipal administration. To secure them costs money, and a state's source of money is its taxing power. There is nothing in the Constitution which exempts persons engaged in religious activities from sharing equally in the costs of benefits to all, including themselves, provided by government.[84]

Frankfurter could not accept as a general principle that the free exercise clause prohibited the imposition of local prior licensing fees on religious evangelizing activity that included the sale of religious literature. He would have required the religious adherent to prove that each individual and specific local ordinance was unjust or unreasonable in its pricing or application, and that the license flat tax "in fact cramps activities pursued to promote religious beliefs."[85] As in *Gobitis,* Justice Frankfurter argued that the Court owed deference to the legislature on social matters such as these. As a matter of principle, he would not strike down a licensing ordinance as unconstitutional "on its face" but would require proof that the taxing power was in fact being abused and had become tyrannical. The burden was thus placed on the religious adherent to prove tyranny; the state had no concomitant burdens of proof, but was accorded prima facie deference.

The dissent in *Jones I* (which became the rationale adopted by the majority in *Jones II* to overturn the decision in *Jones I*) and the majority opinion of the Court in *Murdock* found the imposition of a flat tax licensing fee on persons in the particular position of the Jehovah's Witnesses to be an outright violation of the constitutional guarantee of free exercise. The key to this decision was an analogy to requiring a license tax for comparable mainstream Christian ministers: "The mind rebels at the thought that a minister of any of the old established churches could be made to pay fees to the community before entering the pulpit."[86] Ministers in a church and those in the street are both engaged in "an activity whose sole purpose is the dissemination of ideas."[87] The Court analogized to the offensiveness of a hypothetical law which would exclude ministers from a pulpit if they refused or could not afford to pay a civil licensing fee, and it noted that for the Jehovah's Witnesses, the street is their pulpit. Yet, they are being charged a licensing fee to preach in that pulpit.[88]

When one imagines a licensing tax such as the one sought to be imposed upon Jehovah's Witnesses being imposed upon the orthodox Protestant situation, the evils of the tax become clearer: The tax was for a fixed amount, unrelated to receipts derived from the ministerial activity, and was payable in advance: "It requires a sizeable out-of- pocket expense by someone who may never succeed in raising a penny in his exercise of the privilege which is taxed."[89] The license fees were purely for revenue enhancement, unrelated to the cost of regulating the activity (that is, if any regulation or expense even occurred—none was alleged by the localities). The license requirement thus was basically "a flat tax imposed on the exercise of a privilege granted by the Bill of Rights. A state may not impose a charge for the enjoyment of a right granted by the federal constitution."[90] "Freedom of speech, freedom of the press, freedom of religion are available to all, not merely to those who can pay their own way."[91]

The crucial factor in this debate was the use of different paradigms for "religious activity." The majority of the Court in *Jones II* and in *Murdock* gave careful consideration to the Jehovah's Witnesses' own narratives describing the meanings of their activities, their motivations, and what they understood as their obligations to God. Instead of an isolating focus upon the point of sale, the Court looked at the nature of the activity as a whole, placing it within the context of the outsiders' narratives. Once the Court understood the context, it found that the noncommercial, nonprofit, religiously motivated street activity better fit the paradigm of religious activity than that of commercial activity carried on for profit.[92]

> Petitioners spread their interpretations of the Bible and their religious beliefs largely through the hand distribution of literature by full or part time workers. They claim to follow the example of Paul, teaching "publickly, and from house to house." Acts 20:20. They take literally the mandate of the Scriptures, "Go ye into all the world, and preach the gospel to every creature." Mark 16:15. In doing so they believe that they are obeying a commandment of God. . . .
> The hand distribution of religious tracts is an age-old form of missionary evangelism—as old as the history of printing presses. It has been a potent force in various religious movements down through the years. This form of evangelism is utilized today on a large scale by various religious sects whose colporteurs carry the Gospel to thousands upon thousands of homes and seek through personal visitations to win adherents to their faith. It is more than preaching; it is more than distribution of religious literature. It is a combination of both. Its purpose is as evangelical as the revival meeting. This form of religious activity occupies the same high estate under the First Amendment as do worship in the churches and preaching from the pulpits. It has the same claim to protection as the more orthodox and conventional exercises of religion.[93]

The Court in *Murdock* acknowledged the complexity of the regulatory issue due to the competing analogies (peddler versus preacher) applicable to the activity.

It considered its examination of the context crucial to the analysis of the issue, and it rejected the notion that *any* sincere, religiously motivated conduct must be protected as a matter of course.

While advocating a finely tuned analysis of the religious context of the adherent's activity, the Court at the same time upheld a less deferential analysis of the statute at issue because that statute was patently unconstitutional. A general governmental regulation that burdens religious activity when applied should be declared unconstitutional if its unconstitutionality is obvious from the written text of the law (i.e., "on its face"). The First Amendment freedoms of speech, press, and religion "are in a preferred position."[94] Given this preferred position, such freedoms are to be preserved and protected by legal presumptions against legislation which limits them and legal presumptions in favor of these freedoms. An overbroad or vague regulation, for example, can result in prior restraint and suppression of these important freedoms. Therefore, any regulation applied to punish or restrict an exercise of these freedoms is legally presumed to be improper. To survive strict scrutiny it must be narrowly targeted to a specific and serious danger proven to be posed by the exercise of the right.

In rejecting the free exercise analysis used by the Court in *Gobitis* and *Jones I*, the Court adopted other guiding presumptions and principles it deemed more suitable to resolving conflicts between free exercise rights and regulatory needs. By way of summary, these analytical principles are

1. First amendment freedoms—freedom of speech, freedom of religion—are "in a preferred position." Thus, the fact that a regulation is of general applicability and does not target religion is immaterial to the issue of the constitutionality of its *application* to a religious practice.
2. The Court would not defer to the legislature when constitutional freedoms are at stake. Legislation which regulates them must be "narrowly drawn to prevent or control abuses or evils arising from the activity" and the Court will inquire searchingly into the issue. When a statute is not narrowly drawn, it is per se unconstitutional on its face and the burden cannot be placed on the religious adherent to prove the fact of a prohibitive burden in each instance or application.
3. The totality and nature of the religious activity will be contextualized and examined, giving due consideration to the Other's narratives, explaining what they are doing and why. The paradigm of religious activity is not limited to what the present-day mainstream of society considers "religious." Rather, the range of analogies must be expanded to include a broader history of religious movements and in particular of dissenting religious groups.

Parents, children, and the state: *Prince v. Massachusetts* (1944)

In *Prince v. Massachusetts*, the Court upheld the criminal conviction of a Jehovah's Witness under child labor laws for permitting her nine-year-old ward to distribute religious literature with her on public sidewalks.[95] The Court had received the case on appeal from the Massachusetts State Supreme Court, and an analysis of these proceedings below is helpful in understanding the full import of the U.S. Court's decision.

The Massachusetts Supreme Court in *Prince* had agreed with the defendant Prince that the child labor laws "in a broad sense . . . were directed at the regulation of certain ordinary street trades." Thus, the state court had admitted that the child's religious evangelism did not fit within the paradigmatic child labor law violation. Yet, the Massachusetts Supreme Court held that "this will not justify us in excluding from their operation [the operation of the child labor laws] acts that come within the literal terms and that may involve the very evils intended to be curbed." Note the court's equivocal use of the term "may." No "evil" to the child could be proven at trial. The prosecution (and the courts) relied solely upon an interpretation of the statute as including noncommercial distribution of religious literature, which in turn was premised literally upon the ban against the "sale" of literature by girls under the age of eighteen.

The Massachusetts Supreme Court in effect acknowledged the state's inability to show that any "evil" was or would occur under the free exercise circumstances at issue: "It seems apparent that they [the "evils"] may or may not exist in particular instances according to the circumstances just as they may or may not exist in particular instances where the selling is of publications of a secular nature."[96] But this overbreadth, and the regulatory burden it would impose upon the religious worship of the child and the guardian's raising of the child in accordance with the family's religious obligations, had been of no moment to the Massachusetts Supreme Court, which considered the regulation to be only "slight" and "incidental":

> We think that freedom of the press and of religion is subject to incidental regulation to the slight degree involved in the prohibition of the selling of religious literature in streets and public places by boys under twelve and girls under eighteen. . . .[97]

In light of the child's assertion that her street evangelizing was a central religious obligation and a vital aspect of her worship of God, the prohibition of this evangelism as "child labor" in effect acted as a bar to her practicing her religion until she reached the age of eighteen. This result is hardly an "incidental" burden.

The Court, in an opinion by Justice Wiley Rutledge, agreed with the state court's rulings. Although only one year earlier it had held that the street evangelism of the Jehovah's Witnesses was central to their religion, the Court in *Prince* completely deferred to the state in overruling both the guardian's and the child's express wishes to allow the child to fulfill her religious obligation to evangelize. The record in *Prince* showed that the girl considered herself a devout Jehovah's Witness and had "begged" her aunt/guardian to allow her to help her distribute the literature. Her aunt was with her and watching her the entire time. Other children were on the streets legally shopping with their parents. If the literature had been given away instead of offered for sale the law would not have applied.[98]

Ignoring the precedents set and the analytical processes used in *Cantwell*, *Murdock*, and *Jones II*, the Court in *Prince* found that child labor in selling papers on the streets was a harm which the state had a vital interest in preventing, based upon its *parens patriae* power to protect the health, safety, and welfare of the child. In essence, the child was banned by the Court from preaching her religion and fulfilling her religious obligations to evangelize based upon nothing more than vague assertions of harm and the primacy of the state's power of *parens patriae*. Indeed, the Court in *Prince* stated dramatically, in an often-quoted paragraph:

> Parents may be free to become martyrs themselves. But it does not follow they are free, in identical circumstances, to make martyrs of their children before they have reached the age of full and legal discretion when they can make that choice for themselves.[99]

Note the strong language of "martyrdom" used to describe the situation in this case, which, after all, involved a nine-year-old girl and her aunt offering religious literature on a public street.

Those justices who had dissented in *Murdock* and *Jones II* a year earlier concurred in the *result* of the *Prince* case but on separate grounds from that of the opinion of the Court written by Justice Rutledge. Justice Jackson, in an opinion joined by Justices Roberts and Frankfurter, concurred on the basis of their *dissent* in *Murdock*, (i.e., for reasons that previously had been rejected by a majority of the Court).[100]

The question remains, What had swayed those Justices who had voted with the majority in *Jones II* and *Murdock* (upholding the importance of context in free exercise analyses and recognizing the role of public evangelizing in the worship of Jehovah's Witnesses) to then prohibit a child, under the protective eye of her guardian, from worshiping God in the way her faith dictated? Furthermore, the Court's use of the strong descriptive term "martyrdom" does not seem consistent with the minimal "labor" involved in this case. One important clue may be found in Justice Murphy's dissenting opinion. The hardship with which the opinion of the Court is concerned may very well not be the hardships encountered in underage employment (which hardships in this case were never specifically shown to exist). Rather, the "martyrdom" is perhaps more likely the hardships faced by a child who belongs to an unpopular, even hated, religious sect, *and* who attempts to spread this faith in public. Justice Murphy, the lone dissenter, hints at this substratum when he notes the lack of evidence to support the Court's decision otherwise:

> To the extent that they [i.e., "the crippling effects of child employment . . . in public places"] flow from participation in ordinary commercial activities, these harms are irrelevant to this case. And the bare possibility that such harms might emanate from distribution of religious literature is not, standing alone, sufficient justification for restricting freedom of conscience and religion. . . . The evils must be grave, immediate, substantial. . . . Yet there is not the slightest indication in this record, or in sources subject to judicial notice, that children engaged in distributing literature pursuant to their religious beliefs have been or are likely to be subject to any of the harmful "diverse influences of the street." . . . Moreover, Jehovah's Witness children invariably make their distributions in groups subject at all times to adult or parental control, as was done in this case. The dangers are thus exceedingly remote, to say the least. *And the*

> fact that the zealous exercise of the right to propagandize the community may re-
> sult in violent or disorderly situations difficult for children to face is no excuse for
> prohibiting the exercise of that right.[101]

If, indeed, this is the sentiment which fueled the decision in the *Prince* case, it
amounts to a protection of children from the disdain of the majority for believing in an unpopular religion.

The rise and fall of the "compelling state interest" test:
Sherbert v. Verner (1963), *Wisconsin v. Yoder* (1972)
and *Employment Div. v. Smith* (1990)

The 1963 case of *Sherbert v. Verner*[102] introduced another variation of the free
exercise test: In order to withstand constitutional challenge, a governmental burden on the free exercise of religion should be justified by a "compelling state
interest in the regulation of a subject within the State's constitutional power to
regulate."[103] Even if such an interest is shown, the government must show that
accommodating the religious exercise would impossibly undermine the state's
interest in the regulation: It is still "plainly incumbent upon the appellees [the
government] to demonstrate that no alternative forms of regulation would combat such abuses without infringing First Amendment rights."[104]

In *Sherbert*, a Seventh Day Adventist worked in a mill that changed to a six-
day work week. Petitioner Adell Sherbert was fired because she could not work
Saturdays, the Sabbath for Adventists. When she was unable to find other work
because of her inability to work Saturdays, she filed for unemployment compensation. Sherbert was denied benefits, however, because she had rejected suitable
work "without good cause."

The Court held that the denial of unemployment benefits to Sherbert
under these circumstances was unconstitutional. The Court held that both direct and indirect, intentional as well as neutral, burdens on the free exercise of
religion are actionable:

> The ruling forces her [Sherbert] to choose between following the precepts of
> her religion and forfeiting benefits, on the one hand, and abandoning one of
> the precepts of her religion in order to accept work, on the other hand. Govern-
> ment imposition of such a choice puts the same kind of burden upon the free
> exercise of religion as would a fine imposed against appellant for her Saturday
> worship.[105]

Accordingly, the existence or extent of an imposition on constitutional rights is
not determined solely by looking at the state's intention, but also by looking at
the *impact* of the application of the law upon the religious adherent.

Having found an infringement of free exercise rights, the Court then looked
to the state to justify the infringement with substantial proof that a compelling
interest was at stake: "[I]n this highly sensitive constitutional area, "[o]nly the
gravest abuses, endangering paramount interests, give occasion for permissible
limitation," [citation omitted]."[106] But the state could only offer the "possibili-

ties" of fraudulent claims and of dilution of the fund by payments to those not able to find work because of religious impediments. No imminent threat of grave abuse or paramount endangerment was advanced.

The Court further reasoned that even if the government had produced evidence materially supporting its fears of fraudulent claims and other such dangers, the state would still have to demonstrate that these dangers could not be addressed in any way other than the current regulatory scheme which imposes on the free exercise right.[107] Seriously undermining the state's assertion of a compelling interest in the *Sherbert* case was the preexistence of a review system to evaluate claims of "good cause" for refusing work, coupled with the reality that under the labor laws of the state, Sunday worshipers would never find themselves in a similar situation:

> Significantly, South Carolina expressly saves the Sunday worshipper from having to make the kind of choice [between religious conscience and work] which we here hold infringes the Sabbatarian's religious liberty. When . . . the textile plants are authorized by the State Commissioner of Labor to operate on Sunday, "no employee shall be required to work on Sunday . . . who is conscientiously opposed to Sunday work; and . . . he or she shall not . . . by such refusal . . . be discriminated against in any other manner." S.C. Code, sec. 64-4.

The Court accordingly viewed its decision as upholding the requirement of "neutrality in the face of religious differences" in that it extended to Sabbatarians the same unemployment benefits as the law afforded Sunday worshipers.

Justice John Marshall Harlan, dissenting in *Sherbert*, would have left the matter to the state. The South Carolina Supreme Court had held that the free exercise clause was irrelevant to the case because the state's action in denying her benefits "places no restriction upon the appellant's freedom of religion nor does it in any way prevent her in the exercise of her right and freedom to observe her religious beliefs in accordance with the dictates of her conscience."[108] In other words, because the state did not directly compel plaintiff to go against her conscience but merely withheld unemployment compensation benefits, there was no unconstitutional state compulsion in this case.

Justice Harlan's dissent argued that the Court should have deferred to the South Carolina Supreme Court's interpretation of the state's unemployment compensation law as affording benefits only in situations of *involuntary* unemployment. "Involuntary" was to be judged from the standpoint of industry, not the religious adherent:

> [The South Carolina Supreme Court] has consistently held that one is not "available for work" if his unemployment has resulted not from the inability of industry to provide a job but rather from personal circumstances, no matter how compelling. The reference to "involuntary unemployment" in the legislative statement of policy, *whatever a sociologist, philosopher, or theologian might say*, has been interpreted not to embrace such personal circumstances.[109]

While acknowledging that in reality there was "involuntary unemployment," the dissenting Justice Harlan in *Sherbert* would have deferred to state's interpretation which had determined that the petitioner's involuntary religious obligations were simply "personal" and "voluntary." The controlling paradigm for the dissent was the fact that a single mother of three children who could not work Saturdays because she could not find a babysitter was similarly denied benefits, although her situation certainly was not "voluntary" and was indeed sympathetically compelling. Hence, there was no unconstitutional discrimination: The state denied Sherbert benefits "just as any other claimant would be denied benefits who was not "available for work" for personal reasons.[110] The ready distinction between an obligation of religious exercise, which is specifically and contextually protected in the Constitution, and other compelling but unprotected personal obligations and necessities was ignored by the dissent.[111]

The 1972 case of *Wisconsin v. Yoder*[112] has been called the high water mark of the compelling state interest test. Yet, as will be seen, the Court's opinion planted seeds of destruction that were to produce a dramatic curtailment of the free exercise right in later cases.

In *Yoder*, the Court, in an opinion written by Chief Justice Burger, held that the free exercise clause prohibited the state of Wisconsin from criminally prosecuting Amish parents who would not send their children to high school, as required by a general law which compelled school attendance until age sixteen. The Amish argued that such exposure would "endanger their own salvation and that of their children" because of their belief that "salvation requires life in a church community separate and apart from the world and worldly influence."[113] Amish values and way of life are at variance with those taught in the high schools, and the Amish argued that the high school years were the "crucial and formative adolescent period of life" when their children had to be instilled with the separatist values of their faith, not worldly values.

Testimony indicated that the Amish children received basic skills and a basic education through the eighth grade, and that thereafter, they received "hands-on" vocational training giving them the skills required to make them productive members of the community. An educational expert witness opined that this combination was an "ideal" system of learning, "superior" to that of ordinary high school.[114]

The test applied by the Court in *Yoder* was basically a "compelling state interest" test: whether the state of Wisconsin had an "interest of sufficient magnitude to override the interest claiming protection under the Free Exercise Clause."[115] In other words, the free exercise clause created a presumption in favor of the religious adherent, but the presumption was rebuttable by the state's proof of a compelling interest. The Court acknowledged the state's crucial interest in and responsibility for educating its citizens: "Providing public schools ranks at the very apex of the function of a State." But the Court also acknowledged that the Amish parents had a religious freedom claim of similar magnitude: "[T]he values of parental direction of the religious upbringing and education of their children in their early and formative years have a high place in our society."[116]

To resolve this conflict of goods, the Court used what it termed a "balancing process" — "The essence of all that has been written and said on the subject is that only those interests of the highest order and those not otherwise served can overbalance legitimate claims to the free exercise of religion."[117] The use of "balancing" terminology to describe the casuistical process used in *Yoder* was unfortunate. Such balancing, if considered in the purely abstract, has connotations of subjectivity and intuitiveness which run counter to the type of discursive justification required in law.[118] The process actually used by the *Yoder* court was not intuitive and conclusory, however, but was grounded in the facts of the case and was logical, justified, and well reasoned. The Court made searching inquiry into the quality and context of the claims on both sides. The Court looked at the Amish way of life as a whole and the role that their hands-on training of their children played in instilling Amish values. The Court emphasized that the Amish had proven that their mode of life was not secular in character and not a matter of personal preference but, indeed, a vital part of their religion: "[T]he Amish mode of life and education is inseparable from and a part of the basic tenets of their religion—indeed, as much a part of their religious belief and practices as baptism, the confessional, or a Sabbath may be for others."[119] Note that the Court's analytical process here is similar to that used in the *Cantwell* and *Murdock* cases. The Court carefully considered the Old Order Amish's own narratives which described the meanings of and motivations for their claimed religious practice. Once the Court understood the context, it then found analogies to more familiar (mainstream) religious practices of similar importance (e.g., Baptism, Sabbath-keeping, etc.) as helpful bridges into understanding the importance placed upon the unfamiliar practices of the Other.

The Court also looked at the overall context of the religious practice: As noted, the children received intensive hands-on instruction, and with that training they were inducted into a productive and self-sufficient community. Furthermore, the evidence showed that the very existence of the historic and productive community would be threatened if the state's compulsory education law was enforced against Amish children past the eighth grade. Such enforcement "would gravely endanger if not destroy the free exercise of respondent's religious beliefs."[120]

The Court then gave searching scrutiny to the state's case supporting its claimed interest in educating its citizens. Like the Amish, the state had the burden of proving the importance of its claim *in this case*. The Court rejected the state's claim that it should defer to its plenary regulatory discretion and control because the refusal to send the children to school was an "action" and not just a religious "belief" and because the regulation was not targeted at a religious practice but was of general applicability.[121] Instead, the Court required the state to support its "sweeping claim" of a compelling interest in having the Amish attend school until they are sixteen years of age. Accordingly, the state advanced two more particular "compelling interests" to support its claim: preservation of freedom requires citizens prepared to participate effectively in the political system; and "education prepares individuals to be self-reliant and self-sufficient participants in society."[122]

But the evidence proving the importance of these claims *in this case* was lacking. Indeed, testimony instead showed that these interests were in fact substantially met when the Amish way of life was taken as a whole. Because of the evidential showing by the Amish, the Court found that the state had the burden of demonstrating "with more particularity" how it would be adversely affected if a religious exemption to the compulsory education law was granted to the Amish. The state could not make such a showing, and thus the Court ruled in favor of the Amish.

The state also had argued that the Court must automatically defer to the *parens patriae* power of the state to act in a child's best interests. In essence, the state was claiming a conclusive presumption in favor of a state's actions against a parent and on behalf of a child. To this, the Court replied:

> Indeed it seems clear that if the State is empowered, as *parens patriae*, to "save" a child from himself or his Amish parents by requiring an additional two years of compulsory formal high school education, the State will in large measure influence, if not determine, the religious future of the child.[123]

As promising as the quoted language and analysis of the *Sherbert* and the *Yoder* opinions are for the just resolution of free exercise conflicts, the seeds of undoing had been planted within the *Yoder* opinion. For the Court took pains to distinguish the state's stake in the *Yoder* case from situations in which the "police power" of the state is involved:

> To be sure, the power of the parent, even when linked to a free exercise claim, may be subject to limitation under *Prince* if it appears that parental decisions will jeopardize the health or safety of the child, or have a potential for significant social burdens.[124]

The *Yoder* court was quite careful to leave intact its decision in the 1944 case of *Prince v. Massachusetts,* in which (as previously discussed) a Jehovah's Witness was found criminally responsible under child labor laws for permitting her nine-year-old ward to distribute religious literature with her on the public sidewalks.[125] The Court distinguished the case of *Yoder* from the *Prince* case on the grounds that the police power of the state was not in question in *Yoder:* "This case, of course, is not one in which any harm to the physical or mental health of the child or to the public safety, peace, order, or welfare has been demonstrated or may be properly inferred. The record is to the contrary. . . ."[126] But the characterization upon which the Court in *Yoder* relies to distinguish *Prince*—that is, the "severe characterization of the evils" inflicted upon the child in the *Prince* case—was devoid of factual proof and supported solely by sweeping generalizations.

Just as the evidence in *Prince* was not as strong against the religious practice as the *Yoder* Court represented, the evidence in *Yoder* put forth by the state against the religious practice was not as inconsequential as the Court represented. As the separate opinion of Justice William Douglas in *Yoder* indicates, the picture painted in the majority opinion of an "idyllic agrarianism" is not true to the record. Justice Douglas was concerned that the state's police power interest in protecting the future welfare of the Amish children was not given its due consideration. He argued that Amish children were not being given enough "say" in their educational choices, and he feared that the parental decision to keep a child from high school would "forever bar" the child "from entry into the new and amazing world of diversity that we have today." The child may want to be, for example, "a pianist" or an "oceanographer." Justice Douglas emphasized that "a significant number of Amish children do leave the Old Order" and he was concerned about their "truncated" education.[127] The point, here, is that "police power" issues of child welfare were implicated in *both* cases. The Court misstates the record when it distinguishes *Prince* on that basis: It was not that there was *no* evidence of a child's welfare being affected in the *Yoder* case, but that the Court was either not convinced by it, and/or that it was not enough to overcome an implicit presumption in favor of the Amish (a presumption which was not accorded to the Jehovah's Witness in *Prince*). The precedent set in *Yoder* for free exercise protection would have been far stronger had the Court admitted that the Amish practice was not perfect and idyllic (indeed, what human actions are?) and then explained the Court's rationale for protecting it from encroachment by the state.

Furthermore, the precedent set by the decision in *Yoder* is not as protective of free exercise as it might have been because it specifically endorses the *Prince* decision, rather than overruling it or even ignoring it. The decision in *Prince* is a result of an analytical process which included heavily weighted presumptions against the parent/guardian of a child and in favor of the state, a process radically unlike the process used in *Yoder*. In *Prince*, the state court had deemed the religious dimension of the case "irrelevant"[128] and in effect infused new life into the *Reynolds* standard of review (which likewise had refused to consider religious intent or religious context). Hence, the *Yoder* Court's specific affirmance of *Prince* is problematic in light of the radically different analytical process used by the Court in *Prince*.

In summary, the seeds of nullification planted by Justice Burger in the *Yoder* opinion were the specific endorsement of the *Prince* opinion and the misleading portrayal of the Amish practice in idealistic, idyllic terms which set a false and unrealistic standard for other religious practices to meet in order to qualify for free exercise protection. Furthermore, the emphasis upon a "balancing" process ignored the other casuistical tools of discursive justification that had in fact been used (analogy, presumptions, paradigms, contextuality, centrality, etc.), and it opened the way to a misleading portrayal of the free exercise process as subjective and intuitive.

These seeds fell on fertile soil; the post-*Yoder* history of free exercise protection has been exceptionally minimalist, as attested to by the Court itself in the 1990 case of *Employment Division v. Smith*.[129] In the *Smith* case, the Court rejected modern free exercise jurisprudence and reached back into the nineteenth century to reestablish the free exercise standard espoused in the *Reynolds* case. Briefly,[130] the Court in *Smith* held that members of the Native American Church were correctly denied unemployment compensation benefits when they lost their jobs for participating in Native American Church religious services. Notably, the case arose in the context of this society's "War on Drugs." The claimants were counselors at a drug treatment center, and they were fired for "job-related misconduct" when they partook of sacramental peyote during a Native American Church ritual held on private grounds during off-duty hours. The

Court reasoned that since such ingestion was against the criminal law (even though criminal law was irrelevant to the unemployment compensation issue and they had been neither formally charged nor convicted of a crime), the protections of the free exercise clause were automatically unavailable to them. The Court ignored the "particulars" of the Native American Church practice; the only relevancy was that ingestion of peyote was illegal in Oregon.

In defending the Court's minimal process and weighty deference to the state (amounting in effect to a conclusive presumption in favor of the state), Justice Antonin Scalia, writing the opinion for the Court, noted that the Court has

> never invalidated any governmental action on the basis of the *Sherbert* test except the denial of unemployment compensation. Although we have sometimes purported to apply the *Sherbert* test in contexts other than that, we have always found the test satisfied. [Citations omitted.] In recent years we have abstained from applying the *Sherbert* test (outside the unemployment compensation field) at all.[131]

Justice Scalia thus concluded that the "sounder approach" would be to recognize reality and simply eliminate the compelling state interest test. Citing the 1879 *Reynolds* case, Justice Scalia reinstated the "no exception" standard and asserted that to hold to any other standard would promote the spread of anarchy.

Justice Scalia dismissed the long line of free exercise precedents beginning with *Cantwell* by recharacterizing them as "hybrids." Ironically, the bridge-building efforts to find a way to understand the religious practices of Others were used by Justice Scalia to ultimately nullify the precedential effect of these cases. Where the Court had taken pains to make the behavior of the Other more familiar through analogy to other areas of law, Scalia instead saw this use of analogy as the *principle* on which the cases were decided. In other words, Justice Scalia confused *process* with substantive *principle*. Thus, for example, where the Court in *Cantwell* used the process of analogy to compare political speech with religious evangelizing and selling (in that both had the tendency to arouse hostile reaction), Justice Scalia reinterpreted this analogical process to mean that the case had been decided on the free speech *principle*, with free exercise being of no importance to the case. Justice Scalia's interpretive move in *Smith* effectively nullified fifty years of evolving free exercise clause protection by declaring that the cases finding such protection had in reality been decided upon rights and legal principles other than the free exercise clause. In an opinion concurring in the result of *Smith*, Justice Sandra Day O'Connor yet rejected Justice Scalia's reasoning as a departure from settled jurisprudence.[132] Justice Harry A. Blackmun, dissenting, called Justice Scalia's approach a "wholesale overturning of settled law concerning the Religion Clauses of our Constitution."[133]

Yet, the door to a more contextual, casuistical process of resolving free exercise conflicts may have been opened a crack in the 1993 case of *Church of the Lukumi Babalu Aye, Inc. v. City of Hialeah*.[134] In this case, a unanimous Court sent a clear signal that government may not target a nondominant religious group under the guise of a generally applicable law. In order to reach this result, the Court did not defer to the democratic process, but of necessity had to have looked behind the announced secular purposes of the ordinance (prohibit cruelty to animals and protect the health, safety, and morals of the public). All justices agreed with the result of the case: A Hialeah city ordinance that banned ritual animal sacrifice, a practice central to the Santeria religion, was unconstitutional under the free exercise clause. What the justices could not agree upon, however, was the analytical process used to reach that decision.

Justice Anthony M. Kennedy wrote the opinion of the Court. Kennedy paid careful attention to the context in which the ordinance was passed. He explained the background of the Santeria religion as an absorption of Cuban Roman Catholicism into the traditional African religion of the Yoruba people, who were brought to Cuba as slaves. "The Santeria faith," noted the Court, "teaches that every individual has a destiny from God, a destiny fulfilled with the aid and energy of the *orishas*. The basis of the Santeria religion is the nurture of a personal relation with the *orishas*, and one of the principal forms of devotion is an animal sacrifice."[135]

Traditionally, Santeria has been practiced in secret. Adherents were persecuted in Cuba, where the religion was illegal. Santeria was brought to the United States by Cuban refugees, who continued to practice the religion under secrecy until, in 1987, the Church of Lukumi Babalu Aye rented property in Hialeah and openly announced its plans to establish a place of worship, as well as a school, museum, and cultural center. Reaction from the Hialeah community was swift and negative. An "emergency" public meeting of the city council was held, at which a resolution was adopted reflecting the residents' "concern" that the ritual practices of the Santeria religion were "inconsistent with public morals, peace or safety."

In the portion of Kennedy's opinion which was joined by only one other justice,[136] Kennedy probed more deeply into the factual circumstances of the case and especially looked to evidence which pointed to the purpose of the ban on animal sacrifice:

> Relevant evidence includes, among other things, the historical background of the decision under challenge, the specific series of events leading to the enactment or official policy in question, and the legislative or administrative history, including contemporaneous statements made by members of the decision-making body. These objective factors bear on the question of discriminatory object.[137]

This probative process allowed the consideration of evidence revealing a pattern of animosity toward Santeria: City councilmen, for example, asked, "What can we do to prevent the Church from opening?" and declared that followers of Santeria "are in violation of everything this country stands for."[138]

But such a process is vital for answering questions far broader than whether the purpose of the law was discriminatory. Examining the particulars of the law such as public comments and concerns, events surrounding the law, statements by members of the legislative body, and so on, points to the paradigmatic harm that the law was meant to address. Even in the absence of "religious bigotry," the paradigms are important for considering how closely the religious practice matches the paradigmatic harm which the law was meant to address (recall, for example, the comparison between the paradigmatic harms addressed by child labor laws, and the situation of the Jehovah's Witness child on the public sidewalk with her aunt in the *Prince* case).[139]

Ultimately, the process of analogy provided the principal support for the Court's unanimous decision. One source of analogy was other similar religious practices: Animal sacrifice during religious ritual has "ancient roots" and can be found in Judaism before the destruction of the Temple. Analogies between the Santeria animal sacrifice and other forms of permitted animal killing, however, were overwhelmingly persuasive because they tended to show that the category of ritual sacrifice was both underinclusive and overinclusive by comparison with excepted practices and the stated purpose of the law. The city ordinance banning animal ritual sacrifice was passed only after the council was assured by the Florida attorney general that a city ban on ritual sacrifice of animals did not conflict with the requirements and exemptions of the state law on animal cruelty. According to the attorney general, the city's ban was permissible because animal sacrifice was not considered "necessary" killing which would be exempted under state laws; it was done "without any useful motive, in a spirit of wanton cruelty or for the mere pleasure of destruction without being in any sense beneficial or useful to the person killing the animal."[140] The garden and the wilderness in this case proved easy to bridge, however, by referencing analogous instances of animal treatment and killing that were considered legal and appropriate: hunting, fishing, kosher slaughter, euthanasia of strays and unwanted animals, medical experimentation, use of a live animal as bait or to train greyhounds, private slaughter for food, and so on. Indeed, the Court found so many analogous exceptions that it determined the ordinance against animal sacrifice was a blatant gerrymander: "[R]eligion alone must bear the burden of the ordinances. . . . The ordinances 'have every appearance of a prohibition that society is prepared to impose upon Santeria worshipers but not upon itself.'"[141]

This is not to say that the facts of the case were lopsidedly in favor of protecting the free exercise claim, however. After a nine-day trial, the district court had found several compelling state interests that justified the ban on animal sacrifice, including the following: a "substantial" health risk because the animals are "often kept in unsanitary conditions"; "emotional injury to children who witness the sacrifice"; and the method of killing in Santeria animal sacrifice was found to be "unreliable and not humane" and under "conditions that produce a great deal of fear and stress in the animal."[142] Under the limited analytical process avowed in the *Smith* case, such compelling findings would normally have presented an almost insurmountable hurdle for a religious adherent challenging a law with arguably neutral language and enacted under the usually sacrosanct banner of public health, morals, and children.[143] But whether or not the Court's analysis and opinion in the case of *Church of the Lukumi Babalu Aye* were meant to signal an expansion of the *Smith* process, constitutional scholar (and attorney for the church in the *Lukumi* case) Douglas Laycock notes that the process used by the Court in this case has begun to shape the interpretation of *Smith* in the lower courts: The *Lukumi* opinion "appears to have given real content to the requirements of neutrality and general applicability."[144]

In the meantime, political reaction to the Court's decision in the *Smith* case had been steadily building. In 1993, Congress passed the Religious Freedom Restoration Act[145] (RFRA) to broaden free exercise protection beyond the minimum accorded by the Court's ruling in the *Smith* case. As noted in the House Report on the Bill:

> H.R. 1308, the Religious Freedom Restoration Act of 1993, responds to the Supreme Court's decision in *Employment Division, Department of Human Resources of Oregon v. Smith* by creating a statutory right requiring that the compelling governmental interest test be applied in cases in which the free exercise of religion has been burdened by a law of general applicability.[146]

The report particularly singled out for criticism Justice Scalia's reliance on the opinion in *Gobitis*, noting not only that that opinion had been overruled by the Court in *Barnette*, but also that the Court's decision in that case had had tragic repercussions in society, "precipitat[ing] widespread violence against Jehovah's Witnesses including the beating of Jehovah's Witness children on school grounds."[147]

The Religious Freedom Restoration Act restored the compelling interest standard used in such cases as *Sherbert* and *Yoder*. It did not cure the underlying problem of how to apply that standard, the problem of what *process* can be infused into free exercise jurisprudence in order to accommodate fairly the competing goods at stake. Justice O'Connor, for example, used the compelling state interest test in an exceedingly deferential manner to reach the same conclusion as the majority of the Court in *Smith*.[148] Indeed, as noted in the above discussion of the *Yoder* case, the same standard has been held to embrace the deferential process used in *Prince* as well as the searching scrutiny used in *Yoder*. This underlying problem had not been resolved by RFRA.

The effort to protect religious exercise was thrown into further disarray in 1997, when the U.S. Supreme Court declared RFRA unconstitutional in the case of *Boerne v. Flores*.[149] Congress, according to the Court, had exceeded its power under the Fourteenth Amendment when it made the RFRA standard applicable to the states. The Court furthermore reaffirmed its commitment to the "no exception" standard it had announced in the *Smith* case. The practical effect of *Boerne* is to leave protection of religious exercise in the hands of the fifty states when state and local laws and policies are at issue. Indications are that something similar to the vague "compelling state interest" test will be the states' favored option, whether by a state religious freedom statute or by court interpretations of the state constitutions.[150] Accordingly, the goal of this project remains the same, and remains viable, whether under a "compelling state interest" statutory standard or under state or federal free exercise case law: to produce a foundational free exercise jurisprudence, a basic underlying process by which to apply a compelling state interest test. Without such a process, the test is a "shell" with no content and no meaningful, helpful directive as to how to conduct a compelling state interest review. This project asserts a casuistical free exercise process that can easily be overlaid onto the compelling state interest test or used to further flesh out the so-called neutrality and general applicability test of the *Lukumi* case, giving the tests needed and useful guideposts and avoiding the appearance of arbitrariness created when different underlying processes cause different results under the same free exercise test.

The Process of Casuistry

The analytical tools central to the casuistical process (analogy, context, presumptions, and paradigms) actually have already been informally introduced in the discussion of the various "bridge-building" techniques used by the
Court in the *Cantwell, Barnette, Jones II, Murdock, Sherbert, Yoder,* and *Church
of the Lukumi Babalu Aye* cases (and used by the dissenting justices in *Gobitis,
Jones I,* and *Prince* cases). In the following sections casuistry will be more formally defined and its use in both ethical and legal decision making will be discussed. The casuistical method of conflict resolution will be examined and described in detail, noting the importance of principles, paradigms, presumptions,
and "the particulars."

The process of casuistry

Kenneth E. Kirk defines casuistry simply as "no more than the attempt to extend
the principles of morality to unforeseen cases and new problems."[1] Kirk notes
that "unswerving rigidity in morality is bound to shipwreck upon the rocks of
common sense."[2] Indeed, the inability or the failure to make principled distinctions between when a law is applicable and when in the interests of justice it
should not be applicable will bring "the whole authority of the law into question,
and shak[e] it to the foundation."[3] While it is axiomatic that in law the qualities
of clarity and certainty are highly valued, if taken to an extreme the virtue of certitude can overtake and eclipse the ultimate good of justice. This is the present
state of the law governing free exercise cases. Justice Scalia in the *Smith* case determined that clarity, certainty, and an emotivist[4] valuing of the neutral objectivity of procedural order were preeminent values in a free exercise jurisprudence, and he thus saw only two practical options: a highly deferential (if not
conclusive) presumption either in favor of the government or in favor of the individual religious claimant. With the choices thus starkly defined, the Court

chose the government over what it viewed as the anarchy of the individual. Kirk describes the challenge to those who would eschew the extremes of "rigorist intransigence" and anarchical laxity as follows:

> The problem is to find a method by which the verdict of common-sense—[for example,] that a "lie" is sometimes the lesser of two evils, and so in the circumstances blameless and even laudable—may so be combined with the Christian condemnation of lying in general as to offer a principle upon which perplexities of this kind may be solved without, on the one hand opening the door to widespread laxity, or on the other inflicting intolerable hardship upon innocent individuals in abnormal circumstances.[5]

Such a middle course can be provided by casuistry. Casuistry offers a viable, credible alternative because it was developed primarily to deal with the hard cases: cases which did not quite fit within the established parameters of a rule, cases in which the forced fit of a rule would resemble the proverbial Procrustean bed. Casuistical reasoning is particularly useful in resolving cases in which there are conflicting goods or competing principles at stake.[6] Free exercise cases normally present just such a classic situation of conflicting laws, that is, conflicts between the individual rights spelled out in the free exercise clause of the First Amendment and the demands of society set forth in a generally applicable statute.

As has been demonstrated in the prior chapter's analysis of free exercise reasoning, the basic process of casuistry is well familiar to the legal system. In the traditional common law case method, for example, the case at bar is resolved by comparing it to prior cases touching on the same issues which have already been decided by the courts and printed in court reports. Prior court decisions (including contextual facts, process used, relevant principles applied by the court, precise "holding" or decision reached, opinion on appeal, etc.), called "precedents," are to be applied consistently to decide factually similar cases pending at bar. Indeed, where the facts of a conflict are squarely within the paradigm cases which illustrate the rule of law, such conflicts rarely reach the courthouse as formal legal actions because of the certainty of their outcome. Where the facts of a pending case are dissimilar enough from the paradigmatic cases, however, the outcome may not be quite so clear. Should the rule be extended to cover the present case, or would the interests of justice be better served if a different paradigm was used and a different, competing rule was applied to the case instead? Thus, the context of the case fuels the reasoning process, and, depending on the facts of a case, different precedents which better account for the equities of the context may apply.[7]

Aristotelian moral philosophy is instructive, for this system of reasoning is considered foundational for Western casuistry.[8] Aristotle acknowledges that rational principles rule, not the whim of the individual; otherwise there is danger of subjectivism or favoritism. Yet, principles here are by no means themselves tyrannical. Being treated justly is just as important to Aristotelian justice as acting justly.[9] Aristotle posits equity as a corrective of universal justice where the strict application of the law would be unjust. Thus, there is a working tension between the abstract and the particulars in Aristotelian ethics, which Aristotle accepts as the nature of legal as well as ethical reasoning. Neither justice nor ethics is a precise science, encompassing a search for absolute and universally fixed principles.[10]

Casuistry thus plays a prominent role in both legal and ethical reasoning: The particulars of the case are crucial to the determination of the legality or morality of the conduct. The casuist does not reason "from the top down," applying absolute principles categorically across the board.[11] Indeed, the casuist points out that there are few, if any, absolute principles: Even to such an absolute prohibition in the Ten Commandments as "Thou shalt not kill," exceptions driven by competing principles and goods have been carved out, for example, in matters of self-defense, just war, capital punishment, and so on.[12]

Thus, casuistry recognizes the practical limits to absolute rules. In casuistry, primary emphasis is placed upon a nuanced and sensitive analysis of the context, to give fair and in-depth consideration of all the competing goods and principles at stake.

The tools of casuistry

Albert R. Jonsen and Stephen Toulmin describe casuistry as a process of reasoning by which to make justifiable decisions in hard cases where there are competing goods (principles, values, precedents) at stake. Casuistry is:

> the analysis of moral issues, using procedures of reasoning based on paradigms and analogies, leading to the formulation of expert opinions about the existence and stringency of particular moral obligations, framed in terms of rules or maxims that are general but not universal or invariable, since they hold good with certainty only in the typical conditions of the agent and circumstances of action.[13]

This definition is helpful in that it lists several of the "tools" of casuistical reasoning: paradigms, analogies, rules, attention to the conditions of the agent and the circumstances of the action. From this definition, as well as other general descriptions of the casuistical process by Toulmin and Jonsen, Kirk, and other theologians and ethicists, four basic steps of casuistical reasoning can be discerned.

Step (1) is a careful analysis of all of the particulars regarding the circumstances of the case. The casuist's first question is not "What are the rules?" but, rather, "What is going on here?" This is probably the most crucial part of the casuistical process. As noted by Toulmin and Jonsen:

> The casuists drew on the traditional list of circumstances—"who, what, where, when, why, how, and by what means." . . . They also take note of the "conditions of the agent": does fear for one's life, for one's reputation, for one's goods, justify a lie? . . . The cases are filled with qualifications about greater or lesser harm, more or less serious injury, more or less imminent danger, greater or lesser assurance of outcome.[14]

Kirk emphasizes that the casuist must have an open mind, an eye for complexity, an active and empathetic imagination, and a willingness to try to understand the

situation from the point of view of another. Without such an effort to contextual-
ize the case, a crucial moral aspect of that case may be missed.[15]

Step (2) is the reliance upon paradigm and analogy to get to the heart of the
morally relevant features and principles at issue. What is important to note,
here, is the move from abstract laws and principles to paradigmatic illustrations
of those laws. These paradigms concretize and embody the essence of the evil or
harm which the moral law was most clearly meant to avoid or prohibit, and/or
the essence of the good which the law was most clearly meant to promote. Kenneth Kirk notes that "every principle, to be morally operative, must be accompa-
nied by illustrations and examples," and that "such principle is partially illuminated by the known instances in which it holds good."[16]

Step (3) is a comparison of the context and the particulars of the pending
case with relevant paradigmatic cases illustrating potentially applicable principles. This is a crucial step in practical argument:

> Practical arguments depend for their power on how closely the present circum-
> stances resemble those of earlier precedent cases for which this particular type
> of argument was originally devised. . . . In the language of rational analysis,
> the facts of the present case define the grounds on which any resolution must
> be based; the general considerations that carried weight in similar situations
> provide warrants that help settle future cases. So the resolution of any problem
> holds good *presumptively*; its strength depends on the similarities between the
> present case and the precedents; and its soundness can be challenged (or *re-
> butted*) in situations that are recognized as *exceptional*.[17]

Paradigms illustrate a moral principle at its most certain application. Hence, the
closer on a continuum the pending case is to relevant moral paradigmatic cases,
the more certain and clear the ethical decision is about the pending case. Con-
versely, the further one travels from the paradigm cases, the more uncertain is
the ethical pronouncement. As Jonsen and Toulmin note, "[l]east susceptible
of being argued against were the paradigm cases; the further one moved away
from the paradigm, the more arguable—in terms of pro and con—the case
became."[18]

"Paradigm cases," note Jonsen and Toulmin, "create presumptions that
carry conclusive weight, in the absence of exceptional circumstances."[19] Miller
further explains that

> presumptions hold generally and for the most part, but not absolutely. We pre-
> sume, as a common place, that they [presumptions] ought to orient our re-
> sponse to a situation. Such presumptions or moral orientations may give way
> when they conflict with rival duties in a situation of genuine moral perplexity,
> or when their applicability is extended beyond their normally circumscribed
> situations.[20]

If a situation at hand mirrors the paradigm situation/case, then the burden of
proof is on the party who seeks to go against the applicability of that paradigm
and hence seeks to rebut the presumption. "[A] presumption imposes on the
party against whom it is directed the burden of going forward with evidence to
rebut or meet the presumption. . . ."[21]

Legal presumptions can create impossibly high hurdles for challengers to the system. Indeed, the assigning of a presumption can be the determining factor of a case. In free exercise cases, the fact of prima facie illegal behavior (albeit religiously compelled) has at times raised a conclusive, irrebuttable presumption[22] of guilt against the religious adherent, especially when the *Reynolds* standard is applied to prohibit consideration of competing free exercise values and the religious context of the behavior. In the Courts' decisions favoring the free exercise claimants in *Cantwell*, *Murdock* and *Jones II*, *Sherbert*, and *Yoder*, no presumption was given to the government that its interest in the regulation was compelling *under the facts of that case*. In contrast, as has been seen in the *Prince* and the *Gobitis* cases, the government was accorded, as a practical matter, a conclusive presumption in favor of the overall compellingness of its general interest to regulate in the area. The Court disregarded evidence presented by the free exercise claimants which was attuned to the specifics of the religious context, as well as the state's interest at issue *in that case*.

Clearly, free exercise cases are rife with problems of presumptions and burdens of proof, whether implicitly imposed or explicitly applied. Casuistry helpfully reconfigures free exercise cases as conflicts of principles. Two goods are at stake; two legal commands are at odds. Conclusive presumptions (whether explicit, as in *Reynolds* and *Smith*, or implicit, as in *Gobitis*, for example) are inappropriate for either side of the issue. In recognition of the conflicting goods, it seems just to allocate burdens and rebuttable presumptions equitably among the parties. The religious claimant has the burden of proving that the actions at issue are part of a bona fide religious practice, which is a threshold showing in order to invoke free exercise protection. Once this showing has been made, all connotations and implicit presumptions of guilt and the concomitant burdens the notion of "defense" impose on the claimant should give way to a more equalized conflict of principles situation.

On the one hand, the government is no longer accorded a broad deference amounting to a conclusive presumption. The state must come forward with evidence tending to show that the paradigmatic harm is present in this case, and that there is no less restrictive means by which to accomplish the state's purposes. If the law itself contains exceptions and exemptions, the failure also to exempt the religious practice must be explained and justified in order for the state to show that it does indeed have a compelling interest in prohibiting the religious exercise. The state, in sum, must now shoulder the burden of producing evidence that *in this case* the religious practice must be regulated and cannot otherwise be accommodated. It is this step that has proven the difference between, for example, the Court's majority opinion and the dissenting opinion in *Prince*, as well as in *Sherbert*.

On the other hand, because there are conflicting goods at stake, the free exercise claimant also must come forward with evidence indicating where along the continuum the religiously compelled action for which she is claiming constitutional protection lies in relation to the applicable paradigms favoring free exercise protection. The evidence, for example, should tend to show that the practice/obligation is central to the religion (and not of trivial impact). The evidence may also tend to bridge the garden and the wilderness by showing comparable secular practices which are not prohibited or regulated. Or, the evidence may need to show that the practice does not cause or result in the type of paradigmatic harms which are *not* accorded protection under the rubric of religious freedom and hence which the state *does* have a paramount interest in preventing. These paradigmatic harms include harms to a specific person (human sacrifice, assault, etc.) or to the discrete property of another (destroying the property of "heretics").[23]

Stated in another way, free exercise cases at the outset present the courts with a conflict of principles situation, and a casuistical process would require each side to come forward with evidence of its conformity with the accepted parameters of an applicable paradigm. Once conformity is shown, a casuistical process would then allocate rebuttable presumptions favoring the applicability of each paradigm so shown to apply to the case. Accordingly, each side would also have the burden of coming forward with evidence that tends to show why the other side's "good" is not applicable or should not prevail *in this case.*

In law as in ethics, the presumption is in favor of the paradigm and the burden of proof is on the party challenging its applicability. As one legal treatise on evidence has described it: "[A]nything worthy of the name 'presumption' has the effect of fixing the burden of persuasion on the party contesting the existence of the presumed fact."[24] Note that in law the broad phrase "burden of proof" actually refers to two different burdens. As explained by McCormick, one burden is that of producing evidence on an issue; the other is the burden of persuasion on an issue.[25] As already discussed, the burden of coming forward with evidence is on all parties in a free exercise case since it presents the hard situation of potentially conflicting goods. But the burden of persuasion need not be assigned until the case is at its close and ready to be decided.[26] In free exercise cases this might be the preferred procedure; the burden could then be assigned on the basis of which party had aligned itself within the circumscribed situation represented in the paradigm, thereby placing the ultimate burden of proof on the party challenging the applicability of the paradigm in this case. For example, in the *Yoder* case the state's claimed good at stake was the need for an educated, self-supporting citizenry. The evidence indicated that in that case the Amish situation had met and fulfilled that good. Furthermore, the Amish had shown that their practice was of central importance to their religion and religious way of life.[27] The intrusion of the statutory obligation was not trivial; it was not a matter of throwing rice at a wedding. In contrast, the state had shown that its interest in the education of its citizens was indeed important, but it had failed to show the presence of this compelling interest *in that case.* Furthermore, some of the harms it alleged (what happens to students who leave the community? what of the Amish children's lost opportunities and wasted talent potential in, for example, physics or opera?) seemed, on a continuum, closer to the paradigmatic scope of parental authority and an area in which the state typically does not micromanage. In sum, the Amish had met their burden of coming forward with evidence showing the applicability of free exercise protection, while the state failed to produce evidence indicating that the paradigmatic good of its regulation was not being met in this case. The ultimate burden of proof rested on the state, then, because it was challenging the free exercise paradigm which now had been accorded a presumption in favor of its applicability.

Note how, under a free exercise casuistry, the original structure (at the initial stage of litigation, known as the "pleadings," in which the parties clarify the main point of the lawsuit) of the free exercise case as a conflict of principles can crumble into a virtual "no contest" when the paradigmatic good of the statute is compared with the actual context of the religious practice. Although the letter of the law may not be technically met, using a casuistical process it may be discovered that the spirit of the law is indeed satisfied.

Several categories of paradigms potentially must be considered in a free exercise case, including but not limited to: the paradigmatic harm to be avoided by the specific governmental regulation; paradigms presented by other similar situations which are exempted, excepted, or otherwise not covered by the regulation, and how the religious practice might be comparable to these situations; social harms and the nature of the societal good of "order," which when threatened would tend to justify government intervention and regulation over against the free exercise right (these paradigms will be explored in the next chapter); and the nature and scope of religious activities forming the central core to be protected under free exercise paradigms (worship and one's relational obligations to one's God tend to be of highest importance, for example).

The nature and content of these latter paradigms will be explained and explored in the next chapter. At this point in the argument, it is most important to note that in a conflict of principles situation such as that presented by a free exercise claim, conclusive presumptions are inappropriate, both sides have the burden of coming forward with evidence, and an ultimate assignment of a burden of proof will not likely be made until the proofs and the contexts are related to the paradigms appropriate to the case. This means that claims whose particulars are closest to those normally encompassed within the paradigm would carry the more conclusive weight.

Step (4) in the casuistical process is the final resolution of the case. This may be reached through a combination of processes: an accumulation of evidence and an evaluation of the weight and strength of that evidence; an application of the contextual particulars to the relevant principles and paradigms; and an analogy to determine which of the competing paradigm(s) is/are most applicable to the pending case, and which ultimate resolution is in the overall best interests of justice. The detailed case analysis in chapter six of the Native American Church's use of sacramental peyote is included to further illustrate how the process of coming to a resolution works. This process is not subjective, arational, or beyond discursive justification; if it appears to be so, then the casuist has not done her job. For, as Jonsen and Toulmin note, a casuist's resolution of a case was "required to carry conviction with an experienced professional audience."[28] In the case of a legal judgment, that decision must not be written to persuade only the bar and the judiciary, but also the parties to the case, as well as the general public. The judge must thus be a skilled rhetorician, one who constructs arguments "intended to convince hearers of the rightness . . . of a course of action."[29]

Avoiding the abuse of casuistry

Casuistry is principled decision making, not anarchy. Yet, the perception of "laxity" lingers.[30] Hence, any argument for the adoption of a casuistical free exercise jurisprudence must directly confront such criticisms. How can a casuistical free exercise jurisprudence avoid deteriorating into such "abuse"?

One guiding principle must be to not lose sight of the forest for the trees. Any interpretation of facts and application of a principle to those facts ultimately must remain true to the essence and spirit of the legal principles. Fancy rhetorical and definitional maneuverings are just not credible in the long run if the spirit of the principle is violated by its interpretation. Thus, the appearance of laxity, either for or against the religious adherent, must be avoided. Aristotle provides some helpful guidance and parameters in these types of cases:

> When the law speaks universally . . . and a case arises on it which is not covered by the universal statement, then it is right, where the legislator fails us and has erred by over-simplicity, to correct the omission—to say what the legislator himself would have said had he been present, and would have put into his law had if he known. Hence, the equitable is just, and better than one kind of justice—not better than absolute justice, but better than the error that arises from the absoluteness of the statement. And this is the nature of the equitable, a correction of law where it is defective owing to its universality.[31]

Aristotle's notion of "saying what the legislator himself would have said" served, for him, as guidance for the limits of what could be done in the name of equity. Although such mind reading sounds impossible to a relativist, skeptical, modern world, the general spirit and intent of a moral/law can be gleaned, especially with the assistance of paradigmatic illustrations of the laws at stake. If the facts of the particular case do not seem to fit the spirit of the law (as determined with help from an analysis of its historic context and driving concerns, as well as the law's paradigmatic examples), and yet the case still happens to fall under the rubric of the literal prohibition, Aristotle would find that the application of equity was justifiable. The key, here, is the notion of equity as "corrective justice" and not a technical loophole. Aristotle tellingly has described equity as a form of *justice*, not laxity or compassion. Absolute justice remains the highest form of justice, but where the spirit of the absolute, universal law seems to be violated by its application to the particular circumstances, equity may step in to prevent an injustice from occurring. Aristotle recognizes that absolutely applying an absolute principle can lead to *injustice*. Notably, a free exercise conflict presents an even more compelling situation than that posed by Aristotle's equitable justice, for free exercise cases involve *conflicting laws* (Constitution versus statute) and not simply an equitable claim for an exemption from a universal law.

Another concern is that casuistry creates a "slippery slope." People who hear of a vindication of a free exercise right might no longer see a need to obey the law with which the right conflicted, and/or they might argue as a matter of course for the religious "loophole." The "slippery slope" concern, however, is mitigated by the paradigmatic, contextual, and principled approach of casuistry:

Sincerity of belief, religious context and framework, and the essence of the legal principle, for example, all must be considered. The religious claimant, as well as the government, have burdens to meet. This approach, it is to be emphasized, is one of principled justice between competing goods, and not anarchical relativism.[32]

Finally, there is an obligation on the part of the courts to fully develop the facts and the context of the religious practice and fully explain the competing principles and equities involved in the decision. The perception of unfairness or laxity is just as harmful to justice as actual impropriety itself. Careful, detailed explanations and good communications are the main keys to avoiding misunderstandings and misinterpretations.[33]

In summary, casuistry is far more common in practice than is generally realized or acknowledged. Because there are in reality few, if any, "absolute" principles, even the most rigorist ethic necessarily entails a process to recognize competing "goods" and competing principles. If such justice is not accomplished formally, it will sneak in surreptitiously and ultimately undermine the very foundations of authority. As Kirk notes, the more perfectionist or rigorist the moral code is, the greater the chance that laxity will creep into its application. Rigidity creates the inevitable need for improper laxity. Once the existence of, indeed the practical *necessity* for recognizing, competing goods and principles is acknowledged, the focus then can rightfully switch from *whether* casuistry should be done to *how* to do "good" free exercise casuistry and thereby avoid the dangers of laxity. The problem is not casuistry, but (as Kirk and Jonsen and Toulmin argue) it is a tyranny of absolutes which create laxity and legal injustice.

The distinction between belief and practice is an example of "bad" casuistry, developed and relied upon by the Court to escape the problem posed by the false premise of an absolutely fixed and invariable free exercise right. In the case of free exercise jurisprudence, the fear of an absolutist free exercise principle led to laxity in preserving its protection (i.e., automatic deferral to the legislature on matters involving religious behavior).

Developing a range of "content" for a casuistical jurisprudence

As John D. Arras notes, casuistry is "an engine of thought that must receive *direction* from values, concepts, and theories outside of itself." Casuistry is a process that requires contextual and principled input. Casuistry, therefore, is not "theory-free."[34] The first question, then, must be, Where do the values, paradigms, presumptions, and theories of a free exercise jurisprudence come from? Sources for principles and paradigms which may be used in a casuistical jurisprudence to resolve free exercise conflicts will be sought in the history and the philosophy of the movement toward religious freedom in the West. These initial questions will be explored in chapter 3.

Law and Dis-orderly Religion

*Typologies of the Relationship between
Conscience and the State*

The purpose of this chapter is to search beyond the confines of the "black letter law" for paradigms and principles basic to a free exercise casuistical
analysis. The chapter will begin by introducing four types or models, within the
context of Western Christian theology and tradition, for the relationship between
conscience and state authority. For each type, the supporting biblical, patristic,
and other theological sources will be explored in depth, including extensive
quotes from primary material. This foundational material will include theory
drawn from the movement toward religious toleration in seventeenth-century
England, as well as writings from the American Founding Era that offer a fertile
source of paradigms and principles for a free exercise casuistry.

H. Richard Niebuhr undertook a similar task, albeit with a different central
topic. In *Christ and Culture*, Niebuhr presents five typologies of the relations between Christianity and civilization. His acknowledgment of the weakness of
using typology, as well as his defense of his process, is equally applicable to this
project:

> A type is always something of a construct. . . . When one returns from the hy-
> pothetical scheme to the rich complexity of individual events, it is evident at
> once that no person or group ever conforms completely to a type. Each histori-
> cal figure will show characteristics that are more reminiscent of some other
> family than the one by whose name he has been called, or traits will appear that
> seem wholly unique and individual. The method of typology, though histori-
> cally inadequate, has the advantage of calling to attention the continuity and
> significance of the great *motifs* that appear and reappear in the long wrestling of
> Christians with their enduring problem. Hence it also helps us to gain orienta-
> tion as we in our own time seek to answer the question of Christ and culture.[1]

Similarly, the four types developed in this project help us gain an orientation
into the question of the conflict between conscience and the state. Moreover, I
contend that free exercise jurisprudence must reject as models the types which

have justified religious persecution (the levitical type) or a disregard for non-dominant religious practices and obligations (duly ordered authority type and sometimes the enlightenment type). Of all four types, the two kingdoms type most suitably honors both the individual's duty of conscience and important state interests.

Introduction: Four types

The foundational scriptures of Christianity reflect the complexities that continue to haunt the issue of religious freedom.[2] Broadly speaking, the texts of the Hebrew Bible and the New Testament present three divergent typologies for the relationship between sacred duties of conscience and obligations to the civil state: the two kingdoms, duly ordered relationships, and levitical types. The fourth type, enlightenment, is grounded in the Christian tradition but premised more upon reason than scriptural text.

The essence of the two kingdoms type is that the secular and the sacred are separate kingdoms with distinct powers, jurisdictions, and responsibilities; the laws needed to keep the civil peace and to help society flourish are concerned with material (person-person and person-property) issues, are pragmatic (not perfectionist), and are less comprehensive than the laws governing the spiritual realm. The good of civil order is achieved under the two kingdoms type when each jurisdiction exercises the power and authority which belongs to it alone.

In contrast, at the heart of the duly ordered relationships type is the equating of order with unquestioning obedience to state authority. The state's enforcement of religious orthodoxy in the name of the good of civil peace and order has been justified by the concept of the Christian ruler possessing a dual mandate to enforce both spiritual and civil laws. The civil ruler is deemed to have received the authority to act as God's earthly agent, wielding His "avenging sword" in furtherance and in defense of the one true faith. In the modern era, the duly ordered relationships type continues to undergird laws and court decisions that compel strict obedience to the law over against any claim for exemptions based upon conscience. Claims of competing religious obligations are mechanically rejected using a dualistic thinking that posits an either/or choice: absolute obedience or anarchy.

Under the levitical type, in turn, civil order is defined in terms of purity. "Disorder" is the result of defilement and contamination. If order is purity, than heresy cannot be tolerated. To a stronger extent than the duly ordered relationships type, the levitical type compels state-imposed religious conformity and the merging of religious law with civil law, for to deviate from purity is to perish. Tolerance under the levitical type is a serious threat to the good order of the state for two reasons. First, such defilement invites swift and severe divine retribution. A notion of corporate guilt underlies the fear of divine retribution: The sins of one are visited upon the many. The entire polis becomes accountable, and liable to punishment, for individual sins including heresy and blasphemy.[3] Second, spiritual error is as dangerous to civil order as a physical uprising. Such error is not harmless; it corrupts the soul and the conscience, thereby affecting citizens' good judgment and ability to reason. Such corruption is as deadly and contagious as a plague and as destructive to society as a terrible flood.

The fourth type, the enlightenment type, is firmly rooted in the Christian tradition although it is not as much premised upon scriptural proof-texts as it is upon Christian tradition and upon reason as a divine gift. While reliance upon appeals to God-given reason and common sense is evident from early Christianity, the enlightenment type did not come into its own in theological debates over state authority until John Locke and William Penn championed its principles during the religious turmoil of seventeenth-century England. Under the enlightenment type, the good of order is achieved by moderation and balance: The essence of this type is an esteem for reason, common sense, and reasonableness. True religion, for example, is that which promotes peace, charity, and goodwill among all persons. A state's use of force in furtherance of spiritual matters is unreasonable and ineffectual, and it promotes strife which disturbs the civil peace. The state has no jurisdiction over faith and ritual; these are left to one's conscience. Under this type, however, religious conscience runs into trouble when its dictates are not viewed as "reasonable."

There are certainly specific instances over the centuries where these four conceptions have overlapped at the edges, but, generally speaking, the categories are useful in sorting out the various theories which the Western Christian tradition has used to understand and define the relationship between state authority and sacred obligations of conscience.

An explanation

What follows next in this chapter will not be to everyone's taste: The argument is highly (perhaps even annoyingly) detailed, and original sources are often quoted at length. The rationale for this can be traced to (perhaps blamed upon) many years of litigation experience: The best evidences in support of a proposition are the very words of the participants themselves. In the religious freedom debate, particularly, a crucial understanding is lost when the debates are paraphrased, rephrased, and summarized: The same words are used to connote radically different ideas, and hence the vagueness of the terms framing the debate is the source of much of the confusion and complexity surrounding the issue of religious freedom within the Christian tradition. The advocates' (for there are no "neutral" theologians in this debate) own words, and word choices, reveal both the context and parameters of their conception of the extent of religious freedom ("macro" view), as well as the meanings and definitions they impart to often-used individual words which make up the debate ("micro" view), that is, terms as basic as "Christian" and "order." Furthermore, extensive exposure to the actual words and word choices of the participants can be helpful clues to motives, prejudices, passions, and attitudes which are driving the debate. In summary, the words themselves are important, and hence, there is indeed a method to my madness!

The two kingdoms type

In the model or type of the two kingdoms, the civil and the sacred reign over distinctly different jurisdictions; respect is due the civil state, but its authority does not extend to the relationship between the individual and her God. Several scriptural writings have been used by Christian advocates of religious liberty to support this concept: "Render therefore to Caesar the things that are Caesar's, and to God the things that are God's" (Matt. 22:21 (RSV)).[4] "My kingship is not of this world; if my kingship were of this world, my servants would fight, that I might not be handed over to the Jews; but my kingship is not from the world" (John 18:36 (RSV)).[5] Proponents of religious freedom also cite the pronouncement of Gamaliel, a Pharisee and "a teacher of the law," in response to the council's arrest of the apostles for preaching: "[K]eep away from these men and let them alone; for if this plan or this undertaking is of men, it will fail; but if it is of God, you will not be able to overthrow them. You might even be found opposing God!" (Acts 5:38–39 (RSV)).

The gospel parable of the tares and the wheat also became a key proof-text for those arguing on behalf of religious liberty.

> The kingdom of heaven may be compared to a man who sowed good seed in his field; but while men were sleeping, his enemy came and sowed weeds among the wheat, and went away. So when the plants came up and bore grain, then the weeds appeared also. And the servants of the householder came and said to him, "Sir, did you not sow good seed in your field? How then has it weeds? He said to them, "An enemy has done this." The servants said to him, "Then do you want us to go and gather them?" But he said, "No; lest in gathering the weeds you root up the wheat along with them. Let both grow together until the harvest; and at harvest time I will tell the reapers, 'Gather the weeds first and bind them in bundles to be burned, but gather the wheat into my barn.'"[6]

Supporters of religious freedom interpret the "field" in this parable to represent the state; hence, separating, uprooting, and destroying the "heretical" is not to be done here ("in the field") but, rather, is the sole responsibility of God when he harvests souls.

Tertullian's *Apology* is illuminative of the early Christian paradigm for the proper limits of state authority. The *Apology* (written approximately A.D. 200) is the early church's response to religious persecution by the Roman Empire. The empire was premised on a duly ordered relationship worldview: Civil order was achieved and maintained through *pax deorum*, "the right harmonious relationship between gods and men."[7] Accordingly, Roman religion merged with the Roman state in a form of civil religion. The result, for those with religious scruples preventing them from participating in the state religious celebrations and worship ceremonies, was persecution as an enemy of the state.

The crux of Tertullian's argument against state persecution is that no "physical" breach of the peace had ever been proven: "But who has ever *suffered harm* from our assemblies? . . . we are as a community what we are individuals [*sic*]; *we injure nobody, we trouble nobody*."[8] Tertullian's vision of the relationship between sacred obligations and the polis is that the state has no legitimate interest in the beliefs and worship of its citizens *unless* those beliefs and practices can be *proven* harmful to other specific members of the community. Tertullian, trained in the law, here deliberately drew upon the judicial process and its reliance upon factual evidence: The "harm" cannot be religious, philosophical or otherwise tenuous and metaphysical, but must be evidentiary, that is, the quality of concrete, specific, evidential, factual proofs as presented in a court of law.

Tertullian believes that rulers, including the Roman Caesar, are "appointed by God," but this does not lead him to condone every act of state as inspired by God. Even "the majesty of Caesar" must be "kept within due limits"; he is still "under the Most High" and thus "less than divine."[9] Tertullian accordingly expresses a basic tenet of the two kingdoms concept, that the authority of the state, while having its source in the realm of the divine, is limited to the realm of the material: State power does not extend over matters of the spirit.

> They [earthly rulers] reflect upon the extent of their power, and so they come to understand the highest; they acknowledge that they have all their might from Him against whom their might is nought. Let the emperor make war on heaven; let him lead heaven captive in his triumph; let him put guards on heaven; let him impose taxes on heaven? He cannot.[10]

Tertullian's *Apology* and his treatise, *On Idolatry*, illuminate the early Christian paradigmatic conception of the duties and relationship of the faithful to society. The Christian, states Tertullian, "is noted for his fidelity even among those who are not of his religion. . . . [T]he Christian does no harm, even to his foe."[11] Christians, Tertullian explains, "reject no creature of His hands, though certainly we exercise restraint upon ourselves, lest of any gift of His we make an immoderate or sinful use. So we sojourn with you in the world, abjuring neither forum, nor shambles, nor bath, nor booth, nor workshop, nor inn, nor weekly market, nor any other places of commerce."[12]

Yet, while Paul and Tertullian both emphasize the (self-limiting) freedom of the Christian and the practical necessity if not actual desirability of maintaining social intercourse with "outsiders,"[13] Tertullian ultimately speaks in greater detail about, and hence seems to place greater emphasis upon, self-limits to protect the faithful from the danger of contagion and infection from outsider contact. For Tertullian, the danger of contamination flows from society to the church, in comparison with the levitical type, in which the few nonconformist believers/worshipers pose the dangers of contamination and divine retribution to the larger society.

On the one hand, Christians have a duty to pay Caesar's taxes (except, for example, the tax that supports the pagan temples).[14] On the other hand, Christians are voluntarily to avoid certain trades, "however gainful," which ultimately further idolatry or other unlawful (to the Christian) actions. Morally culpable agency extends not only to performance of the wrongful activity (idol worship, fornication, etc.), but also to furnishing the *means* by which others in society can perform the sinful acts: "In no case ought I to be *necessary* to another, while he is doing what to me is unlawful."[15] Yet, outsiders are not to be discriminated

against. Tertullian is silent on the obvious option whereby Christian vendors selectively pick and choose the customers to whom they will sell frankincense, for
example: Frankincense was problematic in that it had a multitude of uses, some
evil (use in sacrifice to pagan idols) and some helpful (for medicinal ointment or
Christian burial rites). Rather, Tertullian prohibits all Christian participation in
any art, trade, or profession which generally would tend to include or enable
idolatry or sinful acts.[16]

Tertullian limits social intercourse to those pagan ceremonies which are "at
the service" of friends and fellow citizens (e.g., weddings, namings). If the directed purpose of the social or state activity is to serve an idol, however, the faithful must shun it and remain apart. Tertullian thus interprets Paul's ethic of
service to outsiders accordingly:

> But albeit he [Paul] does not prohibit us from having our conversations with
> idolaters and adulterers, and the other criminals, saying, "otherwise ye would
> go out from the world," of course he does not so slacken those reins of conversa-
> tion that, since it is necessary for us both to *live* and to *mingle* with sinners, we
> may be able to *sin* with them too. . . . To live with heathens is lawful, to die
> with them is not. Let us live with all; let us be glad with them, out of commu-
> nity of nature, not of superstition. We are peers in soul, not in discipline; fellow-
> possessors of the world, not of error.[17]

Thus, according to Tertullian's envisioning of the Christian in a pagan polis, the
Christian mingles but does not actively "sin" with fellow citizens; to avoid participation in sin the Christian must voluntarily refrain ("voluntary" in a civic
sense, of course, since God commands that the action not be done) from doing
what the state otherwise permits, that is, from participating in activities other
citizens enjoy and profit from. The larger, civic "community of nature" is vital to
the purer Christian community, but the Christian community voluntarily re-
frains from full civic participation in that community.[18]

Conventional wisdom posits here a temporal pause in the development of
freedom of conscience, picking up the story again at the upheaval of the Reformation and the rise of modern liberal theory. Cary J. Nederman argues, however, for the advancement, in the Latin Middle Ages, of a theory of liberty
premised within the organic medieval political philosophy of "communal functionalism." Nederman's arguments bear mention, here, because I believe that
this communal theory of reciprocal tolerance emphasizes an important dimension of the two kingdoms type: the mutuality and interdependence of each part
of the "body politic." Damage to one part affects the entirety. Excommunication,
on the other hand, is also reciprocal, depriving the whole of the contributions of
the part.

Medieval functionalism tolerates difference because it is reciprocated by the
freedom to criticize difference. The line of demarcation between the tolerable
and the treasonous is drawn only at the point where civil intercommunication,
functions, and exchanges among the parts of the community are impinged, that
is, where "the legitimate concerns of public order and welfare [are] disturbed."
As summarized by Nederman:

The good of each depends on the ability of everyone to contribute freely to the whole. Hence, respect for difference is a precondition of an adequate communal life—that is, a life of peace and mutual advantage. This means that toleration is not a privilege to be granted or denied at the whim of some superior (as liberals might object) but a necessity strictly entailed by and thus built into the very terms of social and political interaction.[19]

Nederman relies heavily on the writings of John of Salisbury and Marsiglio of Padua for development of the limits to both the tolerance of religious differences and the authority of the church: Separation of the heretic, the religiously heterodox, is to be done only on the spiritual level, not in the temporal domain of communal life. To excommunicate a segment or a member hurts the community itself, for the whole is deprived of the contributions, the interchanges, and the functions of those anathematized.

This notion of communal functionalism helps us to further develop Tertullian's arguments under the two kingdoms trajectory. To the Romans, Tertullian admonishes that Christians are good temporal citizens in that they harm no one by their worship. To his fellow Christians, Tertullian instructs that they are to contribute to society fully, withdrawing from trades and activities only to the extent that these are inconsistent with their religious obligations. Full community participation was so important that Tertullian developed a fine-tuned casuistry of pagan rituals and celebrations: permissible for Christians when they serve their fellow citizens, impermissible when these activities primarily serve and honor the Roman gods.

Thus, the medieval functionalist theory highlights a concern for fostering freedom of religion premised not within the modern notion of individualism, but rather within a communal context, emphasizing the notions of mutual harm, reciprocal benefit, and interdependence within the two kingdoms type. If the state outlaws a person for religiously motivated behavior, the nature of the transgression should be such that it seriously threatens communal functionalism or the "intercommunication of functions among the parts of the community," preventing other members of the community from performing their tasks as necessary for the functioning of the common good.[20]

The Reformation brought about a wholesale sundering of the unity of the Christian church and the issue of religious freedom resurfaced with a new urgency. Martin Luther's sixteenth-century theology reflects a respect for civil law and yet he limits, in theory, the state's jurisdictional authority to external, temporal matters. Luther notes the importance of state law, indicating that "the world is evil" and hence, without secular law and sword, "the world would be reduced to chaos." Luther cites Paul's Epistle to the Romans, chapter 13, for the proposition that "secular law and the sword . . . [are] in the world by God's will and ordinance." "[I]t is God's will," Luther continues, "that the sword and secular law be used for the punishment of the wicked and the protection of the upright."[21] But the state's authority to punish and protect extends only to that which is necessary "to bring about external peace and prevent evil deeds."[22] "Worldly government," notes Luther, "has laws which extend no farther than to life and property and what is external upon earth. For over the soul God can and will let no one rule but Himself."[23] Indeed, the state by its very nature is incapable of competently ruling over matters of religion: The "natural world cannot receive or comprehend spiritual things."[24]

In Luther's theory (in contrast to his response to particular situations), beliefs, heresy, the Church, the salvation of souls, even the banning of books—all these things are beyond the purview of the secular state. Luther directly addresses civil princes who attempt to command obedience in spiritual matters as follows:

> Dear Lord, I owe you obedience with life and goods; command me within the limits of your power on earth, and I will obey. But if you command me to believe, and to put away books, I will not obey; for in this case you are a tyrant and overreach yourself, and command where you have neither right nor power, etc.[25]

Note the inclusion of "material" property that involves or promotes religious worship (i.e., books) within the definition of "spiritual" matters outside the civil authority. Clearly, the term "spiritual" encompasses those material things and physical activities necessary to religion (such as Bibles, reading, distributing, printing, buying, etc.); the dividing line between sacred and secular is not placed squarely between thoughts/interior and actions/exterior.

Luther rejects the argument that since the state's authority extends to punishment of the wicked and the sinful, it has jurisdiction over evil such as heresy.[26] Luther cites the practical consideration that any secular attempt to use the sword to resolve a spiritual issue is doomed to fail. "Heresy can never be prevented by force. . . . Heresy is a spiritual matter, which no iron can strike, no fire burn, no water drown. . . . [F]aith and heresy are never so strong as when men oppose them by sheer force."[27] Spiritual matters can only be affected by the use of spiritual power: "Friend, would you drive out heresy, then you must find a plan to tear it first of all from the heart . . . force will not accomplish this, but only strengthen the heresy. . . . God's Word, however, enlightens the hearts; and so all heresies and errors perish of themselves from the heart."[28] In sum, the state cannot change one's heart, and hence, "no one can become pious before God by means of the secular government."

The force of the Reformation movements splintered Christianity into numerous sects and factions. Most relevant to the American story is the situation in seventeenth-century England. Here, rising religious pluralism and feverish religious activity concomitantly led to rising conflicts among English Roman Catholics, Anglicans, Puritans, Brownists, Baptists (both general and separatist), Quakers, Levellers, and so on.[29] All of these groups took their religious doctrine and theological tenets seriously;[30] hence, it was inevitable that the growing pluralism resulted in growing unrest among dissenting believers forced by state power to abide by established church rules. The ongoing religious debate in seventeenth-century England centered upon which church polity (episcopal, congregational, or none) and which prayers and rituals (Anglican rites of worship, Puritan, or none) would be established and enforced by state authority.[31] The two kingdoms type in seventeenth-century England became the foundation for dissenters' arguments against *both* the Anglican establishment and the Puritan counterestablishment. Interestingly, since both Anglicans and Puritans were children of the Reformation, they did not deny outright the freedom of the Christian conscience. Rather, they gave token acknowledgment to this freedom while at the same time vigorously pressing (albeit from different angles) the danger to civil peace and order should their version of religious establishment lose.

The English Dissenters, seventeenth-century champions of the two kingdoms type, reject the applicability of the biblical example of the Kings of Israel, an example which is central to the competing levitical type espoused by the Puritans. The Dissenters instead draw a clear division between the "time of the law" (Old Testament) and the "time of the gospel." As Roger Williams writes, "The *State* of the Land of *Israel*, the *Kings* and people thereof in *Peace & War*, is proved *figurative* and *ceremonial*, and no *pattern* nor *precedent* for any *Kingdom* or *civil State* in the *world* to follow."[32] The locus of the concern over purity of religion in the levitical type is shifted in the two kingdoms type from the state to the individual churches. The state, the world, is steeped in sin. Yet, the faithful Christian cannot retreat from the world (see 1 Corinthians 5:1–13) but must live in the corrupted world; thus, the effective boundaries against infection and for the maintenance of purity are raised not by the state but by the separate gathering of Christians in their churches. Williams continues,

> The *World* lies in *wickedness*, is like a *Wilderness* or a Sea of *wild Beasts* innumerable, *fornicators, covetous, Idolaters,* &c. with whom *God's people* may lawfully converse and cohabit in *Cities, Towns,* &c. else must they not live in the *World*, but go out of it. . . .[33] *Dead men* cannot be infected, the *civil state*, the *world*, being in a natural state dead in sin (what ever be the *State Religion* unto which *persons* are forced) it is impossible it should be infected: Indeed the *living,* the *believing,* the *Church* and *Spiritual State,* that and that only is capable of infection. . . .[34]

Second, the Dissenters rejected the premise of the duly ordered relationships type that peace and order were dependent upon obedience to earthly authority in all things, including spiritual matters. The civil state has no jurisdiction, and thus no authority, over matters of belief and worship. Civil magistrates properly have jurisdiction only over the outer, over physical property and bodies; the soul is not a concern of the state but a matter for spiritual forces and spiritual means. The Dissenters echo Tertullian when they draw a distinction between the "good subject" of a civil kingdom and a blasphemous subject of the kingdom of Christ. As Williams writes, "a blind *Pharisee*, resisting the *Doctrine* of *Christ* . . . happily may be as good a subject, and as peaceable and profitable to the *Civil State* as any."[35] Furthermore, Williams notes, non-Christians are equally capable of good citizenship:

> And I ask whether or no such as may hold forth other *Worships* or *Religions,* (*Jews, Turks, or Anti-Christians*) may not be peaceable and quiet *Subjects,* loving and helpful *neighbors,* fair and just *dealers,* true and loyal to the *civil government*? It is clear they may from all *Reason* and *Experience* in many flourishing *Cities* and *Kingdoms* of the World, and so offend not against the *civil State*

and *Peace*; not incur the punishment of the *civil Sword*, notwithstanding that in *Spiritual* and *mystical account* they are ravenous and greedy *Wolves*.[36]

This stand on behalf of religious freedom is not unique to Roger Williams. His was not a voice "crying in the wilderness," but, rather, a voice joined with an ever-growing chorus, rooted in early Christian tradition and spreading among Christian Dissenters of the seventeenth century. As William Estep notes, this movement for a broadly conceived religious freedom gained strength in England as Baptists and other Separatists opposed both the Anglican and the Puritan efforts to silence them, banish them, and even execute them in the name of order and orthodoxy.[37]

Thomas Helwys, for example, was "the first in England to demand universal liberty for [religious] exercise."[38] In his treatise, *The Mistery of Iniquity*, published in 1612, Helwys not only argues for religious freedom for all, he also sets forth grounds for distinguishing the proper domain of the civil law.

> [F]or men's religion to God is betwixt God and themselves; the King shall not answer for it, neither may the King be judged between God and man. Let them be heretics, Turks, Jews or whatsoever, it appertains not to the earthly power to punish them in the least measure. This is made evident to our lord the King by the scriptures. When Paul was brought before Gallio deputy of Achaia, and accused of the Jews for persuading men to worship God contrary to the law, Gallio said unto the Jews, if it were a matter of wrong or an evil deed, o ye Jews, I would according to right maintain [support] you, & he drove them from the judgment seat Act.18.12.17 showing them that matters of wrong and evil deeds, which were betwixt man & man appertain only to the judgment seat, and not questions of religion.[39]

Thus, the justification for state interference centers upon wrongs and evil deeds "betwixt man and man." These wrongs and evil deeds are "against the *life, chastity, goods, or good name*" of another.[40] The "Sword of Civil justice," notes Williams, is of "a *material civil nature*, for the *defense* of *Persons, Estates, Families, Liberties* of a *City* or *Civil State*, and the *suppressing* of *uncivil* or injurious persons or actions. . . ."[41]

Examples of spiritual matters over which the state has no jurisdiction center upon a "Liberty in the holy things," such as religion, conscience, worship, one's relationship with God, church matters, religious obligations and duties, and so on. Worship, for example, has been defined and described as "service, subjection, or obedience to such things as are commanded by God. . . ."[42] That the distinction between material and spiritual should not be made in a literal fashion is evident from the following exchange, written anonymously but attributed to Thomas Helwys, between [the persecuting] "Anti-Christian" and the ("true," i.e., separatist) "Christian":

> c. What authority can any mortal man require more, than of body, goods, life and all that appertain to the outward man? The heart God requireth. . . .
>
> a. We do not say that the king can compel the soul; but only the outward man.
>
> c. If he cannot compel my soul, he cannot compel me to worship God, for

God cannot be worshiped without the soul. If you say he may compel me to offer up a worship only with my body, for the spirit you confess he cannot compel, to whom is that worship? Not to God.

Furthermore, "Christian" makes the point that "Magistracy is a power of this world: the kingdom, power, subjects, and means of publishing the gospel, are not of this world." Hence, this example makes clear that material things and activities (such as books, and the printing of books) which pertain to the spiritual and spiritual obligations should not be included among the "material" which the state may regulate.[43] Roger Williams makes a similar point with respect to the taking of oaths:

[A]n *Oath* may be spiritual, though taken about earthly *business*, and accordingly it will prove, and only prove what before I have said, that a *Law* may be civil though it concern persons of this and of that *religion*, that is as the *persons* professing it are concerned in *civil respects* of *bodies* or *goods*, as I have opined; whereas if it concern the souls and religions of men simply so considered in reference to *God*, it must of necessity put on the nature of a *religious* or *spiritual ordinance* or *constitution*.[44]

Thus, the simple declaration in law or by magistrate that a matter, such as an oath, is a "civil" matter is insufficient to resolve the issue of legitimate civil jurisdiction. One must look to the purpose of the action or what underlies it.

The Golden Rule is frequently cited by advocates of religious freedom as a measure for what should and should not be punished as against the civil law:

To inflict temporal punishments, upon any of us thy subjects, for not conforming with decrees that restrain us from the worship that we know to be of God; is it not a breach of that royal law, that commands thee, that *whatsoever ye would that men should do to you, do ye even so to them; for this is the law and the prophets*? And we would in all humility offer to thy consideration, if thy soul were in our souls' stead, wouldst thou be satisfied with the same measure as is now dealt unto us, when neither the God of heaven, nor our own consciences, doth condemn us of any evil intended against thy person or authority? Nor can the greatest of our enemies, make any due proof of any combination or plotting, with any upon the face of the earth, for the disturbance of the public peace.[45]

This petition makes no distinction between laws which compel religious behavior that violates the individual conscience and laws which restrain religiously compelled worship: Both are repugnant to conscience.

Furthermore, this Golden Rule of measure assesses the issue of conscience *from the point of view of the religious adherent*. This key procedural consideration is foundational to the two kingdoms type: The authority and judgment of the magistrate is not automatically acceded to, as in the duly ordered relationships type; nor is the magistrate's judgment (reflecting the Christian "orthodoxy" in power) automatically accepted as to what is a threat to persons and to the state (e.g., infection from heresy, divine retribution for the sin of tolerance, and so on) as in the levitical type.

In summary, the hallmarks of the two kingdoms type (as developed in the writings of Tertullian and Dissenters such as Thomas Helwys and Roger

Williams) are (1) that spiritual and material issues are to be governed by separate religious and civil authorities, and (2) that a respectful questioning of the magistrates' power and jurisdiction is required when the matter at issue is one of religion or religious obligation.[46] If the religious activity does not cause distinct and specific harm to the goods or the person or the civic enjoyments of another, there is a strong presumption in favor of religious freedom. Note the resemblance between the principles of the two kingdoms type and the analyses of the Court in the cases of *Cantwell, Barnette,* and *Yoder.* The Court in these cases took seriously the point of view of the religious adherent, it closely examined the actual threat posed by the religious activity, and it did not defer to the state in determining the proper scope of the state's interest in regulating the religiously compelled behavior.

The second type: Duly ordered relationships and the patristics of empire and establishment

The New Testament has been a primary source for the second model, the duly ordered relationships type. As Paul notes in Romans 13:

> Let every person be subject to the governing authorities. For there is no authority except from God, and those that exist have been instituted by God. Therefore, he who resists the authorities resists what God has appointed, and those who resist will incur judgment. For rulers are not a terror to good conduct, but to bad. Would you have no fear of him who is in authority? Then do what is good, and you will receive his approval, for he is God's servant for your good. But if you do wrong, be afraid, for he does not bear the sword in vain; he is the servant of God to execute his wrath on the wrongdoer.[47]

Since all power is from God, there is a sense of the divine hand involved in the governing of the state. The duly ordered relationships conception of state power becomes fraught with the potential for religious intolerance and persecution the more it becomes heavily laden with imperative connotations of the state as God's direct agent on earth. Such agency sets up the state/magistrate as God's protector and God's avenging arm. Upon the rise of the "Christian state," emphases upon peace and order as divine goods, obedience to higher authority, and the unity of the church, coupled with the connotations of the Christian magistrate as a sword of God, have served to justify employing secular force by a dominant religious group in defense of their religious truth and against perceived heresy and moral laxity.

With the advent of the Holy Roman Empire, the Catholic Church, while yet an institution separate from the secular authorities of the empire, steadfastly maintained its superior, spiritual authority over the Catholic emperors and other rulers, qua Catholics. Church fathers broadened early Christian notions of the authority and jurisdiction of the state at the concomitant expense of claims of freedom of conscience. Theological "wedges" helped to widen the growing fault line between the early Christian paradigm of religious freedom, when the church was itself persecuted, and the theology which began to support a paradigm of religious establishment in the Late Empire through the Reformation period of the late Middle Ages. One such theological wedge was an appropriation into the paradigmatic concept of the authority of the state, the maxim that "error" is not to be supported. Added to this wedge was the following gloss on a Pauline tract: If all power is from God (Romans 13:1–7), then to resist civil authority was to resist God. Theologians in Christian states now implicitly reject the earlier paradigm which emphasized a separation of temporal from spiritual matters, and they instead incorporated a paradigm from the Hebrew Bible which posited the civil ruler as God's avenging sword for the cause of true religion here on earth. Hence, pagan establishment was overthrown in favor of a Catholic establishment; now, it was the pagan temples that were destroyed and the pagan acts of worship that were outlawed and punished by the state.[48]

Furthermore, the civil sword was now used against *other* Christians deemed heretics by the Catholic Church. Augustine laid the groundwork for state intolerance of those whom the Catholic Church considered heretics in his Epistle 93 (written in C.E. 408), Epistle 185 (circa C.E. 417), and to a lesser extent, *Contra Litteras Petiliani* (circa C.E. 400). In these writings, Augustine primarily emphasizes two New Testament paradigmatic events to support the use of civil force against heresy: the "great violence with which Christ coerced [Paul] to know and embrace the truth" and Christ's forceful driving of the money changers from the temple.[49] The former paradigm came to justify the church's use of force to change hearts; the latter paradigm was one of many used to justify the use of force against error and sin which impinge upon the religious realm. Christ's admonishment to "love one's enemies" did not rule out physical force motivated by love: "Not every one who is indulgent is a friend; nor is every one an enemy who smites."[50] One who suffers such discipline is not "blessed" for "suffering persecution for righteousness' sake" in that heretics are not "righteous" but, rather, "suffer persecution for their unrighteousness, and for the divisions which they impiously introduce into Christian unity."[51] In other words, St. Paul's "freedom of the Christian" certainly did not refer to a freedom to continue in one's errant ways.

Having established that the church may use physical force against those who hold erroneous beliefs, Augustine then extended that power to the civil state. The bridge between ecclesiastical enforcement and civil enforcement is the concept of the *Christian* ruler as direct agent of the divine. This new development not only gives Augustine reason to depart from the two kingdoms type for relations between the church and state but also provided a basis upon which to justify a new model for the state's involvement with religious matters:[52]

> But as to the argument of those men who are unwilling that their impious deeds should be checked by the enactment of righteous laws, when they say that the apostles never sought such measures from the kings of the earth, they do not consider the different character of that age, and that everything comes in its own season. For what emperor had as yet believed in Christ, so as to serve Him in the cause of piety by enacting laws against impiety, when as yet the declaration of the prophet was only in the course of its fulfillment, "Why do the heathen rage, and the people imagine a vain thing? The kings of the earth set

themselves, and their rulers take counsel together, against the Lord, and against His Anointed;" and there was as yet no sign of that which is spoken a little later in the same psalm: "Be wise now, therefore, O ye kings; be instructed, ye judges of the earth. Serve the Lord with fear, and rejoice with trembling." How then are kings to serve the Lord with fear, except by preventing and chastising with religious severity all those acts which are done in opposition to the command- ments of the Lord?[53]

In summary, the concept of the Christian king's special obligation to God, as a *Christian* ruler, was the key to Augustine's justification for resort to a different type which mixed church and state, ecclesiastical law with civil law, and, hence, condoned the righting of spiritual wrongs with civil force:

> For a man serves God in one way in that he is man, in another way in that he is also king. In that he is man, he serves Him by living faithfully; but in that he is also king, he serves him by enforcing with suitable rigor such laws as ordain what is righteous, and punish what is the reverse. . . . In this way, therefore, kings can serve the Lord, even in so far as they are kings, when they do in His service what they could not do were they not kings.[54]

Augustine's theory of state authority justifies a broad jurisdictional reach for the Christian king's exercise of authority over his subjects. Augustine does not distin- guish between transgressions against God and transgressions against one's fellow citizens: Both are of legitimate concern to the Christian ruler.

> But so soon as the fulfillment began of what is written in a later psalm, "All kings shall fall down before Him; all nations shall serve Him," what sober- minded man could say to the kings, "Let not any thought trouble you within your kingdom as to who restrains or attacks the Church of your Lord; deem it not a matter in which you should be concerned, which of your subjects may choose to be religious or sacrilegious" . . . For why, when free-will is given by God to man, should adulteries be punished by the laws, and sacrileges allowed? Is it a lighter matter that a soul should not keep faith with God, than that a woman should be faithless to her husband?[55]

Augustine, interestingly, vigorously rejects the levitical type's concern with stain, contagion, and defilement in his writings on the issue of correction of error. Coercion in religious matters is justified not because of levitical fears of contamination and divine retribution; Augustine repeatedly emphasizes that "no man can be stained with guilt by the sins of others"[56] and that "every man shall bear his own burden."[57] Rather than a negative fear of contagion, Augustine's ty- pological concept of the proper role of the state is grounded in a more positive vision of the state as a force, even an agent, for the goods of peace and order: "Great care [is] needed for the maintenance of peace, without which no one will see God."[58] Indeed, peace is "the condition of [our] being"; to find it, one must be "at peace with the law by which the natural order is governed."[59] For there to be peace, there must first be order. For there to be order, there must be duly ordered obedience.

> The peace of the body, we conclude, is a tempering of the component parts in duly ordered proportion; the peace of the irrational soul is a duly ordered re-

pose of the appetites; the peace of the rational soul is the duly ordered agreement of cognition and action. The peace of body and soul is the duly ordered
life and health of a living creature; peace between mortal man and God is an
ordered obedience, in faith, in subjection to an everlasting law; peace between
men is an ordered agreement of mind with mind; the peace of a home is the ordered agreement among those who live together about giving and obeying or-
ders; the peace of the Heavenly City is a perfectly ordered and perfectly harmonious fellowship in the enjoyment of God, and a mutual fellowship in God;
the peace of the whole universe is the tranquillity of order—and order is the
arrangement of things equal and unequal in a pattern which assigns to each its
proper position.[60]

God, of course, is "the source of justice," and it is God himself who confers divine authority on the state to promote peace in the "earthly city." God, for example, exempts the state from the general prohibition against killing in cases of just
war or the death penalty in criminal matters. Accordingly, Augustine refers to the
laws of the state as "the justest and most reasonable source of power."[61] The divine importance accorded to the peace and order of the state can be appreciated
by an examination of the vitality of even the pagan "peace of Babylon" in Augustine's theology.

As the holy Scriptures of the Hebrews say, "Blessed is the people, whose God is
the Lord." It follows that a people alienated from God must be wretched. Yet,
even such a people loves a peace of its own, which is not to be rejected . . .
Meanwhile, however, it is important for us also that this people should possess
this peace in this life, since so long as the two cities are intermingled we also
make use of the peace of Babylon—although the People of God is by faith set
free from Babylon, so that in the meantime they are only pilgrims in the midst
of her. That is why the Apostle instructs the Church to pray for kings of that city
and those in high positions, adding these words: "that we may lead a quiet and
peaceful life with all devotion and love." And when the prophet Jeremiah predicted to the ancient people of God the coming captivity, and bade them, by
God's inspiration, to go obediently to Babylon, serving God even by their patient endurance, he added his own advice that prayers should be offered for
Babylon, "because in her peace is your peace"—meaning, of course, the temporal peace of the meantime, which is shared by good and bad alike.[62]

In sum, the good of peace is such that Christians must serve even "Babylonian"
kings, who, albeit "pagan," still possess a vital "divine authority." To the extent
that this divine authority is exercised by kings who are followers of Christ and
members of the church, the emphasis can be expected to rise concomitantly
on the duty of obedience and the good of the peace and order of a Christian
commonwealth.

Indeed, the Christian magistrate assumes the relationship of a surrogate parent, responsible for nourishing the spiritual development of the state's wards,
that is, its citizens. Augustine emphasizes that the use of force against wayward
heretics is similar to the correction of a wayward child by a stern but loving parent. The New Testament's focus upon "charity" does not mean that sin is to be
tolerated; rather, charity is to be exhibited in the *intent* with which corrective

punishment is carried out. Coercion must be undertaken, not in the spirit of revenge or "with the malice of an enemy," but "with loving concern for [the heretic's] correction."[63] In a departure from the tradition of the early Church, Augustine believed that such force was profitable and successful in turning heretics back to the fold of the church.[64] The use of force by civil authorities,

> when it assists the proclamation of the truth, it is the means of profitable admonition to the wise, and of unprofitable vexation to the foolish among those who have gone astray. For there is no power but of God: whosoever resisteth the power, resisteth the ordinance of God; for rulers are not a terror to good works, but to the evil.[65]

Calvin's reformation theology reiterates Augustine's conception of the imperatives of the duly ordered relationships type. Calvin insists upon the spiritual duty of the state to protect "right religion"—that is, the Reformed faith. He promotes the ability and propriety of Christians serving as civil rulers,[66] and he indeed describes the "civil magistracy" as "a calling not only holy and legitimate, but far the most sacred and honorable in human life." Calvin imbues kings with the honorable title of "patrons and protectors of the pious worshiper of God." Civil rulers are "ministers of Divine justice," employed in "a most sacred function, inasmuch as they execute a Divine commission."

> [Even pagan philosophers] have all confessed that no government can be happily constituted unless its first object be the promotion of piety, and that all laws are preposterous which neglect the claims of God and merely provide for the interests of men. Therefore . . . Christian princes and magistrates ought to be ashamed of their indolence if they do not make it the object of their most serious care. We have already shown that this duty is particularly enjoined upon them by God; for it is reasonable that they should employ their utmost efforts in asserting and defending the honor of Him whose vice-gerents they are and by whose favor they govern. And the principal commendations given in the Scripture to the good kings are for having restored the worship of God when it had been corrupted or abolished. . . . These things evince the folly of those who would wish magistrates to neglect all thoughts of God, and to confine themselves entirely to the administration of justice among men, as though God appointed governors in his name to decide secular controversies, and disregarded that which is of far greater importance—the pure worship of himself according to the rule of his law.[67]

Calvin acknowledges that there is a distinction between spiritual government and civil government:

> [M]an is under two kinds of government—one spiritual, by which the conscience is formed to piety and the service of God; the other political, by which a man is instructed in the duties of humanity and civility, which are to be observed in an intercourse with mankind. They are generally, and not improperly, denominated the spiritual and the temporal jurisdiction, indicating that the former species of government pertains to the life of the soul, and that the latter relates to the concerns of the present state. . . . For the former has its seat in the interior of the mind, whilst the latter only directs the external conduct; one may be termed a spiritual kingdom, and the other a political one.[68]

And, indeed, Calvin professes to categorically reject any attempt "to seek and include the kingdom of Christ under the elements of this world": "[T]he spiritual kingdom of Christ and civil government are things very different and remote from each other."[69] But Calvin's line of demarcation separating the spiritual from the civil is defined in such a manner that separation becomes, for all practical purposes, the exception and not the rule. Calvin includes within the political jurisdiction over "external" conduct "the enactment of laws to regulate a man's life among his neighbors *by the rules of holiness.*"[70] This notion that "holiness" rules external conduct is then coupled with the view that, since all power is of God, the governments of the two kingdoms "are in no respect at variance with each other."[71] The result is quite different from that of the two kingdoms type: Civil and religious are no longer separate kingdoms with different jurisdictions, but instead are one. Hence, a civil law that commands against God's law is no command.[72] The civil government "is designed, as long as we live in this world, to cherish and support the external worship of God, to preserve the pure doctrine of religion, to defend the constitution of the Church, to regulate our lives in a manner requisite for the society of men. . . ."[73] Calvin recognized the inherent contradictions in his position, and he proactively parried anticipated objections:

> Nor let anyone think it strange that I now refer to human polity the charge of the due maintenance of religion, which I may appear to have placed beyond the jurisdiction of men. For I do not allow men to make any laws respecting religion and the worship of God now any more than I did before, although I approve of civil government which provides that the true religion contained in the law of God be not *violated and polluted* by public blasphemies with impunity.[74]

While Calvin rejects a levitical model for the relationship between God and the civil state, he reimbues the position of the Christian civil magistrate with that very same levitical concern for purity/defilement by according the magistrate with sacred responsibility of a gatekeeper protecting what is pure from what is contaminated. This levitical leaning toward notions of pollution may lie at the heart of Calvin's seemingly contradictory positions on the nature and jurisdictions of religion and the state. At times his language and arguments reflect more than simply the concept of duly ordered relationships; they begin to encompass levitical typological conceptions of defilement when Christian leaders do not obey God by enforcing holiness.[75] "True religion," Calvin writes, may be "violated and polluted" by public blasphemies which go unpunished by civil authority.[76] If Christian rulers fail in their duty, not only are their people injured, but the rulers "even offend God by polluting his sacred judgments."[77] After noting that the "pure worship" of God is of far greater importance than merely secular concerns, Calvin criticizes "men of turbulent spirits" who "wish that all the avengers of violated piety were removed out of the world."[78] Ultimately, Calvin's conception of the relationship among God, state, and individual conscience relies upon the duly ordered relationships type, with a blurring over into the levitical type that even further justifies and ensconces state powers and jurisdiction over religious matters and beliefs.

In seventeenth-century England, the Church of England (Anglicans) firmly defended their religious establishment using the duly ordered relationships type. Their arguments for order and obedience closely mirrored those of Augustine in his fight against the Donatists.[79] The Church of England's concern was not driven by levitical fears of pollution or contamination ("every error doth not pollute all truths" writes Joseph Hall[80]), but by fears of anarchy. God's laws of obedience, hierarchy, and obedience to hierarchy created the order necessary for the divine good of peace. Puritans, on the other hand, challenged the Anglican establishment using the levitical type by casting the Anglican organization, rituals, and other established religious uniformities as vile abominations infecting the health of the state and rendering the state vulnerable to God's retributive wrath.

The Church of England grounded its response to claims of freedom of conscience by Puritans, Brownists, and other dissidents in Augustinian themes: the threat disunity and anarchy posed to the divine goods of peace and order (both civil and ecclesiastical); the parental role of authority (both church and Christian ruler) to guide members and to correct error; the scriptural duty of obedience to authority; and the imperfection of individual judgment, especially judgment which defies authority. In turn, dissidents challenged the rules and polity of the Church of England with cries of *sola scriptura* and charges that the church's traditions were purely of human fabrication. One Anglican response was that even scriptural reading required interpretation, an act of human reason. Hooker's explanation of evil reveals a worldview that can easily classify heretics and others who deny the authority of the church as suffering from a weakness of will and thus in need of correction, not tolerance or freedom. Hooker writes:

> In doing evil, we prefer a lesser good before a greater, the greatness whereof is by reason investigable, and may be known. The search [for] knowledge is a thing painful and the painfulness of knowledge is that which makes the will so hardly inclinable thereunto. The root hereof divine malediction whereby the instruments being weakened wherewithall the soul (especially in reasoning) doth work, it prefers rest in ignorance before wearisome labor to know.[81]

Thus, failure to abide by the Anglican way is a sign of weakness of reason and will.

Hooker excoriates the dissidents' reliance upon earnestness and zealousness of spirit as "marks" or proper proofs of their correctness:

> Most sure it is, that when men's affections do frame their opinions, they are in defense of error more earnest a great deal. . . . It is not therefore the fervent earnestness of their persuasion, but the soundness of those reasons whereupon the same is built, which must declare their opinions in these things to have been wrought by the holy Ghost, and not by the *fraud* of that evil Spirit which is even in his illusions strong. After that the fancy of the common sort has once thoroughly apprehended the Spirit to be author of their persuasion concerning discipline, then is instilled into their hearts, that the same Spirit leading men into this opinion, does thereby seal them to be God's children, and that as the state of the times now stands, the most special token to know them that are

> God's own from others, is an earnest affection that way. This has bred high
> terms of separation between such and the rest of the world, whereby the one
> sort are named *The* brethren, *The* godly, and so forth, the other [are simply]
> worldlings, timeservers, pleasers of men not of God, with such like.[82]

The Church of England classified the experiences of personal inspiration and
extreme zeal as unreasonable, and hence examples of fallen, unreliable human
understanding. Lack of "reasonable" behavior and thought, and a belief that
emotion and zeal were special tokens of the Spirit, were indicia of souls on the
wrong path and in need of discipline and correction.

This does not mean, however, that the Church of England denied "the freedom of the Christian conscience." Rather, again echoing Augustine, "freedom of
conscience" is, by definition, not at issue in cases of error. There is no freedom
to err, any more than there is a freedom to sin. "To go against the conscience is
sin; to follow a misinformed conscience is sin, also."[83] The Church of England
extended toleration to dissenters, but only to the following limited extent: (1)
purely private belief[84] (outward conformity was required for "public spiritual affairs of the Church of God"[85]), and (2) the opportunity to petition/protest a
claimed error by the church through the regular channels of Church authority.[86] Richard Hooker's conception (written in 1593) of the Church of England's rule-making and governance process is a mirror image of the civil process
for deciding disputes. The "freedom" of the disputant was to submit the con-
tention to "higher judgement" for resolution, with a concomitant duty, binding
upon all parties, to abide by the outcome. To extend "freedom" of conscience
any further than this was to court anarchy and destroy the divine good of
peace.[87] Thus, Hooker's "freedom of conscience" was not a modern zone of individual protection but simply a very slim "right to be heard" with the duty to
abide by the ultimate decision.[88]

The dissenters were troubling the peace of church and state over mere trifles,
"indifferent" matters, such as church organization, government, ceremonies, and
external rites. These matters/rules were necessary for peace and good order, but
none were "things necessary unto salvation."[89] As Anglican Bishop Jeremy Taylor
argues, no one's conscience should be troubled enough over such indifferent
things as to justify anarchy and the destruction of public peace, order, and unity:

> Men pretend conscience against obedience, expressly against St. Paul's doc-
> trine, teaching us to "obey for conscience sake;" but to disobey for conscience
> in a thing indifferent, is never to be found in the books of our religion. . . .
> But there are amongst us such tender stomachs that cannot endure milk, but
> can very well digest iron; consciences so tender, that a ceremony is greatly of-
> fensive, but rebellion is not; a surplice drives them away . . . but their con-
> sciences can suffer them to despise government, and speak evil of dignities, and
> curse all that are not of their opinion, and disturb the peace of kingdoms, and
> commit sacrilege, and account schism the character of saints. . . . To stand in
> a clean vestment is not so ill a sight as to see men stand in separation; and to
> kneel at communion, is not so like idolatry, as rebellion is to witchcraft. . . .
> For the matter of "giving offenses," what scandal is greater than that which
> scandalizes the laws?[90]

As noted by Augustine, the divine good of peace which is a blessing given by God via the civil state cannot avail if disobedience and anarchy reign. Thomas Hooker states it plainly:

> Without order there is no living in public society, because the want thereof is the mother of confusion, whereupon division of necessity follows, and out of division inevitable destruction. The Apostle therefore giving instruction to public societies requires that all things be orderly done.[91]

"Order" and "obedience": herein lie the keys to understanding the theological[92] worldview upon which the Church of England based its intolerance of dissident reformers. Order meant a hierarchical order,[93] the obedience of the lower to the higher; the Christian King was at the apex of this order, owing no allegiance but to God.[94] Thus, the hierarchy envisioned by the Anglicans is a single pyramid with the Christian King as the supreme earthly authority. The Church of England and the government of England are of a piece, because the country is a Christian country, governed by a Christian ruler to whom both owe allegiance. Diverse Christian churches and public religious rituals within the same polis make no more sense than plural governments and plural kings would.[95] That is not to say that spiritual matters are indistinguishable from civil matters: England's elaborate, separate systems of ecclesiastical courts and civil courts are an example of the separateness. Yet, the boundaries are murky and often merge. "The church and the state," writes Joseph Hall, "if they be two, yet they are twins! and that so, as either's evil proves mutual. The sins of the city, not reformed, blemish the church: where the church hath power and in a sort comprehends the state, she cannot wash her hands of tolerated disorders in the commonwealth."[96] Civil contributes to the spiritual by serving as a physical enforcement arm of the ecclesiastical laws when a violation of them is threatening enough to the civil peace.[97] And the spiritual realm tests the validity of civil laws.

> *Human laws are measures* in respect of men whose actions they must direct, howbeit such measures they are, as have also their higher rules to be measured by, *which rules are two, the law of God, and the law of nature.* So that laws human must be made according to the general laws of nature, and without contradiction unto any positive law in scripture. Otherwise they are ill made.[98]

As noted, the linchpin keeping spiritual and civil jurisdictions in order is the Christian King, apex of the hierarchy: In this earlier version of "checks and balances" on power, the King is the one person who can keep the civil and the spiritual powers from encroaching upon each other's jurisdictions.[99] In such a hierarchical, ordered system, honoring nonconforming religious obligations was simply inconceivable. The arguments against conscientious exemptions to laws which imposed uniformity in public religious ritual are instructive in that they echo fears shared by all ordered states. Anglican Bishop Jeremy Taylor writes, in 1661:

> [W]hat remedy can there be to those that call themselves "tender consciences?" I shall not need to say, that every man can easily pretend it; for we have seen the

vilest part of mankind, men that have done things so horrid, worse than which the sun never saw, yet pretend tender consciences against ecclesiastical laws. But I will suppose that they are really such; that they, in the simplicity of their hearts, follow Absalom, and in weakness hide their heads in little concenticles, and places of separation, for a trifle . . .

If you make a law of order, and, in the sanction, put a clause of favor for tender consciences, do not you invite every subject to disobedience by impunity, and teach him how to make his own excuse? Is not such a law, a law without an obligation? May not every man choose whether he will obey or no? and if he pretends to disobey out of conscience, is not he that disobeys equally innocent with the obedient; altogether as just, as not having done anything without leave; and yet much more religious and conscientious? "Quicunque vult" is but an ill preface to a law; and it is a strange obligation that makes no difference between him that obeys and him that refuses to obey.

But what course must be taken with "tender consciences?" Shall the execution of the law be suspended as to all such persons? . . . [F]or if the execution be commanded to be suspended, then the obligation of the law by command is taken away, and then it were better there were no law made. And, indeed, that is the pretension, that is the secret of the business; they suppose the best way to prevent disobedience is to take away all laws. It is a short way indeed; there shall then be no disobedience; but, at the same time, there shall be no government: but the remedy is worse than the disease; and to take away all wine and strong drink, to prevent drunkenness, would not be half so great a folly.[100]

Thus, in words echoed by Justice Scalia in the *Smith* case some three hundred years later, Bishop Taylor champions the duly ordered relationships type's preoccupation with obedience to civil authority as the key to order. Law cannot brook anything less than complete uniformity. The issue of considering an exemption from a law, for one who has a religiously based objection to obeying it, is quite starkly an either/or proposition: either obedience or anarchy.[101]

In summary, Anglicans premised the establishment of the Church of England upon the duly ordered relationships type. The Christian King is God's direct agent charged with enforcing God's laws, including those dealing with religion. Order and obedience overwhelmed any real notion of freedom of conscience. Such freedom was thought of as unnecessary in a Christian commonwealth, where, by definition, the laws would be in accord with clear scriptural mandates and the natural law. The duly ordered relationships type typically accords governmental action a strongly favorable, if not conclusive, presumption of legality, authority, and propriety. The duty of the good citizen is to obey.

The levitical type

Puritans of the seventeenth century premised their levitical typology of the relationship between conscience and the state upon their reading of the covenantal relationship between God and the Israelites, his chosen people, and most particularly the paradigm presented in the story of their dwelling in the promised land of Israel when the laws of religion and "state" were one. Under the levitical type, God's laws are also the laws of the state; breach of the covenant by worship of any other gods was a severe transgression against both God and country. The levitical concept as developed by the Puritans is chiefly characterized by a sense of contamination and defilement from direct contact with *or* tolerance of "false" religious worship. Mere tolerance of such false worship severely violates both God and his covenant, and thus jeopardizes the very welfare of the state by inviting divine retribution. Hence, as already noted, a basic characteristic of the levitical type is the notion of "corporate guilt": the sins of the one are visited upon the many. If the state does not keep the behavior, including the religious worship, of its citizens pure, God's harsh and swift retribution against the state is considered inevitable. (The fate of Sodom and Gomorrah is a frequently cited example of such retribution.)

The Puritans' position on religious freedom was developed in seventeenth-century England in response to Anglican claims for establishment.[102] Although the Puritan conception of the relationship among religion, civil government, and individual conscience is driven by different considerations than the duly ordered relationships type relied upon by the Anglicans, the Puritans reached the same (intolerant) result. Puritan arguments (especially those originating from the American colonies in which the Puritans had establishment power) did reflect a duly ordered relationship emphasis on order, peace, obedience, and God as the source of all authority. What complicates Puritan conceptions of the relationship between religion and the state is the additional emphasis upon order as *purity*. The *civil* fate of the polis is directly dependent upon the religious purity of that polis. Tolerance is not a civic virtue but an evil.

In 1646, Nathaniel Hardy (described as a "popular preacher with presbyterian leanings"[103]) made the following remarks in a fast sermon before the English Parliament:

> The power of Religion lies in its purity, and purity in its unity: diverse kinds of grain in one ground, of beasts in one yoke . . . are forbidden in the Law; and shall diverse Religions be allowed in the Gospel? I have read indeed of a *Turk*, who resembled the diversity of Religions in his Empire to the variety of flowers in a garden; but Christian Magistrates must account them as weeds, which if not plucked up, will soon overtop the flowers of Orthodox doctrine . . . Mixtures in, are the undoubted bane of sincere worship. . . . What, then can be more perilous for the people, then to have liberty, or rather a licentiousness of transgressing Religions bound, to the eternal hazard of their souls? It is the offense here charged upon the Princes of Judah, *they were like them that remove the bound.*[104]

This last reference to the "Princes of Judah" was taken by Nathaniel Hardy from Hosea 5:10–12: "The Princes of Judah were like them that remove the bound: therefore I will pour out my wrath upon them like the water."[105] The Prophet Hosea, continues Hardy,

> does not altogether excuse the people [for their sin of idolatry], but chiefly accuses the Princes as being the authors [of the idolatry], and so guilty of the people's sin. Guilty they were . . . by conniving at and suffering [i.e., putting up

with] them in their idolatry . . . He that having power, corrects not others
faults, contracts them to himself . . . [T]hey did not censure those who removed their neighbors' bounds. . . . [I]f the head be full of ill humours, the
whole body fares the worse.[106]

A major danger of mixing the pure with the heretical is that the orthodox
will be infected or contaminated by the heterodox; the two do not simply coexist
side by side in a civil society. Rather, heresies are like a "Gangrene or canker":
"The canker is an invading ulcer, creeping from joint to joint, corrupting one
part after another, till at length it eats out the very heart and life."[107] Heresies
corrupt the "most active faculty of the soul; they do defile and corrupt the conscience: Now this is amazedly dangerous. . . . Diseases falling among the vital
spirits, are most quick, and most dangerous; Errors are never more pernicious
then when they drop into the conscience."[108] Heresies are also compared to
"poison into the spring" and to a "corrupting and defiling flood": "it presently
defiles the pure waters, spoils the grounds, leaves filth and slime and mud behind it."[109]

The duty of the Christian magistrates (here, Parliament) is clear. Puritan divine Obadiah Sedgwick (1600?–1658) suggests in this fast sermon before Parliament in 1646 several actions be immediately taken to protect the country:

> By a peremptory abhorring, and crushing of that flood-begatting maxim, viz., a
> Catholic liberty and toleration of all opinions. . . . By a public declaration
> against all heresies and blasphemies, known to be spoken and printed. [He ap-
> proves of the measures taken in the "Low-Country" where the state] packed
> away those seducers with exile and publicly condemned and committed their
> pestiferous books to the fire. . . . By making some standing Laws against such
> opinions, which can be proved to be heretical and blasphemous. . . . By
> using your Coercive power with such methods and proportions as the real safety
> of truth and souls doth require, and the repression of dangerous errors doth
> need.[110]

Across the Atlantic, the Puritan Massachusetts Bay Colony was similarly
seized with a sense of urgency over the dangers that heresy and errors of belief
could pose. Among the laws enacted by the colonial government in 1646
(around the time of the fast sermons quoted above) were laws holding persons in
"contempt" for being absent from "public worship," and providing a punishment
of death for persistence in denying "the Holy Scriptures to be the word of God,
or to be attended to by illuminated Xtians."[111] For "the safety of the commonwealth, the right administration of justice, the preservation of the peace, & purity of the churches of Christ therein, under God," magistrates as well as
deputies of the General Court had to be orthodox believers.[112] The preamble to
an anti-Anabaptist law (enacted in 1644) cites fear of infection among the
grounds for the law:

> Forasmuch as experience has plentifully & often proved it since the first arising
> of the Anabaptists, about a hundred years since, they have been the incendi-
> aries of commonwealths, & the infectors of persons in main matters of religion,
> & the troublers of churches in all places where they have been, & yet they who

have held the baptizing of infants unlawful have usually held other errors or heresies together therewith. . . . & whereas diverse of this kind have, since our coming into New England, appeared amongst ourselves, some whereof have (as others before them) denied the ordinance of magistracy, & the lawfulness of making war, & others the lawfulness of magistrates & their inspection into any breach of the first table [referring to the notion that the Ten Commandments were presented by God upon two tablets, the first pertaining to one's relationship with and duties to God, the second containing commandments which govern person-to-person relationships], which opinions, if they should be connived at by us, are like to be increased among us, & so must necessarily bring guilt upon us, infection & trouble to the churches, & hazard to the whole commonwealth. . . .[113]

This preamble reflects the levitical characteristics of "corporate" guilt for individual heresy, danger of infection from heretical opinions, and threat to civil peace ("incendiaries of common wealths") posed by errors of belief. Interestingly, the Anabaptists' arguments were apparently premised upon the two kingdoms type, with an emphasis upon the lack of authority of the state over matters of religion or the relationship between God and man (as contained on the first tablet of the Ten Commandments).

In the colonies, Puritan John Cotton waged a written debate with Rhode Island founder Roger Williams over the legitimacy of persecuting "heretics" with a civil sword. Cotton's writings further illustrate the levitical type's characteristics. When churches "pollute themselves" by false worship, God punishes "not only degenerate Churches, but also the Civil State for this wickedness." Indeed,

> when the Church comes to be Planted amongst them, If then Civil States do neglect them, & suffer the Churches to corrupt, and annoy themselves by pollutions in Religion, the staff of the Peace of the Commonwealth will soon be broken, as the Purity of Religion is broken in the Churches.[114]

In the Puritan example, heretics or false Christians are actually more of a threat to civil peace and safety than non-Christians such as "Jews or Pagans." These non-Christians can be "tolerated" by the state (as long as they do not "openly blaspheme the God of heaven & draw away Christians to Atheism or Judaism"[115]), whereas Christian apostasy and heresy are "pollutions of Religion" which can cause the "Church and People of God [to] fall away from God," whereupon "God will visit the City and Country with public calamity, if not captivity for the Churches' sake."[116]

Cotton continues, "If offenses to the Church do provoke wrath against the Civil State, it is no confusion in the Civil State to punish such."[117] This concern is summed up by Cotton's response to Roger Williams's assertion that "a false religion will not hurt a civil state":

> [T]here may be a Law made for the establishing of true religion: and it though be violated, yet the *Discusser* [referring to Roger Williams] will say, no civil Law is violated, because no Law concerning the second Table is violated. But that is his mistake, to think the civil Laws concern only the outward Estate of the People, and not their Religion. That is a civil Law whatsoever concerns the good of

the City, and the repulsing of the contrary. Now religion is the best good of the City: and therefore Laws about Religion are truly called civil Laws, enacted by civil Authority, about the best good of the City, for the promoting, and preserving of that good of the City.[118]

Cotton's vision of the ground of civil peace must be considered if one is to understand the levitical rationale against religious tolerance. First, civil peace is threatened by God's wrath against the state that tolerates heresy: "That dreadful example of God's vengeance upon Civil States for tolerating and practicing Image-worship, is a serious and loud warning to all Christian States to beware of such seducing spirits . . .[119] Second, the levitical type treats spiritual harm as equal to, if not greater than, the physical harm done by robbers and murderers, because the harm is infectious and the damage done to the soul is eternal. Speaking rhetorically of Roger Williams, Cotton asks,

> And why does he not as well observe the unmercifulness of such States and Laws, as suffer petty thieves, and liars to live in their Towns and Cities: but will not suffer willful murderers, & violent robbers to live among them? . . . [S]uch as . . . do go on to subvert the Foundation of Christian Religion and to subvert and destroy the souls of God's People, and stoutly rob them both of the means of grace here, and of the inherited glory hereafter, they are worse than willful murderers, or violent robbers. . . . which, being so, me thinks, such as do more mischief, are less tolerable, then they that do less. It is true, that they are more deeply wounded-sinners, are more to be pitied, suppose the depth of their wounds reach none but themselves; but if they be infectious, and Leprous, and have Plague sores running upon them, and think it their glory to infect others; It is no want of mercy, and charity, to set such at a distance: It is a merciless mercy, to pity such as are incurably contagious, and mischievous, and not to pity many scores or hundreds of the souls of such, as will be infected and destroyed by the toleration of the other.[120]

Thus, heretics who otherwise obey the laws of the "second tablet" and who are respectful of the persons and goods of others still are not good subjects of the civil state, since they infect or threaten to infect the souls of their fellow citizens. The duty of the Christian magistrate is to protect the sheep from the wolves (heretics): This is not "persecution for conscience's sake" but rightful punishment of error that threatens the safety of the citizens.[121] Two essential prerequisites to achieving civil order, therefore, are the distinguishing of heresy from truth and the separation of heretics from the populace. Note that Cotton assumes that the true religion is easily discernable from error.[122]

Thus, the safety and the health of the state and its citizens are just as dependent upon the well-being of religion as they are upon the well-being and protection of persons and property. Under the levitical type, the state cannot draw a boundary line between the physical/outer and the spiritual/inner. The Christian magistrate and the Christian state properly and, indeed, necessarily, must govern both. The result is a drastic curtailment of religious freedom.[123] Yet, the growing social importance and cultural acceptance in America of the good of religious freedom is evinced by the inability, even under the levitical type, to simply disregard it. The Puritan theocracy, for example, enforced the dominant religious orthodoxy, yet claimed to honor freedom of conscience because it did not physically "force" a conversion: As long as false Christians did not vocally, in writing, or otherwise openly challenge the orthodoxy, and attended the prescribed worship services with the rest of the community, they were free to believe as they liked. Similarly, Native Americans and other non-Christians, while not "compelled" to the Christian faith,[124] were prohibited from "blaspheming" God and from "pawwaw[ing] or perform[ing] outward worship to their false gods or to the devil upon any land or ground which is proper to the English."[125] These examples are indicative of a phenomenon characteristic of the treatment of the religious freedom issue in the modern era: While religious freedom may be honored in theory as an important societal value, the reality of its political existence is quite dependent upon the ruling conceptions of order, of the proper extent of civil authority, and of definitional parameters of what religious freedom itself means.

In summary, under the levitical type the good of religious freedom is all but eclipsed by the need for purity (uniformity). The government must maintain strict boundaries; to allow any deviance from the laws is to invite disaster. Under the levitical type there is a paramount fear of contamination of the corporate body by the deviate beliefs and activities of the few. In the two kingdoms type, state intervention is appropriate at the point where religiously compelled behavior caused particular and demonstrable physical harm to the person, property, or citizenship rights of another. Under the levitical type, in contrast, the harm which is actionable by the state is far more tenuous and metaphysical, as evinced by the vague notion of corporate contamination.

The enlightenment type: A transition into modernity

Elements of this fourth type for the interaction between state authority and religious conscience have existed since the early church: arguments in support of freedom of religion that are grounded in balance, moderation, justice, reason, and common sense. These elements did not coalesce into a discernibly separate and independent type, however, until the religiously turbulent seventeenth century. As used in this thesis, the descriptive name "enlightenment" does not carry connotations of antireligion, anti-Christian, atheistic secularism, secular humanism, or any other similar caricatures.[126]

The themes of moderation, justice, reason, and common sense did not spring forth full grown from the heads of Enlightenment thinkers. Rather, theological arguments and pastoral admonishments based upon common justice and reason are relied upon by such earlier Christian writers as Tertullian and Luther. The difference between these earlier writings and the philosophers and theologians working within the enlightenment type lies not in the substance of the actual arguments, but, rather, in the underlying assumptions supporting the arguments: The earlier types are premised primarily within a worldview that deems humans to be utterly sinful and depraved, with severely limited human faculties. This viewpoint differs from the Enlightenment's tendency to view human reasoning as an endowment of the Creator and a means to know his will, together with a belief in progress and a faith in humanity's ability to act with moderation and balance. Yet, it is important to note the similarity of the main thrust of the arguments for religious freedom made by the two kingdoms and enlightenment types, premised though they are in separate worldviews, for it is this overlap which paved the way for a coalition between these two types during the Founding Era.

Tertullian's arguments in *The Apology*, premised upon the unreasonableness and injustice of majority persecution of a religious minority, should be examined in some detail, for these were destined to be repeated by later advocates for religious freedom.[127] Tertullian's points are: (1) Christian religious beliefs and practices interfere with no other citizen; (2) Christians otherwise are loyal citizens and support the emperor and the secular state;[128] (3) as a practical matter, religious devotion and worship cannot be compelled but can only be freely given;[129] (4) the state suffers incalculable loss when otherwise-good citizens are punished;[130] (5) the law (and hence, the state) loses legitimacy when citizens charged with a crime perceive that the law is unfair and the legal system can not or will not hear evidence concerning the injustice of its charge against them.[131]

Martin Luther's writings on the secular state generally emphasize the importance of using common sense and reason in the administration of government and in the enforcement of civil laws. While these writings are not engaged in a debate over religious tolerance or liberty of conscience, they are still instructive in that the writings advocate the use of reason and understanding in interpreting and applying law (albeit written by a theologian who held a strong conception of the fallenness of human nature). For example, Luther reminds those in civil authority that justice cannot be equated with an unswerving enforcement of the letter of the law. Quoting Proverbs 28:16, Luther notes that "A prince that wanteth understanding will oppress many with injustice." Thus, he explains,

> No matter how good and equitable the laws are, they all make exceptions of cases of necessity, in which they cannot be enforced. Therefore a prince must have the law in hand as firmly as the sword, and decide in his own mind when and where the law must be applied strictly or with moderation, so that *reason may always control all law and be the highest law and rule over all laws.* . . . I say this in order that man may not think it sufficient and an excellent thing if they follow the written law or the legal advisors; more than that is required.[132]

Luther sums up his tract on secular authority with the following admonition: "[K]*eep written laws subject to reason, whence they indeed have welled from the spring of justice,* and not make the spring dependent on its rivulets, nor take reason captive to the letter."[133] Luther, here, assumes a certain degree of reliability in human reason; indeed, justice *depends* upon it.

As already noted, Roger Williams argues that "all *Reason* and *Experience*" have shown that non-Christians are equally capable of being good citizens as "true believers."[134] Richard Hooker, preeminent Anglican theologian of the late sixteenth century, similarly does not disparage humanity's capacity to reason; "reason" is not "an enemy unto religion" but, rather, is "a necessary instrument, without which we could not reap by the scriptures perfection, that fruit and benefit which it yields."[135] Isaac Backus, Separate Baptist in Massachusetts during the Founding Era, argues that "reason and revelation agree" that the power of government is properly limited to the defense of persons and property.[136] Yet, Hooker's theological conception of the authority of the state is grounded primarily in the duly ordered relationships type, whereas Tertullian, Williams, and Backus write primarily from the perspective of the two kingdoms type.

Given that arguments based upon reason and common sense have been included in the arguments of rather theologically diverse writers, it should come as no surprise that the Enlightenment itself was quite philosophically complex. Indeed, as noted by Henry F. May, the Enlightenment, particularly in America, was not a monolithic movement but rather consisted of four distinct threads. May finds two propositions common to all four threads, however, and thus from these the enlightenment type shall draw its basic premises: "first, that the present age is more enlightened than the past; and second, that we understand nature and man best through the use of our natural faculties."[137] Basic to the enlightenment type is a conception of order as the rule of reason, that is, order is achieved when reason, not force, rules. Anarchy reigns when the state is governed by sheer brute power and without the use of reason, that is, without the rule of just laws which are comprehensible and equally applicable to all. Extremism, irrational laws, emotionalism, and dominance by the strong over the weak are serious threats to society. (Hence, the emphases in the U.S. Constitution on checks and balances, separation of power, and in the Federalist Papers on the good of religious pluralism to thwart the arbitrary use of power.) Irrational, unreasonable laws are those which are unenforceable, impractical, inconsistent in treatment (i.e., violate the Golden Rule), favor the powerful, and/or are beyond the proper jurisdiction of the state. A prime example is the test oath requirement, which forces a person to take an oath of allegiance to a religion or religious doctrine with which her conscience cannot agree, and which is a spiritual matter over which the state has no authority or jurisdiction.

The enlightenment type insists upon the "primacy and sufficiency of reason," even in judging matters of religion. As May notes,

> [I]t was impossible that revelation could, as enthusiasts had suggested, run contrary to reason. Thus reason must judge revelation, first by the consistency and rationality of its content, and second, by applying to its witnesses the same tests that should be applied to any evidence.[138]

On the one hand, this emphasis upon reason and rationality often renders unintelligible religious experiences, practices, and requirements; and what is unintelligible becomes too easily discounted and dismissed. On the other hand, the enlightenment type's insistence upon consistency enshrines a Golden Rule policy of religious freedom: Give unto others the same religious freedoms and rights which you demand for yourself. In the United States, the term "tolerance" has traditionally indicated a favored, even an established, religion which allows another unfavored religion to exist. No religious group should be merely tolerated, because all religious groups are accorded equal respect under the law. To do otherwise would be inconsistent and hence unreasonable and irrational; further-more, a rule of reason is overthrown in favor of a rule of the powerful (the domi-nant religious group wins).

These aspects of the enlightenment type are illustrated in John Locke's trea-tise, "A Letter Concerning Toleration," and in William Penn's 1687 tract, "The Reasonableness of Toleration and the Unreasonableness of Penal Laws and Tests," both of which were written in response to the political turmoil in seven-teenth-century England caused by religious intolerance. Striking a theme simi-lar to the two kingdoms type, John Locke emphasizes the jurisdictional distinc-tion between the religious and the secular powers. But the two kingdoms type is theologically driven, emphasizes the fallen state of the world (and hence the inability of the "material" to comprehend the "spiritual"), and is grounded in scriptural proof-texts. Locke's treatise, in contrast, is more philosophical and pragmatic than strictly theological, emphasizes humanity's innate ability to rea-son (deemed a divine gift), and has a notably sparse citation to scriptural au-thority. Yet, Locke's treatise is not secular or irreligious in a twentieth-century sense; rather, Locke's vision of religious tolerance is premised upon a normative view of religion as essentially that which governs the "regulating of men's lives according to the rules of virtue and piety."[139] To Locke, "purity of manners" and "holiness of life" is the essence of religion. All else is "pretense": dogma, doc-trines of faith, ritual, ecclesiastical organization, "external pomp."[140] Locke will-ingly acknowledges that such matters may be of the utmost importance to others and notes that observance of things believed "necessary to the obtaining of God's favor" "is the highest obligation that lies upon mankind."[141] For these very rea-sons, all persons should be left free in matters of faith and in matters of sacred rites, for each needs to do what is deemed necessary to save one's soul.

In contrast to Augustine, Locke believes that force is ultimately of no avail in achieving a saved soul; force cannot convince a person to sincerely believe something against her own conscience. In contrast with the levitical type, Locke denies that the welfare of society is in any way dependent upon the country's en-forcement of the true faith and worship. "It does not follow," states Locke, that because idolatry is a sin "it ought therefore be punished by the magistrate. . . . The reason is, *because they are not prejudicial to other men's rights, nor do they break the public peace of societies.*"[142] The commonwealth has neither interest in nor jurisdiction over offenses against God, "but only the injury done unto men's neighbors, and to the commonwealth."[143] Such injury does not include contagion from "idolatry, superstition, and heresy."[144] Locke specifically re-jects the notion, common to the levitical type, that the law of Moses (whether "moral, judicial, or ceremonial") has any application to Christians or a Christian country.[145] He furthermore denies that any special or distinct obligations for religious enforcement are conveyed upon a magistrate who happens to be Chris-tian.[146] Nor is a Christian ruler privy to any special insights by virtue of his position. "Princes, indeed, are born superior unto other men in power, but in nature, equal. Neither the right nor the art of ruling, does necessarily carry along with it the certain knowledge of other things; and least of all of the true religion."[147]

The good of public peace is attained when civil society operates according to the Golden Rule: Religious groups cannot seek toleration when they are out of power, only to enforce their orthodoxy when they attain such power. "Nobody therefore . . . neither single persons, nor churches, nay, nor even commonwealths, have any just title to invade the civil rights and worldly goods of each other, upon pretense of religion."[148] A religious matter is to be "confined within the bounds of the church, nor can it in any matter be extended to civil affairs; because the church itself is a thing absolutely separate and distinct from the commonwealth. The boundaries on both sides are fixed and immoveable."[149]

As noted, this "boundary" is premised upon a religious worldview that cherishes reason and reasonableness and concomitantly disdains "all that heat, and unreasonable averseness of mind" and "fiery zeal" that is characteristic of religious "zealots" who "persecute" the unorthodox.[150] True Christianity is that which "[preaches] of the duties of peace and good-will towards all men; as well towards the erroneous as the orthodox . . . and . . . ought industriously to exhort all men, whether private persons or magistrates . . . to charity, meekness, and toleration."[151]

William Penn's tract is a complicated blend of arguments from both the two kingdoms and the enlightenment types, and in a sense it anticipates a similar marshaling of support by James Madison in his "Memorial and Remonstrance" of 1784. Penn's writing reflects a Christian enlightenment argument that "scripture, reason, common sense, and antiquity" do not offer conflicting views of truth, but instead reinforce each other.[152] Penn condemns as *both* unchristian *and* unreasonable those who disturb the public peace by prosecuting those who otherwise "lived peaceably and obediently toward the Government" except that they violated a penal law which "debars men from the free Worship of God." As Penn writes in 1687,

> Having thus established the truth of Religious Toleration upon the Foundations of Scripture, Reason, Authority and Example, certainly the wonder must be very great among discerning Persons, that men who boast a more refined Profession of Christian Religion, who aspire to Peace, to Love, to Moderation, and Truth toward all men, should with so much passion and bitter animosity, exercise their hatred upon their Brethren, for the niceties of different Opinions. . . .[153]

To summarize, Penn cites the scriptural arguments of the two kingdoms type, the Enlightenment authority of "Natural Reason," and practical lessons learned from history, as all being united in support of religious freedom.

Both Penn and Locke offer instructive detail concerning the limitations on the jurisdiction of the civil magistrate. Locke draws a bright dividing line between the civil rights of all citizens and the power of the church over the heretical and unorthodox. "Let no man's life, or body, or house, or estate, suffer any matter of prejudice upon these accounts [mode of church worship]."[154] Among the civil privileges due all citizens, Locke includes such matters as being "permitted to either buy or sell, or live by their callings; that parents should . . . have the government and education of their own children; they should [not] be excluded from the benefit of the laws, or meet with partial judges. . . ."[155]

Thus, for one religious group to distinguish from another in civil matters, such as marketplace or livelihood, would be an intrusion upon the civil peace and a violation of the other's civil rights. Indeed, Locke goes so far as to state that those who practice and preach civil intolerance (i.e., those who "teach that 'faith is not to be kept with heretics'") are themselves not to be tolerated by the civil magistrate.[156]

Lockean tolerance on the one hand is not just for Protestants only: "[N]either pagan, nor Mahometan, nor Jew, ought to be excluded from the civil rights of the commonwealth, because of his religion. The Gospel commands no such thing . . . And the commonwealth, which embraces indifferently all men that are honest, peaceable, and industrious, requires it not."[157] Yet, the Lockean "Golden Rule" and goodwill toward all has its curious limits: Locke specifically rejects tolerance of Catholics or atheists, based upon nothing more than their beliefs.[158] Both of these groups, according to Locke, pose an innate threat to the state. No atheist can be trusted because atheists do not believe in an afterlife or a judging God, and, thus, they lack the necessary external control which limits their behavior.[159] Catholics, on the other hand, pledge their allegiance to a foreign ruler, the pope, and thus they cannot, by definition, be loyal citizens of the commonwealth.[160] In contrast, Roger Williams (a theologian of the two kingdoms type) does not appear to make a distinction among believers: "Idolaters, False-worshipers, Antichristians . . . must be let alone in the world to grow and fill up the measure of their sins, after the image of him that hath sowed them, until the great Harvest shall make the difference [referring to the parable of the tares and the wheat, see Matt. 13]."[161] Locke, in these instances, abandons the enlightenment type's insistence upon evidence and rational argument,[162] and instead he incorporates an approach from the duly ordered relationships type: Since Catholics and atheists are not duly ordered toward the King or God, they are conclusively presumed to fall outside of the basic, minimal requirements for an ordered, peaceful society.

In reality, religious toleration, in the colonies as well as in Britain itself, quintessentially was limited to Protestants: Catholics were specifically excluded from English toleration by test oath requirements,[163] and, indeed, the Toleration Act of William and Mary (1689) excluded not only Catholics, but also anyone "that shall deny in his preaching or writing the doctrine of the Blessed Trinity. . . ."[164] Jews, those without creeds, unitarians, and others who denied the doctrine of the Trinity thus were excluded from the "ease and benefit" of the Toleration Act. Hence, Locke's theory of toleration would have been more inclusive than the actual English situation, but far less inclusive than Roger Williams' Baptist/Dissenter vision of religious freedom.

William Penn's tract argues for a religious freedom that specifically includes "popery" and favorably cites historical incidents of religious tolerance of Jews and "witches."[165] Religious freedom, furthermore, clearly extends beyond a literal distinction between "belief" and "action." Penn, in the following passage, speaks of religiously motivated "exercises" as included within the freedom of conscience:

Infinite are the sayings of the Primitive Fathers and Men of Learning, their Successors, who have all along condemned the forcing of Conscience, or *compelling Men to do a thing which is contrary to their Conscience, or to abstain from such Exercises as they in Conscience esteem necessary and profitable for their Salvation:* all centering in the utter detestation of all manner of Violence and Imposition in matters of Religion.[166]

Penn analyzes the nature of law and what is necessary for the legitimization of laws. "Law," he writes, "must be Honest, Just, Possible, convenient to Time and Place, and conformable to Religion and Reason." The penal acts of intolerance are found wanting on all counts.[167] In contrast to the levitical and the duly ordered relationships types, the enlightenment type does not accord the civil magistrate a strong presumption of legitimacy or wisdom when it comes to determining what is required for the civil peace. Reason, reasonableness, logic and consistency are the rules used to judge the legitimacy of an exercise of jurisdictional power by the magistrate. These tools are natural endowments of nature, and they are not unique to, and indeed may be sorely lacking in, the civil ruler. The rule of law, and not the rule of a person, is key.

Locke readily acknowledges that a magistrate may indeed overstep his bounds. Locke furthermore acknowledges that "obedience is due in the first place to God, and afterwards to the laws . . . [I]f the law indeed be concerning things that lie not within the verge of the magistrate's authority . . . men are not in these cases obliged by that law against their consciences."[168] Locke continues:

> [F]or the political society is instituted for no other end, but only to secure every man's possession of the things of this life. . . . Thus the safeguard of men's lives, and of the things that belong unto this life, is the business of the commonwealth; and the preserving of those things unto their owners is the duty of the magistrate; and therefore the magistrate cannot take away these worldly things from this man, or party, and give them to that; nor change property amongst fellow subjects, *no not even by a law,* for a cause that has no relation to the end of civil government; I mean for their religion; which, whether it be true or false, does no prejudice to the worldly concerns of their fellow subjects, which are the things that only belong unto the care of the commonwealth.[169]

Thus, the mere fact that a law regulating religion exists does not empower the magistrate to intervene in a religious matter. No deference is given the magistrate's judgment of what is necessary for the public good, for such judgment cannot confer upon him a law-making power he does not have, nor can it justify an exercise of power that encroaches upon inalienable rights retained by the people.

One standard by which Locke judges the appropriateness of the magistrate's actions is logical consistency: whether the prohibited religious act is otherwise lawful "in the ordinary course of life." "Whatsoever is lawful in the commonwealth, cannot be prohibited by the magistrate in the church. Whatsoever is permitted unto any of his subjects for their ordinary use, neither can nor ought to be forbidden by him to any sect of people for their religious uses."[170]

Even if a matter is apparently one of legitimate civil concern, the magistrate's judgment as to that fact is not presumed infallible:

> But those things that are prejudicial to the commonweal of a people in their ordinary use, and are therefore forbidden by laws, those things ought not to be permitted to churches in their sacred rites. *Only the magistrate ought always to be very careful that he do not misuse his authority, to the oppression of any church, under the pretense of public good.*[171]

Locke then raises the next logical question: "But what if the magistrate believe that he has a right to make such laws, and that they are for the public good; and his subjects believe the contrary? Who shall be judge between them?"[172] Locke's only answer was to leave the matter to "God, alone; for there is no judge upon earth between the supreme magistrate and the people."[173] When the issue of religious freedom during the Founding Era is explored next, it will be seen that the Constitution provided for just such a contingency.

The scope of religious freedom under the First Amendment: Theories and paradigms reflecting the two kingdoms type

We have now completed a general review of the models or trajectories within the Christian tradition for sorting out the complex relationship between the authority of the state and the freedom of conscience. In the next part, we will examine the history and theories of America's Founding Era for the presence and persuasiveness of the two kingdoms and enlightenment types in the discussions over the proper relationship between conscience and the state.

At this point it might be helpful to comment on the methodology, purposes, and goals of this section on the Founding Era. Casuistry, whether in ethics or in legal reasoning, operates at the intersection of the abstract (principles, ideals, laws) and the particulars. On the contextual level, facts and circumstances flesh out the parameters and reflect instances of applicability of abstract ideals. The two are combined in paradigmatic situations in which the principles and the application of the principles are clear. The casuistical method of necessity incorporates methodologies and analytical processes from diverse disciplines (law, history, anthropology, philosophy, theology). Yet, the method is not governed by the rules of any one particular academic discipline. Historians familiar with criticisms of intellectual history might squirm at the emphasis here upon principles as espoused in the writings of various figures involved in the debates over religious freedom. Within their discipline, arguably, historians have rightly questioned a former guiding premise of intellectual history that "the force of beliefs and ideas is somehow related to their cogency, to the quality of the argumentation that supported them, or to the universality of their appeal."[174] Historian Bernard Bailyn made this statement with reference to intellectual historians of the Revolution who "attributed an elemental power to these abstract ideas of Locke" and somehow transformed these ideas "into political and psychological imperatives."[175] This book, however, presents a thesis dealing with law and the principles, paradigms, and general types forming and guiding that law (the exemplary as well as the *rejected*). Thus, here, principles and abstractions (the Constitution, laws, the Bill of Rights, judicial opinions, etc., and intellectual arguments concerning these) *do* matter, for in matters of law, forensic arguments, word choices, and principles have consequences.

Another valid methodological question posed by social historians in the face of historical analysis based upon the political thought of selected historical figures is "whether these leaders truly reflected popular attitudes in their own day. . . . [W]ere these ideas universally held, or did they belong to an exclusive *avant-garde* leadership?"[176] In seeking free exercise paradigms and principles (again, the exemplary as well as the rejected are equally important), the key is not what lies unspoken in hearts but what "archetypes" emerged during the public debates over what the public law should be.[177] Thus, the above question should instead be stated, Were these arguments of public currency?

Another question along similar lines can be posed with respect to the ascertainment and analysis of paradigmatic situations in a particular historical period such as the Founding Era. John Phillip Reid is a lawyer-historian who has studied and written on the Revolutionary period, and his comments on "doing" history that has a forensic aspect to it is instructive here. Reid writes:

> Law and history must be approached with caution. Although often mixed, they do not mix well. To employ history as legal precedent is to tempt the anger of Clio. To use legal briefs, litigation, or forensic confrontation as historical evidence of motivations is to run the risk of distortion and misinterpretation. . . . All too often what an individual says while engaged in a forensic argument tells us not what that person thinks but what he wanted someone else to think. Historians cannot rely upon an argument of facts as evidence of events that have occurred or explanations of why those events occurred. It may be—in truth it is most likely—that a forensic argument of facts is evidence only of what the arguer wanted someone to believe had occurred or why it had occurred.[178]

The term "forensic" has two connotations, one relating directly to cases before the courts, the other, more generally, referring to public arguments over laws, governmental policy, constitutional issues, and so on. The public controversy over the extent of legal protection for religious freedom is thus quintessential "forensic confrontation." Accordingly, public writings and statements made by advocates for or against adoption of a particular type or paradigm (or combinations thereof) of religious freedom, whether the "facts" of the paradigm are actually "true" or not, are of central importance to the casuist endeavoring to determine principles and contexts which framed the religious freedom debates of the Founding Era, culminating in the passage of the First Amendment.

By way of illustration of Reid's point, using Tertullian's writings as an example, it is not whether the early Christians were *in fact* good citizens and good neighbors, but rather that Tertullian thought it relevant and important to assert "good citizenship/neighborliness" as fact, that is revealing and noteworthy to the casuist of religious freedom. As Reid says, it is "not so much reporting a fact as using a fact to make an argument,"[179] and what Tertullian was arguing was not so much "an argument of fact," but an "argument of law" (i.e., these facts of our behavior toward our neighbors are what should be of concern to the Roman state, and nothing else).

Hence, what Isaac Backus (for example) may have written privately in his diary about religious freedom is not as germane to a free exercise casuistry as what he publicly advocated and asserted about the nature of religious freedom. For it is the public debates which reveal the major types, paradigms, and principles which framed and formed the core of the religious freedom controversy, and they reveal those that in the end emerged with enough power to furnish the political momentum behind the enactment of the free exercise clause. The factual aspect of the argument is important not so much for the underlying "truth" of it, as for what it reveals about the type being advocated; these factual arguments furnish contexts within which the advocated principles are imagined to apply (or not apply), and they furnish examples of the kinds of facts to be considered relevant when applying the principles.

In summary, then, the following arguments from the Founding Era are not offered for the underlying "truth" of the factual arguments asserted, but rather for the types, paradigms, and principles they presented to the public forum in legal furtherance of the right to religious freedom.

Prominent and representative advocates for a broadly conceived freedom of conscience during the Founding Era include James Madison, Thomas Jefferson, Isaac Backus, and John Leland. The arguments made by these men in favor of religious freedom span a spectrum from the two kingdoms type to the enlightenment type. Their public writings will now be examined in detail in order to understand their insights into the complexity of the relationship between state and conscience during this crucial period.[180]

Of the above group, Thomas Jefferson's theories followed the enlightenment type most consistently. Jefferson authored the Virginia Bill Establishing Religious Freedom in 1777, which, after years of controversy, was finally adopted in January of 1786 by an overwhelming vote of 74-20.[181] The language of the Statute of Virginia for Religious Freedom is more restrictive of religious freedom than the Bill of Rights: In contrast to the broad "free exercise" of religion terminology of the First Amendment, Jefferson's statute is directed primarily to religious beliefs and opinions.

> *Be it enacted by the General Assembly,* That no man shall be compelled to frequent or support any religious worship, place, or ministry whatsoever, nor shall be enforced, restrained, molested, or burthened in his body or goods, nor shall otherwise suffer on account of his religious opinions or belief; *but that all men shall be free to profess, and by argument to maintain, their opinion in matters of religion* and that the same shall in no wise diminish, enlarge, or affect their civil capacities.[182]

Yet, the Virginia statute offered a broader liberty than that of Lockean toleration. In the preamble to this statute, Jefferson implicitly rejects the duly ordered relationship aspect of Lockean toleration theory which denies civil tolerance to atheists and Catholics as a matter of principle:

that to suffer the civil magistrate to intrude his powers into the field of opinion and to restrain the profession or propagation of principles, on the supposition of their ill tendency, is a dangerous fallacy, which at once destroys all religious liberty, because he being of course judge of that tendency, will make his opinions the rule of judgment, and approve or condemn the sentiments of others only as they shall square or differ from his own.[183]

Jefferson's preamble emphasizes the distinction between actions and beliefs/opinions, deeming actions to be the only proper concern of the state:

that it is time enough for the rightful purposes of civil government, for its offices to interfere when principles break out into overt acts against peace and good order.[184]

In his *Notes on the State of Virginia*, written in 1782, Jefferson gives greater detail as to the extent of the state's jurisdiction over a religious matter, and his line here is drawn at a point quite familiar to the two kingdoms type:

The rights of conscience we never submitted, we could not submit. We are answerable for them to our God. The legitimate powers of government extend to such acts *only as are injurious to others*. But it does me no injury for my neighbor to say there are twenty gods, or no god. *It neither picks my pocket nor breaks my leg.*[185]

A quintessential Enlightenment philosopher, Jefferson was bound to a worldview in which all was ultimately in harmony, and thus he remained "convinced [that man] has no natural right in opposition to his social duties."[186] Yet, his Enlightenment philosophy also predicated a process of continual inquiry and of questioning all assumptions. "Fix reason firmly in her seat," he wrote, "and call to her tribunal every fact, every opinion. Question with boldness even the existence of a God."[187] "Reason and free inquiry," Jefferson notes, "are the only effectual agents against error. . . . If it [free inquiry] be restrained now, the present corruptions will be protected, and new ones encouraged. . . . Reason and experiment have been indulged, and error has fled before them. It is error alone that needs the support of government. Truth can stand by itself."[188] Jefferson further cites to the successful disestablishment "experiments" in the states of New York and Pennsylvania, and he observes:

Religion is well supported; of various kinds, indeed, but all good enough; all sufficient to preserve peace and order; or if a sect arises, whose tenets would subvert morals, good sense has fair play, and reasons and laughs it out of doors, without suffering the state to be troubled with it. . . . They [the states] have made the happy discovery, that the way to silence religious disputes, is to take no notice of them.[189]

Hence, while drawing a seemingly bright line between religious actions and religious beliefs, Jefferson also advocated the Enlightenment's emphasis upon the primacy of reason which continually questions, tests, and inquires. In the case of religious freedom, therefore, it is not at all clear that Jefferson and other public advocates of the enlightenment type would have enforced the distinction made between actions and beliefs as strictly, deferentially, and automatically as subsequent U.S. Supreme Courts have done with respect to the bright boundary line first espoused in the *Reynolds* case.

James Madison's public advocacy on behalf of religious freedom incorporates aspects of both the enlightenment type and the two kingdoms type. Madison authored the "Memorial and Remonstrance" in opposition to a bill, introduced by Patrick Henry into the Virginia General Assembly, which sought to provide state funding to "Teachers of Christian Religion."[190] Although this bill would have treated all Protestants alike, favoring no one Christian sect over another (one version of religious freedom which had public currency at the time), it was opposed by Virginia Dissenters, including the Baptist General Committee, as well as by James Madison's "Memorial and Remonstrance." The Baptist General Committee passed the following resolution against the assessment bill in August 1785:

> That it be recommended to those counties, which have not yet prepared petitions to be presented to the General Assembly against the engrossed bill for a general assessment for the support of the teachers of the Christian Religion, to proceed thereon as soon as possible. That it is believed to be repugnant to the spirit of the gospel for the legislature thus to proceed in matters of religion; that the holy author of our religion needs no such compulsive measures for the promotion of his cause; that the gospel wants not the feeble arm of man for its support; that it has made and will again through divine power make its way against all opposition; and that should the legislature assume the right of taxing people for the support of the gospel it will be destructive to religious liberty.[191]

This reaction against that version of religious liberty, which would have favored Christianity in general but preferred no sect in particular, was widespread. While pro-assessment forces submitted eleven memorials with a thousand signatures in support, the opposition submitted "more than one hundred petitions" and about twelve thousand signatures.[192] Indeed, the demonstration of popular opinion was so overwhelmingly against the bill to support Christian educators that "the pending bill was at once abandoned without further struggle."[193]

Madison's "Memorial and Remonstrance" declared the assessment bill in support of Christianity to be "a dangerous abuse of power." Among the reasons given for opposing such a bill are arguments taken from the enlightenment type: that religion is purely a matter of "reason or conviction" not "force or violence"; rights of conscience are inalienable; as a matter of logic and precedent there is no *de minimis* exception to encroachment on inalienable rights — either the civil state has or doesn't have the jurisdictional authority to usurp such rights; "moderation and harmony" are fostered when laws do not "intermeddle" with religion; and as a practical matter, a law such as this which is "deemed invalid and dangerous" by "so great a proportion of the citizens" is unenforceable and thus will demean and diminish the government's authority in general.[194]

Notably, however, the "Memorial and Remonstrance" presents arguments equally premised in the two kingdoms type: The claims of civil society are secondary to the duties "which we owe to our Creator"; the civil magistrate is not a competent judge of religious truth; the Christian religion is not dependent upon the "powers of this world"; state support of religion hurts the "purity and efficacy of Religion"; and state exercise of jurisdiction over religious matters is an "affront" to the "holy prerogative" of the "Supreme Lawgiver of the Universe."[195]

Equality of citizenship is a recurring theme in the "Memorial and Remonstrance." This concern is rooted in the enlightenment type's emphasis upon reason, reasonableness, and rationality: Subjecting one religious group to "peculiar burdens" and giving to other groups "peculiar exemptions" reflects an arbitrary favoritism. The equality argument made in the "Memorial and Remonstrance" bears close scrutiny for understanding its nuances and complexities: This is crucial to a fuller understanding of the expected relationship between conscience and the state. The starting premises respecting equality and equal rights in matters of religious freedom are that: (1) "equality . . . ought to be the basis of every law," and (2) equality becomes a greater concern as the efficacy or validity of the law becomes more questionable. Relative to these starting premises, in the case of the Virginia bill in support of Christian teachers, three distinct objections were made. First, in order of basic, fundamental considerations, is the lack of jurisdiction over religion and religious duties, which are matters for the individual conscience, inalienable and hence nondelegable to the assembly. Since the assembly fundamentally lacked authority to enact such legislation, the validity of the bill was questionable; therefore, the basic inequalities of the law became even more offensive and objectionable. The bill, which called for the establishment and support of the "Christian Religion," improperly favored one religion, Christianity. This raised an issue of inequality because

> all men are to be considered as entering into Society on equal conditions; as relinquishing no more, and therefore retaining no less, one than another, of their natural rights. Above all are they to be considered as retaining an *"equal* title to the free exercise of Religion according to the dictates of Conscience."[196]

Once the citizenship rights of the members of any one religious group are enhanced, it "degrades from the equal rank of Citizens all those whose opinions in Religion do not bend to those of the Legislative authority."[197] Furthermore, initial acceptance of unequal citizenship rights opens the door to even greater incursions: "Who does not see that the same authority which can establish Christianity, in exclusion of all other Religions, may establish with the same ease any particular sect of Christians, in exclusion of all other sects?"[198]

The bill also exempted two specific religious groups from its coverage and requirements, thereby improperly granting Mennonites and Quakers "extraordinary privileges." At first glance, this objection would seem to rule out any statutory exemptions for a religious group from an otherwise generally applicable law. The context within which this dispute played out, however, indicates that the reach of the principle may not be as far and wide as some might want to take it (i.e., *all* exemptions violate the equality of citizenship standard). In particular, what is singled out for reprobation in the "Memorial and Remonstrance" is that there are seemingly no differing circumstances justifying the exemption for Quakers and Mennonites, and, indeed, other less "favored" or perhaps less powerful sects stand *in the same religious position on that issue* as the two favored sects. The dissenting but "disfavored" sects such as the Baptists, for example, also held firmly to the two kingdoms type rejecting such governmental interference in religion. "Are the Quakers and Mennonites the only sects who think a compulsive support of their Religions unnecessary and unwarrantable? Can their piety alone be entrusted with the care of public worship?"[199] The argument against exemptions for only certain religious groups among many similarly situated religious groups should neither displace nor detract from the vitality and primacy of the main point: that the bill is void *ab initio* because it is beyond the scope of the authority of the assembly to enact a law affecting freedom of conscience.[200]

The enlightenment type focuses upon the goods of moderation and balance and the dangers of extremism and emotionalism. Rather than supporting suppression of emotional or seemingly fanatical religious groups, however, the enlightenment type in the Founding Era supported civic moderation in response to such groups. Indeed, in the enlightenment type, religious pluralism can be a positive, substantive good because it decreases the likelihood of domination by a powerful faction. Society is thus best preserved, not by the heavy-handed suppression of the varieties of religious beliefs and practices, but, rather, by the encouragement of such religious differences.

Specifically, in *Federalist No. 10*,[201] James Madison wrote of the dangers of factionalism, which leads persons with common passions and interests to unite and zealously promote their agenda to the detriment of the civic rights of other citizens. But rather than curing society of diversity's vexations and animosities by curbing (or eliminating) liberties in order to promote societal conformity, Madison instead proposed that efforts should be made to *increase* societal diversity.[202] The greater the number of people involved in the republican form of government, "the less likely a group can form a faction large enough to oppress other individual citizens or groups of citizens." Notably, Madison continues, "[a] religious sect may degenerate into a political faction in a part of the Confederacy; but the variety of sects dispersed over the entire face of it must secure the national councils against any danger from that source."[203] Madison further expounds upon the importance of religious diversity to the health of the republic in *Federalist No. 51*: "In a free government the security for civil rights must be the same as that for religious rights. It consists in the one case in the multiplicity of interests, and in the other in the multiplicity of sects."[204]

All of the types are vitally concerned with achieving and preserving order and avoiding its opposite, anarchy. Madison, in accord with the enlightenment type's vision of "order" as the rule of reason, defines anarchy as the arbitrary imposition of raw power, as when a majority oppresses a minority by incursions on inalienable and fundamental rights of citizenship. As Madison wrote in *Federalist No. 51*: "In a society under the forms of which the stronger faction can readily unite and oppress the weaker, *anarchy may truly be said to reign* as in a state of nature, *where the weaker individual is not secured against the violence of the stronger*."[205]

As already noted, Madison's public advocacy of religious freedom reflects elements of both the enlightenment type and the two kingdoms type. He emphasized the need for balance, moderation, and reason, coupled with a negative view of human nature which recognizes that the basic human tendency is toward factionalism, selfishness, and a lust for power. Indeed, William R. Estep credits the passage of religious freedom guarantees such as the Virginia bill and the First Amendment to a coalition between advocates of what I have been referring to as the two kingdoms type (Estep calls them religious dissenters) and what I have termed the enlightenment type (Estep calls them the "rationalists," referring to such politicians as Jefferson and Madison).[206] As noted in 1790 by John Leland, the opposition to the Virginia bill to assess all citizens for preachers and religious teachers was joined by "the Presbyterians, Baptists, Quakers, Methodists, Deists, and covetous."[207] "Bible Christians and Deists," notes Leland, "have an equal plea against self-named Christians, who (because they are void of the spirit and ignorant of the precepts of the gospel) tyrannize over the consciences of others, under the specious garb of religion and good order."[208]

John Leland (1754–1841), a Baptist preacher born in Massachusetts, figured prominently in the political struggles in both Virginia and Massachusetts for religious freedom, as well as for an inclusion of a guarantee of religious liberty in the U.S. Constitution.[209] The public, political activist writings of Leland and another Massachusetts Baptist, Isaac Backus, echo the Christian tradition of the two kingdoms type. As Leland notes in 1790:

> [T]he Gospel Church takes in no nation, but those who fear God, and work righteousness in every nation. *The notion of a Christian commonwealth should be exploded forever*, without there was a commonwealth of real Christians. Not only so, but if all the souls in a government were saints of God, should they be formed into a society by law, *that society could not be a Gospel Church, but a creature of state*. . . . Here, let it be observed, that religion is a matter entirely between God and individuals. No man has a right to force another to join a church; nor do the legitimate powers of civil government extend so far as to disable, incapacitate, proscribe, or in any way distress, in person, property, liberty, or life, any man who cannot believe and practice in the common road. A church of Christ, according to the Gospel, is a congregation of faithful persons, called out of the world by divine grace, who mutually agree to live together, and execute gospel discipline among them. . . .

> The legitimate powers of government extend only to punish men for working ill to their neighbors, and in no way affect the rights of conscience. . . . The very idea of toleration, is despicable; it supposes that some have a pre-eminence above the rest, to grant indulgence; whereas all should be equally free, Jews, Turks, Pagans, and Christians.[210]

Leland reflects that strand of the Christian tradition which emphasizes the basic sinfulness of all persons, including public officials. He advocates against legal provisions which adopt the duly ordered relationships type and improperly imbue government leaders with a parental-like wisdom, and even special divine assistance or guidance, in their exercise of authority over subjects and citizens.

> [G]overnment is an evil, but . . . in fact, a necessary evil, to prevent greater evils. . . . How extensive this government is, is a point in which legislators,

philosophers, and men in general, are greatly divided. Some suppose, that when government is formed and organised, those in office have power to make all civil, municipal, sumptuary and religious laws, and that any disregard of those laws is a moral evil: they seem to pin their life, liberty, property, body and soul on the sleeve of the rulers, and abundance of those in power love to have it so. If rulers were infallible in wisdom and goodness, there would be no danger in this scheme, but as all Adam's children are a bad breed, the scheme is very exceptionable.[211]

Leland's theological grounding in the two kingdoms type leads him to advocate against such exercises of governmental power as the regulating or imposing of a Sabbath by civil law,[212] the hiring and payment of chaplains for the legislatures as well as the military,[213] and the making of civil laws against purely moral evils (confusing sins with crimes).[214] These issues are more familiarly discussed in terms of the establishment clause. For our free exercise purposes, however, it is important to note that—in accordance with Madison's admonition that the more suspect a law is, the greater its scrutiny should be with respect to infringing upon religious liberties—such governmental regulations as the enforcement of Sunday Sabbath and laws against "sins" (moral evils which are not direct crimes against the person or property or civil liberties of another individual) should come under greater scrutiny when applied against those who do not comply because of competing (Saturday Sabbath) or conflicting religious obligations.

Leland's writings reflect the medieval communal functionalism aspects of the two kingdoms type. "The legitimate designs of government," argues Leland, are "to preserve the lives, liberties and property of the many units that form the whole body politic." It is only in this work of preservation and of preventing physical harm to others that rulers can be considered "God's ministers," albeit "[a]ll have sinned," including such rulers.[215]

Leland advocates for a definition of "liberty of conscience" that considers the point of view of the religious adherent:

> To be definite in expression, by the liberty of conscience, I mean, the inalienable right that each individual has, of worshipping his God according to the dictates of his conscience, without being prohibited, directed, or controlled therein by human law, either in time, place, or manner.[216]

Yet, ever mindful that the religious individual is also a fallen "child of Adam," Leland firmly rejects the anarchy of the individual and sets parameters for the exercise of religious freedom. "Freedom," notes Leland, "does not authorize one man to destroy the freedom of another, but that freedom is to be governed by the laws of good order."[217] For example, one of the religious sects "might arise in a mob, and rob, confine, or kill others. Here then is work for the magistrates; the lives, liberties, and property of the people are destroyed, which the government was formed and supported to protect."[218]

Furthermore, one's right to perform duties of conscience ends where these duties impose on the freedoms of life, liberty, and property, or the rights of citizenship, of others. Thus, Leland advocates for the rejection of claims by powerful factions in Massachusetts that *their* consciences *require* the imposition of their religious duties upon the entire commonwealth:

> In the year 1780, when the constitution of Massachusetts was formed, the third article of the bill of rights occasioned a long and close debate. A gentleman, at the head of his party, said: "We believe *in our consciences that the best way to serve God, is to have religion protected and ministers of the gospel supported by law, and we hope that no gentleman here will wish to wound our tender consciences."* The plain English of which is: "Our consciences dictate that all the commonwealth of Massachusetts must submit to our judgments, and if they do not, they will wound our tender conscience." Had a Jew and a Turk been in the same convention, and founded a plea on tender conscience—the first, to abstain from hogs' flesh, and the last, to abstain from wine, would the gentleman have been so careful of hurting the soft feelings of the son of Isaac, and the son of Ishmael, that he would have abstained from pork and wine all his days? And yet the Israelites were forbidden to eat swine's flesh, and the Nazarites and Rechabites were forbidden to drink wine, in the sacred volume, the Bible; but where shall we turn to the page, in that blessed book, which gives orders to the rulers of the world, to make any laws to protect the Christian religion, or the support of preachers of it? Why is my liberty judged? and why am I condemned by another man's conscience?[219]

Interestingly, the religious "freedom" argument by Massachusetts Christians in support of their religious establishment, so roundly criticized by John Leland, has found new currency among modern advocates for greater unity between their church and the state on issues such as organized and sponsored prayer in public schools.

Isaac Backus is another American Separatist/Baptist preacher whose advocacy for legal protections and preservation of religious liberty during the Founding Era reflected arguments from the two kingdoms type.[220] Backus, for example, advocates the essential distinction, within the two kingdoms type, between civil and ecclesiastical government.[221] He describes several "essential points of difference" between the two. First, forming a constitution and appointing rulers is a matter of "human discretion" and we are required to submit to civil government "as an ordinance of men for the Lord's sake." Civil rulers have no more authority than that which the people are able to give them; the people have no powers over religious matters to give to the civil ruler. Matters of religion, described quintessentially as "what [God's] worship shall be, who shall minister in it, and how they shall be supported," are solely within the prerogative of God, and hence withheld from the state.[222] Second, the weapons of the two are different: "the church is armed with *light and truth* to pull down the strongholds of iniquity . . . while the state is armed with the *sword* to guard the peace and civil rights of all persons and societies."[223] Third, civil power is exercised in the name of the civil state, whereas "all our religious acts are to be done in the *name of the Lord Jesus.*" Accordingly, Backus's public, forensic arguments criticize the founding Puritans of the Massachusetts Bay Colony for confounding the civil with the religious by attempting "to pick out all they thought was of universal and moral equity in Moses' laws and so to frame a Christian commonwealth here."[224]

Backus published a pamphlet in response to a sermon of Mr. Philips Payson that was preached to the Massachusetts Assembly in Boston. Payson's sermon had sounded an alarm against religious liberty with arguments premised on the duly ordered relationships type. According to Mr. Payson,

> The importance of religion to civil society and government is great indeed as it keeps alive the best sense of moral obligation, a matter of such extensive utility, especially in respect to an oath, which is one of the principal instruments of government. . . . Let the restraints of religion, once broken down, as they infallibly would be, by leaving the subject of public worship to the humors of the multitude, and we might well defy all human wisdom and power, to support and preserve order and government in the State.[225]

Backus agrees that Christianity is important to the success of the civil state, and he retorts that he "is as sensible of the importance of religion and of the utility of it to human society as Mr. Payson is." Backus furthermore agreed that fear and reverence are "the most powerful restraints upon the minds of men." Where Backus and Payson disagree is the appropriateness of the use of legal force in support of Christianity: Payson, arguing from the duly ordered relationships type, declared that religious freedom would destroy the "restraint of religion" over human distempers.[226] While agreeing with Payson that "religion has been the life of New England," Backus vehemently disagrees that "*human laws about religious worship* have been our life," but, instead, such human laws "have been most deadly to us."[227]

Notably, Backus uses the term "Christian" in his public advocacy of religious freedom in a manner which is sharply different in meaning from the scope of power, duty, and authority intended to be conveyed when the defenders of the "Standing Order" use the term. Backus lists "the many mistakes and corruptions which have been covered with that lovely name [i.e., Christian]" including: "the conceit that religion gives the subjects of it a right of dominion over the persons and properties of others,"[228] and "the conceit that the sword" is "consecrated to the Christian cause so that those who had got it into their hands were to enforce their religious sentiments thereby."[229] These "corruptions" of Christianity are evident in both the duly ordered relationships type and the levitical type.

Backus, like Leland, argued that the issue of religious freedom cannot in justice be decided solely according to the majority's view of what is necessary to the good of society or of society's order.[230] Backus finds irony in the claim of orthodoxy by majority vote, since "Our Lord tells us plainly that *few* find the narrow way while *many* go in the *broad way*."[231] The matter of religious liberty must instead be considered from the viewpoint of the religious adherent, for, notes Backus, "where the *wolf* is judge the poor *sheep* always trouble the water."[232]

Backus, here, points to the common experience of the dissenting Baptists in New England. Public supporters of church establishment over against a broadly based religious freedom often portrayed the dissenting Baptists (or "Separatists," as Backus referred to his gathering of the faithful) as motivated by "lusts," "covetousness," and "weakness," rather than by conscience,[233] and as being disturbers of the peace.[234] He responded to these charges by placing the cause of any disturbance upon those who defined "peace" as acquiescence in a loss of liberties and rights, and "disturbance" as objections to this incursion:

> We have been very far from perfection in our behavior therein [referring to "our controversy about religious liberty"], but we have not been accused of disobedience to government and of disturbing the public peace because of our ever invading the rights of others but only because we will not give up our own. It is because we have chosen sufferings rather than to sin against God. We believe that attendance upon public worship and keeping the first day of the week Holy to God are duties to be inculcated and enforced by his laws instead of the laws of men.[235]

Defenders of the Standing Order churches furthermore had accused the Separatists of law breaking for their refusal to abide by the civil law which taxed citizens for religious maintenance. Backus answered that these civil laws were not properly within the scope of civil power, and "[c]ovenants which are contrary to God's word ought not to be kept." Backus continues,

> It is the majority of the people, be they saints or sinners, which make these covenants [contracts to ministers to serve the town], and *John* gives this as a distinguishing mark of *false prophets* that *they are of the world, therefore speak they of the world, and the world heareth them.*[236]

Supporters of established religion also argued that the common people cannot be trusted with religious freedom and freedom of conscience because even as it was, "the Lord's-day is awfully profaned." Backus publicly challenges his opponents on their "facts," noting somewhat sarcastically:

> This is indeed a terrible story, but many a *Jesuit* has told as frightful a one, about the consequences of letting common people have the Bible; and with as much truth as this. For all the argument turns upon this point, That because many have *abused* liberty therefore we must not let people *use* it.[237]

Here, Backus has changed the emphasis; yes, there will be some abuses (even though in these particulars his opponents' charges against the Baptists are false), but even so, a broadly conceived religious freedom is not a favor, dependent or contingent upon the perfect behavior of each and every minority, dissenting, religious group. Rather, religious liberty is an inherent right. Indeed, Backus argues that the key difference between the New England Standing Order and the dissenters thereto "lie[s] in this, that common people claim as good a right to judge and act for themselves in matters of religion, as civil rulers or the learned clergy." Backus concedes that it is often a mark "both of wisdom and humility" to appoint the more knowledgeable to "judge and act for us . . . in temporal things." But to relinquish this authority in religion "is a most dangerous snare."[238]

Thus, Backus explicitly rejects the duly ordered relationships type that claims that rulers know best, and he implicitly rejects that aspect of the levitical type which holds that religious toleration is dangerous because it contaminates the civil state and the proposition which follows therefrom, that those in power (clergy, rulers) determine the orthodoxy. Backus furthermore explicitly rejects those aspects of the levitical type which mandate the civil separation of the "pure" from the "others."[239] Backus *rejects* the argument that, even if civil laws cannot be made establishing religion for religion's sake, civil laws can be enacted regarding religion and conscience for the safety and order of the state:

> And though we have great cause of thankfulness for the light to distinguish things more clearly which has lately been granted and that our honored rulers have discovered so much of a regard to equal religious liberty, yet lest the same should be fully allowed, I hear that some plead that if rulers have no right to establish any way of religious worship for its own sake, they have a right to do it for the good of civil society. The import of which plea, in my view, is just this, viz., That because religion is a means of great good to human society therefore rulers ought to improve their power to destroy the means in order to accomplish the end! . . . [I]t is evident that the sword is excluded from the kingdom of the Redeemer and that he gave this as sufficient proof why it did not interfere with the government of civil states, *John* xviii, 36. And it is impossible to blend church and state together without violating our Lord's commands to both. His command to the church is, *Put away from among yourselves that wicked person.* His command to the state is, *Let both grow together until the harvest,* 1 *Cor.* v, 13; *Matt.* xiii, 30, 38–43.[240]

Religious freedom is clearly not limited to matters of belief only; Backus explicitly describes it as including the freedom to think, speak, *and* practice one's religion. He criticizes, for example, those who in the name of Christian unity expected a dissenting minister to keep unpopular opinions and practices "'private to himself' and neither *openly* hold them up nor *practice* them." Backus argues his point in terms of the Golden Rule:

> But we may boldly appeal to his conscience that he would not call it *charity* nor a *catholic temper* for another sect to allow him only to *think* for himself but not to *speak* his thoughts; or if he spake them, yet not to *practice* upon them lest it should offend others.[241]

On the other hand, Backus's public advocacy of religious freedom explicitly rejects any penchant toward excesses or anarchy. Sounding much like Jefferson on this issue, Backus denies that there is anything in our nature that is incompatible with governmental rule. "Freedom is not acting at random but by reason and rule."[242] He disagrees with those enlightenment philosophers who place the beginnings of society and government within a "social contract" whereby some freedoms are given up in exchange for the benefits of society. Humans first lost their liberty, Backus argues, not with the formation of a civil government, but "by breaking rules of government." This is because "true government" cannot interfere "with true and full liberty." The original sin was an aspiration for liberty "beyond our capacity or out of the rule of our duty." Although Backus may disagree with the "social contract" version of societal formation, his arguments in the main are compatible with James Madison's political theory of "checks and balances" and "separation of powers" wherein the very structure of government must contain built-in protections against the human tendency to abuse power. Human nature, Backus agrees, is governed by a "dreadful distemper":

> Observe well where the distemper lies; evil imaginations have usurped the place of reason and a well informed judgment and hold them in such bondage that instead of being governed by those noble faculties, they are put to the horrid drudgery of *seeking out inventions for the gratification of fleshly lusts which war against the soul.*[243]

Backus argues that Christianity is essential to a "well-regulated" government in civil states: Christianity is of "importance and benefit" to society because Christ espoused a universal rule of equity—his laws promote civic virtues such as "yielding to all their dues, faithfulness in every station, benevolence to all, and the working of ill to none." Furthermore, Christians are promised Christ's help in living this Christian life as well as the visiting of "wrath, distress, and anguish upon every soul that doeth evil."[244] There is nothing in the former set of virtues with which any of the various enlightenment philosophies, including the most radical, would or could disagree. Backus explicitly declares:

> Reason and revelation agree in determining that the end of civil government is the *good* of the governed by defending them against all such as would work *ill to their neighbors* and in limiting the *power* of rulers there. And those who invade the religious rights of others are *self-condemned*, which of all things is the most opposite to *happiness*, the great end of government, *Rom.* xiii, 3–10; xiv, 10–23.[245]

Major differences certainly exist between the two kingdoms type and the enlightenment type with respect to the latter matter of the existence of divine help and divine punishment. But these theological and philosophical differences would, under Backus's public arguments (and the two kingdoms type in general), be beyond the power of the sword of civil government to effect.[246] Indeed, Backus refers approvingly to Roger Williams's arguments for a broadly applicable freedom of conscience, noting that Williams

> contended earnestly for *impartial liberty* for the consciences of Papists with others, as to matters of worship, so far as might be consistent with the safety of government and the rights of individuals and that none but spiritual weapons should be employed against mere errors in judgment of any kind. But the fathers of the Massachusetts [*sic*] called this liberty "dangerous principles of separation."[247]

"Papists," as Roman Catholics were called at that time, were commonly feared and reviled, and, indeed, they were considered to be agents of the Antichrist (the Pope). Together with the close proximity of Catholic Quebec, memories of the French and Indian War, and ongoing fears and mistrust of Catholic missionaries among the Native American tribes in New England, the very mention of religious freedom for Roman Catholics in a piece publicly advocating religious freedom is thus quite significant for its inclusiveness.[248]

Finally, Backus had an apocalyptic theology which looked to the Second Coming in his lifetime, and it was at this Second Coming that *Christ* (and not a fallen mankind) would initiate a proper Christian nation. Hence, his vision of the *future* of the United States, as McLoughlin notes, was not that of a separated two kingdoms but of a kingdom united through and by Christ.[249] But this vision of a future Christian nation was not in the imperative mood, was not a matter that Christians themselves should, or could, establish. Until the Second Coming, the proper relationship between government and freedom of conscience was as set forth in the theology of the two kingdoms type.

> But when the *spirit of life from God shall enter into them, the kingdoms of this world* will soon become *the kingdoms of our Lord and of his anointed, and the ark of his testament will be seen again, Rev.* xi, 3–19. Then *the Spirit that is upon him and the Words of his mouth shall not depart from his seed forever, Isai.* lix, 19–21. The magistrate's sword is to punish none but such as work ill to their neighbors, *Rom.* xiii, 1–10. And when the influence above described shall extend so far as to restrain those who would *hurt and destroy,* the sword will be entirely laid aside, *Isai.* ii, 2–5, and iv, 5, 6 and xi, 9, 10. Amen; even so, come Lord Jesus.[250]

While I have given extensive examples of the presence of the two kingdoms and enlightenment types in arguments for a broad right to religious freedom in the Founding Era, the question remains: Are there any paradigmatic examples or cases of a religious exemption from a generally applicable law during this period? Michael W. McConnell notes that the historical evidence tends to point to the conclusion that the free exercise clause was in fact understood at the time of its enactment to encompass religious practices, including those which went against generally applicable legislative proscriptions. To quote the conclusions of McConnell's article:

> Indeed, the evidence suggests that the theoretical underpinning of the free exercise clause, best reflected in Madison's writings, is that the claims of the "universal sovereign" precede the claims of civil society, both in time and in authority, and that when the people vested power in the government over civil affairs, they necessarily reserved their unalienable right to the free exercise of religion, in accordance with the dictates of conscience. Under this understanding, the right of free exercise is defined in the first instance not by the nature and scope of the laws, but by the nature and scope of religious duty. A religious duty does not cease to be a religious duty merely because the legislature has passed a generally applicable law making compliance difficult or impossible.

> The language of the free exercise and liberty of conscience clauses of the state constitutions, from the early Rhode Island, Carolina, and New Jersey charters to the new constitutions passed after 1776, strongly supports this hypothesis. These constitutions curtailed free exercise rights when they would conflict with the peace and safety of society. These "peace and safety" provisos would not be necessary if the concept of free exercise had been understood as nothing more than a requirement of nondiscrimination against religion.

> Moreover, in the actual free exercise controversies in the colonies and states prior to passage of the first amendment, the rights of conscience were invoked in favor of exemptions from such generally applicable laws as oath requirements, military conscription, and ministerial support. Many of the framers, including Madison, a majority of the House of Representatives in the First Congress, and the members of the Continental Congress of 1775, believed that a

failure to exempt Quakers and others from conscription would violate freedom of conscience.[251]

The religious exemption from military service is an instructive example for two reasons: the issue was current and the exemption was highly unpopular. A dissent written in 1787, in response to the ratification of the U.S. Constitution by the Pennsylvania Convention, includes the following among its many objections:

> [T]he rights of conscience may be violated, as there is no exemption of those persons who are conscientiously scrupulous of bearing arms. These compose a respectable proportion of the community in the state. This is the more remarkable, because even when the distresses of the late war, and the evident disaffection of many citizens of that description, inflamed our passions, and when every person, who was obliged to risque his own life, must have been exasperated against such as on any account kept back from the common danger, yet even then, when outrage and violence might have been expected, the rights of conscience were held sacred. At this momentous crisis, the framers of our constitution made the most express and decided declaration and stipulations in favor of the rights of conscience[252]: but now when no necessity exists, those dearest rights of men are left insecure.[253]

The author of this dissent does not overstate the crisis caused by nonresistant sects in Pennsylvania during the Revolutionary War. It was, indeed, a most searing clash of conscience over against the needs of the state, a clash in which faithful members of the nonresistant churches predictably suffered, often harshly, at the hands of a society that was making great sacrifices in a fight for its very existence and deeply resented their noninvolvement. Hence, the stakes were high, the public was in a furor, and yet, these very facts were still not sufficient to resolve cleanly or ultimately the matter against those who refused to fight in the war.

In Pennsylvania the crisis was most acute, for the traditional peace churches, including "Mennonites and Dunkers, Schwenkfelders and Moravians, as well as Quakers," formed a significant, albeit politically powerless, minority of the population at the time of the Revolution.[254] What the nonresistant sects could not, under conscience, do for the common cause was fight, make weapons,[255] or pay military taxes. What in good conscience they could contribute to a war effort (as they had done in the French and Indian War) was to help refugees, contribute to poor relief, provide food and other such nonmilitary supplies, provide horses and wagons, and serve as teamsters to transport these supplies.[256]

Nonresisters also acknowledged their responsibility to pay *general* taxes. Instead, however, Pennsylvania developed a "tax on conscientious objectors as an equivalent to military service and intended for military purposes," a tax which was problematic for two reasons: first, conscience was still violated because the money funded the war effort directly, and second, the fine was severe and punitive, amounting to a confiscation. The tax was meant as a punishment and was not of a realistic amount, but, rather, an amount meant to make up the entire difference between the small monies the colony had and the large amount needed to train, supply, and pay troops to fight the war.[257] By 1777, each colony had in place a large-scale draft for men between the ages of eighteen and fifty-three. Conscientious objectors were to get substitutes or pay the confiscatory fine.[258] When conscientious objectors could do neither, the pent-up frustration and fury of the populace over the war itself became directed against the nonresistant sects.[259] Yet, after all this, the legal protection for liberty of conscience was not discredited and, indeed, it was being advanced in tracts calling for a Bill of Rights amendment to the Constitution.

Several aspects of the situation of the nonresistant sects in Pennsylvania during the American Revolution are instructive to a free exercise casuistry. First, the importance to the state or the urgency of its need, in and of itself, does not cancel out freedom of conscience. Second, the fury of the citizenry against religious dissenters, alone, does not justify the cancellation of liberty of conscience. Third, religious dissenters cannot escape all obligations to the state thereby, but they must assist the state in other vitally relevant ways which would be amenable to conscience. Finally, the state should work with religious dissenters in establishing the least restrictive alternative ways to meet the needs of the state, imposing requirements that neither violate their conscience nor are punitive or confiscatory.

I have here the story of the coalescence of supporters of the two kingdoms and enlightenment types to form a political force powerful enough to overcome centuries of established church traditions. Political forces today seeking to reestablish Christianity and limit the free exercise of non-Christians[260] rely upon an argument that may be summed up in the familiar phrase, "This is a Christian country." While accurate as a general descriptive phrase (the majority of the population of the United States of America have always been some form of Christian), as a model for interpreting the Constitution and as a mandate upon which we are to conform our laws, it is decidedly bewildering. Evangelicals, Quakers, and the traditional peace churches (Mennonites, for example) argued for a broad freedom of religion premised within the two kingdoms type: Their Christian tradition embraced a universal freedom of religion. Those Christians who had traditionally held the authority of state (Congregationalists in Massachusetts, Anglicans and the upper crust of eastern Virginia) naturally argued to conserve that traditional authority and pronounced that anarchy and chaos were inevitable should the hierarchical order be leveled. Thus the phrase, "This is a Christian country," begs the questions, "Whose Christianity?" and "Which of the myriad of Christian traditions?"

As we have seen, the two kingdoms type applied religious liberty to all persons, not just Christians, and it held that government action in religious matters was *void ab initio* for lack of power and jurisdiction. As described by Eckenrode, the main argument in Virginia for Patrick Henry's bill was "that religion is necessary to the welfare of the State and the supervision of the State necessary to religion. Holding such an opinion, many good people considered the definite separation of church and state as a blow at the existence of religion."[261] Here we have the hallmark of the duly ordered relationships type. If the hierarchical order is not maintained, if the authority of the state can no longer compel the people to a modicum of religious support, and if adherence to Christianity and the authority of the church is honored on a voluntary basis, then the vital relationships are all askew. The formerly ordered pyramid of hierarchical relationships is crumbled, and, by definition, chaos and anarchy now reign.

To this, Madison made his famous reply that the "true question" was "not is Religion necessary–but are Religious Establishments necessary for Religion? No."[262] What we have trouble fathoming today is that in the Founding Era one could express deeply religious sentiments and wholehearted support for the Christian religion, while still advocating universal religious freedom and the voluntarist principle of the two kingdoms type.

The language of the First Amendment provides, "Congress shall make no law respecting an establishment of religion, or prohibiting the free exercise thereof." Furthermore, article VI, section 3, states, "no religious test shall ever be required as a qualification to any office or public trust, under the United States." In this chapter I have argued that the guiding principles and paradigms of the enlightenment type and the two kingdoms type are most appropriate to a free exercise casuistry, given the broad language and concepts of the no religious test clause and the free exercise clause. These two types are firmly grounded in the Western Christian tradition and were the models from which Madison, Jefferson, and religious dissenters premised the fullest protection of religious freedom (while still remaining consonant, of course, with good order). When the language of the U.S. Constitution and the evolving constitutional protections of the various states is considered, the tide of intolerance was dramatically turning and the momentum of the Founding Era was favoring broadly based free exercise rights, even for the despised and feared Roman Catholics.[263]

For example, letters of respect and reassurance from President George Washington to religious groups, who during the Colonial and Revolutionary Eras were considered anathema and even feared as a real danger to the peace and good order of society, reflect the new mood of religious freedom and inclusiveness during the Founding Era. As Gaustad notes,

> By 1789 the nation had a new civil structure which, among other things, gave greater authority to the central government. . . . How safe were the liberties of individual citizens under this unproven government, and specifically, how secure was one to worship, or not worship, as he or she chose? . . . The issue was not so much George Washington's personal religious position . . . but the policies of the chief executive with respect to America's already pluralistic people. Thus, (1) Baptists, (2) Presbyterians, (3) Quakers, (4) Roman Catholics, (5) Jews, and (6) others all wrote to President Washington, first to offer congratulations on his election, but second usually to express anxious hopes concerning the safety of their own liberties in the realm of religion. To each group, Washington replied with even-handed respect, giving assurance to all, even those previously persecuted and disdained, that the new government of the United States would give to "bigotry no sanction, to persecution, no assistance. . . ."[264]

Here, Washington rejected the role that would have been placed upon him, by either the levitical type or the duly ordered relationships type, to enforce orthodoxy in religion for the order, safety, and well-being of the new nation.

Accordingly, in this chapter I have rooted the two kingdoms and enlightenment types firmly within the history of the Western Christian tradition and I have shown that these trajectories were influential in the Founding Era and the basis of the American tradition of religious freedom. And I thus contend that the two kingdoms type in particular provides legitimate, helpful tools and principles for a casuistical free exercise jurisprudence appropriate and necessary for our own time—a time of bewildering religious pluralism and far-reaching government regulation.

How would a free exercise casuistry work? At the very least, a free exercise casuistry requires the elimination of strong, conclusory presumptions for the enforcement of the law and against the religious adherent claiming free exercise protection. Anti–free exercise arguments premised within the duly ordered relationships type and/or the levitical type must be scrutinized closely for indications that the religious norms and assumptions of one religious group are not being used to prohibit the free exercise of another religious group.

Principles and analyses premised within the two kingdoms type and the enlightenment type should provide the parameters and process used in deciding free exercise issues. The greatest free exercise protection, under these types, should be accorded to religiously compelled practices and actions of *worship*. Freedom of worship is a core value which emerges in both types, albeit not the only value or religious matter to be protected under the rubric of "free exercise."

Furthermore, as noted in both types, the religious adherent is not thereby to succumb to anarchy. The basic limiting premise of the free exercise clause, as indicated by the two kingdoms type and the enlightenment type, is that the free exercise protection does not extend to actions which cause harm to the person, property, or privileges of citizenship of another in the name of one's own religious freedom/obligation. The least persuasive competing interest of the state, in turn, is that which is nebulous or dispersed, a matter of the "good of society" or of general interest but no specific harm to pinpointable, specific individuals. Indeed, underlying a prohibition enacted for the good of society is often a levitical notion of contamination: The evil must be contained with the strongest of boundaries or the infection will spread throughout society. The religious exercise, if its specifics produce no direct harmful impact upon a cognizable, nameable person or piece of property, should be protected. The free exercise clause, after all, was founded upon traditions, types, and paradigms which recognized and respected the importance of divine obligations.

The Religiously
Encumbered Self

As Kenneth Kirk reminds us, the casuist must have an open mind, an eye for complexity, an active and empathetic imagination, and the skill to approach a situation from numerous viewpoints. In the next two chapters I will examine potential stumbling blocks to a casuistical free exercise jurisprudence: unexamined assumptions about the nature of self as moral agent (explored here in chapter 4), and societal boundary tightening in times of paranoia (see chapter 5). Each is a foundational assumption that can prove misleading to the extent that that assumption is not shared by the religious group in question. Unexamined, such assumptions will hinder the casuistical process, for the successful use of the process depends upon the quality of the effort to consider the issue from the viewpoint of the Other. An imagination limited to a moral self that is unencumbered and free to choose its obligations, or one that accepts the basic premises of a society-wide paranoia, is an imagination that will miss essential aspects of a free exercise conflict. Hence, these chapters make explicit two of the most common unexamined assumptions in order that the process of casuistry might be undertaken in a more mindful self-awareness.

The right of free exercise, as has been discussed in chapter 3, is premised on the binding obligations of religious worship and conscience. Michael Sandel has criticized the Court's approach to issues of religious liberty for being premised instead upon a liberal ontology of the self which he calls "voluntarist." The voluntarist conception emphasizes a "respect [of] persons as free and independent selves, capable of choosing their ends for themselves."[1] Under this classic liberal view of civil rights, what is required to be protected is simply the "individual's right to choose his or her beliefs":

> [The voluntarist case for neutrality] thus casts religious liberty as a particular case of the liberal claim for the priority of the right over the good and the self-image that attends it. Respecting persons as selves defined prior to the religious

convictions they affirm becomes a particular case of the general principle of respect of selves prior to their aims and attachments.[2]

The voluntarist view of the self offers far less protection of the individual's freedom of conscience than was contemplated in the Founding Era.

> Where freedom of conscience is at stake, the relevant right is to exercise a duty, not make a choice. . . . Religious liberty addressed the problem of encumbered selves, claimed by duties they cannot renounce, even in the face of civil obligations that may conflict. . . . [T]he observance of religious duties is a constitutive end, essential to their good and indispensable to their identity.[3]

Thus, unexamined assumptions about the "self" can pose a barrier to a nuanced understanding of a free exercise conflict.

As Charles Taylor has noted, it is at the ontological level where "we face important questions about the real choices open to us."[4] In other words, how we view the self, acting as moral agent, will inevitably affect our interpretive options when a statute and a religious act conflict. Taylor further explains the modern liberal view of the self as follows:

> The ethic central to a liberal society is an ethic of the right, rather than the good. That is, its basic principles concern how society should respond to and arbitrate the competing demands of individuals. These principles would obviously include the respect of individual rights and freedoms, but *central to any set that would be called liberal would be the principle of maximal and equal facilitation.* This does not in the first instance define what goods the society will further, but rather how it will determine the goods to be advanced, given the aspirations and the demands of its competing individuals. *What is crucial here are the procedures of decision.* . . .[5]

Central to this theory of liberalism, therefore, are an atomistic view of individuality and a vision of law as the process that enables people to choose their own good. Accordingly, the role of the law under the voluntarist conception of religious liberty simply is to provide a process that allows individuals the freedom to pursue their own private religious goods. While this sounds like a fair and just arrangement, the process breaks down when a nondominant religious group's obligations of conscience entail "choices" that puzzle, annoy, or even outrage the dominant culture.

Frameworks: An exploration of the religiously encumbered self

Standing in stark contrast to the liberal ontology of the self as having free choice over life's goods is the encumbered self of the religious adherent as she actually functions within her religious worldview and her religious community. What is lost in the voluntarist conception of religious liberty is the fact that a religious practice is not an isolated and optional act but an integral part of a belief system, or of what Charles Taylor defines as a "framework."

The framework theory is important to free exercise jurisprudence for its added insight into the psyche of the true believer, the religiously encumbered self, the person whose world construct cannot be easily altered by making a choice that is alien to that construct. The term "framework" connotes cornerstonelike stability and permanency: Major demolition or reconstruction work is necessary in order to change a framework of a building, for example. And if the changes made in the framework are not done carefully and with adequate support, the entire structure will collapse. As used by Taylor, framework:

> define[s] the demands by which [persons] judge their lives and measure, as it were, their fulness or emptiness. . . . [A] framework is that in virtue of which we make sense of our lives spiritually. Not to have a framework is to fall into a life which is spiritually senseless.[6]

Taylor notes the vital role which a framework plays in the life of every human being:

> Frameworks provide the background, explicit or implicit, for our moral judgements, intuitions, or reactions. . . . That is, when we try to spell out what it is that we presuppose when we judge that a certain form of life is truly worthwhile, or place our dignity in a certain achievement or status, or define our moral obligations in a certain manner, we find ourselves articulating inter alia what I have been calling here a "framework.[7]

Thus, refraining from religiously motivated behavior because the rest of society deems it to be illegal or even criminal does not necessarily present the same simple choice between goods. Being compelled by law to act in a manner that violates one's religious beliefs will, if involving matters fundamental enough to the belief system, threaten the very framework by which one has structured one's life. Indeed, to individualize the issue in this way is to further trivialize the impact, for what may be threatened is the very integrity and coherence of the religious community itself, and the units (such as the family unit) which make up that community.

A framework is holistically, primarily, and essentially a *qualitative* (and thus descriptive and substantive) matter, not a list of "dos and don'ts." Frameworks are, in a sense, that by which we measure all other matters and the compass by which we steer. Teleological goals, "the good," horizons, provide the structure of our framework; these are seen as extraordinary, "incomparably higher than the others which are more readily available to us."[8] These goods are not mere "choices" but are fundamental to our being for they "command our awe, respect, or admiration."

> And this is where incomparability connects up with what I have been calling "strong evaluation": *the fact that these ends or goods stand independent of our own desires, inclinations, or choices, that they represent standards by which these desires and choices are judged.* These are obviously two linked facets of the same sense of higher worth. The goods which command our awe must also function in some sense as standards for us.[9]

Here, Taylor aptly describes the encumbered condition of the religious self. Indeed, the tendency for religious adherents is to discount the merely human and to give greatest authority to what is perceived to be a/the transcendent. Such religiously encumbered selves are premised within belief systems that may affirm the member's ability to communicate with God (by inspiration and prayer) and know what God expects of her. The belief systems also, for example, may accept mediators between God and humanity as part of God's ways of working: Sacred texts and divine visionaries are accepted mediators cloaked with the authority of God or the transcendent. The laws of society, in comparison, could be seen as less authoritative and binding if they must be obeyed at the cost of disobeying a divine law.[10]

Severe existential crises result when there is a tension between one's religious framework and societal laws. Internally, a crisis may arise when an "unchallengeable framework" itself poses demands which one can fully meet only at great sacrifice and peril, if at all. Yet, one must meet those demands, for the cost of failing to do so is terrible: "irretrievable condemnation or exile . . . being marked down to obloquy forever, or being sent to damnation irrevocably. . . ."[11] Alternatively, the religiously encumbered self is thrown into a void when a framework is damaged or destroyed as a result of the pressure of external (legal) influences or forces. In this case, rather than penalty or crisis brought on by the internal workings of the religious system's framework, it is the framework itself that has shattered and the self that had formerly been structured by that religious worldview ruptures along with it. "[T]he world loses altogether its spiritual contour, nothing is worth doing, the fear is of a terrifying emptiness, a kind of vertigo, or even a fracturing of our world and body-space."[12]

The consequences when a framework is damaged or destroyed are severe because our framework is integral to our identity: Our framework is the source against which, or by which, we judge what is important to us as a person. If a framework loses its authority or integrity, one's identity and orientation to life itself are lost.

> My identity is defined by the commitments and identifications which provide the frame or horizon within which I can try to determine from case to case what is good, or valuable, or what ought to be done, or what I endorse or oppose. In other words, it is the horizon within which I am capable of taking a stand.

> People may see their identity as defined partly by some moral or spiritual commitment. . . . What they are saying by this is not just that they are strongly attached to this spiritual view or background; rather it is that this provides the frame within which they can determine where they stand on questions of what is good, or worthwhile, or admirable, or of value. Put counterfactually, they are saying that were they to lose this commitment or identification, they would be at sea, as it were; they wouldn't know any more, for an important range of questions, what the significance of things was for them.[13]

Thus, the stakes are highest for devout religious adherents in free exercise conflicts where cornerstone frameworks are at stake. Yet, the legal system does not appear to appreciate that the controversial behavior is not the result of a simple isolated personal choice to do wrong.

Given the above, it should come as no surprise that a religious community would be likely to choose to risk criminal punishment by the state, a form of martyrdom, over a disintegration of their religiously based framework and the accompanying psychological and spiritual free fall which would follow. Indeed, irrebuttably forcing religious adherents into making a choice between one's God and one's country will only serve to damage feelings of loyalty to the society. What allegiance could a person maintain toward a government that has made her a criminal for obeying her God, especially when the Bill of Rights states in plain language that she is free to exercise her religious obligations? Such a person (or community) could not help but feel betrayed by the laws and the legal system.

With this insight, the true stakes in a free exercise controversy become clear: The nature and scope of protection offered by the free exercise clause is not only for the benefit of nondominant religious groups, but it may indeed help preserve the peace and tranquility of society as a whole. For the government should not be in the business of coercing some of its citizens into a choice between their God and the laws of the country, without at least affording them a full and fair opportunity to be heard, without searching for a less restrictive alternative, and without producing honest and forceful reasons for their criminalization if the issue goes that far. To do otherwise is to invite civil disobedience, perhaps even civil unrest and rebellion.

During the 1860 debates over outlawing Mormon polygamy in the Utah Territory (where the Mormons made up the overwhelming majority of the populace), Representative Keitt echoed these very concerns over the social cost, the continued legitimacy of the government, and the survival of basic constitutional ideals, when the government forces sincere religious adherents to choose between their God and their country:

> And what will you gain by this enactment? You must carry it out through Mormon juries and Mormon agencies, or you must suspend trial by jury, and declare martial law. With the inhabitants of Utah, as you declare, tied to polygamy by social institutions and religious fanaticism, do you expect to uproot it and waste it through their agency? *It is embedded in their social and religious structure, and you can only tear it up by upheaving that structure and scattering it to the winds.* Are you prepared to start the Government on this crusade against manners and morals? Are you willing to clothe it with power to ravage the Territories, to substitute the sword for trial by jury, and to carry out, by flame and violence, an indictment against a whole community? If these people are the crazy fanatics you charge them to be; if they are the religious zealots we are told they are, then your war is against opinion, and nothing but extermination will close it. You may pile statute upon statute, up to the very skies; you may send forth laws, backed by armed legionaries, but if a hostile religious opinion confronts them, both statute and law will fall to the dust worthless and dead, unless the bayonet steps in and terminates the conflict. Is a result like this worth the fearful aggrandizement of the Federal Government?[14]

The more fundamental the religious practice is to its framework, and the more rigid the framework is (i.e., little or no authoritative provisions for doctrinal change to accommodate the demands of a changing prevailing culture), the more certain it will be that laws that are in conflict with the framework will be deemed to be overruled by what the religious community believes to be a higher law and a higher good.

In a 1991 law review article analyzing the decision in *Employment Divsion v. Smith*, Richard K. Sherwin argues that rendering an entire segment of society outlaw in the absence of "principled judicial discourse" encourages that segment to confront the police/enforcing powers in acts of civil disobedience or even of violent rebellion. Sherwin asks whether a religious believer, "thrust beyond the margins of society," has any stake left in that society. Indeed, how can such a person "reasonably be expected to submit to his own demise?"[15]

The explanation of "frameworks" and the exposition of the necessity for a contextual approach to free exercise issues call for some editorial comment, emphasis, and refinement in two areas at this point: (1) the issue of secular perfectionism, and (2) a response to the Court's stand against what it has termed a "centrality of the religious practice" standard.

It is readily acknowledged that a perfectionist, unchallengeable framework is not solely the domain of the religious. Secular perfectionist frameworks also abound, such as those of long-distance runners, professional musicians, workaholics, members of radical political movements, and so on. The primary differences between the secular and the sacred are: (1) The religious adherent is motivated and directed by what her God has commanded. The arational belief that a sacred source is responsible for and requires certain behavior differentiates the religious from the secular perfectionist frameworks. (2) Religious practices are accorded a specific mention and thus a special status in the Constitution, a status not offered to all perfectionist frameworks.[16]

Yet, modern culture seems far more tolerant of secular perfectionists than it is of religious perfectionists. Children, for example, who begin athletic training at very young ages before their bones are solidly formed, are vulnerable to severe and crippling injuries and endure much pain in the pursuit of their Olympic (or NFL or prima ballerina) dreams. These children in effect forfeit their childhoods to their quest for perfection. Olympians Shannon Miller and Kim Zmeskal, for example, continued to train and compete while minors despite severe injuries during their careers. Children often sustain injury in the course of training for and playing individual and team sports. Yet, the dominant culture praises an overeager child's dedication to being the best there is, ignoring the certainty that some small percentage of children will be seriously hurt, even crippled for life, as a result of their pursuit. Nor would it seem likely that the government would prosecute parents of such perfectionists for child abuse.[17] If it is un-American to ban children from training for and competing in dangerous sports like football, gymnastics, or dance, why, then, is it not equally un-American to prohibit a child from pursuing perfection in her religious duties? At the very least, it seems that an inquiry into the context and framework of the religious community be undertaken in order to assess realistically the potential for harm within that framework as a whole, as well as look to similar secular circumstances to ensure that the religious group is not being persecuted under a double standard.

My next point, that practices which are fundamental to the religious framework should be accorded the greatest consideration, has been vigorously criticized from both sides of the free exercise debate. On the one hand, religious adherents are fearful of being judged by inappropriate norms. One court, for example, declared a Christian Scientist's use of spiritual healing methods to be a religious obligation of minimal import because the use of conventional medical treatment was not considered a "sin" and does not result in "divine retribution" under the Christian Science theology.[18] To avoid this type of outcome and in the name of deference to religion, the Supreme Court has recognized that courts are not competent to decide theological questions.[19] Justice Scalia, on the other hand, in the 1990 *Smith* case rejected a "centrality of belief" standard under the logic that judging where a particular idea fits within the framework of a religious community involved the same impropriety and judicial incompetence as the judging of theological claims. But under this banner of "deference" to religion, the Court in *Smith* eliminated all judicial exemptions to generally applicable laws.

Without a burden or limit (such as "centrality") placed on the religious adherent's claims, Justice Scalia argued, a terrible burden is placed on the state to prove it has a compelling state interest in regulating the behavior, no matter how trivial the regulatory burden *or* the religious practice is to the religion. Thus, Justice Scalia's argument against the propriety of and ability to determine the centrality of a particular practice to the religion is a vital underpinning to his theory of legislative preeminence. The reasoning supporting the move eliminating the compelling state interest test is as follows:

> Nor is it possible to limit the impact of respondents' proposal by requiring a "compelling state interest test" only when the conduct prohibited is "central" to the individual's religion. [Citation omitted.] It is no more appropriate for judges to determine the "centrality" of religious beliefs before applying a "compelling interest" test in the free exercise field, than it would be for them to determine the "importance" of ideas before applying the "compelling interest" test in the free speech field.[20] What principle of law or logic can be brought to bear to contradict a believer's assertion that a particular act is "central" to his personal faith? Judging the centrality of different religious practices is akin to the unacceptable "business of evaluating the relative merits of different claims." [Citation omitted.] As we reaffirmed only last term, "[i]t is not within the judicial ken to question the centrality of particular beliefs or practices to a faith, or the validity of particular litigants' interpretation of those creeds." [Citation omitted.] Repeatedly and in many different contexts, we have warned that courts must not presume to determine the place of a particular belief in a religion or the plausibility of a religious claim.[21]

Justice Scalia is certainly correct that judging the centrality of a practice or activity to the religious framework is dangerous business. There is unfortunately much room for abuse on both sides of the issue. It is horrible to contemplate judges and juries deciding what is and is not central to an Other's religion based upon their own normative understandings of what religion should be. Yet it is equally horrible to envision religious groups with anarchical, antisocial, and/or

antigovernment leanings making free exercise claims to gain freedom from obedience to a law they resent rather than freedom to fulfill a sacred obligation to
God.

The widespread criticism of the *Smith* decision is directed at the draconian
solution to such a threat: the elimination of free exercise exemptions. Notably,
no party briefed and no evidence was heard on the appropriateness of the use of
a compelling state interest test to determine claims for free exercise exemptions.
Neither side had requested the Court to reconsider the *Sherbert-Yoder-Thomas*
standard in the *Smith* case. The Court's *sua sponte* rejection of the test apparently sprang from its own conceptions about religion and religious practices and
from its clear distaste for free exercise issues. In the end, the argument essentially
distilled into a quite revealing comment made at the close of the opinion: "[I]t *is
horrible to contemplate* that federal judges will regularly balance against the importance of general laws the significance of religious practice."[22]

The "horrible" that seems to lurk behind the Court's rejection of the compelling state interest/least restrictive alternative standard is the nightmarish vision of the courts and the government buried under an avalanche of trivia. The
process is simply too one-sided: If someone doesn't like a law or regulation, all
they have to do is claim a religious exemption from it. Such a claim immediately
places the burden on the government to justify each and every regulation with a
compelling interest, and even then, it has the burden of proving that there is no
other less restrictive alternative to the regulatory intrusion upon the religious
practice. Under Justice Scalia's scenario, the government is held hostage, the
helpless victim of wildly diverse individual claims of religious obligations, all of
which it now must spend time and resources to defend against and ultimately
probably accommodate. In other words, free exercise exemptions ineluctably
lead to the anarchy of the individual conscience.

The problems, here, are the Court's projections of monstrous Otherness
onto nonmainstream religious people, and its either/or (no exemptions/anarchy)
dualistic portrayal of the options. After all, the court system had survived quite
well during the fifty years in which a more protective free exercise standard had
been employed. And forgotten in the free exercise fray was the fact that all courts
regularly "do the impossible" in the course of a day's work: determine the best
interests of a child in a custody case, assess what dollar amount to place on an individual's pain and suffering, balance risk against utility in a products liability
case, determine fault in a negligence case and intent in a criminal case, and so
on. By comparison, the *Smith* Court's claims of horribleness and fears of impossible difficulty are indeed thin.

The real issue is how to eliminate the spurious, discourage the trivial, and
avoid the theological, while still doing justice to those who are bound by conscience. The courts have never had difficulty rejecting spurious religious freedom claims made not to protect sacred obligations, but to evade the law. Voluntary restraint on the part of both the religious adherent and the government will
help to lessen trivial religious claims, as well as government stonewalling for
trivial reasons. The advantage to a casuistical free exercise analysis is that both

sides have the burden of proof. Neither the government nor the claimant has the advantage of holding a trump card. They each must build their case on the merits of the context.

The requirement of centrality in free exercise cases would be better understood in the context of Charles Taylor's notion of framework. What must be avoided, at the very least, under the free exercise clause is the disintegration of a religious community because a governmental law prohibits a practice fundamental to the framework of that religion *without* a compelling interest in doing so, and without proof that there is no less restrictive alternative that would accomplish the same government interest. The religious adherent bears the burden of proving the central place that the contested practice has in the overall framework of the religion. On this issue, the government and the courts are indeed incompetent to judge the truth of the theological framework, and it is highly inappropriate for the government to bring in expert witnesses on religious norms to show that the believers have faultily constructed their religious framework.[23] But the claimant must be prepared to prove to a skeptical court that this claim is not the trivial equivalent of "throwing rice at a wedding" (to use Justice Scalia's example), and that the burden on her ability to fulfill serious, sacred obligations under her religious framework will be substantial and grave. Both sides must keep in mind the mutual respect that law and religion must have for each other if the goods of civil peace and order are to flourish.

The classic liberal ontology of the self as unencumbered and free to choose its good neither accurately characterizes nor adequately protects the religiously encumbered self. Overemphasis on the liberal ontology of "self" as voluntaristic has, furthermore, created confusion over the nature of free exercise claims. The right of free exercise, as Sandel indicates and as has been discussed in chapter 2, is not premised on a right to choose but on the obligations of conscience and of worship.

The concept of frameworks is important to a casuistical free exercise jurisprudence because it underscores the need to look at the religiously compelled behavior within the context of the religion as a whole, on its own terms. Isolating a religious practice and judging it by a standard derived from an alien framework does not give a true picture of the practice, nor of its actual impact. Within the framework itself, for example, there may be practices, rules, and beliefs which serve to minimize the harm which the law was meant to address.

Finally, a liberal ontology which views the self as unencumbered and free exercise as simply a matter of freedom of choice has led to confusion over the boundaries of the free exercise right and has distracted judges by implicating irrelevant considerations of equal treatment. A process focused upon justice as an equal opportunity of choice (or an equal opportunity for action or inaction) will be concerned with the justice of imprisoning one man found guilty of the act of polygamy while "those who make polygamy a part of their religion are excepted from the operation of the statute."[24] A process, however, that properly recognizes that the heart of the free exercise right is duty of conscience, will not be troubled or sidetracked by irrelevant issues such as equality of choice (which places an action done with criminal intent to flaunt the law on equal footing with a religiously compelled action). Rather, judicial attention can be solely focused upon the competing principles at issue in a free exercise claim: the religiously compelled obligation and the framework within which it occurs, and the societal good meant to be advanced or protected under the statute.

Societal Boundaries, Paranoia and Ill Humor, and the Role of the Courts under the Free Exercise Clause

I demand more evidence before I accept as true a statement which gives me pain, than I do in the case of one which gives me pleasure. . . . The danger therefore that likes and dislikes will blind us to truth . . . as regards the judgments and inquiries of conscience . . . *is* very real indeed.

— Kenneth E. Kirk, *Conscience and Its Problems: An Introduction to Casuistry.*[1]

A s discussed in earlier chapters, understanding the context of a free exercise issue is the crucial first step to a casuistical free exercise jurisprudence. One impediment to understanding "what is going on" is a liberal ontology which assumes a self free to choose, and hence it defines the free exercise problem as a matter of freedom of choice. The reality of the compulsion of the religious obligation is lost. A second impediment is societal: paranoia that fuels legislation when important societal boundaries are perceived to be threatened.

The wilderness trope, discussed previously in the introduction, is a helpful tool with which to analyze this problem of boundaries. Wilderness is demonic, according to the negative aspect of the wilderness myth, because of its unboundedness; evil, the devil, thrives in this "terrible, chaotic openness." Society, confronted by such anarchy, is driven to contain the chaos with boundaries, for "[o]rder is produced by walling, channeling, confining."[2] As described by Jonathan Z. Smith, "[t]he walled city is a symbolic universe which serves . . . as an 'enclave,' a 'strategic hamlet' against the threat of the boundless, chaotic desert. The desert . . . is an active threat, constantly seeking to breach the walls."[3] Yet, the people of the wilderness often view themselves as the pure remnant, seeking a wilderness refuge from the unholy, impure mainstream. Such a group does not view its behavior as uncontrolled, but, rather, as *more* obedient to God's will and thus *more* virtuous and law abiding than the societal mainstream.

Boundaries are crucial. A society is defined by its boundaries and, indeed, by the very struggle to maintain them. If boundaries did not exist, a society could not exist. Our society no longer confronts the physical, geographical wilderness as did the Israelites, or the Puritans, or the westward Euro-American migrants. Yet, the struggle over boundaries, the struggle over both how and where the walls of society shall be constructed to keep out the chaos and the demons, rages on.

How to establish the boundary presents itself in the tension between self-regulation and governmental regulation. Informal conformity to societal norms (in behavior, thought, dress, and so on) is enforced by one's neighbors, peers, employer, coworkers, family, or even the ethics committee of one's professional association.[4] The penalty suffered by the deviant is isolation, ostracism, verbal and/or symbolic condemnation. In a church setting, for example, the punishment could be excommunication, and in a club, the loss of membership rights.

A perennial question in the struggle for order and virtue is whether reliance on the self to conform and refrain from evil is sufficient, or are stronger measures needed? The issue was of deep concern to the Puritans:

> Having thrust themselves into a new and unformed world, they had the responsibility to create there stability and order. . . . Given the power of darkness in the wilderness, could Puritan society rely on individual conscience to maintain itself, or did it require strong and authoritarian institutional support?[5]

As fear of a perceived evil mounts, and as the dominant culture feels that its own informal ostracism is an inadequate control or punishment, the majority naturally tends to seek direct formal (government) regulation of the offending behavior and belief.

Our modern society increasingly opts to draw and enforce its boundaries through legal power and authority. When a person is found guilty of and punished for socially deviant behavior, the community

> is making a statement about the nature and placement of boundaries. It is declaring how much variability and diversity can be tolerated within the group before it begins to lose its distinctive shape, its unique identity. . . . [O]n the whole, members of a community inform one another about the placement of their boundaries by participating in the confrontations which occur when persons who venture out onto the edges of the group are met by policing agents whose special business it is to guard the cultural integrity of the community.[6]

The framers of our Constitution, shrewd observers of human nature, understood the temptations of such legal power. They accordingly designed a system of checks and balances controlling all exercises of governmental power, consciously and deliberately devising a power separation among the legislative, the executive, and the judicial branches, with the individual retaining power in the form of the individual rights protected in the Constitution.

This governmental system can be analyzed in terms of its functions in establishing and maintaining society's formal boundaries. The legislatures, as representatives of the community, define the boundaries. The law enforcers (including governors, the president, administrative agencies, federal and state attorneys general, and prosecutors) have a primary role in maintaining those boundaries. The role of the judiciary is to preside over trials and other court proceedings ("boundary-maintaining devices") and apply the relevant law to the facts to determine whether a breach of the boundaries has occurred.[7] The courts were deliberately made independent from the enforcers (the executive branch) and the boundary makers (the legislative branch). The courts of justice, being a separate branch of government, theoretically give the entire system the impartiality necessary for legitimacy. The independence of the courts, the "blindness" of justice, protects the integrity of the boundary-making and boundary-maintaining (or policing) process by ensuring fundamental fairness in the prosecution of persons accused of socially deviant behavior.[8]

The courts normally are to defer to the boundary makers on questions concerning the wisdom of the policy establishing the boundary line. Only the barest minimum of rationality will support the legislative enactment. Policy and political decisions are the domain of the legislature, and the courts are usually obligated to accept and apply the statutes strictly in accordance with the letter and intent of the law. Indeed, the courts play a key role in boundary maintenance by applying the law to socially deviant behavior and exacting punishment for such deviation.

Our societal boundaries, however, are formed not only by legislation passed by a majority of the representatives. Our constitutions (including the state constitutions, but referring primarily to the U.S. Constitution) are the foundations and guideposts for all other boundaries. The Bill of Rights and other similar constitutional provisions form a perimeter of protection for individuals, which the governments, state and federal, must respect: Neither boundary makers, nor boundary enforcers, may erect a narrower societal boundary which excludes (and thereby penalizes) persons who engage in constitutionally protected behavior.[9] In other words, the boundaries may not be constructed or interpreted in such a way as to render constitutionally protected behavior as socially deviant. The battle lines over social deviance, therefore, are often fought at this constitutional perimeter.

One of the functions of the courts is to act as guardian over this constitutional boundary.[10] Judges ensure that the policing agents do not tread upon the procedural protections afforded under the Constitution to those accused of social deviance. Before one is to be ostracized from and punished by society, society must, by fair proceedings, prove beyond a reasonable doubt that the defendant is guilty of the deviant behavior. Furthermore, the courts afford substantive protection in the sense that they oversee the boundary makers to ensure that society's definition of deviance (as found in statutes and other policy decrees) has not prohibited, penalized, or otherwise improperly circumscribed constitutionally protected behavior. The constitutional perimeter is by no means a solidly fixed line of protection, however: Behavior that is considered to be socially deviant will only be protected to the extent that the courts believe that the Constitution was meant to protect it.

The judicial branch's vital role as protector of the individual's right to free exercise under the Constitution becomes clearer when the social phenomenon of defining and proscribing socially deviant behavior is better understood. For the characterization "socially deviant" is not necessarily something inherent in (or naturally attributable to) the behavior itself, but is a label devised and placed upon such targeted behavior by the mainstream society.[11] Since the legislature (at society's urging) has created and imposed the label "criminal," it necessarily follows that not all actions which are deemed criminal are intrinsically or even equally evil and harmful. The societal boundaries created by a criminal statute should therefore not be imbued with magical quality when they clash against the protective boundaries created by the Constitution's free exercise clause.

Labeling and punishing deviant behavior may not serve merely to protect society from actual, realizable, tangible harm: "[I]t is by no means evident that all acts considered deviant in society are in fact (or even in principle) harmful to group life."[12] Labeling behavior as deviant may also be used to create societal scapegoats who help cement social cohesion and identity in times of flux:

> The deviant individual violates rules of conduct which the rest of the community holds in high respect; and when these people come together to express their outrage over the offense and to bear witness against the offender, they develop a tighter bond of solidarity than existed earlier. . . .

> The deviant act, then, creates a sense of mutuality among the people of a community by supplying a focus for group feeling. Like a war, a flood, or some other emergency, deviance makes people more alert to the interests they share in common and draws attention to those values which constitute the "collective conscience" of the community.[13]

Thus the deviants placed behind geographical prison walls and metaphysically outside of the societal boundary for society's own protection in reality may be a necessary component, in the symbiotic sense, of the very society which banished them from its midst. As Jonathan Z. Smith notes, chaos is never overcome in the myths; neither can deviance ever be completely cured or conquered in society, for society would then need to form yet another boundary by which to create and define itself.[14]

I do not question the propriety and the necessity of the use of legislative power to define what is deviant and to enact laws to protect society from that deviance. While thus recognizing the necessity for boundaries, however, it is important to focus on the extent to which the numerically dominant or the most politically powerful in our society should be given free reign to punish or ostracize (or even eradicate, as occurred, for example, in the Roman persecution of Christians, the Inquisition against heretics, the persecution of the Ghost Dance religion, etc.) the religiously deviant for the sake of defining boundaries.

The likelihood of such boundary clashes increases in times of social stress. Unusual societal flux causes fear, and a fearful, paranoid society greatly is tempted to take extreme measures to protect itself by tightly drawing in its boundaries. During periods of panic, society may select a nondominant segment and an activity identified with that segment, and imagine itself to be seriously threatened by that Otherness:

> Societies appear to be subject, every now and then, to periods of moral panic. A condition, episode, person or group of persons emerges to become defined as a threat to societal values and interests; its nature is presented in a stylized and stereotypical fashion by the mass media; the moral barricades are manned by editors, bishops, politicians and other right-thinking people.[15]

A society inflamed is not likely to encourage its politicians to act rationally. Legislators hoping to win points with the voters and to avoid being branded as "soft" by opponents may be unable or unwilling to enact reasonable measures designed to address the actual harm; nothing less than broadly drawn prohibitions with harsh penalties may suffice to eradicate the menace. The full power of the government, both legislative and enforcement, may become intensely focused upon protecting society from the perceived threat. Furthermore, the extent of the threat posed by deviant behavior, and the amount of punishment required to fit the crime, may also be distorted by religious perceptions and interpretations by a culturally dominant group, whose understandings may not be shared by the deviant minority.[16]

Legislation, regulations, and other policy-making vehicles such as prosecutorial discretion[17] when propelled by paranoia may place pressure upon individual rights and seek to limit individual protections under the Constitution, all in the name of the greater societal good. It is the court's duty to safeguard the integrity of the procedural process, as well as protect from encroachment the substantive right to the free exercise of religion protected by the Constitution. This duty becomes no less important when society attempts to rein in the perimeters of its boundary in times of paranoia.

Accordingly, the questions the courts should be asking are those particularly suited to the judicial proceeding, which is designed to question all assumptions and get to the heart of a controversy through the introduction of hard proof in the form of factual evidence relevant to that particular dispute. Establishing the nexus between the harm sought to be avoided by the legislature and the ultimate results and effects of the individual religious practice is a vital key in distinguishing paranoia from substantially harmful situations. Not only is legislation and prosecution likely to cast a wide net,[18] punishing both harmful and beneficial instances of the taboo behavior; a paranoid society has also been known to target subjects and situations which in fact promote the very societal value which the panicked society believes to be under threat. For example, in the case of the Native American Church's use of sacramental peyote, all particularized evidence indicated that church membership fostered the same goals as those sought to be achieved by the drug laws: freedom from addiction and a productive existence.[19] Certainly if the religion/religious practice tends to *foster* the same goals as the statute, then the free exercise clause mandates non-interference. This is especially true where a legal destruction of that religious practice would result in the very harm which the law was meant to prevent, for example, a relapse into alcohol addiction precipitated by the loss of one's spiritual support. For what the

Court in *Reynolds* did not recognize when it addressed the free exercise issue is the potentially radical difference between an antisocial, "criminal" intent and action, and a religious intent and action.

Even if it is agreed by all parties that there is a substantial personal detriment suffered in the performance of the religious duty, to what extent is it legitimate for government, against the will and sincere belief of the believer, to save that believer from her God?

Paranoia as a societal phenomenon was not unknown to the framers of the Constitution. Indeed, in *The Federalist No. 78*, Alexander Hamilton refers to such matters as "ill humors" which occasionally overcome society, and he explains the role of the judiciary during such times.

Hamilton in *The Federalist No. 78* generally discusses the role of the federal judiciary under the Constitution. Much quoted by conservative legal scholars lately is Hamilton's description, in *No. 78*, of the judiciary as "the least dangerous branch." But Hamilton viewed the judicial branch as the weakest, not because it was without significant authority to check the legislative and executive branches, but because the judicial branch had neither the power of the purse nor the means to physically enforce its decrees (a job of the executive branch).

The judiciary was given the power and assigned the vital task of protecting the people from the legislature when it overstepped its constitutional boundaries:

> No legislative act, therefore, contrary to the Constitution, can be valid. To deny this would be to affirm that the deputy is greater than his principle; that the servant is above the master; that the representatives of the people are superior to the people themselves; that men acting by virtue of powers may do not only what their powers do not authorize, but what they forbid. . . .

> [T]he courts were designed to be an intermediate body between the people and the legislature in order, among other things, to keep the latter within the limits assigned to their authority. The interpretation of the laws is the proper and peculiar province of the courts. A constitution is, in fact, and must be regarded by the judges as, a fundamental law. It therefore belongs to them to ascertain its meaning as well as the meaning of any particular act proceeding from the legislative body. If there should happen to be an irreconcilable variance between the two, that which has the superior obligation and validity ought, of course, to be preferred; or, in other words, the Constitution ought to be preferred to the statute, the intention of the people to their agents.

> Nor does this conclusion by any means suppose a superiority of the judicial power to the legislative power. It only supposes that the power of the people is superior to both, and that where the will of the legislature, declared in the statutes, stands in opposition to that of the people, declared in the Constitution, the judges ought to be governed by the latter rather than the former. They ought to regulate their decisions by the fundamental laws rather than by those which are not fundamental.[20]

Hamilton was well aware of the passions of the moment which may drive a majority against a minority. Hamilton did not use the modern descriptive term "paranoia" but instead described the phenomenon in terms of "ill humors" which may cyclically infect the people:

> This independence of the judges is equally requisite to guard the Constitution and the rights of individuals from the effects of those ill humors which the arts of designing men, or the influence of particular conjunctures, sometimes disseminate among the people themselves, and which, though they speedily give place to better information, and more deliberate reflection, have a tendency, in the meantime, to occasion dangerous innovations in the government, and serious oppressions of the minor party in the community. . . . [I]t is easy to see that it would require an uncommon portion of fortitude in the judges to do their duty as faithful guardians of the Constitution, where legislative invasions of it had been instigated by the major voice of the community.[21]

The Mormon situation in the late nineteenth century is an example of societal ill humor: Prosecutors proposed, and courts adopted, clever practices and theories aimed at hastening "justice" (i.e., convictions) and harshening penalties. Proof of the crime of cohabitation became "ridiculously easy." Prosecutors began dividing the essentially single crime into smaller and smaller units in order to get multiple punishments. Utah's judges disregarded laws prohibiting an unwilling wife from testifying against her husband and jailed Mormon women who so refused. Scholar Edwin Firmage quotes an 1888 eyewitness report to the House of Representatives that six wives, three with infants, were jailed together in a tiny cell with no floor for refusing to name the fathers of their children.[22]

The experience of Jehovah's Witnesses in the mid-twentieth century further illustrates the extent to which an ill-humored society will use generally applicable laws to counter religious deviance. The Court in *Gobitis* deferred to the power of the legislative majority to determine the extent to which Jehovah's Witnesses could practice their religion and fulfill what they deemed to be divine mandates. This judicial deference, however, led to greater acts of persecution under the guise of law enforcement by the majority. The decision in *Barnette* overruling *Gobitis* recognized that when the Court abdicates its responsibilities by failing to searchingly scrutinize such cases and instead automatically defers to the democratic majority, this deference simply confirms and even feeds the righteousness of the fearful populace in pursuing its containment of religious deviance.

Alexander Hamilton recognized that an important aspect of active judicial discernment in constitutional claims was the message such searching scrutiny sent to legislators and prosecutors. Thoughts of incursions into areas protected by the Bill of Rights are thus deterred. The damage done to the rights of the individual in a situation of paranoia is thereby limited, for the judiciary puts an end to vendettas before they get out of control.

Hamilton's remarks are quoted here at length:

> But it is not with a view to infractions of the Constitution only that the independence of the judges may be an essential safeguard against the effects of occasional ill humors in the society. These sometimes extend no farther than to the injury of the private rights of particular classes of citizens, by unjust and par-

tial laws. Here also the firmness of the judicial magistracy is of vast importance in mitigating the severity and confining the operation of such laws. It not only serves to moderate the immediate mischiefs of those which may have been passed but it operates as a check upon the legislative body in passing them; who, perceiving that obstacles to the success of an iniquitous intention are to be expected from the scruples of the courts, are in a manner compelled, by the very motives of the injustice they meditate, to qualify their attempts. This is a circumstance calculated to have more influence upon the character of our governments than but few may be aware of. The benefits of the integrity and moderation of the judiciary have already been felt in more States than one; and though they may have displeased those whose sinister expectations they may have disappointed, they must have commanded the esteem and applause of all the virtuous and disinterested. Considerate men of every description ought to prize whatever will tend to beget or fortify that temper in the courts; as no man can be sure that he may not be tomorrow the victim of a spirit of injustice, by which he may be a gainer today. And every man must now feel that the inevitable tendency of such a spirit is to sap the foundations of public and private confidence and to introduce in its stead universal distrust and distress.[23]

Rather than fulfilling the expectations of the framers of the Constitution by performing the judicial branch's appointed function of protecting the minority from the majority's ill humors, however, the *Reynolds* Court instead catered to such humors. As one scholar has observed, "*Reynolds* is . . . a prime example of using law to protect the majority against religious outrage."[24]

Some congressmen who participated in the debate over the original anti-polygamy bill in 1860 had predicted that the escalation in civil rights abuses against the Mormons would occur should Congress prohibit the religious practice of the Mormons. They offered astute insights and prophetic warnings that the government would ultimately stretch the Constitution beyond the breaking point to stamp out the sincere religious belief. Representative Thayer noted, with rhetorical flourish:

> I say, as a penal statute it is powerless. I will not go into the argument now to show why it ought not to be enforced, or the cruelty of attempting to enforce it against these men, who never could understand why the bill was enacted. I will not go into the argument about the expense of millions that it would cost this Government to enforce it; or that it would give the Mormons reason to charge that we have made use of persecution against them, driving them to the mountains and hunting them like partridges, or that it would inevitably prolong the existence of the institution which it proposes to abolish.[25]

The result of the congressional prohibition was as these congressmen had predicted. The Mormons entrenched in a response comparable to the Quakers' response to the Puritan persecutions centuries earlier: steadfast loyalty to their religion and a willingness to martyrdom. James L. Clayton writes:

> For several years following its public announcement in 1852, there was no question among the Mormons as to legality or constitutionality of polygamous marriages. Because it was a commandment from God, Mormons assumed polygamy was immune from governmental interference because the First

Amendment guaranteed the "free exercise" of religion. Once Congress took steps to proscribe polygamy, however, the Mormon attitude toward polygamy hardened considerably. Most worthy male Mormons, not just the elite, were now to enter into the covenant, and the eternal nature of this doctrine was emphasized over and over again.[26]

Historian Klaus Hansen observes that "[i]t is not improbable that had it not been for the anti-polygamy crusade, this relic of barbarism . . . might have died with a whimper rather than a bang."[27]

Ironically, the challenge of adjudicating free exercise claims is not, as hinted by Justice Scalia in the *Smith* case, the arationality and incommensurableness of outsider religions and the inability of the judicial system to contend with such matters. The more serious problem for free exercise jurisprudence historically has come from the dominant society's own phobias. The problem is not the Court's inability to discern the difference between a Native American Church sacramental peyote ritual and a marijuana "pot party," but society's ability to accept the difference as a principled one. This is the crucial question for modern free exercise jurisprudence: Should pragmatism driven by fear of societal backlash and anger outweigh the good of justice? I think the example of the Framers can be instructive on this issue. John Adams, after all, was the attorney who successfully defended British soldiers charged with murder in the Boston Massacre, much to the revulsion of the Boston patriots.[28] As already noted, James Madison defined anarchy as majority oppression of the weak, as "in a state of nature." And pursuant to the enlightenment paradigm, moderation was the key to achieving the order necessary for a society to flourish.

Accordingly, I propose that especially when a free exercise case arises out of a larger societal context which has aroused unusual phobic reaction and emotion-laden rhetoric, the Court in turn must be exceptionally careful in its efforts to understand and analyze the religious framework within which the religiously compelled behavior is situated. The Court must be similarly careful in its consideration and analysis of the societal good at stake. Is the law overinclusive and/or is there a less burdensome way to achieve the good intended by the statute? Is it underinclusive, are there comparable or analogous instances of the activity that are not regulated? What is the nexus, if any, between the religiously compelled action and paradigmatic harm anticipated by the statute? Something distinct, discrete, demonstrable, and tangible (harm to persons, property, or interference with the common civic enjoyments of citizenship of a discrete individual, for example) must be at stake.

A Critique of the Court's Free Exercise Clause Jurisprudence In the U.S. Supreme Court Case of *Employment Division v. Smith*

Casuistry is not offered here as *the* magical solution to all free exercise con-flicts. As Kirk acknowledges, "It will scarcely be supposed that any system of casuistry . . . could ever be fool-proof."[1] Ambiguities will always be present in marginal cases. But what casuistry does most successfully is at least separate the easy cases from the hard ones. If the paradigmatic good of the statute is accom-plished, or if the spirit and intent of the statute (as indicated by its paradigms) are not violated by the religious practice considered within the context of the belief system as a whole, then in fact there is no conflict.

In this chapter I analyze the 1990 case of *Employment Div. v. Smith* as one of the "easy" cases. The Court, however, ignored the particulars of the Native American Church practice; the only relevancy was that ingestion of peyote was technically illegal.[2] Thus, I will explore the particulars of the *Smith* case in great detail, placing the facts in their larger, societal context (i.e., contexts of the un-employment compensation law of Oregon, of risks which society does allow, of drug ingestion which has society's regulatory approval, etc.). Such a searching scrutiny of the factual record of the *Smith* case highlights the Court's radical dis-regard of such particulars.

The "particulars" of the *Smith* Case

Smith v. Employment Division:
Through the administrative agency

Alfred Smith and Galen Black, former or recovering[3] alcoholics, were coun-selors at Douglas County Council on Alcohol and Drug Abuse Prevention and Treatment (ADAPT). ADAPT is a private treatment organization which oper-ated under the theory that addiction is a disease and "the only responsible and prudent course of recovery for an alcoholic and/or addict is total abstinence."[4]

Smith and Black were both members of the Native American Church and had ingested sacramental peyote during a religious ceremony. John Gardin, director of ADAPT, determined that *any* use (including religious use) of alcohol or nonprescribed drugs was job-related misconduct. ADAPT, therefore, treated the ingestion of the sacramental peyote as a relapse and told Smith and Black that they had a choice between being fired or undergoing an "intensive program of personal counseling" in a residential treatment center, at their own expense and on unpaid leave.[5] They both refused such treatment on the grounds that there was nothing wrong with them. Neither had broken their abstinence, other than to partake of a minor amount of the sacramental peyote as participants in the ritual worship service. Gardin fired them.

The Supreme Court case of *Employment Division v. Smith* began simply as two separate administrative hearings concerning the denial of unemployment benefits to Black and to Smith. The administrative hearing focused on the limited issues relevant to unemployment compensation, such as "job-related misconduct."[6] Expert testimony was admitted by written affidavit. The parties, therefore, had no opportunity to cross-examine these expert witnesses. No evidence was introduced by the state and no legal issues were addressed relating to the criminality of the claimants' ingestion of sacramental peyote, or to whether imposing the criminal law on believers of the Native American Church would further any compelling state interest.

The referees[7] at the separate hearings for Smith and Black (hereinafter, the "claimants") determined that each was entitled to receive unemployment compensation benefits. The Employment Division of the Department of Human Resources (which administers the unemployment compensation program in Oregon) appealed up its own administrative ladder to the Employment Appeals Board (EAB), which reversed the decision of the division's referees.

The EAB determined instead (based upon the facts of record at the limited administrative hearings before the referees) that the knowing ingestion of "an illegal drug" by a drug treatment counselor was *"wilful [sic]"* job-related *misconduct* detrimental to the employer's interests.[8] When confronted with the claim in the *Smith* case that Smith's free exercise rights[9] would be violated by the denial of unemployment benefits, however, the EAB abandoned the realm of unemployment law, where the free exercise right would have normally been measured against the state's unemployment compensation interests. Instead, the EAB bootstrapped a broad, otherwise irrelevant *criminal law* interest onto the narrow unemployment issue. By doing so, the EAB felt justified in finding that the religious motivation for such ingestion was then, in turn, totally irrelevant to the *unemployment compensation* case. The EAB concluded that the state had an overriding "compelling . . . interest in the proscription of illegal drugs,"[10] which eclipsed whatever free exercise right Smith may have had.

Normally, unemployment benefits could not be withheld simply because of criminal behavior: "Indeed, the Employment Division conceded below that 'the commission of an illegal act or conviction of a crime is not, in and of itself, grounds for disqualification from unemployment benefits.'"[11] The state had successfully injected the element of criminal law into this unemployment case for the sole purpose of thwarting the claimants' free exercise defense to the unemployment disallowance for willful misconduct. But neither Black nor Smith had ever been charged with a crime. The administrative hearing by definition could not delve into the relevance of any justifications that existed for the state's criminal prohibition of peyote, when applied to sacramental use by the Native American Church. What little evidence had been considered regarding the state's justification for classifying peyote as an illegal drug and applying that criminal law against members of Native American Church was minimally received only through untested written affidavits, if at all.

In summary, the disallowance of the unemployment claims was a two-step process. Initially, the denial rested upon the civil determination that the counselors had knowingly and willfully ingested the sacramental peyote as part of their religious beliefs, and that, even though such ingestion was on their own private time, it was *job-related willful misconduct*. The job-relatedness factor was found to be present because the claimants were accused of setting a bad example for the treatment center's addicts. And notably, although they would partake of the peyote ceremony only a few times per year, the ingestion was apparently not considered an isolated incident[12] which would have qualified the claimants for compensation, precisely because it had been done as part of religious worship, which, however infrequently, would be repeated.

The second step in the analysis of the compensation claim was to consider whether, in denying them unemployment benefits for engaging in religiously motivated behavior, the state had violated the claimants' constitutional rights. It was at this point that the criminal aspect of the use of the sacramental peyote was introduced by the Oregon attorney general as a counterweight to the claimants' constitutional rights.

The full import of the denial of unemployment compensation and the rejection of the constitutional right to free exercise of religion in this case becomes clearer when placed in stark contrast to other instances where benefits were or would be granted. If the claimants had been Catholic, for example, and had taken wine at communion (which also would have been considered a "relapse" by ADAPT), they would have been fired and initially denied unemployment benefits for job-related willful misconduct. But, since the taking of wine is not a crime in Oregon, their federal, First Amendment free exercise right would have overridden any interest the state would have had in denying them benefits.

If the claimants simply had suffered a relapse and were fired, as opposed to having taken part in a religious ritual, they would have also been entitled to unemployment benefits. Moreover, persons who are fired for job-related misconduct attributable to "personal reasons" are also deemed eligible for unemployment benefits. The claimants' brief to the Supreme Court listed several such examples: a worker who left his job to help his stranded wife and was fired when he refused to return to work and leave his wife with a broken-down vehicle; a worker who was fired for fighting with another worker; and a worker who quit his job because of his wife's medical condition.[13]

And, as noted above, criminal behavior that is not directly job related would not disqualify one from receiving unemployment benefits. Claimants cited, for example, to the case of a Portland State University professor who was fired after his conviction "for conspiring with others to explode devices designed to damage or destroy certain federal buildings."[14] The professor was held to be entitled to unemployment benefits, because it was "off-duty" conduct, and not "misconduct in the course and scope of employment."[15]

In another Oregon case, a person was fired for running a red light and causing an accident in the course of his employment as a courier service driver. The driver was entitled to unemployment benefits because the court found no rational support for the administrative agency's conclusion that such conduct evidenced a willful disregard of the employer's interest.[16]

In the Oregon state courts

Smith and Black appealed their denial of unemployment benefits to the intermediate appellate court in Oregon, which reversed the decision of the EAB. The court found that the state's refusal to pay unemployment benefits was a "substantial burden" on religion. The appellate court also found that the state's interest, asserted as "protecting the Unemployment Compensation Fund from depletion by those who are undeserving due to their own conduct, e.g., those who quit or are fired without good reason," was not compelling enough to justify the burden placed on religious practice.[17] But the appellate court remanded the case back to the agency because it felt there had been insufficient fact-finding with respect to whether the ingestion of peyote was pursuant to a sincerely held, bona fide religious belief.

The Oregon Supreme Court heard the case on the Oregon attorney general's appeal from the intermediate appellate court. Oregon's highest court overturned the appellate court's remand to the agency for further evidential hearings, because it felt that no further fact-finding was necessary. The court, on the record before it, directly addressed the freedom of religion claims. The free exercise analysis of the state supreme court is related here in detail in order to highlight its attitude toward the individual's right to freedom of worship. It is precisely these governmental bodies to which the U.S. Supreme Court wishes to give deference, and thus their attitudes and processes bear further examination to determine whether such deference on issues involving the guarantees of the federal Bill of Rights is well placed.

After noting at the outset that "[t]he states were the original guarantors of religious freedom for their citizens," the Oregon Supreme Court dismissed the religious exercise claim for *lack* of protection under the Oregon Constitution.[18] The court found that it was the employer, not the state, who interfered with the claimants' right to worship by firing the claimants for job-related misconduct. The state's unemployment statute,[19] which had furnished the basis for the decision to deny the claimant's unemployment benefits, was not to blame. The unemployment benefits statute was "completely neutral toward religious motivation," and this neutrality was present "both on its face and as applied."

The determination that the statute was "neutral" in its application is curious in light of the above examples where unemployment benefits[20] were granted. When viewed from the perspective of the religious rights protected under the state constitution (i.e., using the freedom to worship as the norm by which to judge neutrality), the unemployment laws are not applied neutrally: As pointed out in the claimants' briefs, "religious worship" is given far less consideration than such exemptions and excuses as good faith errors, recurring negligence, lack of wrongful intent, fist-fighting for personal reasons, or medical relapses. Indeed, one who plots to blow up a federal building may receive unemployment compensation, but one who engages in an illegal act as part of religious worship cannot. Religious motivation puts one at a decided disadvantage, for one's religious intent is considered to be "wrongful" simply because the behavior itself is "intended."

The Oregon Supreme Court gauged neutrality from the point of view, not of the constitutional right, but of the statute under scrutiny. The statute itself was the norm, not the constitutional right.

> The statute and the rule are completely neutral toward religious motivations for misconduct. If the statute or the rule did discriminate for or against claimants who were discharged for worshipping as they chose, we would be faced with an entirely different issue.[21]

Thus, one way that an Oregon rule or statute would be deemed in violation of Oregon's constitutional protection of religious freedom is if the enactment specifically stated, "Anyone discharged for religious behavior cannot be eligible for unemployment benefits." But, apparently, if the statute also said, "Anyone fired for bona fide good faith religious behavior *shall* be eligible for benefits," the court would consider that "discrimination *for* . . . claimants," which would also be a problem under Oregon's analysis.

"Neutrality" to the court meant that the same outward action would be treated the same, that all drug counselors who knowingly and freely and deliberately ingest peyote are all equally ineligible for unemployment benefits. The court saw no meaningful distinction between one who ingests sacramental peyote in worship and one who, knowing it is illegal, deliberately chooses to break the law and ingest peyote for merely recreational purposes. "Neutrality" means, therefore, that the religious motivation and context are not just irrelevant; they are actively disregarded. The significance and meaning of the religious experience is discounted; the behavior is punished as if harm to society, not worship of one's deity, was intended. Under the Oregon Supreme Court's analysis, one who breaks the law as an active religious worshiper is at a severe disadvantage: Such worship has been equated with, indeed defined as, deliberately engaging in "misconduct," and thus automatically presumed as having "wrongful intent." No consideration is given for the mitigating factor of a spiritual, rather than an antisocietal, motivation. The inescapable outcome is that spiritual motives are equated with antisocietal motives.

Despite the protection of the individual's right to worship guaranteed to the citizens of Oregon under the state constitution, these rights are subordinated to the business interests of the employers under the unemployment compensation system. One can be fired from one's job for worshiping God according to the dictates of one's religion, and the state must abide by and defer to the employer's decision and deny the protection of the unemployment safety net. The pressure of having no state unemployment benefits to cover immediate bills, or even bus fare to go to job interviews, according to the Oregon Supreme Court, is not enough to consider the *state's* denial of unemployment benefits as a *burden* imposed *by* the state on the practice of religion. Thus, the court concluded:

> Claimant was denied benefits through the operation of a statute that is neutral both on its face and as applied. The law and the rule defining misconduct in no way discriminate against claimant's religious practices or beliefs. If claimant's freedom to worship has been interfered with, that interference was committed by his employer, not by the unemployment statutes.

> Under the Oregon Constitution's freedom of religion provisions, claimant has not shown that his right to worship according to the dictates of his conscience has been infringed upon by the denial of unemployment benefits. . . . [H]ere, it was not the government that disqualified claimant from his job for ingesting peyote. And the rule denying unemployment benefits to one who loses his job for what an employer permissibly considers misconduct, conduct incompatible with the job, is itself a neutral rule, as we have said. . . . *[W]e do not believe that the state is denying the worker a vital necessity in applying the "misconduct" exception of the compensation statute.*[22]

After rejecting the claim under the Oregon Constitution, however, the Oregon Supreme Court found that the claimants were entitled to unemployment compensation under the free exercise clause of the federal Constitution. The court considered the U.S. Supreme Court cases of *Sherbert v. Verner* and *Thomas v. Review Board* to be controlling on the issue of denying unemployment benefits for religiously motivated behavior.

Next, the court looked to the state's interest in *not* allowing unemployment compensation to be paid to the claimants. The court considered the EAB's finding of a compelling state interest "in proscribing the use of dangerous drugs," but found criminal law to be *inapplicable* to the unemployment situation:

> The state's interest in denying unemployment benefits to a claimant discharged for religiously motivated misconduct must be found in the unemployment compensation statutes, not in the criminal law statutes proscribing the use of peyote. [Footnote omitted.] The Employment Division concedes that "the commission of an illegal act is not, in and of itself, grounds for disqualification from unemployment benefits. ORS 657.176 (3) permits disqualification only if a claimant commits a felony in connection with work ***. (T)he legality of (claimant's) ingestion of peyote has little direct bearing on this case.[23]

Having dismissed the relevance of the criminality of the activity, the court found that the state's sole interest in denying benefits was to protect the financial well-being of the compensation fund from a rash of religiously based claims. Citing again to *Sherbert* and *Thomas*, the court found that such financial interest was not compelling enough to override the constitutional free exercise right. It remanded the case back to the EAB to carry out the directive to award Smith and Black unemployment benefits.

In the U.S. Supreme Court Smith I:

The State of Oregon (Employment Division of the Department of Human Services) sought review of the Oregon Supreme Court's decision to the U.S. Supreme Court on the ground that the state supreme court had misinterpreted the breadth of federal constitutional rights under the free exercise clause. The free exercise right, argued the state, did not protect the individual as much as the Oregon Supreme Court thought it did. Harking back over one hundred years to the *Reynolds*[24] analysis, the state argued that since the action is theoretically criminal, there is *no* need for the state of Oregon to prove any sort of interest in regulating the particular situation presented by the religious practice.

The State of Oregon methodically structured its argument to the Court to mirror, and thus to trigger, the *Reynolds* analysis. The state's brief to the U.S. Supreme Court targeted and underscored the state's interest in enforcing its criminal drug laws, although the *Smith* case arose in the unemployment context, where the criminality of the claimants' conduct was irrelevant and where the administrative hearing did not take evidence on or address the issues relevant to criminality.

> [B]ecause the conduct is prohibited as a matter of criminal law . . . then these claimants had no free exercise right to engage in the conduct. . . . When the state has regulated the conduct itself and, as in this case, has outright prohibited it, Sherbert [the analysis adopted by the Court in the case of *Sherbert v. Verner*] doesn't apply. You don't even get . . . [to] the analysis that requires the state to prove a compelling state interest. . . .[25]

The deputy attorney general of Oregon, at oral argument before the U.S. Supreme Court on behalf of the State of Oregon in *Smith I*, offered broad, sweeping assertions as "proof" of the evils of peyote. These assertions are noted in detail, for they provide a glimpse into the attitude of the state of Oregon toward the religious right being asserted and the nature of the proof offered by the state against the religious practice.

> Oregon, like all states, has determined that there is a compelling need to deal with the problems of drug abuse. . . .
>
> Peyote is a Schedule I drug in Oregon. It is—that means that it has determined that there is no safe use for it. It cannot be used safely even under the care of a physician and that there is great susceptibility to drug abuse. . . .
>
> In order to accommodate the religious practice would [sic] undermine the state's compelling interest in at least four different ways. First, peyote is dangerous to the user and to those who come in contact with it. That's the very reason why the state has criminalized it in the first place.
>
> It is also dangerous to the community which must tolerate its presence within it. Peyote produces an hallucinogenic state similar to that produced by LSD. All fifty states and the federal government categorize [sic] peyote has [sic] dangerous. The dangers posed by peyote are indifferent to the motivations of the user, and the state should be no less concerned about the dangers posed to a re-

ligious user than to the dangers posed by the drug—by one who uses it for recreational purposes or for personal enlightenment.

Once peyote is made lawful for some purposes, as these claimants contend they have a right to require the state to do, then the problem of controlling drug trafficking is significantly compounded. Peyote only grows in the Southwestern United States, primarily Texas and parts of Mexico. It would be difficult to distinguish meaningfully between traffic for lawful purposes and traffic for unlawful purposes.

The simple fact is that once some people have a right to possess peyote, there is an increased risk the drug will fall into the hands of those who do not have that right. There is a risk that others will commit crimes against persons who possess peyote lawfully in order to obtain it from them.

These claimants, like eighty-nine percent of the Native American population in Oregon, reside in urban areas, and that merely compounds the risk that the presence of the drug in the community will mean that it will fall into the hands of persons who cannot possess it.

The record in this case includes an affidavit from Stanley Smart, who is a road chief, who conducts the peyote ceremony. He indicates that it is not uncommon for him to conduct as many as four peyote ceremonies a week. That means that at any given time, Mr. Smart is in the possession of a large amount of peyote, and he makes himself thereby a target for those who would mean to obtain the drug from him for unlawful uses.[26]

These assertions sound important, but is the rhetoric supported by data, detailed analysis, or other contextual information? Or was the basis asserted by the State of Oregon for the prohibition of the sacramental use of peyote bolstered mainly by fear, popular misconceptions/prejudice, and/or political expediency? Note that the state's arguments echo the concerns of the levitical paradigm respecting purity and contamination, the need for strong boundaries to prevent infection, as well as the concerns for hierarchical authority and obedience which characterize the duly ordered relationships paradigm.

The U.S. Supreme Court in *Smith I* did not ask these questions. The Court focused only upon textual parameters of the Oregon criminal statute which prohibited the possession, but not the use, of peyote. Although the Court agreed that, "as a matter of state law, the commission of an illegal act is not itself a ground for disqualifying a discharged employee from benefits,"[27] taking its cues from Oregon's arguments, the Court also became fixated with the illegality of the act itself. Justice Stevens, in the opinion for the Court in *Smith I*, took up the state's concern that the Oregon Supreme Court disregarded the state's criminal law out of a misreading of the prior unemployment compensation decisions such as *Sherbert*:

Whether the state court believed that it was constrained by *Sherbert* and *Thomas* to disregard the State's law enforcement interest, or did so because it believed petitioner to have conceded that the legality of respondent's conduct was not in issue, is not entirely clear.[28]

The Court remanded the case to the Oregon Supreme Court and asked the court to answer a single question of Oregon law: Was the ingestion of peyote by a communicant during the sacred ceremony of the Native American Church considered "possession" under the Oregon drug laws, and therefore theoretically a crime under Oregon law?

Justice Brennan wrote a dissent in *Smith I*, with Justices Marshall and Blackmun joining. As bluntly described by Justice Brennan, claimants Black and Smith "were fired for practicing their religion."[29] Justice Brennan condemned the tortured analysis which searched outside of the unemployment compensation statute to an entirely different area of law, in order to find a validating purpose for the denial of unemployment benefits, especially where the Oregon Supreme Court itself had disavowed any such criminal law interest in its unemployment compensation statute.

On remand, the Oregon Supreme Court noted that it had been commanded to clarify the legality of the claimants' use of peyote. The court concluded "that the Oregon statute against possession of controlled substances, which include peyote [footnote omitted], makes no exception for the sacramental use of peyote. . . ."[30] In a footnote, the court simply noted that facially "[n]either the statute nor the regulation make an exception for religious use of peyote, nor do they by reference adopt the exemption found in federal law. . . .[31]" The court then, however, cited to numerous other statutes which had express exemptions for sacramental peyote use.

The state attorney general interpreted the above to mean that in this particular case the *use* (ingestion) of peyote by members of the Native American Church during the peyote ceremony would theoretically be considered as criminal *possession* and therefore illegal as defined in the statute. The state advanced its interpretation of the Oregon court's opinion in its petition for certiorari to the U.S. Supreme Court for another hearing on the issue of free exercise protection for theoretically criminal conduct. Overlooked in the state's brief was footnote three of the Oregon Supreme Court's opinion:

> If disqualification from unemployment compensation hinged on guilt or innocence of an uncharged and untried crime, it would raise issues of the applicable mental state and of changing burdens of proof for which the compensation procedure is neither designed nor equipped. Because no criminal case is before us, we do not give an advisory opinion on the circumstances under which prosecuting members of the Native American Church under ORS 475.992(4)(a) for sacramental use of peyote would violate the Oregon Constitution.[32]

In this footnote, the Oregon court directly refused to decide what the Supreme Court had asked of it: whether the use of peyote was criminal under the specific circumstances of a Native American Church ritual. The court's recitation of the insurmountable difficulties in assessing criminality in an administrative hearing, which clearly was not designed to fully and fairly consider the issue, injects a note of common sense into the debate which went unheeded.

The problems expressed in footnote three of the opinion, above, are noteworthy: The highest court of the State of Oregon had withheld its judgment on its own constitutional issue because there was no criminal case before it. The court rightly recognized that the case arose in the unemployment context and was restricted by that hearing format. The Oregon court furthermore declared that, not only was the administration of unemployment compensation not set up to resolve criminal law issues, but also that the state had no interest whatsoever in upholding the policies of its criminal law within the context of the unemployment compensation system.

Under the notion of federalism, the U.S. Supreme Court should have deferred to the wisdom of the state on issues of state law. Here, the highest court in the State of Oregon declared Oregon criminal law to be irrelevant to the unemployment compensation claim, both as a matter of law and as a matter of practicality (due to the confines of the unemployment context). An *amicus curiae* brief in support of respondents argued to the Court that it had granted the petition to hear this case improvidently, since the Oregon Supreme Court's determination rested on an issue of state law by which the U.S. Supreme Court was bound. The brief also noted that for the Supreme Court to decide the free exercise claim upon Oregon criminal law would mean that it would be issuing an "advisory opinion" not based upon an actual criminal case or controversy fully litigated below at the hearing level.[33] Yet, undaunted by its own conservative judicial norms, the U.S. Supreme Court determined for itself[34] what the state's interests should be (i.e., the criminal law) in assessing the free exercise claim. Such prosecutorial and judicial behavior is consistent with the "moral panic" syndrome: "Reaching" to make a point is an indication that perhaps something besides logic and rationality is fueling the decision-making process. Thus, a careful scrutiny of the basis for the Court's ultimate decision is in order.

Before the analysis of the U.S. Supreme Court's final decision as rendered in *Smith II* can be undertaken, therefore, it is necessary to conduct an in-depth analysis of the Oregon attorney general's case (both evidence and arguments) against allowing any exemption under the free exercise clause for benefits to be paid to claimants who were fired for the religious ingestion of sacramental peyote.

Limits on the free exercise of religion: Peyote as a hallucinogenic drug which must be absolutely prohibited because of the dangers it causes to the user and to society

The state's arguments against finding a free exercise exception to the unemployment laws for the religious use of peyote amounted to the following: (1) peyote is a Schedule I drug, and as such, it has no safe use; (2) the drug is dangerous to the user; (3) the drug is dangerous to those who come in contact with the user; (4) society will be harmed because controlling illegal drug trafficking in peyote will be compounded in difficulty by any religious use exemption; and (5) criminal activity will increase against those who have the right to possess the drug. Such bald assertions do not rise to the level of "evidence," however. The telling aspect of this case was the amount, and nature, of the proofs offered by the state in support of its asserted interest in preventing any sacramental exceptions.

The state's brief began what should have been a presentation of evidentiary proofs of its compelling state interest in banning sacramental peyote by stating: "It should be unnecessary to detail the public and private devastations caused by drug use and drug abuse in this nation." In support of this general statement, the state cited to such politicized efforts as presidential antidrug campaigns, a congressional declaration of "National Drug Abuse Education and Prevention Week," and antidrug legislation.

What to the claimants was a sacrament was to the state a crown or button of a cactus plant which, "when dried and chewed, produces a psychedelic effect." "Peyote," according to the state, "indisputably poses severe dangers to human health and well-being." In support of its position, the state offered generalized textbook laboratory descriptions of the physical effects of the drug mescaline:

> Low doses of mescaline produce "dilatation of the pupils, increased blood pressure and heart rate, an increase in body temperature, EEG and behavioral arousal, and other excitatory symptoms" similar to those produced by amphetamines. Mescaline also produces vivid hallucinations, usually both visual and auditory, and can cause temporary psychosis. High doses lead to "severe hypertension, a toxic acute brain syndrome (manifested by disorientation), a clouding of consciousness, and convulsions," as well as death or respiratory failure probably caused by "vasospasm of isolated cerebral arteries."[35]

In addition to the generalized textbook pronouncements of potential personal harm, the Oregon attorney general offered two affidavits as evidence of the need to ban all use of peyote. Joseph R. Steiner, a counselor in a private practice that focused on issues of chemical dependency, authored the first affidavit. Steiner, when reciting his qualifications, mentioned neither firsthand knowledge of the Native American Indian ceremony, nor any direct treatment experience with either Native Americans or members of the Native American Church. The focus of Steiner's written testimony was the importance of total abstinence from all drugs for a recovering alcoholic. Steiner quoted textbook sources for the proposition that peyote was a powerful hallucinogen and that there was "no way to accurately predict how any user will react on any given occasion to mescaline." Steiner portrayed religious use of drugs, whether alcohol or peyote, as a self-deception.

> The purpose of elaborating on the extreme mood and mind altering effects of peyote are several. One is to make clear that peyote is a powerful and potent agent which does have sometimes long-lasting negative effects on its user with no predictability as to when that could happen. A very important reason for clarifying peyote as a mood/mind altering substance is to make clear that it does, in fact, distort the perceptions of the user.
>
> This distortion of perception and the subsequent effects on judgment is in and of itself very risky for the alcoholic, as the alcoholic may use alcohol in order to deal with the negative effects of peyote, convincing him/herself that "alcohol will help", "only a little won't hurt" (or matter), or that he/she needs alcohol in order to be okay.

The risk factor is significantly increased if the alcoholic is involved in the relapse process. . . . All recovering alcoholics experience the relapse process at
times while remaining abstinent. The risk is related to how seriously entrenched the relapse is in the alcoholic, and whether he/she has the resources
to maintain sobriety after experiencing the use of such a potent hallucinogen as
is peyote. . . .

Another major concern is how a recovering alcoholic/addict may convince
him/herself that use of peyote (or wine or any other mood/mind altering substance) for religious, ceremonial, spiritual, or any other reason is acceptable.
The alcoholic who has truly accepted the powerlessness over alcohol and other
drugs and admitted to his/her life's unmanageability (both of which are considered necessary in order to initiate recovery), probably knows that *any* [Steiner's
emphasis] use of a mood or mind altering chemical may trigger a drinking
episode or the renewed use of other drugs. To convince him/herself that alcohol or other mood/mind altering drug use is acceptable, the recovering alcoholic would have need to reactivate his/her denial system. . . . The question
must be asked whether a recovering alcoholic who wants to participate in a religious ceremony and use wine, peyote, or other mood/mind altering substance
is already involved in this relapse process, with an activated denial system, and
whether this would make that person even more vulnerable to loss of control of
use. . . .[36]

Steiner does allow one exception to total abstinence: drugs prescribed by a
physician.

Steiner indicated that alcohol addiction is a physiological process, but then
ignored the physiological differences between ingesting peyote and drinking alcohol. Terence Gorski's affidavit, on behalf of the claimants, addressed this aspect directly: "There is no clear-cut evidence that peyote impacts on the same
neurological or neurochemical systems as does alcohol." Steiner's affidavit had
gone into the record without benefit of questioning or cross-examination.
Steiner could not be challenged directly with Gorski's statement and could not
be asked the basis for his unsupported and generalized opinion to the contrary.
What was clear was that to Steiner, the religious experience of the Native American Church was simply an excuse to lapse back into old patterns of addiction.

John DeSmet, then director of the Alcohol Dependence Treatment Program at a Veterans Administration medical center, authored the other affidavit
relied upon by the Oregon attorney general. DeSmet's prior assignment was at
an army fort, as clinical director of its alcohol and substance abuse center. His
clinical interest was focused on the "denial system" of an alcoholic. DeSmet also
did not list any personal contact or experience with Native American Church
peyote ceremonies, nor with the personal treatment of any persons who were
members of the church.

In summary, DeSmet's position was that a drug is a drug, whether it was
used for religious purposes, for medical purposes,[37] or for recreational purposes.
His analogies, however, were with the pain-killing drugs used for medical
treatment—presumably (for he was not specific in any of his examples) such
highly addictive drugs as codeine or morphine. DeSmet nowhere addressed the

particular potential (or lack thereof) for abuse of the peyote drug; certainly, it is not a drug being used for medical treatment by doctors currently, and thus it could not have been within the experience upon which he relies so heavily.

DeSmet completely discounted the religious motivation and spiritual experience of an individual in his statement, essentially agreeing with Steiner that religious drug use is just an episode of denial:

> If an individual uses such drugs knowing full well that the ingestion of such a drug is against the personnel policy of the organization to which he or she belongs, then such use must be interpreted as having severe occupational and vocational consequences. This use despite severe occupational consequences constitutes relapse according to Gorski's model. . . .

> Mr. Gorski indicates that the use of peyote in small quantities for spiritual ends does not necessarily constitute a relapse. I would *suggest* [38] that the small quantities are irrelevant. This is a potent mood and mind altering drug.[39]

DeSmet's affidavit implicitly rejected the notion that the ingestion of sacramental peyote could be a bona fide religious experience: "The drug produces hallucinations. The hallucinations are intended to produce a spiritual experience." In other words, what one experiences is not really a communion with God, but a chemically induced physical reaction. DeSmet exhorts peyote cult members to go out and find another God to worship:

> Commen [sic] sense and this history of medicine shows [sic] that it is reasonable and prudent for individual [sic] to take the medically safer course. To insist that one has the right to wine at a Catholic religious experience or peyote in a Native American religious experience, at [sic] that this ingestion does not increase the likelihood of relapse is not consistent with the available experience of this practitioner. When a former heroin addict is placed in the hospital for a surgical procedure and administered an opiate derivative to manage the pain in the post- surgery process, the cells do not disregard the ingestion of another opiate just because it is for medical reasons; the cells do not distinguish the reasons for which the drug was taken. Centuries of tradition in medical practice would indicate that the safe, reasonable, prudent, common sense approach would be for individuals to find other ways to manage pain or achieve religious and spiritual highs without the ingestion of mood altering chemicals.[40]

DeSmet was not subject to cross-examination as to this statement. If he had been, certainly one would have questioned his references to "centuries" of medical tradition or his comparison of heroin with peyote. Additionally, one also could have questioned the statement that the cells do not distinguish the reasons for the taking of a drug: Have there been any studies showing that the reaction (physical and behavioral) to a drug such as peyote is always unaffected by the psychological state of the person as he ingests the drug? Was his statement based upon his own "common sense" or upon some relevant medical studies?

These affidavits and highly generalized textbook descriptions, heavily relied upon by the attorney general at the U.S. Supreme Court level where the case focused upon criminality, supported a case for protecting an individual from himself, or for justifying the employer's argument that "good cause" existed to fire the drug abuse counselors. But these evidentiary materials did not support the state's claims of drug trafficking problems, potential harm to bystanders or to the public in general by the Native American Church ceremony, or other *criminal* law considerations as later touted by the attorney general.

In rebuttal to these generalized statements as to the personal harm caused by peyote ingestion, Dr. Robert Bergman, psychiatrist and former national chief of Mental Health Programs for the Indian Health Service, submitted an affidavit which stated:

> The Native American Church, and its ceremony involving the use of peyote, is the single most effective manner of treatment for Indian alcoholism and other drug abuse. . . . Whereas the abuse of alcohol leads to terrible effects upon the mental and physical health of the individual and upon surrounding friends and family, it is extremely rare for the use of peyote in a Native American Church ceremony to lead to any such negative effects. The hallucinogenic effect of the drug has generally been exhausted by the time the religious ceremony is complete.[41]

Dr. Bergman's opinion was based, not upon isolated laboratory tests of mescaline or upon generalized textbook theories or upon experience with heroin addicts, but upon direct personal experience in treating members of the Native American Church, as well as in his capacity as director of the Indian Health Service. Anthropologist Omer C. Stewart, who had studied the peyote religious ceremonies since 1937, submitted an affidavit which stated:

> The peyote ceremony is in no way a substitute for alcohol. In fact, the peyote ceremony assists a participant in resisting the use of alcohol by providing a sense of self-awareness and faith. I believe it is fair to say that nothing has been shown to be as effective in combatting the negative effects of alcoholism as the use of peyote in an Indian religious ceremony.[42]

To counter arguments as to the beneficial use of sacramental peyote, the attorney general claimed the impossibility of monitoring each and every ceremony to be certain that a safe dosage was given, and, indeed, he cited to the impossibility of determining what such a dosage might be. The state claimed harmful excessive entanglement in religious worship might result.[43] One does not hear about such regulatory entanglements as monitoring Christian church services for overdosage or abuse of alcohol in "dry" regions of this country where sacramental wine exemptions are politically given, or even of the dangers of giving alcohol in the form of sacramental wine to children as young as seven years of age. And with respect to ensuring that each person receives a "safe" level of alcohol during the service, to an alcoholic there is perhaps no safe level. Yet, exemptions for sacramental wine exist. These exemptions may be premised upon the common experience of sacramental wine, or upon a higher comfort level with the known. If so, it would seem that evidence and narratives of those experienced in the ways of the Native American Church could have served a useful educational function, lessening the Otherness of the church and its practices. The Court virtually ignored these narratives, however.

Both the Oregon attorney general and the U.S. Supreme Court ultimately placed great emphasis on the importance of "uniformity" and "comprehensiveness" in the War on Drugs. Their concern (correlating with the basic tenets of the levitical paradigm) was the threat of contamination: If sacramental peyote was permitted, religious use might spread out into prohibited misuse. This concern is not unique to religious use alone. *Any* qualification, no matter what the purpose, entails that same risk. Yet the concerns over misuse have not led to a complete ban on all uses whatsoever. An elaborate exemption system accommodates important societal uses of regulated drugs, coupled with close regulatory controls which are meant to reduce the chances of misuse. Thus, the drug laws in fact are not strictly prohibitive bans but actually permit certain uses within limited circumstances. The federal program, which is essentially duplicated at the state levels, provides such exemptions for "legitimate medical, scientific, research, or industrial channels. . . ."[44] "Legitimate and approved religious use" could be added to the list of protected societal uses of controlled substances. But unless the Court actively gives notice that it will protect the rights of nondominant religious groups to freely exercise their religion, the legislature may or may not take steps to accommodate politically unpopular practices or groups.[45]

Registered and regulated practitioners receive exemptions for the use of controlled substances in their professional capacities. A "practitioner" is defined as

> a physician, dentist, veterinarian, scientific investigator, pharmacy, hospital, or other person licensed, registered, or otherwise permitted, by the United States or the jurisdiction in which he practices or does research, to distribute, dispense, conduct research with respect to, administer, or use in teaching or chemical analysis, a controlled substance in the course of professional practice of research.[46]

A clergyman/"road chief" could be subject to the same regulatory safeguards, in order to meet fears of illegal trafficking.

Statutory requirements must be followed in the granting of a registration to distribute a controlled substance. 21 U.S.C.A. Section 823 (b) provides that the attorney general may deny an application for registration if he finds it against the public interest. Factors which are to be considered in determining whether the public interest will be served by the granting of a particular application are:

(1) maintenance of effective control against diversion of particular controlled substances into other than legitimate medical, scientific, and industrial channels;
(2) compliance with applicable State and local law;
(3) prior conviction record of applicant under Federal or State laws relating to the manufacture, distribution, or dispensing of such substances;
(4) past experiences in the distribution of controlled substances; and
(5) such other factors as may be relevant to and consistent with the public health and safety.[47]

Procedures for denying, revoking, or suspending a registration are contained within 21 U.S.C.A. Section 824; labeling and packaging regulations, including the sealing of containers, are set forth in 21 U.S.C.A. Section 825; production quotas are provided for in 21 U.S.C.A. Section 826. Registrants are subject to stringent record-keeping and order form requirements (see 21 U.S.C.A. Sections 827 and 828). Practitioners whose in-house controls are lax, and thus allow slippage of controlled substances into unauthorized hands, would lose their registration. Similarly, practitioners who themselves dispense controlled substances in situations beyond their limited area of approval are subject to criminal prosecution.[48]

These controls provide "neutral" criteria for reducing the spread of controlled drugs into uncontrolled areas of use. Theoretically they could be made applicable to, and would be effective in, controlling such spread whether the use was in a five-hundred-bed major hospital with several thousand employees, or in a religious ceremony supervised by a registered "road man" of the Native American Church. But it is the Court's responsibility to provide the impetus for the protection of free exercise rights where legislative initiative has lagged.

Indeed, as persuasively argued by the claimants in their brief to the U.S. Supreme Court in *Smith II*, the religious exemption of sacramental peyote did not present the Court (or the State of Oregon) with a unique regulatory situation fraught with unknown risks: Criminal antidrug statutes in eleven states contain specific exemptions for sacramental peyote use. In fact, federal regulations specifically exempt peyote use from the proscription of the federal drug laws, and twelve other states incorporate those federal exemptions. Other states, such as California, have judicial protection for the Native American Church's use of sacramental peyote under constitutional rights to freedom of worship.[49]

The State of Texas, the only place in the United States where peyote cactus grows, has an established, successful program which controls and regulates the distribution of sacramental peyote. The Texas statutory exemption contains a requirement that persons who distribute peyote to members of the Native American Church must "register and maintain appropriate records of receipts and disbursements in accordance with rules promulgated by the director." Other Texas statutes contain provisions for minimum security controls, inspections of premises and records, qualifications for registration, requirements for selling peyote to authorized persons, requirements for reporting peyote sales, etc.[50]

The claimants in *Smith* pointed out that, according to the records of the federal Drug Enforcement Administration (DEA), "[t]he amount of peyote seized in illegal trafficking and analyzed by the DEA between 1980 and 1987 was 19.4 pounds."[51] Thus, not only was the Texas system of distribution and control efficient, the state's allegation of trafficking problems was clearly unsupported in the record.

But the Oregon attorney general argued that no religious use exemption whatsoever could be carved out because the state's ban on peyote was absolute. Thus, its health and safety interests were identical with respect to *all* uses:

> Whether the drug is used in a religious ceremony, medicinally, for secular personal enlightenment or for recreation, a user's objective is to produce a hallucinogenic state. As already described, the physiological and psychological responses to peyote ingestion pose serious health hazards. Those health hazards are indifferent to the user's motivation for using the drug. The state, accordingly, is entitled to be as concerned with religious peyote as it is with any other religiously-motivated conduct that threatens human health.[52]

To the attorney general, sacramental peyote was just a harmful drug. Peyote was a hallucinogen, not a sacrament: The religious experience was in reality nothing more than a chemically induced hallucination. The government, as representative of the majority, was asserting a "need" to prevent this nondominant group from voluntarily experiencing the physical side effects of its religious rituals. The government of the majority must act to protect these people from their God.

One can further uncover the norms underlying the Oregon attorney general's concern by placing that concern within the broader cultural perspective for comparison. The expression of intense governmental interest in protecting an individual from causing personal harm through religious practice becomes less persuasive when one notes that the State of Oregon still permits individuals to engage in such risky activities as tobacco smoking, consuming alcohol and coffee, gun ownership, hunting, motorcycling, rodeo riding, rock climbing, spelunking, hang gliding, football, and flying ultralights. One is free to undertake such dangerous activities as these and risk the consequences; however, one will be punished by the state for practicing one's religion because the state believes that the religious worship has dangerous side effects which can cause harm to the religious believer.

Such a discrepancy in result suggests the political (as opposed to evidential) nature of the regulation, and it demonstrates the need for a more searching scrutiny of the governmental action where it impacts upon nondominant religious worship. Proscribing behavior which is the focus of a societal paranoia is an entirely proper, even necessary, governmental activity. But regulation which springs from a political process which is fueled by paranoia may be illogical, irrational, and overbroad. And in a *constitutional* democracy, paranoia alone should not be enough to deny someone a fundamental constitutional right to worship God. Yet, the state argued that the Court must defer to that political process even when constitutional rights are at stake: "Neither this Court nor the state courts should substitute their judgment as to the harmfulness of using peyote for that of the Oregon legislature."[53]

And the state was "preaching to the choir," for the U.S. Supreme Court proved to be a highly receptive audience. The attorney for the claimants, Smith and Black, pointed out to the Court at oral argument in *Smith I* that "[t]he most disturbing suggestion that the state makes in this case is that they can extinguish a free exercise guarantee simply by labeling conduct as criminal." The response by one justice was that it was "more than labelling it" because there was "a statute that makes it a crime to use certain drugs."[54] This exchange calls to mind the philosophical debate over where the law comes from: Is there something "more," something inherent, intrinsic to the behavior itself (i.e., according to a natural law) which the legislature simply discovers and the legislation reflects, or does the legislative process and judgment itself create the criminal status of the behavior when it decides to regulate it (a positivist conception of the law)? To the justice, the state statute which declared the conduct "criminal" had "more" behind it than simply a legislative determination that such conduct would be called "criminal." A statute does not "label" conduct as criminal; rather, the conduct itself is inherently criminal, and the statute merely recognizes this fact.

One justice at oral argument in *Smith I* insistently hammered at the claimants' attorney that this case claimed "a free exercise right to engage in criminal conduct" or "a free exercise clause right to . . . use drugs."[55] In other words, the claimants were simply looking for an excuse to do something that was naturally and intrinsically wrong.

The state and the Court consistently referred to peyote not as "sacramental peyote," but as a "drug" or a "hallucinogenic drug" or a "Schedule I substance" whose ingestion was, first and foremost, criminal. At oral argument in *Smith II*, however, the Oregon attorney general discussed the use of alcohol by Christian churches in terms of "sacramental wine."[56] This discrepancy in language also reveals the otherwise unstated norm which informed the judgment of the state in this case. Neither the state nor the Court ever really seriously considered the sacredness of the peyote; in the eyes of the state and the Court, its criminal status destroyed its sacramental status.

The Oregon attorney general frequently cited to the legislative judgment that peyote was a "Schedule I" substance as hard evidence of the need to have a complete ban on all use of peyote. The state considered the Schedule I categorization as tangible proof that the ingestion of peyote causes the highest magnitude of harm and that no religious accommodation could be at all tolerated. And at oral argument, a justice picked up on the use of "Schedule I" as proof of the evils of peyote:

> QUESTION: Well, Mr. Dorsay, do you say that the State of Oregon can't rely at all on the fact that the peyote is shown as a Schedule I drug? That the facts behind that have to be proved all over again?[57]

A citation to Schedule I status was also the response given when a justice at oral argument questioned the difference (as mentioned above) between, for example, a hospital exemption and a religious use exemption. The justice pointed out that the potential illegal trafficking problems from allowing religious use also existed when hospitals used controlled drugs for medicinal reasons. The deputy attorney general's response was to simply state that the drug was a Schedule I drug and *therefore* not safe for *any* use and subject to high risk of abuse.

The comparison to other, allowable (i.e., non–socially deviant) exemptions to the antidrug laws, as suggested by the justice at oral argument, provides helpful insight in discerning between the real interests and the phantom fears of the state (and ultimately of the U.S. Supreme Court), which were behind the denial of religious exemptions. Librium, for example, although a commonly prescribed drug, has a high potential for abuse. Librium use poses a documented risk that the user will cause physical harm to others:

> Librium may produce a paradoxical rage reaction, i.e., an excited and exhilarated state whereby the individual may become a danger to himself and to others. This reaction has been manifested in isolated instances by a hostile and irritable mood to a point where the person taking Librium has become violent and has physically threatened the lives of others.[58]

Librium is also pleasant to take, and the great weight of evidence shows that it produces "psychic dependence."

In contrast, there was *no* evidence presented to indicate that the ingestion of sacramental peyote produced any threatening behavior to others whatsoever. Peyote's severe side effects have been found to self-regulate its use, and the ingestion of sacramental peyote does not promote drug abuse.[59] As noted by Justice Blackmun in his dissent in *Smith II*:

> The use of peyote is, to some degree, self-limiting. The peyote plant is extremely bitter, and eating it is an unpleasant experience, which would tend to discourage casual or recreational use. . . .(T)he eating of peyote usually is a difficult ordeal in that nausea and other unpleasant physical manifestations occur regularly. Repeated use is likely, therefore, only if one is a serious researcher or is devoutly involved in taking peyote as part of a religious ceremony. . . .[60]

Conclusive evidence has documented illegal trafficking in Librium by pharmacists: From 1960 to 1965, over fifty-four thousand capsules were unaccounted for among fourteen pharmacies alone, and thirty-five prosecutions for 132 illegal buys were made. But the illegal traffic in peyote, even with twenty-three states having exempted it for use by the Native American Church, proved to be *de minimis*.

Librium is a drug with "substantial potential for significant abuse,"[61] yet patients take it essentially unsupervised: Although technically "under medical supervision" because prescribed by a doctor, the drug is completely within the patient's control as to who takes it, when, how often, and what amount. In contrast, the road chief of the Native American Church always controls the administration of the sacramental peyote, which is done only as part of the sacred ceremonies. The Native American Church forbids any other use of the sacrament.

To counterbalance Librium's societal negatives and detrimental health effects, what is its benefit? Librium is primarily used to treat anxiety and tension and other problems such as muscle spasms where "emotional factors" are present.[62] Treating anxiety and depression is useful, and thus to society the drug is worth the substantial risks. The worship of God apparently is not as useful, and thus it is not worth even the most minimal risks.

The state heavily relied upon peyote's classification as a Schedule I drug (lack of acceptable safety for any use) to make its case that the drug deserved a uniform prohibition. In order to circumvent the fact that twenty-three other states had chosen to exempt sacramental peyote (which tended to make the Oregon attorney general's actions against the claimants look unreasonable), the state portrayed this Schedule I classification as a product of a deliberate determination by the Oregon legislature. But in fact the "Schedule" to which the state referred originated in overarching federal antidrug legislation, and, as I shall indicate below, there is evidence that the federal classification of Schedule drugs was as much a political decision as a medical/scientific one.

The federal classification of controlled substances ranges from Schedule I, which is intended to contain the most dangerous drugs and therefore has the most restrictive controls and the severest penalties, to Schedule V, which regulates substances which need the least amount of control. The following factors must be considered in deciding whether, and how, each substance is to be classified:

1. Its actual or relative potential for abuse.
2. Scientific evidence of its pharmacological effect, if known.
3. The state of current scientific knowledge regarding the drug or other substance.
4. Its history and current pattern of abuse.
5. The scope, duration, and significance of abuse.
6. What, if any, risk there is to the public health.
7. Its psychic or physiological dependence liability.
8. Whether the substance is an immediate precursor of a substance already controlled under this subchapter.[63]

Schedule I, as noted, is the most restricted, most heavily penalized and regulated category of drugs. A substance is regulated under Schedule I if:

A. The drug or other substance has a high potential for abuse.
B. The drug or other substance has no currently accepted medical use in treatment in the United States.
C. There is a lack of accepted safety for use of the drug or other substance under medical supervision.[64]

Marijuana and peyote were specifically listed in the statute as Schedule I substances.

Sacramental peyote was given an exemption under federal regulations, but the Oregon attorney general in the *Smith* case dismissed the exemption as a misinterpretation of what is required under the First Amendment.

[T]he federal government [meaning, here, the federal agency which administers the War on Drugs] has taken the position that the regulatory exemption for peyote was merely a product of the agency's perception of congressional will; that in fact the agency lacks authority to create such exemptions; and that, in any event, congressional members were wrong: The Free Exercise Clause does not require government to exempt religious peyote or other drug use from valid and neutral criminal laws of general applicability.[65]

One federal circuit court, however, has held that there was legal justification for federal regulatory exemption of peyote under Sections 811 (1) and (4) (listed above) of the federal drug law itself. The federal circuit court applied the law to the facts of Native American use of sacramental peyote: "Both the lessened potential for abuse in the religious context and the history of religious use of peyote support the exemption."[66]

The courts in fact have held that the Schedule classifications are *political*, not scientific or medical. But as long as such classifications are the least bit rational, the courts defer to Congress's judgment:

In determining penalties, the legal classification of a drug does not have to match its medical classification . . . for Congress may consider other issues not involving a drug's medical properties. In addition, the penalties do not need to be graduated according to the potential harm of the drug.[67]

Indeed, it seems as though political considerations have a greater priority than the benefits of medical use when it comes to the regulation of "politically disfavored" controlled substances such as marijuana. As Judge Skelly Wright has noted,

> Placement in Schedule I creates a self-fulfilling prophecy . . . because the drug can only be used for research purposes . . . and therefore is barred from general medical use. But if Dr. Cooper's [acting assistant secretary for health] statement [that marijuana has no currently accepted medical use] is meant to reflect a scientific judgment as to the medicinal potential of marihuana [*sic*], then the basis for his evaluation should be elaborated. Recent studies have yielded findings to the contrary: HEW's *Fifth Annual Report to the U.S. Congress, Marihuana and Health* (1975), devotes a chapter to the therapeutic aspects of marihuana, discovered through medical research. . . . Possible uses of marihuana include treatment of glaucoma, asthma, and epilepsy, and provision of "needed relief for cancer patients undergoing chemotherapy."[68]

The point here is not to engage in a debate over this country's drug policies, but, rather, to note how politicized the regulation is. By relying heavily upon the Schedule I classification in its argument against an exemption for sacramental peyote, the State of Oregon was *not* citing to medical or scientific proof, but simply to another political judgment which may have been fueled by societal paranoia.

From all of the foregoing, one can reasonably conclude that the state failed to present any hard evidence whatsoever which would justify banning the sacramental peyote ceremony of the Native American Church, or justify withholding unemployment compensation from Native American Church members Smith and Black when they were fired for practicing their religion. The question then remains, What was the real interest of the state in holding out for a complete ban? The reason appears to have had nothing to do with the Native American Church practice directly, for there were simply no particularized facts which would justify the vigorous declarations made by the Oregon attorney general against the ritual.

Smith II: *The U.S. Supreme Court brings* Reynolds *back into the future*

Justice Antonin Scalia delivered the opinion of the Court.[69] From the very first sentence of his opinion, it is clear that criminal behavior and the drug war are the Court's targeted agenda: The issue Justice Scalia presents for the Court to decide is framed, first and foremost, as an issue of free exercise clause rights versus a "general criminal prohibition."

> This case requires us to decide whether the Free Exercise Clause of the First Amendment permits the State of Oregon to include religiously inspired peyote use within the reach of its general criminal prohibition on the use of that drug, and thus permits the State to deny unemployment benefits to persons dismissed from their jobs because of such religiously inspired use.[70]

Justice Scalia's choice of the phrase *"requires us"* is curious in this case, on two counts. First, as mentioned above, the U.S. Supreme Court was not "required" to reach the criminal law issue. The Oregon Supreme Court itself had declared the Oregon criminal law to be irrelevant and impossible to apply to the unemployment compensation scheme. But the U. S. Supreme Court in *Smith II* adopted the assertion of the Oregon attorney general that the Oregon Supreme Court had definitively held that "respondents' religiously inspired use of peyote fell within the prohibition of the Oregon statute. . . ."[71]

Thus, Justice Scalia made a determination of state law which, on the most obvious and simple reading of the Oregon opinion, the highest court of that state had refused to make. Certainly the U.S. Supreme Court is the final arbiter of federal constitutional law. But although the Oregon Supreme Court had declared that the federal free exercise clause compelled the awarding of unemployment compensation funds, this decision regarding the First Amendment was premised on the state law determination that the criminal conduct (upon which the U.S. Supreme Court became fixated) was irrelevant *under state law*. The much-publicized conservative notion of "federalism" was overlooked in the Court's strain to establish the desired precedent.

Second, the statement that the Court was "required" to decide the case defied the fact that the case was no longer an active controversy when the Supreme Court had agreed to hear it a second time. The case was moot, for a consent agreement had been reached with ADAPT, the claimants' employer. According to the federal Equal Employment Opportunity Commission consent decree, ADAPT agreed that religious use of peyote would not be considered employee misconduct.[72] The unemployment compensation issue was thus taken care of, being that Smith and Black had been denied compensation because they were fired for "employment related misconduct" and *not* because they had committed any crime.

Justice Brennan made this point in his dissent to the Court's opinion in *Smith I*:

> Respondents Smith and Black were fired for practicing their religion. . . . This Court today strains the state court's opinion to transform the straightforward question that is presented [regarding unemployment compensation] into a question of first impression that it is not. . . .
>
> The state court could find no legislative intent expressed in the unemployment statute to reinforce criminal drug-abuse laws. Although we are not bound by a state court determination that a state legislature was actually motivated by a particular validating purpose, [citation omitted] we have never attributed to a state legislature a validating purpose that the State's highest court could find nowhere in the statute. . . .
>
> The Court avoids this straightforward analysis. . . .[The Court] poses two entirely implausible interpretations of the opinions below and overlooks the only natural one.[73]

The Court's insistence upon rendering an opinion in *Smith II*, in light of the *second* opinion by the Oregon Supreme Court which specifically notes the impossibility of determining the criminality of conduct through the state's unemployment compensation scheme, is thus all the more inexplicable. Normally, these circumstances would have been sufficient for the Court to decline to spend its valuable and limited time on a case.

Indeed, the case was again almost rendered moot when the Oregon State Board of Pharmacy voted an exemption to the Oregon drug law for religious use of peyote by the Native American Church. In consternation, the Oregon attorney general told the board that such an exemption was against the *establishment clause* of the Constitution. The board, at his urging, suspended the rule, and the attorney general's controversy was saved.

> MR. DORSAY [attorney for claimants Smith and Black]: The Board of Pharmacy did exempt the religious use of peyote. That exemption was withdrawn upon the advice of the Attorney General that it might violate the Establishment Clause, or for other reasons.
>
> Question [from a justice]: It might moot this litigation, I suppose.[74]

Apparently, the Oregon attorney general wished to have it all ways: The free exercise clause would not offer the nondominant religious adherent any relief from a generally applicable law, and yet, under the attorney general's version of the establishment clause, neither could those of a minority religious denomination seek specific legislative or administrative redress. These people, for whom the First Amendment religion clause protections were written, were to be crushed in between them instead.

Another curious aspect of Justice Scalia's opinion is his misstatement of what the claimants were requesting of the Court. He wrote:

> [Respondents] contend that their religious motivation for using peyote places them beyond the reach of a criminal law that is not specifically directed at their religious practice, and that is concededly constitutional as applied to those who use the drug for other reasons. . . . Respondents urge us to hold, quite simply, that when otherwise prohibitable conduct is accompanied by religious convictions, not only the convictions but the conduct itself must be free from governmental regulation.[75]

Neither in the respondents' briefs, nor during oral argument, did the claimants ever make these broad assertions. Rather, they consistently and forcefully argued for the application of the "compelling state interest" test: The state certainly could regulate religiously motivated behavior, but it must justify its regulations before they can be imposed to prohibit such constitutionally protected conduct. This test had been the law under *Yoder*, and it was the law in unemployment compensation cases such as *Sherbert*.[76] The claimants had never sought complete freedom from all regulation; in fact, they introduced extensive evidence that the Native American Church was successfully regulated in Texas as to peyote distribution. All the claimants wanted was the same unemployment compensation consideration afforded to the Oregon professor who was convicted of conspiring to blow up federal buildings. But Justice Scalia's opinion for the Court rarely referred to the unemployment compensation issue. The opinion instead read as if Smith and Black had been fully and fairly tried under the Oregon drug law, and as if they were now seeking absolute dispensation for their wrongdoing under the free exercise clause.

Justice Scalia revisited earlier cases interpreting the free exercise clause, and he concluded that the free exercise protections apply only to the limited situation where the government has specifically labeled the targeted activity as religious on the face of the regulation and has failed to provide a separate, nonreligious reason to justify the prohibition. Otherwise, the free exercise clause affords no independent protection whatsoever.

> The only decisions in which we have held that the First Amendment bars application of a neutral, generally applicable law to religiously motivated action have involved not the Free Exercise Clause alone, but the Free Exercise Clause in conjunction with other constitutional protections, such as freedom of speech and of the press. . . or the right of parents . . . to direct the education of their children. . . . Some of our cases prohibiting compelled expression, decided exclusively upon free speech grounds, have also involved freedom of religion. . . . And it is easy to envision a case in which a challenge on freedom of association grounds would likewise be reinforced by Free Exercise Clause concerns. . . .
>
> The present case does not present such a hybrid situation, but a free exercise claim unconnected with any communicative activity or parental right. Respondents urge us to hold, quite simply, that when otherwise prohibitable conduct is accompanied by religious convictions, not only the convictions but the conduct itself must be free from governmental regulation. We have never held that, and decline to do so now. There being no contention that Oregon's drug law represents an attempt to regulate religious beliefs, the communication of religious beliefs, or the raising of one's children in those beliefs, the rule to which we have adhered ever since *Reynolds* plainly controls.[77]

Although it has been found to exist in the Constitution under the liberty provisions of the Fifth and Fourteenth Amendments to the Constitution, the right to "direct the education of one's children" is certainly not textually stated in the Constitution. Accordingly, one would not normally deem the right to be equal in importance to those enumerated in the Bill of Rights. But in order to all but expel independent content from the free exercise clause, the Court had to overcome the hurdle posed by the case of *Wisconsin v. Yoder*, the Amish high school education case which specifically dealt with a generally applicable criminal prohibition. Accordingly, the Court elevated "control over a child's education" (apart from the religion clauses) to the lofty status of a favored, separate, and independent constitutional right. This elevation in status was accomplished at the expense of a First Amendment protection textually plain on its face: the right to freely exercise one's religion.

In summary, the religious practice violated the generally applicable drug laws of the State of Oregon, and any practice which is a crime automatically loses free exercise clause protections. The government must be allowed to regulate for the good of everyone, and it cannot be concerned with the myriad of religious practices in this pluralist society. The Court's opinion in *Smith II* mirrors the considerations and the process of the duly ordered relationships paradigm. As is characteristic of that paradigm, Justice Scalia (as did seventeenth-century Anglican Bishop Jeremy Taylor[78]) champions obedience to civil authority as the key to order. The arguments by the State of Oregon, and the exchanges among the attorneys and the justices at oral argument (as previously discussed), further reflected the fear of contamination and the concern for purity echoed in the levitical paradigm. Under either paradigm, law cannot brook anything less than complete uniformity. A consideration of religiously based objections to obeying it presents quite starkly an either/or proposition: either obedience or anarchy.

Societal boundaries and the war on drugs

The Court's decision in *Smith II* is centered upon such emotionally charged, fear-laden topics as illegal drugs, "strange" religious practices, the anarchy of individualism, and moral relativism. These topics are also heavily colored by, if not fundamentally infused with, fear that the activity in question will contaminate the rest of society. During times of paranoia, society severely tightens its boundaries, and clashes between an individual's civil rights protections and restricted boundary lines inevitably result. The abnormal becomes the rule for the day. The routine and accepted procedural processes and protections, the normal mode of doing things, are discarded in favor of the quick, crushing blow that is absolutely vital in order to "save" society. Such blows are often overbroad, indiscriminately attacking harmful, neutral, and even beneficial behavior. Although such crusades use law as a major weapon, they are fundamentally illogical and irrational. In this section I will examine the *Smith II* case for actions which might indicate overreaction or paranoia.

As indicated, the *Smith II* case was flawed procedurally. The case no longer presented a live controversy, for the consent agreement among the parties made it moot. The Oregon Supreme Court, moreover, had declared the case to be an unemployment compensation case and not a criminal case. Putting this case on the Supreme Court docket went against conservative notions of procedural propriety, for the case was simply an "advisory opinion" and not a true controversy.

Even more troubling is the lack of factual evidence grounding the broad conclusions asserted by the Court. All evidence specifically regarding the Native American Church's peyote ceremony and religious practices indicated that, rather than inducing drug addiction and unproductivity in its members, church participation produced the exact opposite: The Native American Church was highly effective in helping its members combat alcoholism. The attorney general never introduced any specific factual evidence (as opposed to political rhetoric) of any tangible *societal* harm whatsoever caused by the use of sacramental peyote; the negative evidence in the case only concerned the effect on the individual who ingested the sacrament. Thus, the total factual argument of the Oregon attorney general distilled down to the arrogant assertion that he must prohibit an act of worship which posed a low risk of permanent physical injury in order to protect a person from his God.

The opinion in *Smith II* creatively rewrote free exercise precedent. Cases such as *Yoder* and *Sherbert* had established a compelling state interest test, which eschewed the *Reynolds* process of according the government a conclusive presumption and instead instituted a process that scrutinized the needs and interests of the government. Yet, the root precedent advocated by Justice Scalia was the *Reynolds* opinion, which in turn was decided during a time of fearful overreaction to the threat of Mormon "barbarians" in the wilderness. Both in *Smith* and in *Reynolds*, the Court worried about the need to protect society from the anarchy of individual conscience. Indeed, Justice Scalia wrote that *suppressing* religious practices was a means of fulfilling the framer's intent of *encouraging* diversity.

> Any society adopting such a system [which would apply the compelling interest test to all actions thought to be religiously commanded] would be courting anarchy, but that danger increases in direct proportion to the society's diversity of religious beliefs, and its determination to coerce or suppress none of them. Precisely because "we are a cosmopolitan nation made up of people of almost every conceivable religious preference," [citation omitted] and precisely because we value and protect that religious divergence, we cannot afford the luxury of deeming *presumptively invalid*, as applied to the religious objector, every regulation of conduct that does not protect an interest of the highest order.[79]

Madison, however, defined anarchy as *majority* oppression of the weak (minorities). As Madison wrote in *Federalist No. 51*:

> In a society under the forms of which the stronger faction can readily unite and oppress the weaker, anarchy may truly be said to reign as in a state of nature, where the weaker individual is not secured against the violence of the stronger. . . .[80]

In summary, then, the Court's opinion interpreting the free exercise clause does not make sense procedurally or factually. What, then, was the impetus behind the holding in *Smith II*? As indicated above, one viable interpretation of the case is to view it as a radical effort at boundary drawing. The case is not really about two members of the Native American Church who were fired from their jobs because they ingested small amounts of sacramental peyote. Rather, it is about the current fear not only of drugs (the illegal ones), but also of the anarchy (or so-called moral relativism) which is expected to result when individuals are guided by their own consciences rather than the majority's view of what is legal/moral. The drug culture (at its height in the late 1960s and 1970s) epitomizes the intersection of these two aversions, particularly where *religious* use of drugs is concerned.

Indeed, the true "folk devils" in this case perhaps were not the Native American Church members themselves, who might simply have been the unlucky scapegoats. The Oregon attorney general and the U.S. Supreme Court cited to and seemed to emphasize the specter of religious use of hallucinogenic drugs as symbolized by such folk devils as Timothy Leary and the Rastafarians.

Implicit was the notion that such religious claims are simply fraudulent efforts to escape the brunt of the federal drug war.[81]

At oral argument, the attorney for the claimants found himself having to argue two cases: one for the peyote religious ceremony and another against the marijuana religious ceremonies of other faiths, which faiths, of course, were not a party to the case and for whom there was no fact-finding readily available.

> QUESTION: How about marijuana use by a church that uses that as part of its religious sacrament?
>
> MR. DORSAY: Well, see, I think we can get into a lot of examples, and I don't want to go down that road too far because we don't—
>
> QUESTION: I'll bet you don't.
>
> (Laughter)
>
> MR. DORSAY: —have the facts here.
>
> (Laughter)
>
> MR. DORSAY: But the fact is, and a number of courts have looked at marijuana, and they have concluded that marijuana contributes substantially to the law enforcement problem. That has been the distinguishing factor in a number of cases. This drug does not contribute to the law enforcement problem . . .
>
> QUESTION: Only because the law is not enforced. I mean, you know—
>
> MR. DORSAY: Well, why is the law not enforced?
>
> QUESTION: . . . . —I am, I am not comforted by the fact it doesn't— . . . cause a law enforcement problem. I don't know what that means.
>
> MR. DORSAY: Well, what it means is it doesn't contribute to the use of other drugs. It doesn't undermine the federal government or the nation's law enforcement efforts for other drugs. It doesn't get into the distribution system. It is not one of the drugs that is looked to by other people as a recreational substance.
>
> QUESTION: But why can't the state consider it itself as the law enforcement problem?
>
> MR. DORSAY: Peyote itself?
>
> QUESTION: The very use, even in religious services. Just as the state may consider the very use of marijuana, regardless of whether it pollutes commerce or anything else, as being itself a problem. We don't want it used. Why can't—
>
> MR. DORSAY: The state can look at it as the problem itself, but we're—it is my position, strongly, that they have to justify that position by showing some actual harm. Otherwise there would really be no free exercise right, because the state could outlaw any kind of conduct and say—
>
> QUESTION: So long as it does generally, I think—why isn't that right?[82]

It was the "rightness" which was being upheld here. Essentially, the antidrug statute became a universal[83] moral command, to which the Supreme Court would permit no relativist exceptions.

Of emotivism, anarchy, and free exercise jurisprudence

As discussed earlier, the modern philosophy of emotivism contrasts the objectivity of "facts" with the subjectivity of "values." As MacIntyre writes:

> Questions of ends are questions of values, and on values reason is silent; conflict between rival values cannot be rationally settled. Instead, one must simply choose—between parties, classes, nations, causes, ideals. . . . [T]he choice of any one evaluative stance or commitment can be no more rational than that of any other. All faiths and all evaluations are equally non-rational; all are subjective directions given to sentiment and feeling.[84]

Accordingly, such "masters" of facts as bureaucrats (primarily business bureaucrats, but MacIntyre also includes governmental bureaucrats) have risen in status and power in society, for their choices are seen to rest upon "hard" criteria which produce objectively reached and objectively defensible results: "For . . . no type of authority can appeal to rational criteria to vindicate itself except that type of bureaucratic authority which appeals precisely to its own *effectiveness*.[85]

Objective "effectiveness" furthermore includes legislative output (i.e., laws). The emotivist aura of objectivity has similarly been placed upon the will of the majority; its "hard" and "rational" criteria are the majority vote which elected the legislature and the majority vote within the legislature which passed the statutes. Society thus becomes bifurcated

> into a realm of the organizational in which ends are taken to be given and are not available for rational scrutiny and a realm of the personal in which judgment and debate about values are central factors, but in which no rational social resolution is available. . . .[86]

The emotivist "twist" to the Court's opinion in *Smith II* is that "organization" is society and the legislature its "bureaucrats." The key move is the almost complete equation of the organization's "ends" with the laws passed by the elected legislative body. Hence, these laws are "not available for rational scrutiny."

The result is a perceived binary opposition between the realm of the personal (the right to the free exercise of religion) and the "ends" or laws of the society (i.e., the will of the majority expressed through legislation). The factions perceive the only available choices to be an alignment for subjective " individual liberty" on the one hand or for the objectivity of "legislative deference" on the other:

> But in fact what is crucial is that on which the contending parties agree, namely that there are only two alternative modes of social life open to us, one in which the free and arbitrary choices of individuals are sovereign and one in which the bureaucracy is sovereign, precisely so that it may limit free and arbitrary choices of individuals.[87]

And, indeed, this is the way the Court painted the issue in the *Smith* case: Either the anarchy of the individual religious conscience would rule, or the government bureaucracy must be left alone to regulate as it deems necessary for (what Justice Scalia characterized as) society's best interests. There could be no middle course, because judges would then be faced with the impossible task of "weigh[ing] the social importance of all laws against the centrality of all religious beliefs."[88]

But the claimants, Smith and Black, were not playing by these emotivist rules and were not asserting a right to anarchy in the name of religion. Indeed, as noted in the above statement of facts, a curious mistake in Justice Scalia's opinion is his misstatement of what the claimants were requesting of the Court. He wrote his opinion as if they were claiming automatic and complete freedom from the criminal law simply because their conduct was religious. But neither in the respondents' briefs, nor during oral arguments, did the claimants ever make these broad assertions. Rather, they offered detailed factual justifications for their claim that the free exercise clause should take precedence over the state regulation, and their arguments demonstrated the religious practice's lack of harm to society and the contribution of the Native American Church to the well-being of its members.

Justice Scalia, however, framed his opinion in *Smith* as would an emotivist who fears utter anarchy:

> Can a man excuse his practices to the contrary [of the law] because of his religious belief? To permit this would be to make the professed doctrines of religious belief superior to the law of the land, and in effect to permit every citizen to become a law unto himself.[89]

Justice Scalia's logical stance rendered the context of the peyote religion irrelevant; the only facts of concern were that there was a law and the religious activity would break it. "Anarchy" based upon individual religious beliefs cannot be permitted, period.

> The government's ability to enforce generally applicable prohibitions of socially harmful conduct, like its ability to carry out other aspects of public policy, "cannot depend on measuring the effects of a governmental action on a religious objector's spiritual development." To make an individual's obligation to obey such a law contingent upon the law's coincidence with his religious beliefs, except where the state's interest is "compelling" — permitting him, by virtue of his beliefs, "to become a law unto himself," — contradicts both constitutional tradition and common sense.[90]

Justice Scalia premised this result upon the assumption that legislative determinations of what is "socially harmful conduct" are objective (in the emotivist sense) and thus cannot be disturbed on account of subjective religious beliefs. In order for society to function effectively, the courts must defer to the legislature's objective authority.

Any middle ground, such as the compelling state interest test, even if limited by a requirement that such a test would apply only if the practice was "central" to the religion, would have to be rejected as impossible to perform, given the pure subjectivism of the individual's religious stance. Courts cannot judge the plausibility of a religious claim, and they cannot be in the business of evaluating the relative merits of differing religious practices over against a statute or regulation, *because there is no basis for choosing.* Most revealing is Justice Scalia's parting quip in response to Justice O'Connor's search for a middle ground between the (bureaucratic) criminal law and the (individual) protection of the free exercise clause of the Constitution. For this conclusory remark reveals Justice Scalia's assumption that the gap between the two is so incommensurable, and the fact of this incommensurability is so obvious and commonsensical, that it is ludicrous to even argue about a middle ground. "It is a parade of horribles because *it is horrible to contemplate* that federal judges will regularly balance against the importance of general laws the significance of religious practice."[91]

Note the subtle shift of focus from the substantive free exercise standard (the compelling state interest test) to the process applying that standard (the *balancing* of the state's interests against the free exercise right). Justice Scalia's concern is the perceived subjectivity of balancing.[92]

Justice O'Connor, in a separate opinion concurring in part and dissenting in part, had objected to Justice Scalia's emotivist dismissal of the compelling state interest test. She noted that his "parade of horribles," that is, his list of approximately eleven broad areas of governmental regulation over which free exercise claims for exemptions have been litigated, does not indicate that courts (and thereby the government) would be helpless captives of religious believers. Instead, Justice O'Connor interpreted these cases as examples of her point that the choice is not simply between anarchy and societal order; there is indeed a practical, workable middle ground for decision making. She contends that the very fact that a compelling state interest test had been used in those so-called horrible cases "demonstrates . . . that courts have been quite capable of strik[ing] sensible balances between religious liberty and competing state interests."[93] Justice Scalia, however, retorted that such "sensible balances" have been struck "only because they have all applied the general laws, despite the claims for religious exemption."[94] In other words, Justice Scalia considered it his duty in this case to cut through the "sham" of the compelling state interest test to reveal what an emotivist "knows" to be the hard "reality."

Ironically, the potential subjectivity of an intuitive balancing process is illustrated by Justice O'Connor's own use of it in *Smith*, where she rejected the weighty evidence in support of the free exercise claim in favor of the rhetoric supporting the War on Drugs. But Justice O'Connor's flawed use of the process of balancing does not ineluctably compel the abandonment of the substantive compelling state interest standard. A casuistical process is well suited to resolving conflicts of principles such as those represented by free exercise claims. More than simply "balancing," casuistry offers discursive justifications in terms of analogies, paradigms, principles, and particulars. In the *Smith* case, the state's lack of hard data against the use of sacramental peyote, coupled with the evidence which tended to show that the Native American Church was successful in fulfilling the paradigmatic goals of the War on Drugs (nonaddiction, productive lives, etc.), would have discursively justified a finding in favor of the claimants.

Indeed, the *Smith* decision itself lacks any discursive justification for favoring the state's position in this case, other than the conclusive presumption accorded to the government's War on Drugs and the assumption that anarchy will result if the government is not to be conclusively obeyed. This approach reflects the logic and underlying values of the duly ordered relationships and the levitical paradigms. Order, on the one hand, is defined in terms of obedience to the law. On the other hand, order is also described in terms of purity and boundary maintenance. An undercurrent of fear of contamination and a fierce desire to maintain the purity of the boundaries of the drug laws is reflected in the government's briefs, the oral arguments, and the Court's opinions. Conclusive deference to governmental authority, procrustean efforts to maintain the purity of boundaries established by legislation, and emotivist tendencies such as those exhibited in the jurisprudence of the *Smith* opinion are all troublesome primarily because they blind one to the existence of additional viable ways of defining and resolving the problem, as well as to the possibility of errors by the governmental system. For in emotivism (as in the levitical paradigm and the duly ordered relationships paradigm) there are only stark, either/or, choices. If the Court in *Smith* had instead engaged in a casuistical process appropriate to the two kingdoms and enlightenment paradigms, the government would not have had the benefit of the conclusive presumption, and the opinion's "discursive justification" would have focused upon, for example, the particulars of the Native American Church's sacrament, the paradigmatic goods intended to be fostered by the War on Drugs, and the nature of the state's interest in regulating the religious practice.

Governmental Intervention in and Punishment for the Use of Spiritual Healing Methods

> The greatest dangers to liberty lurk in insidious encroachment by men of zeal, well-meaning but without understanding.
>
> —Justice Louis Brandeis, dissenting in *Olmstead v. United States*.[1]

The U.S. Supreme Court's minimalization of free exercise protection in deference to government regulations left core issues unaddressed and raised new questions. For example, punishment and deterrence are the two most-often-cited objectives of criminal law. Yet, modern judges and prosecutors have rarely exhibited any thoughtful concern over the justice and far-reaching ramifications (for both the believer and society) of punishing sincere believers as criminals for worshiping and obeying their God. And little attention has been given to the actual effectiveness of the threat of punishment as a deterrent. What are the stakes for religious adherents when the government prohibits behavior which they hold to be spiritually mandatory? Why have some courts and commentators portrayed the free exercise conflict as one between good (the government) and evil (the religious adherent)? Is the conflict between the law and one's religion by its very nature a matter that can be resolved easily by the adherent, who could simply quit her "illegal" spiritual affiliation and find herself a church that is less "offensive"?

Just as the *Smith* case should have been an easy nonconflict under a casuistical free exercise jurisprudence, the matter of the use of spiritual healing methods by parents presents an example of a hard case. On the one hand, I will argue that criminalization of Christian Science parents whose children have died despite their spiritual healing efforts is not appropriate, for the parents do not have the paradigmatic *mens rea* or culpable intent that characterizes manslaughter/child abuse cases. Rather, typically, the parents had intended the best for their child. On the other hand, civil interventions on behalf of children may very well be justified, raising issues of paternalism. The parent's religious values (including, it must be emphasized, their conception of beneficence) and the value of personal autonomy directly clash with the state's conception of beneficence. In cases such as this where there are directly conflicting principles at stake, casuistry has no easy or clear answers. Yet, I submit that the casuistical process, with its emphasis on context, use of analogy, and critique of underlying assumptions, offers the fairest method of dealing with this most difficult of cases.

Accordingly, this chapter begins with a casuistical analysis of the context and the conflicts involved when the state criminalizes parents whose use of spiritual healing methods on their children have failed with tragic consequences. Because of the complexity, the influence as precedent,[2] and the relatively long and interesting history of this genre of free exercise cases, I will analyze the many particulars in detail. My purpose is not to rewalk the battleground over states' rights and *parens patriae* obligations versus the parents' rights. Rather, I look at the particulars using the tools of casuistry discussed earlier: what paradigms come into play, what boundaries are at stake and how are they being described and protected, what analogies were used, what processes? These matters are examined both from the historical context of the spiritual healing issue as well as within the modern context of the case of *Walker v. Superior Court*. I hope thereby (in the spirit of Justice Brandeis) to add some further understanding by which the government's well-meaning efforts to require allopathic medical care may be guided.

Historical background: Criminal laws and cases regarding a parent's use of religious healing

In turn-of-the-century America, Christian Bible-based faith healers and spiritual healing religions such as Christian Science became cultural lightning rods, attracting controversy and the contempt of orthodox society. One indication of the ferment is that, of the twenty-six editorials run by the *New York Times* on "religious affairs" in 1899, seventeen (or 65 percent) explicitly concerned the topic of "faith healing."[3] These editorials spared no invectives in their denunciations of faith healing: One typical editorial, for example, called the Church of Christ, Scientist a "grotesque cult."[4] The *New York Times* deemed newsworthy, and thus routinely covered, sermons and seminars by both medical and mainstream religious "orthodoxy" which condemned faith healing.[5] Between 1899 and 1904, the *New York Times* also highlighted local and out-of-state instances of faith healing failures in its news coverage,[6] as well as prosecutions arising out of such "failures."[7]

It is in this context of cultural lightning rod that the germinal cases addressing the conflict between religion and laws criminalizing parents who fail to use licensed (i.e., allopathic) medical care need to be examined.

The criminalization of religious healing: From common law to statutes

Under the common law, it was questionable whether a duty to provide medical care existed.[8] The common law only had required that a parent feed and shelter a child: A parent, for example, who starved a child or abandoned a child outside in harsh weather, thereby causing its death, was criminally culpable under the common law of manslaughter.

With the growing professionalization of nineteenth-century medicine (and, as will be discussed, the successful efforts of the American Medical Association (AMA) to establish allopathic medicine as the legal practice of medicine), the courts in the late nineteenth century increasingly faced the issue of whether the common law parental duty to supply shelter and food could be extended to include medical care. There are two legal reasons why the courts at this time experienced some discomfort over the faith-healing issue. The first applied to the problem of criminal convictions based upon evolving common law doctrines: The U.S. Constitution prohibits *ex post facto* laws, that is, a criminal conviction for an action which was not a crime when it was committed. A court's decision that a common law criminal offense included the failure to perform a new duty (such as the provision of allopathic medical care to children) came dangerously close to imposing a standard of behavior *ex post facto*.

Second, religious healing cases typically were brought against parents who were loving and attentive, and otherwise had cared for their child. Such defendants did not fit comfortably within the traditional criminal child neglect paradigm. As noted in one 1880 treatise on tort law:

> In a crime, *the most conspicuous and inseparable element is the intent*; in a tort, on the other hand, the intent is usually of subordinate importance; sometimes of no importance whatever. The State will not punish an act as a crime unless there is an evil intent either actually indulged or imputable. Where there has been no purpose to disobey the public laws, there cannot, in general, be a crime. A murder lies not in the killing, but in accomplishing a murderous purpose. If one knock another down purposely it is a crime; but if carelessly, it is only a tort. . . . But there may be negligence so gross as to be criminal; the criminal inattention to the rights and safety of others, supplying the intent.[9]

From the above, it is plain that the law, at least as of 1880, had required a rather severe and heinous level of wantonness to be present in order to warrant a *criminal* conviction. One way to describe this serious level of "criminal inattention" is as a deliberate intent to do evil or cause harm which in the execution of the act results in greater actual damage or causes more severe injuries than the defendant had actually intended. Because the initial action had a "bad intent" (an intent to do serious harm) to begin with, the law held the defendant criminally responsible for the natural consequences of that act even if the severity of those consequences was not specifically intended.[10]

Religious healing cases depart from this criminal negligence paradigm. Parents typically have no intent to cause harm;[11] their intent is to heal their children. In order to fit the religious healing cases within a criminal negligence standard, the courts either had to disregard the context and the beneficial intentions altogether, or they had to assume, and thus to superimpose, a "bad intent" on otherwise sincere and loving parents. Criminal statutes which explicitly made it a crime to fail to provide allopathic medical treatment for children were early examples of a "strict liability" type of crime: A defendant who simply does (or fails to do) a particular act, regardless of whether he or she had a criminal state of mind (or *mens rea*[12]), was conclusively presumed to be guilty of a crime.

Criminal cases involving faith healing most often implicated the death of a person and thus came under the heading of the criminal law known as "homicide." Not all deaths or killings are crimes; the issue to be decided in a homicide case is whether the defendant's behavior with respect to the death of another rises to the level of a punishable offense against the common good. Assuming that the defendant actually legally caused the death of another, a homicide might still not be culpable if it was either justifiable or excusable, in which case the defendant is not guilty of a crime. At the other end of the culpability spectrum, a defendant is guilty of the most serious crime, murder, where the defendant has deliberately and intentionally killed another, without a legally recognized excuse such as self-defense.

While "manslaughter" is a lesser crime, it is still a grievous one. Manslaughter is less serious because the defendant has been found to act less deliberately. If one kills in the heat of passion, for example, it would be voluntary manslaughter.[13] The criminal law considers "involuntary manslaughter" (also known as "criminal negligence") to be the least culpable form of criminal homicide. Yet, it must be noted that even at this level, criminal negligence is still *criminal*. Criminal prosecutors usually brought their prosecutions for deaths associated with faith healing under involuntary manslaughter, which was defined generally as follows:

> Involuntary manslaughter is where the death is unintentionally caused:
>
> (a) In the commission of an *unlawful act* not amounting to a felony, nor likely to endanger life, *or*
> (b) By *culpable neglect of a legal duty*, as
>   (1) By *negligence* in performing a *lawful* act
>   (2) By *neglect* to perform an *act required by law*.[14]

An initial legal obstacle to prosecution of parents who used faith-healing methods to treat their children was whether there even existed a legally enforceable duty to provide medical care for children when they became ill. Prosecutors who charged a faith healing parent with involuntary manslaughter had to prove that faith healing was an "unlawful act" per se, under (a), above, or that the parents had a clear and firm legal duty to call an allopathic medical doctor when their child became ill, under (b)(2), above. Although an extrapolation from available reported opinions indicates that prosecutors most frequently charged a violation under (b)(2), reasoning that the failure to obtain the normative medical help was an illegal act (of omission), the notion, under (b)(1), that the parents were negligent in their choice of religious beliefs and practices also permeates the faith healing cases. Thus, one key to understanding the stakes involved in the faith healing criminal manslaughter cases is the conflicting conceptions of the parents' duties to their children. The law created a conflict between the duty, indeed the religious *obligation*, of the parents to raise their children in accordance with the requirements of their religious beliefs, and a duty to provide orthodox, allopathic medical care.

In summary, the key difference between the paradigmatic child abuse or neglect case and the faith healing case is, as noted by one legal commentator of the time, that the failure of faith healing parents to provide medicines was due to "conscientious scruples" and not from "any desire to avoid the performance of their duties."[15]

With this very general background in mind, I will now explore the particular results and reasonings in some early faith healing cases.

The Wagstaffe case

The earliest faith healing case found in the legal literature of either the United States or England is the case of *Regina v. Wagstaffe*,[16] alleging a common law felony of manslaughter for failing to provide proper medical attention to a fourteen-month-old daughter. The Wagstaffes were members of a small religious community in London called the Peculiar People. Two noteworthy features of this church were complete trust in the Bible and their belief "in the healing power of God."[17] The jury at London's Central Criminal Court—The Old Bailey—found them not guilty of the charge. Most of the factors found in this case reoccur in later faith healing cases; the difference between the process used in this case versus the later cases, however, is quite important.

The testimony in *Wagstaffe* conclusively established, and indeed emphasized, that the parents were loving and attentive. "The mother," we are told by a witness, "devoted most of her time to it [the child]," and the father "was very kind and affectionate." The Wagstaffes had two other children who were described as "healthy and well-nourished." A witness (who was a member of the sect), the elders, and the parents had all mistaken the deceased child's "inflammation" for teething problems.[18]

The Wagstaffes were sincere and honest in their belief in faith healing as premised in the Bible: They had had their child anointed with oil by "the elders" as noted in the fifth chapter of the epistle of St. James,[19] and they felt that the child would benefit from their faith and anointing. Significantly, their healing methods were not simply grounded in the Bible, but also in their own practical experiences. The witness noted that the church members had "proved it [the healing power of God] for ourselves many times" and she herself claimed to have been healed of smallpox, among other diseases.

Judge Willes, as noted by the reporter, Mr. Cox, "spoke with profound respect for any belief honestly entertained in religious matters." The judge thought it "right" for the jury to consider the text of the epistle upon which the religious sect relied in its views on faith healing, in order to evaluate the reasonableness and culpability of the parents' conduct. He commented to the jury that "this was a case where affectionate parents had done what they thought the best for a child, and had given it the best of food."[20] Judge Willes's remarks should be read against the testimony of a surgeon called to the stand to give evidence for the prosecution. The surgeon had testified that "*in all probability* the child's life *would have been saved* if medical advice had been early obtained. The symptoms must have been very urgent, as any ordinary person must have seen."[21] The surgeon's own course of treatment would have been leeching and the administration of some "antinomial wine."

The issue for the jury to decide was whether the parents "were guilty of gross and culpable conduct in not resorting to those means for its [the child's] benefit by lack of which its [the child's] death was occasioned." The judge noted that the issue of "gross and culpable negligence" in this case was "a very wide question," and he then took the jurors through a fine casuistry of the issue of culpable conduct in the faith healing context.

"Insane" religious beliefs, such as, for example, where the parents believe that they have a religious duty to starve their child, are clearly culpable. On the issue of the "insanity" or "absurdity" of beliefs, however, Judge Willes ruled that the words of the epistle of James were admissible evidence to show that the beliefs of the Peculiar People were based in the common Bible and not the result of insanity (insane delusions?) or "morbidity." Dishonestly held beliefs would cancel out any notion that the parents had "acted for the best." A belief that was "so absurd in itself that it could not be honestly obtained" would also be evidence that the parents had not reasonably acted for the good of their child[22] Hence, the testimonies explaining the beliefs and the experiences of the parents and their church community regarding faith healing were permitted to be considered by the jury as relevant to Judge Willes's concerns that the religious belief be "honest," not be absurd, and not have been derived out of an insane condition.

The judge's approach to what could be considered reasonable behavior under the law was deliberately broad and respectful. Indeed, he felt that this approach was dictated by the letter and the spirit of recent legislation which established religious tolerance in England. Judge Willes took great pains to note the varying beliefs concerning medical healing which have been held through the ages: Religious beliefs in Catholic countries might result in the taking of a sick child to a shrine, whereas two hundred years ago in England, it was thought that the king could heal. In reciting these differences and in pointing out that a conviction for manslaughter could very well turn upon the customs of the area where the charges were laid, the judge aimed to broaden the jurors' notions as to reasonableness. He certainly did *not* encourage them, in their judging of these prisoners, to use their (the jurors') own personal and limited purview (both medical and religious) as a yardstick by which to judge what was a proper healing custom. Indeed, the judge's emphasis was on the history of diversity of opinion in the area of medical treatment:

> [A]ll the reasoning in the world would not justify a man starving a child to death [for religious reasons]. But when a jury had to consider what was the precise medical treatment to be applied to a particular case, they got into a much higher latitude indeed. At different times people had come to different conclusions as to what might be done with a sick person. . . . There was a very great difference between neglecting a child in respect to food, with regard to which there could be but one opinion, and neglect of medical treatment, *as to which there might be many opinions.*[23]

In contrast, the prosecutor had opened the case with the remark that "these were times of toleration, and anyone was entitled to entertain any *opinion* he chose on the subject of religion." The prosecutor then tried to confine tolerance of "religion" to matters of religious *faith/opinion* and thus *exclude* all religious practices. He argued for a bright, absolute dividing line on the issue in order to avoid what he viewed as a slippery slope ultimately resulting in a toleration of religious practices which "go to the extent, for instance, of starving a child."[24]

Premised upon the spirit of religious respect he found represented in the toleration statute, Judge Willes rejected the prosecutor's absolute either/or approach. Instead of an overly protective line arbitrarily drawn between faith and religious practices, the judge (as has been noted) wove a finely nuanced casuistic tapestry of relevant factual distinctions for the jurors to consider in the course of their deliberations on the issue of gross and culpable negligence. Ultimately, the instruction the judge gave to the jury in the *Wagstaffe* case was whether, *given the historic plurality of beliefs concerning medical healing*, the parents had (1) acted reasonably, (2) were caring and affectionate, and (3) had proceeded in accordance with what *they* sincerely believed was in the best interests of their child.

I have described the judge's approach in the *Wagstaffe* case in some detail for two reasons: (1) courts in the United States at that time still frequently cited to such English cases as precedent, and (2) the *Wagstaffe* case presents a marked contrast to what became the dominant approach in the United States. Judge Willes's due respect for the conflict of principles which lies at the heart of this case was derived from a mere statutory declaration of religious *tolerance*; his process for resolving the conflict of principles was rejected by the U.S. Supreme Court in the *Reynolds* case, despite the theoretically *greater* freedom and protection afforded to religious exercise under the First Amendment of the U.S. Constitution. Instead, the American courts ultimately gave absolute privilege to the science of the infant medical profession over centuries-old convictions about religious duty and sacred obligations.

People v. Pierson

The 1903 decision in the case of *People v. Pierson*[25] was a watershed ruling in the area of faith healing. Decided by the influential New York Court of Appeals, the case pioneered a position on faith healing which was adopted by a majority of American courts. Up until the *Pierson* case, the issue could be described as unsettled. After *Pierson*, some courts still continued to hold nonconforming opinions, but courts and commentators alike considered such nonconformance as the minority legal position in this country.

In the New York *Pierson* case, the defendant was indicted for "willfully, maliciously, and unlawfully neglecting and refusing to allow [his sixteen and one half month-old daughter, who died of pneumonia] to be attended and prescribed for by a regularly licensed and practicing physician and surgeon, contrary to the [Penal Code]. . . ."[26] The child apparently contracted whooping cough which developed into pneumonia. The father of the child, a member of the Christian Catholic Church of Chicago,[27] , did not call a medical doctor because he believed that the child would get well by prayer.

The relevant portions of the New York Criminal Code provided for punishment of anyone (i.e., parent or guardian) who "willfully omits, *without lawful excuse* . . . to furnish . . . *medical attendance* to a minor. . . [28] The issues on the appeal were (1) whether "medical attendance" included prayer, and, if not, (2) whether one's religious beliefs could furnish a "lawful excuse" for not providing medical care.

In contrast to the casuistical, finely nuanced jury instructions given by Judge Willes in the *Wagstaffe* case, the trial court in *Pierson* charged

> that, before the jurors could convict the defendant, they must find that he knew that the child was ill, and deliberately and intentionally failed or refused to call a physician, or to give the child such medicines as the science of the age would say would be proper that a child in its condition should have; that, if at the time he refused to call a physician, he knew the child to be dangerously ill, his belief constitutes no defense whatever to the charge made. In other words, no man can be permitted to set up his religious belief as a defense to the commission of an act which is in plain violation of the law of the state.[29]

Recall that crimes traditionally required a "criminal intent" or *mens rea*. The impact that a *religious* intent and context might have on the issue of whether the defendant had the requisite culpable mind, the reasonableness of the use of spiritual healing methods based upon the defendant's experience and the church's success rate, and even the issue of causation (whether medical attendance would have cured the child, and thus whether there was a causal connection, beyond a reasonable doubt, that the failure to call a doctor caused the child's death) were matters which the court barred the jury from considering. Criminal negligence in faith healing cases had now become a strict liability crime; "fault" or "criminal intent" would now be automatically inferred. In effect, conclusive presumptions of criminal culpability and of causation were attached to the fact that religious healing methods were used and a doctor was not called.

The court's treatment of the "medical attendance" issue reflected its vision of modern medical science finally triumphing over religious superstition. The court noted that Hippocrates founded "medical science" five hundred years before Christianity, but that such science made little progress because a belief in divine miracles was so rooted in the populace that the practice of "physic or surgery" was deemed "dishonorable." Indeed, the highest court of the State of New York explicitly condemned the Catholic Church's Lateran Council and several of its popes for having promoted such superstitious belief in miracles of healing. The court furthermore blamed the Roman Catholic Church for Western civilization's slow progress in medical science due to the church's former prohibition against any medical treatment done without the presence of priests and due to the church's promotion of miracles as "the mode of treating sickness recognized by the church."[30]

The court then noted that the eighteenth century (i.e., after the Protestant Reformation and the Enlightenment had freed Europe from the bonds of Roman Catholicism) finally ushered in important scientific discoveries in medicine and surgery. Now, as a result, "throughout the *civilized* world" there are professionalized medical schools where one can get specialized education in the science of medicine. Accordingly, the court interpreted the requirement of providing "medical attendance" to children under the child neglect statute as fulfilled *only* by "regularly licensed physicians" under the separate and distinct medical licensing statute. Thus, in contrast to the opinion in *Wagstaffe*, history was not used to illustrate the plurality of methods and diversity of views on healing, but rather to show the evolutionary superiority of one kind of medical treatment: the model provided for in a separate licensing statute.[31]

The statute had provided a "lawful excuse" exception, but the court did not extend this to apply to religious obligations. Yet, interestingly, there is evidence in the record to indicate that the compulsion of indigency *would* have furnished a lawful excuse. The court in *Pierson* states, "Yet he [Mr.Pierson] did not send for or call a physician to treat her, *although he was financially able to do so*. His reason for not calling a physician was that he believed in Divine healing."[32] To the extent that financial hardship was a "lawful excuse" under the statute, certainly an analogy could have been drawn between that kind of compulsion and the compulsion of religious conscience.

But the free exercise issue gave the *Pierson* court no pause for thought. In contrast to the finely tuned casuistry of the judge in the *Wagstaffe* case, the court in *Pierson* sharply divided the realm of religion from the realm of medicine, and it firmly distinguished the right of religious *belief* from the governmental sovereignty over any and all *action*. Accordingly, failure to obtain the care of licensed medical physicians for one's child became a public wrong against which the right to practice one's religion held no weight whatsoever. The choice of language by the court on this issue affords insight into its general attitude: "He cannot, under the belief or profession of belief that he should be relieved from the care of children, be excused from punishment for *slaying* those who have been born to him."[33] Indeed, the parental duty to consult a licensed medical physician is spoken of in terms of universal law and even natural law. Thus, only an insensible, grossly (even maliciously) negligent and uncaring parent would (1) not know of or acknowledge such a duty or (2) ignore such a duty. Accordingly, the court affirmed the criminal conviction of the defendant.

The *New York Times* was jubilant at the conviction. In an editorial, it declared:

> White Plains is to be congratulated on the intelligence of its jurymen. Mr. J. Luther Pierson . . . is a believer in "faith" as the only proper and efficient remedy for disease, so when his little daughter was attacked by pneumonia, he faithed [*sic*] at her to the best of his ability. . . . The officials of White Plains do not approve of this form of homicide . . . and the jury proved its common sense by bringing in a verdict of guilty as charged. Any other verdict ought to have been impossible, but lamentable experience has shown that it is extremely difficult to secure conviction in such cases. Now that a beginning has been

made, perhaps it will be easier in the future, and if that proves to be true, much gratitude will be due to the White Plains jurymen from the general public.[34]

From the tone and content of this editorial, it seems reasonable to conclude that, generally, jurors' instincts in these cases went against branding and punishing such parents as criminals. Hence, one wonders whether the "common sense" of the jury produced the guilty verdict (as credited by the *New York Times*) or whether the court's strict liability jury charge which eliminated any notions of *mens rea* (or criminal intent) and causal connection in essence served to strip the jury of its deliberative function and forced it into the guilty verdict. The use of faith healing and the failure to call in a doctor created a conclusive presumption of criminal intent, irrebuttable by evidence to the contrary.

The jury in the *Pierson* case had recommended leniency. The trial judge, however, refused to give Pierson a suspended sentence because Pierson "did this deliberately [and] violated the law because he wants to." It bothered the judge that Pierson had not recanted his faith: "The trouble with him is that he takes the ground that he is all right, and will do the same thing over again—he would do it tomorrow." The judge did not fathom that to show or feel remorse would be tantamount to betraying his God and abandoning his faith. Accordingly, the judge fined Pierson the maximum five hundred dollars. When Pierson told the court that he refused to pay the fine, the angry judge sentenced Pierson to serve one day for each dollar he refused to pay (i.e., up to five hundred days in jail).[35] This sentence was 135 days *longer* than the maximum jail sentence under the statute, which called for only one year maximum imprisonment.

Pierson had testified at his trial that he "drew his faith in the efficacy of prayer to heal disease from the fifth chapter of James, and that he believed that if he had called in a physician the child [his deceased daughter] would have been sure to die."[36] Ironically, while Pierson was serving his jail sentence, his two-month-old son died of what appeared to be the same illness that the daughter had, while under the care of a medical physician. The *New York Times*, which had been giving the case front page and editorial page coverage, reported this development on page six:

> Mrs. Pierson came to the jail today and told her husband of the death early this morning of the second child. When he heard of this event he exclaimed: "Oh, my God." Those who heard the exclamation say it was more in the nature of an appeal than anything else. Then husband and wife prayed for a long time.
>
> Afterward Pierson said the child would have lived if the right [or rite?] had not been broken and a doctor allowed to attend it. Prayer, he said, would have saved the child. Mrs. Pierson said almost the same thing. She does not believe in doctors and has never had one in the house. She says she took the child to a physician because of the trouble her husband was in. . . .
>
> It is thought that Pierson may lose his reason. He seems fearfully downcast by the death of the child, and takes much blame upon himself because faith cure was not closely adhered to.[37]

Thus, Pierson was a convicted criminal because he had failed to call a physician to treat his daughter, yet such medical care failed to save the life of his son. Indeed, Pierson took the blame for the death of his son because faith healing had *not* been used. For all of the publicity which surrounded the parents' choice of faith healing for the first child, the news of the second child's death while under the care of an "orthodox" physician was consigned to a short paragraph in the midst of an article on the back pages of the *Times*. Needless to say, there was no *Times* headline, nor an editorial, against the medical profession for "killing" the child. Indeed, almost unbelievably, in the same day's paper which reported on this tragedy and Pierson's terrible mental state, the *New York Times* ran an editorial *berating* the jury in the *Pierson* case for recommending leniency and describing Pierson as *glorying* in his martyrdom and "contented" in this position:

> [W]e cannot help regretting that the jury's inexplicable recommendation to mercy led the judge to place a money penalty on the man's offense instead of the imprisonment which the law also provided. As it happened, the homicidal fanatic refused to pay the fine, and therefore was sent to jail for 500 days, but he went there of his own accord, in a way, and now and always will be able to pose as a voluntary martyr. In other words, it is glory, and not punishment at all that the fellow gets as a reward for his atrocious act, and, as he cares nothing for public opinion as expressed by sane people, and much for the admiration of the "faith cure" fraternity, he is in all probability much more than contented with his present position. If he had been sent to jail directly it would have been a little different. He would still be a martyr in the estimation of his fellow-dupes of every variety, but the element of self-immolation would be wanting, and the dignity of the law would be more clearly vindicated.

> Fines will not intimidate "healers." They earn money too easily and in too large quantities to care for a few hundred dollars [fine], and if, now and then, as in this case, somebody who really believes in one or another of the wretched delusions, goes to prison rather than admit the authority of the courts, the professional exploiters of ignorance and credulity can well afford to smile with glee when they think how the episode will help business.[38]

This editorial, coming on the heels of the searing story of the death of Pierson's son while under medical attendance, borders on incoherency. Furthermore, the notion that somehow the "dignity" of the law must be "vindicated" by putting a sincere religious adherent and a kind and loving parent in jail calls into question the very fairness and justice of the legal system itself.

The editorial exhibits a complete inability to fathom the workings of a religious worldview which puts obligation to God above any secular consideration. In the *Times's* own article, Pierson himself appears not as an attention seeker or a man suffering from a martyr complex, but, rather, a tragic figure desperately caught between duty to his God and a legal system bent on revenge. The *Times's* assertions and rantings, on the same day that it reported the death of Pierson's son under tragic circumstances, reveals that something else is going on here. They are not writing of the man, but of a monster: The *New York Times*, and perhaps the legal system itself, recast Pierson in a demonic archetype.

Faith healing as a monstrous "Other"

Criminal prosecutions do not occur in a cultural or societal vacuum. In this section I will draw upon insights into societal panic and boundary drawing explored earlier in chapter 5. I will not presume to offer any positive answers as to why society seemed to drape Mr. Pierson with the mantle of the demonic Other, but I have some tentative suggestions and musings. The *New York Times* editorial page, as noted above, never passed up an opportunity to vilify faith healers in the strongest language imaginable. But the *Times* was not alone in its condemnation; the newspaper regularly ran news reports of condemnations of faith healing from both orthodox Protestantism and orthodox medicine. Such strong reaction is usually reserved for times when a group perceives that it is seriously at risk. Perhaps faith healing served as a cultural lightning rod for contempt and condemnation because these two powerful societal institutions, church and medical, at that time perceived themselves to be highly vulnerable to the efforts and inroads of faith healing.

As noted, judges do not interpret law, and juries do not convict criminals, in a societal vacuum. Hence, this section will briefly survey the complaints registered in the *Times* and place these concerns into a wider cultural context as noted in some secondary literature.

Religious boundaries

"Mainstream" Protestant Christianity at the turn of the century was reeling from the effect of the forces of modernity: science, biblical criticism, urbanization, and industrialization.[39] Added to these problems was the external challenge posed by successful new religious groups such as Mormons, Holiness Revival, Jehovah's Witnesses, the Salvation Army, and numerous faith healing groups (including Christian Science, some Holiness groups, and New Thought churches). This was a time when the cultural hegemony of mainstream Protestant groups began to weaken; American religious historian Sydney Ahlstrom refers to this era as "The Ordeal of Transition."[40]

Readers of the *New York Times* would certainly have been justified in believing that faith healing groups were becoming quite powerful, and the *Times*, as noted, did all it could to portray that power as threatening. Articles gave the impression, at least, that "faith healing cults" were experiencing phenomenal growth in the New York area and elsewhere. For example, an editorial in 1899 depicted citizens of Hopewell, Pennsylvania, in angry revolt because school officials refused to fire a teacher who had been teaching Christian Science to her students.

> Miss Isabel R. Scott [the teacher] . . . has demonstrated her unfitness for continued employment by constant and lamentably successful efforts to inculcate her pupils with the pernicious doctrine of "Christian Science." To this a large majority of the residents of Hopewell strenuously object, but the Board of Directors happens to be itself infected with the plague of Quimby-Eddyism, and four of its members uphold Miss Scott in her evil practices, thus making her deposition for the present impossible. . . .

The people of Hopewell, finding it impossible or inconvenient to change immediately the personnel of their School Board, have done the next best thing—
established a new and independent school, in which their children will not be
depraved and brutalized by enforced listening to blasphemy and senility dis-
guised as religion.[41]

The inescapable message of the *Times* editorial is that these Christian Scientists
are evil, they are after your children, and they are in positions of power: They
teach in the public schools and they even control school boards.

An editorial in the *Times* in 1900 noted a news release from the Christian
Science church which showed their followers to be "steadily and rapidly increasing." In the face of these "lamentably accurate" numbers, however, the *New York
Times* declared the church to "be showing signs of swift decay," for it is, according to the paper, a movement which can only reap a single crop of converts and
has no staying power. This editorial bore signs of "whistling in the dark" and appeared to be aimed at calming the public's fears over this news of growth.[42]

Indeed, what was of greatest concern to the *Times* (and thus, perhaps, to its
readers) was that Christian Science was attracting bright, intelligent, successful,
upper-class people into its fold. When a former judge gave a lecture on behalf of
Christian Science, the headline screamed: "CHRISTAN SCIENCE DEFENDED BY
A JUDGE: Senator Thurston's Former Law Partner Its Champion; Nearly Two
Million Cases of Healing for [*sic*] Sickness Proves the Truth of the Scientists'
Doctrine, He Declares."[43] A few months earlier, a *New York Times* editorial re-
marked upon a similar lecture held in Chicago's Coliseum, which attracted a
crowd of nine thousand people, "well-dressed" and having the marks of "average
rationality." The *Times* was aghast at a Chicago newspaper's neutral, if not
slightly favorable, comment on the lecture:

> The size and quality of this audience seems to have impressed The Chicago
> Inter Ocean to a really remarkable degree. It declares the impossibility of deny-
> ing that Mrs. Eddy's teaching is on the increase, and, going further, admits that
> Mrs. Eddy's doctrines are accepted by many men and women of recognized
> standing in the intellectual world, and asserts that the great majority of "Chris-
> tian Scientists" are people of high intelligence and education. . . .

> The Inter Ocean doubtless knows that it was just yammering when it sought to
> excuse its failure to do its obvious duty, which is to condemn fraud and false-
> hood wherever found. What is it afraid of, anyway? We can assure the Inter
> Ocean that nothing happens to newspapers that neither have nor pretend any
> respect for "Christian Science" or "Christian Scientists."[44]

Here, to the specter of Christian Scientists holding powerful positions such as
teachers and school board members, the *Times* now added the power of judges
and even newspapers. Also frightening (to the *Times*) was the prospect that this
was not an aberration and that indeed intelligent, "quality" people are adopting
this religion in droves.

One last primary source which shall be used to illustrate the perception of
the power of the Christian Science movement is the contemporary judgment
and observations of Mark Twain. Twain blamed the influence of the Christian

Science Church for causing a several-year delay (from 1903 to 1907) in the publication of his book on Christian Science. Twain feared what he perceived as the growing power and influence of the movement, and he wrote in 1899:

> It is a reasonably safe guess that in America in 1920 there will be ten million Christian Scientists . . . that these figures will be trebled in 1930; that in America in 1920 the Christian Scientists will be a political force, in 1930 politically formidable, and in 1940 the governing power in the Republic—to remain that, permanently.[45]

The foreword to the modern reprinting of Twain's *Christian Science* notes that Twain interpreted the Harper publishing company's refusal to publish the book in 1903 "as suppression and as convincing proof of his opponent's power" and quoted Twain as follows: "The situation is not barren of humor: I had been doing my very best to show in print that the Xn Scientist cult has become a power in the land—well, here was the proof: it had scared the biggest publisher in the Union![46]

Adding to the problems in the *Pierson* case posed by "faith healing" in general (as evinced in the fears expressed in the press, above) was the news coverage of the leader of Pierson's church, Alexander Dowie, which chronicled his personal descent into the realm of the bizarre. In 1901, Dowie declared himself to be Elijah, but then eight days later expressed some doubts and held an election among his deacons and elders to decide the issue. As noted by the *Times*, Dowie found out that he was indeed Elijah by a vote of 249 to 5. Dowie then declared that he spoke "by the full authority of a completed divine commission . . . [and that] he will live until Jesus Christ returns to earth to restore all things."[47] On June 17, 1901 a report in the *New York Times* stated that Dowie believed that he was the target of a plot by physicians to kidnap him, lock him in a detention hospital, and beat him on the head and back "till he should lose all his reasoning powers and become really insane." Dowie wanted the doctors to leave him alone and to stop calling him paranoid.[48]

In 1903, as Pierson's case was pending before the Court of Appeals (New York State's highest court), Dowie again attracted the attention of the *New York Times* with an announcement of a planned "invasion" of New York City with three thousand workers.[49] His followers hired Madison Square Garden (with a seating of sixteen thousand) for the mission, and they contracted for several trains to carry the "Restoration Host" from Zion, Illinois, to New York City.[50] A report on the progress of the invasion noted that Dowie's followers living in the City of Zion alone numbered forty thousand strong. It further noted that Dowie had been arrested "no less than one hundred times" in 1895 for practicing faith curing, but although he was sometimes fined, he was never imprisoned.[51] Ironically, on the very day that the first train left Zion to begin what the *Times*'s front page headline called the "DOWIE INVASION," the New York Court of Appeals reaffirmed Pierson's conviction for criminal negligence in the use of faith healing to care for his child.[52]

The newspapers apparently played no small part in whipping up the populace against Dowie. The *Times* repeatedly dubbed Dowie's visit an invasion and noted his plans for converting at least twenty-five thousand New Yorkers. Dowie's Madison Square Garden religious ceremonies and speeches were continually interrupted by hissing and jeering, and people apparently went for the sole purpose of provoking Dowie by walking out on him in the middle of his talk. The papers reported on this, which apparently encouraged even more dissenters to attend and disrupt the events. A *Times* headnote sectional for this article read, "EXPECTED THE STORM TO BREAK." The article noted that "The reports of the morning meetings had become known through the evening papers and many thousands arrived at night to witness a storm that they knew must break soon."[53]

By October 22, 1903, the headlines were recording Dowie's defeat: "'ELIJAH' OVERAWED BY ANGRY MULTITUDE: Defiance Gone, He Abruptly Closes Services in the Garden. Record-breaking Throng, In Resentful Mood, Sweeps Away Police and Makes Demonstration Against 'Prophet.'" This last crowd was looking for trouble: The paper noted that "the great gathering [of ten thousand persons] was full of pent-up excitement and hostility from the very start." Seven hundred policemen on the scene at Madison Square Garden could not contain the crowd.[54]

Boundaries of science and medicine

In addition to the furor created by the incursion of faith healing sects and cults into territory once dominated by the mainstream Protestant churches, faith healing also trampled upon territory staked out by allopathic medicine in general and the AMA in particular. Allopathic medicine at the turn of the century had assumed the philosophical and political mantle of an orthodoxy, reminiscent of pre-Reformation Catholicism in the Middle Ages or evangelical Protestantism in the mid-nineteenth-century United States. The allopathic medical profession has at times consciously and deliberately defined itself as sole possessor of Truth, and it has used the legal/political arena (with impressive but by no means total success) as a means of enforcing its orthodoxy as against all other alternative healing methods.

> The medical profession, like the clergy but unlike the professions of law and engineering, has exhibited throughout history a dominant establishment frequently challenged by dissident groups of practitioners called in areas of both health and religion, "sects" or "cults."[55]

The history of the AMA's use of political power to obtain legal protection for its branch of the medical profession need not be retold here.[56] As summarized by Gevitz, in making such moves the orthodox medical profession did not distinguish between medical quacks and frauds who knew they were "hoodwinking" the public and unorthodox practitioners whom the orthodox considered to be simply "self-deluded" or "deranged" because they offered an alternative to the allopathic orthodoxy:

> To most orthodox physicians, the motivation of these individuals was essentially unimportant. What was significant was their potential for harm and the neces-

sity of putting an end to their activities. . . . Orthodox physicians viewed it as
their public duty to combat and eliminate these false systems of healing, just as
it was their obligation to crush patent medicine and device quackery.[57]

Such "combat" took the form not only of public relations campaigns, but also
political and legal efforts. The AMA lobbied for medical licensing acts which
limited (under penalty of law) the practice of healing to the followers of orthodoxy. As other alternative medical practioners such as osteopathic or chiropractic physicians made legislative inroads on the AMA monopoly, the allopaths
fought to have the licensing of these groups reviewed by medical boards made
up of allopathic doctors, using allopathic criteria. The AMA in the past had kept
alternative practitioners out of otherwise public (and publicly funded) hospitals
and had banned its members from consulting with the unorthodox, or even from
seeing a patient who was also under the care of one of these alternative healers.
The issue was pluralism versus absolutism, indeed, polytheism versus monotheism. The issue was whether the medical paradigm would be one of evolution
with allopathic medicine as the pinnacle or one of parallel co-existence. The allopathic AMA and its members fought for the evolutionary, monotheistic model.
Other competing groups fought for legal recognition that would permit them at
least the ability to coexist.[58] Notably, in the *Pierson* case the New York Court of
Appeals, in their affirmation of the trial court's conviction of the defendants for
failing in their statutory duty to "provide medical attendance" to their child,
looked to the medical licensing statute for guidance as to what "medical attendance" was required. The parents' care of and attending to the child by prayer
did not qualify, because such care was not within the statutory definition.

Walker v. Superior Court

"Were blisters, leeches and calomel the medical alternative to prayer today,
quite likely defendant's reliance on *Hines* [1874 English criminal case in which
the court absolved parents of criminal charges for using prayer instead of medical treatment for a child's illness] would more fully resonate with this court.
Medical science has advanced dramatically, however, and we may fairly presume that the community standard for criminal negligence has changed
accordingly."[59]

We don't know what we're doing in medicine.[60]

The flurry of criminal prosecutions of parents who used faith or spiritual healing
methods in the early decades of the twentieth century caused Christian Scientists to lobby state legislatures across the country and obtain express statutory exemptions for spiritual healing. Recently, however, these statutory exemptions for
religiously based methods of healing under child abuse laws mandating medical
attention for children are being eroded, if not eliminated, by the judicial
branches at the urging of the executive branches of government (agencies and
prosecutors). Prosecutors, judges, and some legal commentators routinely take
the position that although a Christian Scientist, for example, is legally permitted

to use the services of a Christian Science practitioner, a believing parent can and should be criminally prosecuted for abuse or criminal neglect if a child's healing does not occur.

The influential opinion of the California Supreme Court in the 1988 Christian Science healing case of *Walker v. Superior Court* must be examined in light of this background. Walker was a devout Christian Science parent[61] who was convicted of manslaughter in the death of her 4-year-old daughter from meningitis. In the *Walker* case, the court construed the spiritual healing exemption in a child neglect statute as *unavailable* as a defense in the manslaughter section of the penal code. The court reached this result by labeling the child abuse and neglect statute as merely a vehicle for enforcing child support obligations, and thus it had nothing to do with the purpose of the manslaughter statute, which was the punishment of criminally negligent parents.

The California court inserted its own religious standards for defining and judging the seriousness and importance of a religious obligation, rather than looking to that of the defendant and her church. The court questioned the mother's behavior on *religious* grounds when it noted that a resort to medicine for a Christian Scientist is not a "sin" nor does it result in "divine retribution" (court's own terms). And the court further noted that the Christian Science Church leaves each member to its own conscience and does not "stigmatize" anyone who does use medicine. In other words, adherents to Christian Science are "free" to use medicine because their church does not have the same enforcement tools that mainstream Protestantism or Catholicism has, (i.e., one will not be excommunicated or burn in hell if one consults with a medical doctor).[62] With the court taking such pains to note these theological differences, the court's subsequent insistence that they had no effect on its decision in the case is unconvincing.

The following quote from the U.S. Supreme Court case of *Prince v. Massachusetts* is routinely relied upon to give paramount weight to the state's interest and, indeed, it served that familiar purpose in *Walker*:

> Parents may be free to become martyrs themselves. But it does not follow they are free, in identical circumstances, to make martyrs of their children before they have reached the age of full legal discretion when they can make that choice for themselves.[63]

Accordingly, the *Walker* court showed no interest in addressing the issues of the uncertainty of its standard and the chilling effect this uncertainty might have on religious adherents. The defendant plaintively asked the court, "Is it lawful for a parent to rely solely on treatment by spiritual means through prayer for the care of his/her ill child during the first few days of sickness but not for the fourth or fifth day?" The court, however, summarily dismissed the problem by noting that the law is full of instances where one must "estimate rightly" and that such estimating is simply a matter of "common experience known to the actor."[64] The court exhibited great faith, here, in medical doctors, as well as an insupportable faith in the ability of "common experience" to diagnose all manner of ailments and separate the serious ones from the trivial.

Furthermore, the court did not question the efficacy and the expertise of medical science to heal regardless of the illness. Medical science is accorded a conclusive presumption in any and all events. One commentator has noted the *Walker* court's failure to address the issue of causation, that is, the degree of certainty that medical science would have accurately diagnosed the disease and cured it successfully:

> The court in *Walker* stated that medical science has now advanced to the point where it must be relied upon in every serious case . . . While the court supports its conclusions by stating that medical care has advanced from the days of *Wagstaffe* when leeches and blisters were common medical practice, the court fails to address the fact that the death rate for meningitis in hospitals today ranges from ten to fifteen percent.[65]

Of those who do survive meningitis under medical care, 20 percent suffer brain damage. The court also ignored evidence that "Christian Science has healed medically diagnosed meningitis cases."[66]

And not only did the court expect the defendant to have used "common experience" in order to diagnose as well as a doctor and then to have abandoned her religious convictions in order to bear the risks of forced medical care, she was also expected to have had the research and interpretive skills of a lawyer to predict her risk of criminal exposure, for, according to the court, the defendant should have known that she could not rely upon the plain statutory exemptions for faith healing in the child abuse and neglect statutes. Astoundingly, the court admonished her that "We thus require citizens to apprise themselves not only of statutory language but also of legislative history, subsequent judicial construction, and underlying legislative purpose."[67]

What about the "chilling effect" which this vagueness and uncertainty would have on the practice of religious beliefs such as those of Christian Science? The court simply defines away the problem. Reliance on prayer for minor matters is exempted by the child abuse and neglect statutes, and such minor injuries are not indictable offenses under manslaughter statutes. Thus, reliance on prayer healing for minor matters is religious conduct which is *not* chilled. The only conduct, therefore, that could be chilled is reliance on prayer when a child's life is endangered or the child has died. Since this conduct is *not* protected by the free exercise clause, there is no "chilling" of the right to exercise one's religion freely with respect to this more serious conduct. The court deliberately ignores the difficulties posed by an after-the-fact, results-oriented definition of protected versus criminal conduct. The evasion of the real free exercise issue, the strained logic, and the conclusive, irrebuttable presumption in favor of medical science and against the parent speak louder than the court's careful masking of its decision in formally neutral language: Spiritual healing is now essentially a criminal activity subject to absolute liability if it does not work. Accordingly, the court upheld the criminal conviction of Walker for the death of her four-year-old daughter from meningitis.

Justice Broussard voted for conviction but in a separate opinion criticized the majority's claim that it was simply undertaking a technical statutory interpretation in its opinion, and nothing more. Justice Broussard critiqued the majority court's interpretation, which limited the faith healing exemption to instances of enforcing child support obligations: "[I]t would be absurd to conclude that by adopting that provision the legislature intended only to exempt a parent from a duty to pay for medical care which was not received."[68] He continued,

> There is nothing in the legislative history to indicate that the Legislature sought to eliminate a non-existent duty to pay for medical services which were never rendered or was concerned primarily with reimbursement for medical services paid for by others.

> The religious exemption must be applied to the child endangerment provisions . . . or the legislative intent is totally defeated.[69]

Yet, even Justice Broussard would forgo any exemption for faith healing when it becomes active conduct endangering the child, and he thus ultimately agreed with the conviction of the defendant.

Recent articles in the legal literature commenting upon the faith healing issue have been riding the new wave of intense concern over child abuse. In those articles which have focused negatively on the religion, however, the paradigm for child abuse has been unquestioningly broadened and extended to include the use of spiritual methods of healing *per se*. Some commentators advocate complete removal of all faith healing exemptions in the best interests of the child. As one stated, "It is preposterous to rationalize that deaths resulting from such neglect are 'God's will,' since that same God has provided us with the intellect and technology necessary to sustain and promote optimum health and welfare."[70]

The personal faith of this commentator in a particular sort of God, as well as the faith that she has in medical science, is revealed not only in the above quote, but also in the very first lines of her article:

> Each year, modern medicine saves the lives of countless children who are critically ill. Yet, many children still die from childhood illnesses, despite the availability of specially-trained doctors and advanced medical technology. This paradox arises because some parents do not accept or utilize available health care systems, instead relying upon faith-healing or spiritual treatment (religious treatment) to cure an ill or injured child.[71]

The hostility of another article is also quite apparent from the beginning paragraph:

> [C]hildren in this country are still being martyred on the altar of their parents' religious beliefs. Parents cloaking themselves in the first amendment and its free exercise clause are denying their children medical treatment and those children are dying.[72]

These comments, as well as some of the judges' opinions which have been previously examined, reflect a sharp, bright-line absolutism and justify this stance with emotion-laden language marked by fear, anger, and repugnance. We have indeed witnessed formidable advancements in medicine and medical treatment since the days of *Wagstaffe*. Yet, to what extent have we forgotten how tentative and fragile our medical knowledge is at times? The next section of this chapter will examine common attitudes toward medical science with the guiding thought that only when assumptions as to its invincibility are uncovered and examined can reasoned judgments be made in faith healing cases.

Unexamined assumptions: Myth and modern medicine

The increasingly hostile case law and commentary against spiritual healing is heavily laden with assumptions as to the disinterestedness, objectivity, neutrality, and rationality of the medical viewpoint. The well-established ability of allopathic medicine to cure many diseases and to heal broken bodies is not at issue here. What should be laid bare and explored, however, is the extent to which the phrase "miracles of modern medicine" refers perhaps to something beyond the matter-of-factness of surgical techniques and antibiotics and unconsciously taps into a competing mythical and metaphysical belief system.

Images of parents "sacrificing" their children on the "altar" of their religion are provocative, not insightful. Such language of abomination does not contribute to an understanding of the complexity of the spiritual healing issue, the high stakes for the family involved, and the possible value-laden underpinnings of what are usually assumed to be simply rational and objective medical assertions. One modern assumption is that when human beings throw off their superstitions and courageously face the disenchanted universe, knowing that there will be no supernatural help forthcoming, they then can be freed to take on full responsibility for improving the human condition and for achieving universal justice. Charles Taylor notes that the "grace" which enables the achievement of such transcendence of the flawed, magical past comes to us in the form of reason and scientific detachment: "[W]e see a pervasive belief in our scientific culture that scientific honesty and detachment itself inclines one to fairness and beneficence in dealing with people."[73]

Thus is born the assumption that science is benevolent and fair because it is based upon reason; allopathic medicine is science, and, therefore, medicine takes on the aura of benevolence, fairness, detachment. A logical negative inference that anything which rejects medical science is inherently maleficent, superstitious, undetached (self-interested), and even dishonest is sometimes also drawn. Attacks on Mary Baker Eddy's spiritual healing were commonly *ad hominem*, based not on her results but on various alleged "dishonesties" concerning her *private* life.[74] Along the same lines, the Christian Science practitioners were commonly depicted as motivated by the self-interest of receiving payment for their healing work.[75] In comparison, judgments of the healing abilities or professional motivations of an allopathic physician would probably not be based upon her collection of fees, nor on how she conducted her private life.

What is problematic is not that the assumption of beneficence exists, but that the image of medicine in turn may be unfairly prejudicing free exercise jurisprudence (e.g., where the image of a self-interested spiritual healer using superstition is compared with the image of a kindly family doctor (a Marcus Welby type) using modern science). Medicine is conclusively presumed to be beneficent; religious healing in turn is conclusively presumed to be vacuous.

Interestingly, the public itself seems to have informally opted medically for a modified polytheism rather than a strict monotheism. David Hufford refers to "a hierarchy of resort" as the model for medical treatment in the United States. Orthodox medicine, chiropractic, homeopathic, osteopathic, health food, folk medicines, acupunctures, etc., all are used depending upon the problem and the results received. "Even among those for whom a single health system is dominant, it is rare not to find a variety of health resources used, in different order, for different problems, and at different stages of those problems."[76] "In other words," Hufford notes, "the health culture of the United States is basically pluralistic."[77]

One way of looking at this de facto pluralism is that the public recognizes that allopathic medicine is an art, is not infallible, and has not been able to furnish them with all-healing miracles. Since it has (not surprisingly) *not* been able to solve all health problems, other health systems are also commonly utilized, sometimes as a first resort, sometimes as a last resort. This pluralism has not found its way into the courts, however. Indeed, legislative exemptions for faith healing practices in child abuse and neglect statutes which otherwise mandate medical treatment are increasingly being evaded by the courts by for example, declaring the exemption unconstitutional or by "interpret[ing] these exemptions in such a way as to circumvent their purpose."[78] One commentator on the California Supreme Court's opinion in the case of *Walker v. Superior Court* observed:

> Under *Walker*, all forms of health care other than medicine, including herbal, chiropractic, acupuncture, and spiritual treatment, may potentially constitute grounds for criminal negligence. Thus, the *Walker* court effectively outlaws differing opinions on health care and establishes that medical science is the only legally safe form of health care.[79]

One other indication of the potential for medicine to assume mythic status in faith healing cases is the common image of the doctor as parent. This image is the subject of wide discussion in the field of medical ethics, where it is being examined for its underlying effects upon such matters as who should make decisions concerning a patient's medical care.[80] In *The Physician's Covenant: Images of the Healer in Medical Ethics*, William F. May notes that "images for the healer derive partly from notions of godly action."[81]

> [R]eligious forces . . . pervade our times and, not least, those fateful events which attend sickness, suffering, and death. These events shatter or suspend the ordinary resources that people trust for managing their lives and send them to the doctor in hope of rescue. They clothe the doctor accordingly in the images of shelter and rescue—the parent, the fighter, and others. The full power of these images and the hold that they have over the lay person and therefore the professional does not become clear except that we see them, at least in part, in a religious setting. . . .

We think of ourselves as the children of a secular, scientific age. But looking at the shaman's work in its religious reverberations suggests that latent religious forces are still at work in twentieth-century medicine, religious forces that shape the perceptions and responses that men and women oppose to the crushing power of disease, suffering, and death.[82]

If these images of the medical profession as priest-healer-parent-military general exist within the unconscious realm of judges, juries, and prosecutors, then a parent who rejects medical assistance could, indeed, be perceived as monstrous, an abomination.

As I have repeatedly noted, my aim is not to attack medical science. That would be self-defeating and foolish. Society as a whole needs antibiotics and other medications, internists and surgeons, the expertise of the entire medical profession. But what I am proposing is that medical science (1) be recognized as the imperfect art that it is and (2) not be accorded the status of unerring goodness personified. I am in essence proposing that medical science be demythologized, that the use of medical science should not be conclusively presumed to be beneficent when forced upon families against their wishes. Concomitantly, the use of religious healing methods should not be conclusively presumed to be criminal. Fairness and the importance of religion and of religious values to faith healing families cannot be well served if prosecutors and judges are premising their decisions in faith healing cases upon such assumptions about allopathic medicine.

Children: Isolated integers or an integral part affecting the whole?

As discussed in chapter 4, the stakes can be high for devout religious families in free exercise clause conflicts where fundamental framework matters are in jeopardy. Neither the courts nor some commentators appear to appreciate that the controversial behavior is not the result of a simple isolated personal choice, or even a strong attachment to one's religion. Rather, the behavior at issue may very well be a key structural component of the foundation and framework which form the basis for the religious community's identity, as well as the identity of the families within that community and of the individuals who make up that family.

The government's attitude toward the raising of children in religious spiritual healing families also has little depth of thought behind it, and it ignores the reality of the religious family's (and the religious community's) situation. The government, in the faith healing cases and such cases as *Prince v. Massachusetts*,[83] has taken the position that a child should be protected by the state from certain of the parents' religious practices which the state feels promotes martyrdom, until the child is old enough to choose a religion. The practical difficulties with this position have simply not been addressed, however: What the state is in essence requiring is that parents, and, indeed, the entire church community,

somehow suspend a portion of their framework when raising and otherwise dealing with their children. Life is not that segmentable, and, indeed, frameworks
cannot be manipulated in such a manner. Frameworks are fundamental struc-
tures, the grounding of one's being, and the temporary suspension required by
the court may not be possible. If a religious community and its families cannot
fully practice a core, religious obligation in an integrated manner which includes the children of the community, either the law must be disobeyed or the
religious framework is at risk of disintegration.

Furthermore, and notwithstanding the good accomplished by the children's
rights movement,[84] a child is a bundle of complexities and not simply an isolated, encapsulated, miniature, autonomous individual self. A child is raised,
and learns, only within the contexts of a community: the family and the larger
religious community to which the family belongs, and not simply the civic polis.
Indeed, the "notion of children's rights has limited practical utility. In any child-
care dispute, the conflict is over *whose conceptions of the child's needs should prevail.*"[85] As Taylor notes, "A self can never be described without reference to
those who surround it."[86] And, indeed, one learns the requisite moral and evalu-
ative languages which constitute the framework of the child's self only in conversation with one's parents and one's community:

> There is no way we could be inducted into personhood except by being initi-
> ated into a language. We first learn our languages of moral and spiritual dis-
> cernment by being brought into an ongoing conversation by those who bring us
> up. The meanings that the key words first had for me are the meanings they
> have for *us*, that is, for me and my conversation partners together. . .
>
> So I can only learn what anger, love, anxiety, the aspiration to wholeness, etc.,
> are through my and others' experience of these being objects for *us*, in some
> common space. This is the truth behind Wittgenstein's dictum that agreement
> in meanings involves agreement in judgments.[87]

Indeed, the court has the entire process of instilling moral and spiritual values
backward: A child needs a moral/religious framework as a *start* in life, from
which that child can later build upon, renovate, or even reject. "Train up a child
in the way he should go, and he will not depart from it."[88] But where the state
has forbidden the parents to raise their child up in their religious framework,
what religion or structure has the state offered to replace it? And if the parents
simply exclude the child from a fundamental practice of the otherwise integrated religious framework, the result is a child who develops an inherently contradictory structure/framework. Either way, the child is disoriented at best and
"base-less" at worst. As Taylor explains,

> Later, I may innovate. I may develop an original way of understanding myself
> and human life, at least one that is in sharp disagreement with my family and
> background. But the innovation can only take place from the base in our com-
> mon language. Even as the most independent adult, there are moments when I
> cannot clarify what I feel until I talk about it with certain special partner(s) who
> know me, or have wisdom, or with whom I have an affinity. This incapacity is a
> mere shadow of the one the child experiences. For him, everything would be

confusion, there would be no language of discernment at all, without the conversations which fix this language for him.[89]

It is clear that one's framework is not simply built upon verbal language, but
also upon behavioral language (examples and actions) which conforms to the
verbal language. A child, especially, learns by example, and where the example
differs from what the child is told, the child is confused by the inconsistency.
These crossed signals, in turn, weaken the development of her own framework
and self-identity. Self-definition can only be accomplished by means of a combination of verbal and behavioral language. Taylor alludes to this when he writes,

> It is this original situation [i.e., the achievement of a self-definition through re-
> lation and conversation with others] which gives its sense to our concept of
> 'identity', offering an answer to the question of who I am through a definition of
> where I am speaking from and to whom. *The full definition of someone's identity
> thus usually involves not only his stand on moral and spiritual matters but also
> some reference to a defining community.*[90]

A "stand" implies words backed up by actions, and, indeed, a community defines itself even more loudly by its actions than by its words. For, as the author of
Proverbs observed: "Even a child makes himself known by his acts, whether what
he does is pure and right."[91]

Thus, in summary, to a committed member of a religious community, the
more fundamental the religious practice is to the framework, and the more rigid
the core framework is (i.e., little or no outlet for doctrinal change to accommodate the caprices of a changing dominant culture), the more certain it will be
that laws and regulations which are in conflict with the framework will be
deemed to be overruled by what the religious community believes to be a higher
law and a higher good. A religious practice which is a fundamental part of the
structural framework for the religious community is not simply optional behavior or even a strongly held belief that is open to persuasion or to conversion by
the dominant religious framework. Rather, the practice and the belief behind
the practice are crucial components to the basic identity and the framework
of the individuals and their community. To abandon the practice could plunge
the group into chaos and disintegration. Witness to one's convictions (martyrdom) then seems to be not only a reasonable alternative under these circumstances, but even an imperative.

Mark Twain wrote scathingly of Christian Science. Even so, he understood
the mindset of the religiously faithful parent better than anyone else engaged in
the debate, both then and now:

> I have received several letters (two from educated and ostensibly intelligent per-
> sons), which contained, in substance, this protest: "I don't object to men and
> women chancing their lives with these people, but it is a burning shame that
> the law should allow them to trust their helpless little children in their deadly
> hands." Isn't it touching? Isn't it deep? Isn't it modest? It is as if the person said:
> "I know that to a parent his child is the core of his heart, the apple of his eye, a
> possession so dear, so precious that he will trust its life in no hands but those
> which he believes, with all his soul, to be the very best and the very safest, but it

is a burning shame that the law does not require him to come to *me* to ask what kind of healer I will allow him to call." The public is merely a multiplied "me."[92]

Prosecutors and judges would do well to ponder Twain's insight before they bring the criminal justice system to bear on grieving parents who were doing "the very best" for their children. As I will discuss in a later section, civil intervention to force allopathic medical care upon a child may very well be the best course of action when the child's life is at stake, but even here the government must proceed with respect for the different framework and value system of the family, and in a way that is least intrusive.

The role of spiritual healing in the Christian Science framework.

As noted, a universalizability characterizes the current free exercise standard: The generally applicable statute or regulation is the universal maxim which shall be applied to all, despite the overall religious, not criminal, purpose of the behavior. What appears to be neutral policy, however, in fact has a built-in bias in favor of the normative values and behavioral standards of the majority of the populace. Nondominant religious groups which operate within a different framework may thus find that their unique religious voices have been legally silenced: The framework of the religious system as a whole, as well as probable qualitative differences between paradigmatic criminal situations and sincere religious practices, has been made irrelevant to the workings of criminal justice through the use of conclusive presumptions. Thus, "relevant" evidence at trial increasingly is limited to the narrow focus of whether the religious adherent intended to commit and in fact committed the act which the statute or regulation proscribes, a matter usually readily admitted and thus not really at issue.

Although U.S. Supreme Court justices are key players in setting the boundaries of free exercise protection, they are not the only governmental actors with power over the lives of the religious adherent. Some flexibility still remains within the system, and the arguments in this chapter are directed not only to judges, but also to those who have the power of enforcement discretion and of rule making and standard setting. The many levels of prosecutors as well as the many administrators in child welfare agencies have discretion as to allocation of resources and as to what cases will be pursued and prosecuted; the federal and state legislatures and the many agencies which oversee children's issues have discretion in making and setting standards, policies, and priorities. And, indeed, the Christian Scientists took their circumstances to lawmakers, and they convinced them to include a spiritual healing exemption in child abuse statutes, only to have the courts repeal this protection by strained interpretation. Thus, it is appropriate here to explain the role that spiritual healing plays in Christian Science and to give a voice to that religious community and substance to its framework. For it is contended that the goal of justice in these free exercise situations requires not only that the unexamined assumptions of those who would wield power be brought to light and scrutinized, but also that those in power be open and willing to broaden their horizons by openly engaging the framework and the context of the religious Other.

Let us thus turn to the framework of devoted members of the Church of Christ, Scientist: those who have committed themselves to the work of living the spiritual principles discovered by the founder of Christian Science, Mary Baker Eddy. There are several aspects to the normative Christian Science framework which will be analyzed here not only because they are helpful keys into the mindset and way of life of such devout Christian Scientists, but also because they provide insights which will be helpful in assessing more *secular* considerations relevant to resolution of the free exercise issue. These aspects of the Christian Science framework are: (1) the bright lines which demarcate Christian Science beliefs from that of the normative American mainstream; (2) the *empirical* emphasis, which insists upon demonstrations or outworkings as part of the authority and proof of the spiritual principles; and (3) the total integration of daily life and spiritual belief, of practicality and theology. In a nutshell, Christian Science is a direct counterpoint to a Sunday-morning faith. Rather than merely one among many other focal points of life, the religion of the Christian Scientist entails a most serious commitment to a totally integrated spiritual way of life. Christian Science is not simply a theology; it is a radically different worldview which requires not only thoughtful allegiance but also *application,* in the form of demonstrations of practical results in every area of the adherent's life.

The Christian Science worldview is that of the Western world turned inside out. Only by "upturning" traditional Western assumptions about "reality" can one begin to get a glimpse of what Christian Science's framework and webs of belief may look like.[93] The modern Western normative world construct regards "matter," that is, the world perceived through the five senses, as the locus of all cause and effect. The mental thought processes of human beings, per se, are not capable of directly producing an effect on the "outer" world of matter. Achieving a material effect upon the physical world requires the use of the material, mechanical forces of that outer world. Christian Science, however, sees the spiritual/mental realm of principle as the locus of all cause and effect in the material realm. Thus, it is principle which is truly real, and the appearance of causation, of "effective" power, in the physical/material plane, is just an illusion. The material world is illusion not because it does not exist, per se, but because the spiritual (divine principle) is the ultimate source of power over the material and can correct all error (including sin and sickness and dis-ease). Such "error" only exists because human beings, consciously and unconsciously, continue to believe in these errors and thus give them power, rather than working to eradicate such error with spiritual truth.

Accordingly, Christian Scientists reject as false and illusory any attribution of dominance and causative power to the everyday material world, a power which most others in this culture probably accept in one form or another. The true reality, as seen from the Christian Science perspective, is wholly that of Mind, Spirit, Principle:

> One praying in Christian Science accepts the premise that existence is indeed mental. He sees the Christian battleground as one in which two forces oppose each other. On the one side are the forces represented by a selfish, materially-minded mentality that believes in a world of good and evil, matter and spirit, divine Providence and bad luck, and a life that has both beginning and ending. On the other side of the field is the force of a wholly-benign, all-powerful loving Father-Mother God, who knows no evil and no sets of opposites. Whatever . . . belief [remains] in a combination of good and evil, or Spirit and matter . . . must give way . . . to the spiritual fact.[94]

In a framework which does not admit to the reality and truth of the material and, indeed, sees itself at war even against a dual mentality which admits of both matter and spirit, there is no room for *materia medica*. DeWitt John in *The Christian Science Way of Life* notes how combining medicine and spiritual healing can be harmful:

> It is true that relying concurrently on Christian Science and medicine does not work out well; the two systems are so vastly different in diagnostic approach, in their concept of the nature of disease, and in their healing procedure, that they cannot work in cooperation; this would be unfair to both systems and dangerous to the patient. The fundamental assumptions of Christian Science are opposite to those of medical theory. . . .[95]

One irony of the increasing number of prosecutions directed against Christian Scientist parents is that, of the myriad of religious groups which place primary reliance upon some sort of spiritual method of healing, Christian Science is perhaps the most rationally based and empirically grounded. Christian Science healing is not a test of faith: Healing is not a matter of proving one's faith to God by passively relying upon his unknowable will (faith healing). What Christian Scientists most emphasize is that they practice *spiritual* healing, not "faith healing": Christian Science healing is accomplished by application of what they term scientific principles, because the principles have produced demonstrable results over the course of 125 years of practice, through five or more generations of Christian Scientist families.

To the Christian Scientist, God does not behave as if he were a person, dispensing favors like health and healing at his inscrutable whim, and expecting his creatures to respect his power and dominion by showing unthinking, unquestioning faith in him. Rather, the Christian Science God is Principle: unchanging, constant, all-powerful, and all-loving. This Principle acknowledges and produces only health; sickness and disease are violations of the Principle, and thus the Principle cannot be blamed, and is not responsible, for the existence of these errors. One must therefore attune one's life and thought back to divine principle in order to achieve a healing of the error. Christian Scientists often refer to the principles of mathematics as an analogy to divine principle: If one adds two plus three and gets a total of six, the fault does not lie within the principle of addition.[96] In a Christian Science publication, A *Century of Christian Science Healing*, this point is further explained:

> Christian Science healing is in fact one way of worshipping God. It is an integral part of a deeply felt and closely reasoned view of ultimate reality. This very fact sometimes causes its use of the words "real" and "unreal" to be misunderstood. For when Christian Scientists speak of illness as unreal, they do not mean that humanly it is to be ignored. They mean rather that it is no part of man's true, essential being but comes from a mortal misconception of being, without validity, necessity, or legitimacy. Like a mathematical error which has no substance or principle to support it, sickness is not to be ignored but to be consciously wiped out by a correct understanding of the divine Principle of being. This is the metaphysical basis of Christian Science practice.[97]

A Christian Scientist is a Christian Scientist precisely because she has proven the principles to her own satisfaction through empirical demonstrations in her life. She believes in the principles of Christian Science, not because God, the Bible, Mary Baker Eddy, or the church told her to, but because the principles have worked to heal aspects of her own life. And this proof is not just manifested in the individual's life, but in the lives of family members and church members. Written and verbal testimonials of healings are an important part of Christian Science ritual and practice: Every Wednesday, for example, members of local branch churches across the country gather to exchange witnessing testimony of the outworkings of divine order in every aspect of their lives.[98] Church publications dating from the founding of Christian Science contain written testimony of various sorts of healings.[99] And although it is popular and convenient to dismiss such healings as the inconsequential result of imaginary illnesses, a fair examination of the testimonies belies a quick dismissal.

> The range of conditions healed [as reported in over 7,100 testimonials published from 1969 to 1988] included congenital, degenerative, infectious, neurological, and other disorders, some considered terminal or incurable. These testimonies included over 2,400 healings of children. More than 600 of these involved medically-diagnosed conditions, life-threatening as well as less serious, including spinal meningitis (in several cases after antibiotics failed to help), pneumonia and double-pneumonia, diabetes, food poisoning, heart disorders, loss of eyesight from chemical burns, pleurisy, stomach obstruction, epilepsy, goiter, leukemia, malaria, mastoiditis, polio, rheumatic fever, and ruptured appendix.[100]

This insight is not being offered as ultimate proof that Christian Science theology is "true," but to make two important points relative to the resolution of the free exercise conundrum that spiritual healing has presented. First of all, a religious practice rooted in such intense personal experience is not likely to be abandoned at the mere say-so of the government, and thus the deterrence effect of criminal prosecutions is highly doubtful.

> [T]he student of Christian Science who has accepted its mental and moral discipline and demonstrated for himself the unfailing goodness of God is not likely to look elsewhere for help. It is no sacrifice to forego medical treatment

when one has repeatedly proved that "the word of God is quick, and powerful, and sharper than any two-edged sword." (Hebrews 4:12). Puzzling as the Christian Scientists's confidence is to others, it is rooted in concrete experience and reasoned conviction as well as in the Christian promises. . . . Whole families have relied exclusively on Christian Science for healing through several generations.[101]

Second, albeit the testimonials of healing are "religious documents rather than clinical histories," the numbers of them extending from the nineteenth century up to the present day, and the evidence which they *do* contain, cannot be written off and ignored by the government.[102] Any governmental action which restricts or punishes the use of Christian Science healing *must* contend with this body of personal experience and information. The Christian Scientists have a rightful grievance over governmental evaluations and judgments of their healing as a whole by concentrating on the few highly sensationalized "failures." The present process of judging Christian Science healing is no more fair or accurate than an evaluation of the entire medical profession which was solely premised on patients whose medical treatment had failed. As Williams notes:

> Christian Scientists acknowledge that failures have occurred under their form of treatment just as they have under medical care, in pediatric as well as in other kinds of cases. Physicians argue, understandably, that some who have died might have been saved under their care. Yet there is no evidence that disproportionate numbers of Christian Scientists' children have been lost. In fact, such figures as are available would indicate that the opposite is the case.

> Christian Scientists feel that a greater number of children would in effect, have been "martyred" to medical technology if their parents hadn't had the freedom to turn in a wholly different, spiritual direction for healing. The small number of deaths in Christian Science families are clearly *exceptions* [emphasis in original]—no less tragic than similar occurrences under medical care, but also no more common proportionately and no more criminal.[103]

One further point needs to be made here: the inseparableness of the *spiritual* from the *practical*. Free exercise jurisprudence distinctions between belief and practice are completely alien to, and unintelligible under, this religious system. Sickness is seen as simply a symptom of a larger, underlying, *spiritual* problem: that of living a life which is not in alignment with divine Principle. All physical healing is ultimately spiritual because the true root cause of any material disorder or disease is spiritual dis-ease. Christian Science's "scientific prayer" enables the adherent to attain spiritual at-one-ment with divine order/Principle, at which point healing of life's "errors" (sin or sickness, for example) occurs:

> To a Christian Scientist the real importance of a healing is the light it lets through. The change in physical condition or personal circumstance is only the outward and visible evidence of an inward and spiritual grace—a hint of a perceived spiritual fact. In looking back on a healing, the Christian Scientist is likely to think, not "That was the time I was healed of pneumonia," but "That was the time I learned what real humility is," or "That was the time that I saw so clearly that all power belongs to God." . . . The real change, as Christian Sci-

entists understand it, is from material-mindedness to spiritual-mindedness, from self-centered to God-centered thinking.[104]

Salvation, to the Christian Scientist, is not an otherworldly matter, but a matter of spiritual growth through demonstrations of the Truth principles in this life.[105]

In Christian Science, prayer is not introspective and passive. Prayer is not an audible exercise, or even a heart's whisper to God. Prayer, rather, is "the desire *to do* right."[106] Mere faith and belief will not change one's spiritual situation; there must be daily "striving" to become more in tune with the divine. One cannot expect unmerited pardon for one's sins/errors; such pardon for sins and correction of error can only be obtained by a corresponding radical change in one's life, in both thoughts and practices. One must *demonstrate* the outworking of divine principles, one must undergo a personal reformation and *live* what one has believed and prayed. "It is sad," Mrs. Eddy wrote, "that the phrase *divine service* has come so generally to mean public worship instead of daily deeds. . . . [P]rayer, coupled with a fervent habitual desire to know and do the will of God, will bring us into all Truth. Such a desire . . . is best expressed in thought *and in life*."[107]

Accordingly, criminal punishment for practicing spiritual healing is tantamount to a criminalization of the Christian Science religion. The latter cannot exist without the former, and the framework of Christian Science healing brooks no compromise with *materia medica*. The free exercise distinction between belief and practice is a meaningless, even insidious, construct when applied to criminalize Christian Science parents in these cases: It is a construct of convenience which permits the government prosecutors and judges to avoid confronting the serious, exceedingly complex considerations involved in the issue of spiritual healing in favor of a "quick fix" conviction. The Christian Science community justifiably feels itself to be a target of religious persecution, a situation which cannot change until the legal system develops fairer processes, procedures, and analyses with which to resolve these cases.

Civil interventions and a broadened discussion of "child abuse"

The normative Christian Science family situation simply does not fit the paradigmatic child abuse or neglect situation. Yet, there are situations when a child's life is in danger if medical treatment is not given. This section will explore parameters and justifications for government civil intervention forcing medical treatment upon Christian Science children. This question presents the quintessential hard case, for the results are likely to be tragic whichever way the court moves.

Civil alternatives to criminalization in the context of faith healing have been addressed to some extent in the legal literature: A few articles have criticized the criminalization of spiritual healing, pointing out the unfairness of prosecuting unquestionably loving and attentive parents under child abuse statutes. Such articles have offered solutions such as a strengthening of the spiritual healing exemptions in child abuse statutes. Other articles, showing sympathy for the parents' religious idealism and a competing concern for the health of their children, have proposed civil interventionist solutions short of criminalization including injunctions, temporary state custody in medical emergencies, court supervision, and a separate "non-stigmatizing" statute directed solely at the furnishing of medical care for children.[108]

To these helpful and insightful conversations over what constitutes intervenable neglect and child abuse, this section interjects two additional proposals drawn from a casuistical methodology: using an analogical process by looking to other statutory schemes, as well as to medical ethics itself, for criteria in judging the family situation, and adding to these criteria some contextual nuances highlighting the independent importance of religious practice to the child and to the religiously centered family.

States have child custody acts which help family courts to determine the impossible: what is in the "best interests" of the child with respect to care and custody when such matters are in dispute. Although relevant to a different domain, the factors mentioned in these statutes do list some of society's judgments as to what constitutes a healthy family situation that in turn promotes a child's welfare. Some of these factors (adapted somewhat to fit the spiritual healing situation) include, for example:

(1) Is the child otherwise receiving love and affection, have the parents established healthy emotional ties within the family?
(2 Are the parents otherwise providing the child with food, clothing, and other material needs, are the children of the family "thriving" on the whole?
(3) Is the family situation an otherwise satisfactorily stable environment?
(4) Are the parents "morally fit" and do they provide reasonable guidance and behavioral training to the children?
(5) What is the home, school, and community record of the child? Is the child reasonably well-adjusted at school, making satisfactory progress, in any kind of regular "trouble" that would evince an underlying problem, able to participate appropriately in children's groups and activities?
(6) What are the child's preferences?[109]

As with any such attempt, the above factors are, of course, value laden and open to interpretive abuse. Because the factors are being applied to evaluate the family quality of a nondominant religious group, one very real danger is that normative cultural and religious family values will be read into the criteria and parents whose religious values do not measure up will be penalized. Yet, the criteria are useful in broadening the area of inquiry beyond the narrow confines of whether the parents drive their children to the doctor when they are ill. The criteria at least provide a signal means of determining when the problem is more of a paradigmatic example of child neglect or abuse, and when the crux of the issue is more of a free exercise conflict over healing methods.

Furthermore, the family's success in maintaining a stable and nurturing environment may very well be premised upon its religious framework, which is in turn integrally related to and dependent upon the practice of spiritual healing. As noted above, in a devoutly religious family the spiritual beliefs and practices of the individual, as well as of the family, form the framework upon which their lives are built. Remove or destroy the structural supports, and the entire building crashes. Indeed, in the "best interests of the child" list of criteria, the government itself recognized the importance and value in "the educating and rearing of the child in its religion or creed. . . ."[110]

This is an area in which, clearly, the government should act gingerly, at its peril. The government may be able to furnish a family with food and shelter should these be destroyed in a storm, but the government cannot furnish a family with a metaphysical framework around which to structure their lives and give them meaning and direction. In this realm, what the government destroys, it cannot build back up or replace. Only a stable family relationship and structure can furnish this metaphysical foundation for a child.

One other area of inquiry which is frequently overlooked in free exercise cases involving children is the preferences of the child. This factor receives explicit attention in the child custody context, and it is of equal importance here. If the child has not assimilated the family's spiritual framework, and as a result of a freewill decision (not coerced or brainwashed by social workers or school officials for example) wishes to have medical attention, then the child's wishes should be honored. Alternatively, the wishes of a child who has evinced a commitment to the family's spirituality should likewise be honored. There are two reasons for doing so. One is the already-mentioned importance of framework to the child's overall well-being. The other is the recognition elsewhere in society that a child's perfectionism is to be encouraged, honored, and rewarded, even if that perfectionist behavior entails physical risks and hardships (as noted, especially in athletics). The antagonism which singles out religious perfectionism for criticism is often premised upon the belief that the child has been brainwashed by the parent and thus is incapable of forming an independent desire which needs to be respected. Would the government likewise be interested in preventing the children of athletic stars from becoming hooked on sports because of the likelihood of injury coupled with the possibility of prejudicial parental influence?

A related assumption underlying the actions and rhetoric of those who are in principle against parental use of spiritual healing methods on their children is that the government must do all it can to keep these children alive until they reach the age when they can then choose to adopt attitudes more sensible than their parents. Certainly, testimonies of younger members of the Christian Scientist religious community express sincere devotion to the practice and beliefs of their religion and belie any notion that such children simply have no understanding of what they are doing. These testimonies indicate that children are probably sufficiently capable of understanding and successfully applying the spiritual healing principles taught by (*their*) religion.[111] In such cases, the currently ascending notion of seeking and seriously considering children's input and preferences in the issue of child custody would indicate that respect be given to the child's decisions in areas of religious belief and practice, also.

Courts and commentators who have confronted the issue of religious faith healing in the context of child abuse statutes requiring medical attention have almost unanimously spoken of it in terms of balancing rights: the child's right to life versus the parent's rights to religious freedom and autonomy, versus the state's *parens patriae* rights. I agree with other commentators, however, who generally reject balancing of rights as a particularly unhelpful way of analyzing free exercise issues. The scales of justice are too easily tipped one way or the other by placing one's fingers (i.e., one's assumptions, fears, prejudices, etc.) on them, albeit undeliberately and unconsciously. As should be evident from the above discussion, even to state the issue in terms of a child's right to life is to place an isolated and disproportionate focus upon the relatively few extreme cases, assume that the child herself has no religious interest at stake, and assume that the impact *on the whole* of the religious worldview/framework on the child is one so negative that the child's life is endangered per se.

Instead of a model of balancing scales, it is proposed that a model of a continuum between two extremes or paradigms be utilized. At the positive end of the continuum is a paradigm of a reasonably functioning (physically, mentally, spiritually) family situation. At the negative end of the continuum is a paradigm represented by the archetypal abused child: physically, mentally, and spiritually bruised, beaten, crushed. Dysfunctional parents of all religious persuasions (or none) can be guilty of abuse which approaches the negative paradigm. Religious beliefs, in these cases, are usually not the crux or the source of the problem, and these cases should be judged on their individual facts. Where a particular practice of a religious community is at issue, however, the fair and just response is to look at the religious community's effects and results as a whole. Is there something within the religious framework which minimizes the assumed and expected damage from the practice?[112] For example, if the overall goal of the child abuse statutes is to protect the health of the child, certainly the healthy lifestyle resulting from adherence to Christian Science principles goes a long way to accomplishing that goal. Christian Scientists generally do not smoke or drink, and they strive for positive attitudes and a general moderation in living that would seem to be quite conducive to good health.

The field of medical ethics has been debating and developing parameters for evaluating paternalism in medical situations and thus provides a rich source for analogous insights on the justifiableness of state paternalism in religious healing cases. James Childress notes that "two conditions . . . are frequently invoked to justify medical paternalism": "(1) the defects, encumbrances, and limitations of a person's decision-making and acting, and (2) the probability of harm to that person unless there is intervention."[113] Intervention premised solely upon condition (2), "probable harm," is strong paternalism. "According to this position, paternalistic interventions can be justified when a patient's risk-benefit analysis is unreasonable, even though he is competent and his wishes, choices, or actions are informed and voluntary."[114] Childress contends that the principle of respect for persons (the value of autonomy) requires the rejection of strong paternalism. Only a "limited" or weak paternalism, which requires proving the individual's incompetence before intervention can be allowed, is ethically justifiable.[115] *Both* of the above conditions are necessary to justify *active* paternalism, which is defined as intervention forced upon a patient against express wishes.

Active paternalism is indeed the issue in cases where the government seeks civil intervention to force medical treatment upon faith healing families. The government contends that the belief in and use of religious healing methods is prima facie proof of incompetence. To this, Childress asserts that

> While a person's false beliefs about some circumstances and means may support a finding of incompetence, such beliefs should be distinguished from beliefs about religious or metaphysical matters, which are not empirically verifiable. . . . However much such beliefs may be disputed, *they do not provide grounds for a finding of incompetence.*[116]

Note the assumption that religious matters are "empirically unverifiable." As previously discussed, Christian Scientists claim corroborated testimonies, as well as their own personal experiences, as rational proof that removes their spiritual healing practices from the realm of pure faith and mere metaphysics. Furthermore, a lapse into emotivist logic is likely if all matters within the category of "religious" are consigned automatically to the realm of the "empirically unverifiable." The actual context and particulars of the religious exercise are then too easily ignored, as the more-familiar scientific world view takes over the judgment process.

Courts, pursuant to ethical parameters governing active paternalism, have begun generally to not interfere with adults who remain outside of medical relationships for religious reasons and who refuse lifesaving medical treatment on religious grounds. Childress states the ethic as follows: "My claim is that competent persons . . . have the moral right and have, or should have, the legal right to refuse lifesaving medical treatment for whatever reasons they find appropriate."[117]

A major difficulty with applying medical ethics parameters of justifiable paternalism in spiritual healing cases arises when children become embroiled in the issue. For children, according to the medical paradigm, are assumed (indeed, conclusively presumed) to be incompetent. The very term "paternalism" invokes images of a father deciding on behalf of the child's best interests.[118] A casuistical analysis of this issue would proffer two responses to this.

First, a casuistical free exercise process would deny the state a conclusive presumption in favor of the child's incompetence in free exercise intervention cases. The precedents for respectfully considering the child's own wishes are found in the factors considered in child custody and care matters, as discussed above. Accordingly, neither religious beliefs nor minor age per se (at least above the age of seven) can accord a conclusive presumption of incompetence in order to meet condition (1). The state must bear the burden of proving incompetence. The natural temptation will be for the state to bootstrap a finding of incompetence upon its conflict with the mistaken decision to forgo medical treatment for religious healing methods. But, as Childress indicates, "the *content* of the decision is neither necessary nor sufficient to indicate incompetence, even if it rightly triggers an inquiry into incompetence. If this test were sufficient, it would support strong paternalism under the guise of weak paternalism."[119]

Second, a casuistical process would deny the government a conclusive presumption in favor of the values underlying its paternalism and concomitantly deny what amounts to a conclusive presumption that the values embodied in the religious way of life of the parents are not in the best interests of their children. As Childress notes:

> *Whose* values are relevant and decisive as we try to identify and balance harms and benefits? This question is not identical with the question, "who should make the decision?" Some paternalistic interventions impose *alien* values not accepted by the patient. [This is called "hard" paternalism, and it] overrides the patient's values in the name of other values. Rosemary Carter, who draws this distinction, identifies "hard" paternalists as "those who believe that the subject's conception of the good is irrelevant to determine whether or not to interfere."[120]

Childress cautions that the ranking of values is "itself a value, not reducible to its parts." Thus, Christian Scientists and allopathic medicine both value healing and good health, but the spiritual healing practice which forms an integral part of the daily life of a Christian Scientist is itself a value from which the value of healing is derived. Thus, it is "hard" paternalism, not "soft," when the state imposes allopathic treatment in the name of the shared value of health and healing. "Much paternalism is 'hard' because it imposes a hierarchy of values alien to the patient at that time. It overrides the patient's value-structure."[121]

For children under seven who are presumed incompetent, as well as those over seven who are found incompetent, what values and conditions should determine whether the state's active paternalism (civil intervention) is justified? Condition (2), "probability of harm unless there is intervention," as well as a third condition, "proportionality," should provide the guiding parameters. The second condition, "probability," encompasses both the magnitude of the risk and the probability of harm. In general, notes Childress, "where a harm such as death is irreversible, the paternalist has stronger reasons for intervening to prevent it than where harms are reversible."[122]

Proportionality, in turn, refers to the risk/benefit assessment that the "probable benefit of intervention" outweighs the "probable harm of non-intervention." Here, the pain, suffering, intrusiveness, riskiness, experimental nature, and physical and mental consequences of the involuntary medical treatment are seriously examined. Note that the probable benefits of involuntary hospitalization are reduced by the psychological trauma of forced hospitalization: "[A] patient's experience of pain and suffering as a result of involuntary hospitalization may outweigh the benefits of treatment."[123] In contrast, where the certainty of serious, irreversible harm to a child is great and the chance of a successful cure is high, the presumption of competence can be overridden in that child's case and intervention can be justified.[124] Great care must be taken, however, against the tendency of equating the "usual" medical treatment with what may be "obligatory" in that particular case. "Thus, no treatment as such is obligatory or optional; everything depends on the patient's condition. The only adequate grounds or standards can be found in the ratio of benefits and burdens of the treatment to the patient."[125]

Finally, one general condition applies to all paternalistic interventions: "[T]he least restrictive, humiliating, and insulting alternative should be employed." Using an analogy to civil commitment, Childress explains that, "[w]hile effectiveness is important, it should justify only those means absolutely necessary to prevent the harms or realize the benefits in question for the nonautonomous patient."[126]

In summary, a casuistical analysis is helpful in resolving the hard free exercise issue of whether civil intervention to impose medical care on the children of religious healing families is justifiable paternalism. Casuistry draws upon insights, analogies, and principles from other related fields, such as child custody laws and medical ethics, to offer principles and questions appropriate to a fair resolution of faith healing cases.

The insights in this chapter have not been offered as an excuse to provide blanket justification of any and all religious healing practices. A casuistical free exercise process does not replace one absolutist position with another. Rather, the purpose of this chapter is to add some necessary complexity to what courts and some commentators are considering an open-and-shut matter. These commentators, as well as some of the judges' opinions which have been previously examined, advocate an authoritarian process that disregards the context and fixates upon the tragic death of the child. Few allopathic physicians would survive such a process,[127] particularly if it was justified with emotion-laden language marked by fear, anger, and repugnance.

To some it might seem that the last thing this difficult area needs is further complexity and nuance. This chapter has proposed that when the actual excruciating character of the clash between religion and the government's notion of what medical treatment is best for a child is allowed to emerge in its full complexity, only then will justice most likely be done. Those—on either side—who wish to draw bright easy lines here can do so only, as did the California Supreme Court in *Walker*, with plugs and blindfolds to shield them from the dissonance of their actions. When the pendulum swings in either direction and one set of values completely eclipses the values at the other end, then the decisions become easier to make, but the justice and fairness of them diminish. The dead child becomes an icon for a societal crusade and the parents are made the subject of a social house-cleaning operation aimed at their beliefs and practices.

Any legislative, administrative, or judicial solution to the problem which society perceives is posed by religious-based healing practices must holistically address the religious framework in which the practices occur. Those who would make and enforce governmental policy in this area must be willing to understand and approach the issue from the viewpoint of the religious adherent, and they must be willing to examine their own assumptions and prejudices concerning the issue. Assumptions, for example, as to the infallibility and the beneficence of medical treatment seem endemic to this issue.

The metaphor of "balancing rights" can be misleading and unhelpful in resolving religious healing conflicts. Instead of the narrow confinement to balancing (with all of its present connotations of intuitiveness and subjectivity), I propose a broader, casuistical process of analysis which employs analogy, paradigms, contextual analysis, and presumptions. Such a casuistry could take as a positive paradigm the average caring, nurturing family as described in the "best interests of the child" regulatory criteria in child custody/care matters. A negative paradigm would be the quintessential child abuse and criminal neglect situation at common law, where the parent has evil intent to do harm or is so wantonly careless that she does not care what happens to the child. Unless the situation at issue matches the negative paradigm, the government should not seek criminal prosecutions.

If intervention is justified, the least restrictive and most effective alternative to follow, would be a course of civil interventions such as temporary, limited custody by the state solely for medical care, court ordering of medical care, or routine school screenings, etc. In such interventions, the courts must recognize that what the state is proposing is hard, strong, and active paternalism, justifiable only under the conditions of incompetence/encumbrance, probability of harm, proportionality, and least restrictive alternative. The court furthermore cannot conclusively presume that the proposed medical intervention is beneficent; the state must bear the burden of proof as to the conditions and factors justifying forced medical care.

Casuistical Free Exercise Jurisprudence

A Summary and Some Conclusions

The free exercise standard announced in the *Reynolds* case and reinvigorated in the *Smith* and *Boerne* cases has the advantage of clarity: When religiously compelled behavior violates the letter of a generally applicable law, the obligation under the statute always prevails over the religious obligation. Under this standard, however, the relative goods of clarity and certitude have eclipsed the ultimate good of justice. Kenneth Kirk notes that "unswerving rigidity . . . is bound to shipwreck upon the rocks of common sense."[1] Indeed, the inability or the failure to make principled distinctions between when a law is applicable and when in the interests of justice a competing principle or good should prevail will bring "the whole authority of the law into question, and shak[e] it to the foundation."[2]

I have proposed in this project that a casuistical free exercise jurisprudence, while not perfect, offers a fairer and more just alternative process for resolving the conflict of principles which lies at the heart of free exercise cases. To those who would reject casuistry as a new element, without precedent, and as an arbitrary choice without foundation or authority, I noted that casuistry is quintessentially the process used in common law decision making and hence neither foreign nor arbitrary. I also have offered the arguments in chapter 1, showing the actual (if not acknowledged) use of a casuistical process in deciding the free exercise cases of *Cantwell*, *Barnette*, *Jones II*, *Murdock*, *Sherbert*, and *Yoder* (and the process used effectively and persuasively in the dissenting opinions in the *Gobitis*, *Jones I*, *Prince*, and *Smith* cases).

In chapter 3, furthermore, I have offered a searching analysis of the Christian tradition on the issue of the authority of the state versus obligations of conscience. Four types or paradigms emerged: duly ordered relationships, two kingdoms, levitical, and enlightenment. I examined not only the principles but also the historical contexts in which those principles emerged and were applied. Neither the duly ordered relationships paradigm nor the levitical paradigm contributed to the political development of religious freedom. In fact, they are conspicuously present in periods when even religious tolerance (a concept far narrower than religious freedom) is politically at a low ebb. In contrast, the two kingdoms paradigm and the enlightenment paradigm not only fostered religious tolerance, but also actively contributed to the development of free exercise protections during the Founding Era. In both the enlightenment paradigm and the two kingdoms paradigm, conclusive presumptions are inappropriate: Neither the individual conscience nor the state automatically prevail. The governmental action is given a searching scrutiny to ensure that its application in the given instance is within the realm of its authority. Paradigmatically, the state has least (if any) authority over matters involving the "first tablet": when, where, and how to worship; infractions against the divine (no other gods, keeping Sabbath, etc.); and also, both by implication and by seventeenth-century English dissenter argument pursuant to the two kingdoms paradigm, the form and internal governance of God's church and the qualifications of its ministers. In contrast, the highest interest of the state in prohibiting actions compelled by religious obligation is protection of discrete persons and properties. The vague declaration of the "good" or the "safety" of the state, however, raises suspicions, and the state must meet a high burden of proof to sustain the prohibition.

The process of casuistry was explained in chapter 2. Casuistry is an analytical process that relies upon a nuanced and sensitive contextual analysis to give fair and in-depth consideration of all the competing goods and principles at stake. The successful use of casuistry to resolve free exercise conflicts must contend with two potential stumbling blocks which are endemic to the process: liberal assumptions of the self as an unencumbered moral agent (discussed in chapter 4) and societal boundary drawing during times of "ill humor" (discussed in chapter 5). Assumptions of the self as an unencumbered moral agent do not reflect the reality of the religious self encumbered by divine obligation and not free to choose. More problematic, however, is the role of the courts in protecting religious exercise in times of societal "ill humor." Such times truly test the court's willingness as well as its ability to apply a searching scrutiny to areas touched by societal paranoia. It is during these periods of panic that society enacts and enforces legislation that casts a net far wider than necessary, and neutral and even beneficial examples of the behavior are caught willy-nilly by that net. This is the way a democracy works, and in times of perceived crisis there will be unfortunate victims of overzealous law enforcement. But in instances where the proscribed behavior is religiously compelled, a vital and foundational competing good is at stake and a searching judicial scrutiny of the context of the situation is required. As explained in chapter 5 and illustrated by the examination of the particulars of the *Smith* case in chapter 6, religiously compelled behavior, when examined within its contextual framework, may prove to be neutral as to the harmful results anticipated by the legislation, or it indeed may foster and promote the good that society sought to protect and promote by the legislation.

Casuistry is not a perfect solution to any and all free exercise conflicts, and as seen in chapter 7 there are the truly hard cases where the results will be tragic whichever way the court moves. The fact that a case is hard, however, does not mean that the casuistical process is unhelpful or should be disregarded.

In the hard cases the court has an even greater obligation to the public to develop the facts and the context of the religious practice and to explain the competing principles and equities involved in the decision. The *perceptions* of authoritarian injustice or of an anarchical laxity are just as harmful to the integrity of the justice system as actual impropriety itself. Careful, detailed explanations and good communications are the main keys to avoiding misunderstandings and misinterpretations.

Another concern which must be directly addressed is the fear that understanding the contexts and motives of a religiously compelled action will necessarily and automatically compel a tolerance of it. This is simply not true. Casuistry is not fueled by compassion but by principles and paradigmatic examples illustrating those principles. For example, actions which harm the person or property of another are not to be protected as a matter of law under the free exercise paradigms. The Western tradition recognizing the duties of conscience and the good of religious freedom has not extended this recognition to include interference with the goods and person, and even the privileges of citizenship, of another. Thus, no matter how understandable an anthropologist can make the Aztec practice of human sacrifice of its enemies, such sacrifice is not a religiously compelled action that can ever be sanctioned or tolerated under the free exercise clause. Nor, for that matter, can damage to the property of another (such as damage to a Wiccan altar by those who consider it to be a place of satanic worship) ever be legally permitted in the name of one's religious obligation. Thus there are clear, definable paradigmatic limits to the free exercise right under a casuistical free exercise jurisprudence. The problem is not one of anarchy under the guise of compassionate understanding; rather, the problem is the court's ability to conduct a searching scrutiny with discernment and a willingness to make, explain, and justify the hard decisions to a fearful public and to a faithful "people of the wilderness."

Notes

Preface

1. Montana, for example, has a growing problem with anarchists who refuse to pay taxes and back up their refusal with powerful weapons arsenals.

> What some call paranoia, Greenup [a tax protestor upon whom the article focuses] calls patriotism. He's at the volatile fringe of a burgeoning movement that believes an armed citizenry is the only way to defend against a corrupt government. Militia groups have sprung up nationwide in the past year, boosted by the current anti-government fervor in politics. They train with guns, talk darkly of government conspiracies and prepare for the war they believe will be needed to keep Americans free from a tyrannical New World Order.

Associated Press, "Confrontations With Militias Spread," *Bloomington (Indiana) Herald-Times*, 25 March 1995, p. A7.

2. For example, a news release sent out by the American Center for Law and Justice (ACLJ) advises of a lawsuit they filed on behalf of a medical doctor who objected to a Jefferson County, Kentucky, ordinance which prohibits employment discrimination on account of sexual orientation. The doctor

> contends that his Biblically-based Christian beliefs prevent him from complying with the County's ordinance. The lawsuit contends that because of his sincerely held religious beliefs, Hyman [J. Barrett Hyman, M.D., the doctor/plaintiff] is compelled to deny employment and discharge from employment any person whom he learns is living a homosexual, bisexual, transgendered, or transsexual lifestyle. "This is a case of government attempting to legislate its own view of morality at the expense of the fundamental rights of its citizens," said Francis J. Manion, Senior Regional Counsel of the ACLJ-Midwest, who is representing Hyman in the suit. "We believe the ordinance is not only unlawful, but unconstitutional as well." . . .

> Manion said: "These so-called 'Fairness Ordinances' simply are not fair. These ordinances trample on an employer's constitutional right to the free exercise of

religion. It forces an employer to choose between following the dictates of his conscience and going out of business." . . .

Manion said: "There is a fundamental constitutionally-protected right to freely practice one's religion. The bottom line is that governments cannot be permitted to penalize the practice of Christianity by fining employers who simply want to run their businesses in accordance with their beliefs."

ACLJ News Release, "ACLJ Files Federal Lawsuit Challenging Sexual Orientation Ordinance in Jefferson Co. Kentucky" (Louisville, Ky., dated 23 November, 1999). Obtained at *www.aclj.org* under "News Releases."

3. See articles on FIJA and the activities of FIJA activists in: Todd R. Wallack, "Judges Hit 'Vote Conscience' Jurors," *Dayton Daily News*, 17 September 1994, news section, p. 1A; Tony Perry, "Jury-Power Advocate Runs Afoul of Judicial Clout," *Los Angeles Times*, 5 December 1993, sec. A, p. 3; Leslie Wolf, "Can Jury Void Law? Proponent Faces Jail," *San Diego Union-Tribune*, 6 December 1993, p. B-1; Dawn Weyrich Ceol, "Some Want Juries Told of Right To Nullify Laws," *Washington Times*, 23 November 1990, p. A1; Rene Lynch, "Reformers Want To Give Jurors a Freer Hand," *Los Angeles Times*, 7 September 1993, sec. B, p. 1; Bruce Vielmetti, "Group Urges Jurors To Vote Their Consciences," *St. Petersburg (Florida) Times*, 25 October 1993, business section, p. 9.

Law review articles have also addressed the issue of "jury nullification": Scheflin, "Jury Nullification: The Right to Say No," *California Law Review* 45 (1972): 168; Scott, "Jury Nullification: An Historical Perspective On a Modern Debate," *West Virginia Law Review* 91 (1989): 389. A prominent treatise on the history of the subject is Thomas A. Green, *Verdict According To Conscience: Perspectives On the English Criminal Trial Jury, 1200–1800* (Chicago: Univ. of Chicago Press, 1985).

4. Kenneth E. Kirk, *Conscience and Its Problems: An Introduction To Casuistry*, with an introduction by David H. Smith (Louisville, Ky.: Westminster John Knox Press, 1999; repr. London: Longmans, Green, 1927), 123.

5. Alasdair MacIntyre, *After Virtue*, 2d ed. (South Bend, Ind.: Univ. of Notre Dame Press, 1984), 26.

6. *Id.* at 31–32.

7. *Id.* at 34.

8. *Id.* at 34–35.

9. *Employment Div. v. Smith*, 494 U.S. 872, 890 (1990).

10. Henry S. Richardson, "Specifying Norms as a Way to Resolve Concrete Ethical Problems," *Philosophy and Public Affairs* 19 (1990): 279, 285.

11. *Id.* at 283.

12. In the series of decisions in the case of *Chandler v. James*, for example, Judge Ira DeMent declared unconstitutional a state statute which authorized school authorities to sanction prayer during school activities and school-related events. The court, more particularly, enjoined the public school officials of DeKalb County from encouraging and supporting Christian activity in the public schools, including such ongoing practices as the distribution of Bibles in the classrooms by the Gideons, student-led Christian prayer over school public address systems, Christian prayer over public address systems before athletic games, student-led Christian prayer at graduations, teacher selection of students to lead prayers in the classrooms, and even Bible readings by teachers in the classrooms.

Students had intervened in the case to defend an absolute free exercise right to school prayer, arguing "that the Free Exercise Clause negates the Establishment Clause." *Chandler v. James*, 985 F. Supp. 1068, 1077 n. 17 (M.D. Ala. 1997). The court rejected this position:

If the Free Exercise Clause protected all religious activity, it would not be possible to maintain a civil, pluralistic society. . . . [I]t is easy to see how the absolute protection of religious activity would quickly lead to an establishment of religion. If a school principal's religious beliefs commanded him or her to "save" others and taught him or her that other religions were false, he or she might consider it his or her religious duty to "establish" his or her religion in that particular school. [footnote omitted] And, if the Free Exercise Clause were an absolute, the principal would have a constitutional right to press his or her religious views on students through official school channels. Clearly, the Free Exercise Clause cannot be interpreted as an absolute mandate.

Chandler v. James, 958 F. Supp. 1550, 1555–56 (M.D. Ala. 1997). See also, *Chandler v. James*, 985 F. Supp. 1062 (M.D. Ala. 1997), 985 F. Supp. 1094 (M.D. Ala. 1997), and 180 F. 3d 1254 (11th Cir. 1999) (affirming unconstitutionality both facially and as applied, remanding on portions of the injunctive remedy). See also, William J. Murray, *Let Us Pray: A Plea for Prayer in Our Schools* (New York: William Morrow, 1995). Among other arguments, Murray defines the debate over school prayer as one of competing discomforts: the discomfort of minority faiths or nonbelievers at hearing prayer in school versus the discomfort of Protestant Christians at being prohibited from public prayer. The minority's discomfort, he argues, cannot override the Christian majority's right to religious expression and prayer in public places. Murray, *Let Us Pray*, 188–202. Champions of religious freedom such as John Leland (Virginia Baptist dissenter) and James Madison, however, never framed the issue in terms of competing "personal discomforts," but rather in terms of a solid, basic principle: a universal and inalienable freedom of worship, and the total lack of government power and authority over matters of worship.

13. For example, the defendants in *Chandler v. James* actively resisted the court's earlier judgment against them in the case and even questioned whether the federal judge had proper authority in a first amendment lawsuit:

[C]ertain educators wanted clarification on the question of whether "a federal judge has the authority to tell school officials and administrators in DeKalb County how to handle the issue of school prayer" and "if a federal judge can do whatever he wants to whenever he wants to." . . . Appended to the filing submitted by the DeKalb County Board of Education is a newspaper article titled, "Principal questions judge's authority in prayer lawsuit." Also appended to the filing is a Letter to the Editor over Principal Gary Carlisle's signature which makes plain that Mr. Carlisle believes that only elected officials, and not the judiciary, may traffic in the First Amendment's religion clauses.

985 F. Supp. At 1074.

Introduction

1. Similarly, the normative model of a civil case involving a statutory violation also is premised upon this basic set of assumptions: Did the behavior occur, and if so, what penalty should be assessed? Certainly, by this description of the normative, I do not mean to slight the importance of mental intent. As a practical matter, however, "criminal intent" has been equated with an intent simply to do the act, regardless of the religious motive.

2. Roderick Nash, *Wilderness and the American Mind* (New Haven, Conn.: Yale Univ. Press, 1967); Henry Nash Smith, *Virgin Land* (Cambridge, Mass.: Harvard Univ.

Press, 1978), ix–x.

3. Nash, *Wilderness*, 16.

4. *Id.* at 18.

5. *Id.* at 31–33.

6. *Id.* at 3.

7. *Id.* at 9.

8. Jonathan Z. Smith, *Map Is Not Territory* (Leiden, Netherlands: E. J. Brill, 1979), 109. Smith notes that the desert is called "the land not sown" in Jeremiah (2:2) and the place "in which there is no man" in the Book of Job.

9. Nash, *Wilderness*, 10–13.

10. *Id.* at 17–18.

11. Thomas Tweed, *The American Encounter with Buddhism, 1844–1912: Victorian Culture and the Limits of Dissent* (Bloomington: Indiana Univ. Press, 1992), 111–115, 96–97. Tweed's analysis can be extended to include one further aspect of core values and the commonalities between "insiders" and "outsiders": psychological/moral transference. To what extent does societal preoccupation with the (alleged) absence of a central value in an outsider religious group reflect a transference onto that group of a value defect that is (embarrassingly) lacking in the mainstream culture? My addition to Tweed's methodology is thus the question of whether a sore point necessarily indicates a core value *present* in the culture and *lacking* in the outsider group. Could society's outrage instead perhaps reflect transference of a cultural flaw, reflect a value which is maintained more in the breach and thus a value which critics perhaps do not want to acknowledge is lacking in the dominant culture? By accusing an outsider of such faults, we deflect recognition of the same phenomenon of failure in ourselves. Pointed criticism of an Other for such a fault serves as reassurance that "we" are not like "they." For example, Victorian Protestants criticized the absence of satisfactory amounts of "activism" in the Buddhist religion. Yet, I wonder if this activism was more of a concern because of its *lack* in mainstream Victorian American religion, rather than because this trait was a deeply ensconced *presence*. The picture of religious activism (social gospel, etc.) which Tweed paints of that time period does not confront other popular, yet opposing, phenomena and images of the Gilded Age: laissez-faire capitalism (supported by theological underpinnings), the Horatio Alger bootstrap myth, and the image of eager-to-please mainline clergy making God fit the needs of the middle and upper classes. Could it be that these clergy criticized Buddhism for a "fault" which, albeit unacknowledged, was actually endemic to their own religious practice?

12. This is not meant to limit the viability of the wilderness metaphor solely to that of a descriptive trope. I have elsewhere explored the facets of the wilderness myth which appeared, in all of the myth's ambiguity and polarity, as self-understandings and arguments during the heated polemics of the free exercise conflict over Mormon polygamy. Catharine Cookson, "Myths, Mormons and Moral Panics: A Critique of Governmental Processes and Attitudes in the Free Exercise Case of *Reynolds v. United States*," master's thesis, University of Virginia, 1992. This battle, which centered upon Mormons who made up the majority of the populace in the Utah Territory, erupted into a major national religio-political issue and produced the first interpretation of the free exercise clause by the U.S. Supreme Court, in the 1879 case of *Reynolds v. United States*. The *Reynolds* opinion will be explained and examined in depth later in chapter 1.

13. Paul Ricoeur, *Interpretation Theory: Discourse and the Surplus of Meaning* (Fort Worth: Texas Christian Univ. Press, 1976), 53, 60, 67; by this acknowledgment of debt to Ricoeur, however, I must note that I have not thereby signaled an intent to adopt the technical, precise rhetorical definitions and differentiations of the terms "symbol"

and "metaphor" which Ricoeur discusses therein. I have simply used those terms here interchangeably.

14. The terms "play" and what Gadamer describes as a "fusion of horizons" are concepts developed in Hans-Georg Gadamer, *Truth and Method*, 2d rev. ed. (New York: Crossroad, 1991), 101–10, 306–07, 374–75.

Chapter 1

1. Hereafter, the U.S. Supreme Court will be referred to simply as the "Court" (capitalized).

2. I use the terms "Other" and "Otherness" (capitalized) throughout the text in an anthropological, social scientific sense, denoting the radical sense of difference in the attitude of the dominant mainstream over against nondominant religious groups (i.e., "They" are not like "Us"). I do not use these capitalized terms in their theological sense, that is, to denote a Supreme Being or transcendent Other.

3. Reynolds v. United States, 98 U.S. 145 (1879).

4. Scholars may still be exploring and debating the human benefits and costs of nineteenth-century Mormon polygamy, but there is at least a consensus on the sincerity of the practice: Contrary to the prevailing public opinion of the time, polygamy was not engaged in by the Mormon people as a fraudulent pretext for evading the sexual norms of the time and engaging in a lustful, "perverted" lifestyle. Indeed, to the Mormon faithful of the nineteenth century, marriage, and particularly plural marriage, was a solemn and sacred religious obligation. The Mormons believed that the devout among them were commanded and ordained by God, under penalty of damnation, to enter into plural marriages, for the purpose of populating the highest level of heaven. See generally, Kathryn M. Daynes, "Plural Wives and the Nineteenth-century Mormon Marriage System: Manti, Utah, 1849–1910" (Ph.D. diss., Indiana University, 1991); Kimball Young, *Isn't One Wife Enough?* (New York: Holt, 1954); Leonard J. Arrington and Davis Bitton, *The Mormon Experience: A History of the Latter-Day Saints* (New York: Knopf, 1979), 185–205.

5. See, generally, Edwin B. Firmage and Richard C. Mangrum, *Zion in the Courts: A Legal History of the Church of Jesus Christ of Latter-day Saints, 1830–1900* (Urbana: Univ. of Illinois Press, 1988), 128–36, retracing the legislative history of the Morrill Anti-Polygamy Act of 1862.

6. Reynolds v. United States, 98 U.S. at 150.

7. *Id.* (emphasis added).

8. *Id.* Reynolds appealed the propriety of this charge, claiming that it was an attempt by the court to inflame the passions and prejudices of the jurors. The Supreme Court of the Territory of Utah (at this point "packed" with non-Mormon appointees), however, found that the language was "proper" and noted itself that

> the doctrine that polygamy is right having been shamelessly preached and proclaimed and practiced in this Territory from its first settlement to the present time, in defiance of the statute of the United States against crime, and especially, too, when we remember that this crime has a blighting and blasting influence upon the consciences of all whom it touches, as is everywhere witnessed throughout this Territory.

United States v. Reynolds, 1 Utah 319, 323 (1876).

Ironically, the Mormon "wilderness barbarians" described the home life of their families in the same terms of endearment as more "mainstream" Christians described theirs; family and childrearing had always been of vital importance to the Mormons. As noted by historians Arrington and Bitton:

> The minority of Mormons that practiced plural marriage was bound by the same injunctions that directed the monogamous families: Marriage was a blessing and a duty; children were to be welcomed in quantity (although no one expected unrestrained propagation); they were to be raised gently but firmly by parents who were obligated to teach them religious truths and train them for adult responsibilities; and the family unit was to be at once a school of experience, a haven of affection, and a foreshadowing of and preparation for eternal blessedness. To a large degree this was the standard ideology of family in the nineteenth century, but the Mormons saw it in their own religious framework. For them, the family has always been the basic unit for progress and joy in this life and in the life hereafter.

Arrington and Bitton, *The Mormon Experience*, 205, and see generally, 183–205. See also, for example, Edward W. Tullidge, *The Women of Mormondom* (New York: Tullidge and Crandall, 1877; repr., 1957); and Leonard J. Arrington, *Brigham Young: American Moses* (New York: Knopf, 1985), 313–21. Arrington and Bitton do describe the unique "heartache and suffering" which could attend a plural marriage relationship, but they additionally note the deep spiritual experiences and commitment which were an integral part of the arrangement, and they explain, as well, the practical advantages which accrued. See, generally, Arrington and Bitton, *The Mormon Experience*, chapter 10. They further have observed that while polygamous families experienced their share of trials, sorrows, and unhappiness due to the polygamous arrangement, certainly monogamous marriage "was not a perfect system guaranteeing bliss. . . . [P]olygamy worked about as well as monogamy. . . ." Arrington and Bitton, *The Mormon Experience*, 202–03. See also, Thomas G. Alexander and James B. Allen, *Mormons & Gentiles: A History of Salt Lake City* (Boulder: Pruett Publishing, 1984), 74–77. These pages review the status and lives of Mormon women in Salt Lake City, and they contain an assessment of polygamous marriages.

9. The case apparently had to be tried twice. The first conviction was overturned on appeal by the Supreme Court of the Territory of Utah in 1875 (at 1 Utah 226) because the grand jury panel which had indicted Reynolds was composed of twenty-three persons, whereas the statute required fifteen persons. The appeal from the second conviction is reported at 1 Utah 319 (1876).

10. Reynolds v. United States, 98 U.S. at 161.

11. *Id.* at 162. The two sources which the Court considered authoritative proof of the scope of "religion" protected by the free exercise clause were the Commonwealth of Virginia's statute on religious freedom, William Waller Hening, *The Statutes at Large* (1823), XII, 84–86, and a letter by Thomas Jefferson (author of the Virginia statute) to the Danbury Baptist Association which was dated January 1, 1802. Reynolds v. United States, 98 U.S. at 162–64.

12. Reynolds v. United States, 98 U.S. at 164.

13. *Id.*

14. *Id.*

15. *Id.*

16. *Id.* at 166.

17. See chapter 4 for a discussion of this issue in terms of Michael Sandel's distinction between freedom of choice and freedom of conscience.

18. Stephen M. Feldman argues that the right to religious freedom in this country

has only succeeded in further entrenching the dominant Protestant hegemony, at the expense of nondominant religious groups. Whatever minimal protections have been given to such minority groups, Feldman notes, have only come about when the interests of the out group have converged with the interests of the Christian majority. Stephen M. Feldman, *Please Don't Wish Me a Merry Christmas: A Critical History of the Separation of Church and State* (New York: New York Univ. Press, 1997).

19. *Reynolds v. United States*, 98 U.S. at 164.

20. *Id.* at 167.

21. Note that the logical course which the Court chose to take in order to reach its result in *Reynolds* was by no means preordained. Many Americans, including members of Congress, believed with the Mormons that the protection afforded individuals under the free exercise clause did extend to practices: Congress's efforts to place wording in the antipolygamy measures that specifically denied that polygamy was in any way a religious practice could reasonably be attributed to a belief that religious *practices* were indeed afforded some protection under the free exercise clause.

22. Sweeney v. Webb, 33 Tex. Civ. App. 324, 76 S.W. 766 (1903), writ denied, 77 S.W. 1135 (1904) (citations to the appellate opinion hereafter will be to 76 S.W.).

23. *Id.* at 770.

24. *Id.* Cf. Shapiro v. Lyle, 30 F.2d 971 (W.D. Wash. 1929), app. dismissed, 36 F.2d 1021. *Shapiro* was a Prohibition-era case noteworthy more for the insight given into the extent of governmental regulation of religious groups during Prohibition than for its actual narrow legal holding. Prohibition regulations limited each Jewish family to five gallons of wine each year; one had to prove membership in a congregation and have a legal permit in order to be entitled to receive the wine allotment. To the complaint that the National Prohibition Act unlawfully deprived Jews of the free exercise of religion because it limited their religious use of wine, the court had two interesting responses: 1. The free exercise clause is not a defense for "acts inimical to the peace and good order of society." Thus, one must accept whatever the law allots as in accordance with such good order. To justify this deferral, the court referred to "Thugs of India" who had religious beliefs in assassination, human sacrifices, and suttee by Hindu widows. 2. The court undertook *religious* arguments against the Jewish position:

> Unlimited use of wine was disapproved by prophets of old. See Isaiah 5:11; 28:1–8; Jeremiah 35:5–6. See also Numbers 6:3; Proverbs 20:1; 23:29–31; Judges 13:14; Hosea 4:11—Holy Scriptures.

30 F.2d at 973. Justice Scalia in the *Smith* case, discussed in chapter 6, warned of the horribleness of these types of theological embroilments. There is something deeply offensive about a judge telling religious congregations what their religious requirements "really" are. Justice Scalia's solution, however, was to preclude all discussion on the matter by deferring to the legislation.

25. An earlier case, Pierce v. Society of Sisters, 268 U.S. 510 (1925), upheld the right of parents to send their child to private schools, striking down a state statute that required all children to attend public schools. The basis of the holding, however, was not religious freedom (indeed, one of the appellants was a nonsectarian, private military academy), but the deprivation of the private schools' property rights and the parents' liberty rights to choose a school for their children, without due process of law. The Court found the statute unconstitutional because these private schools were "useful and meritorious" and the state offered no proof of an emergency which required them to close. Thus, the state had no rational reason related to a lawful purpose for the legislation.

26. As this manuscript was going into galleys, I obtained a copy of Shawn Francis Peters, *Judging Jehovah's Witnesses: Religious Persecution and the Dawn of the Rights Revolution* (Lawrence: Univ. Press of Kansas, 2000). This book gives a deeply contextualized account of the Jehovah's Witnesses' legal battles from their point of view. Peters brings the controversies to life with detailed stories from the 1940s era, based upon personal interviews of those involved as well as upon the historian's traditional archival sources.

27. Cantwell v. Connecticut, 310 U.S. 296 (1940).

28 The other charge was for soliciting money for religious causes without prior governmental approval and certification. The Court held that the power of the licensing official to determine whether a cause is religious, and to withhold a permit if he determines that it is not religious, is an improper exercise of censorship. The availability of a judicial remedy for any abuses in the system of licensing would not "save" this regulation, because the system is still one of previous restraint. *Id.* at 303–06.

29. *Id.* at 303.

30. *Id.* at 308.

31. Reynolds v. United States, 98 U.S. at 164.

32. Cantwell v. Connecticut, *supra*, 310 U.S. at 306, 307.

33. *Id.* at 307–08.

34. *Id.* at 311.

35. *Id.* at 309–10.

36. "The danger in these times from the coercive activities of those who in the delusion of racial or religious conceit would incite violence and breaches of the peace in order to deprive others of their equal right to the exercise of their liberties is emphasized by events familiar to all. These and other transgressions of those limits the states appropriately may punish." *Id.* at 310.

37. *Id.* at 311.

38. Minersville School District v. Gobitis, 310 U.S. 586 (1940).

39. *Id.* at 592, n.1. Two helpful, detailed resources on the background and context of the *Gobitis* case and other flag salute controversies of that period are David R. Manwaring, *Render Unto Caesar: The Flag Salute Controversy* (Chicago: Univ. of Chicago Press, 1962), and Leonard A. Stevens, *Salute! The Case of the Bible vs. The Flag* (New York: Coward, McCann & Goeghegan, 1973) (written at the advanced high school and introductory college level). Both of these texts are based upon first person interviews with participants in the controversies, as well as written primary source research. Manwaring's analysis of the *Gobitis* opinion is centered upon a narrow interpretation of Frankfurter's holding, keeping the case in its "proper perspective" as simply a due process case involving secular, general-purposed legislation. For a different appraisal of Frankfurter's analysis and motivations, see Richard Danzig, "How Questions Begot Answers in Felix Frankfurter's First Flag Salute Opinion," *The Supreme Court Review* 1977: 257–74.

As noted above (n.26), Shawn Francis Peters's book, *Judging Jehovah's Witnesses: Religious Persecution and the Dawn of the Rights Revolution*, is the latest work on this topic and includes an analysis of the works I've cited here.

40. Minersville School District v. Gobitis, 310 U.S. at 591.

41. *Id.* at 595. Richard Danzig explains Frankfurter's judicial restraint in the flag salute cases (*Gobitis* and *Barnette*) as arising from an inflated view of the state's interest.

On their face, the government actions questioned in *Gobitis* and *Schneider* [Schneider v. State, 308 U.S. 147 (1939)] prescribed flag saluting and proscribed littering. If judges and other observers saw larger issues at play it was through individual acts of inflation. The facts presented by these controversies were like flaccid balloons waiting to be pumped up by those who interested themselves in the matter. The size the cases would reach when full blown, the heights of abstraction to which they would be lifted, would be determined by the heat of the principles with which they were injected and by the energy and intensity with which Justices pumped them.

Danzig, *The Supreme Court Review* 1977, at 266.

By the term "inflation" Danzig also includes the use of differential focusing to frame the question or issue of the case in terms which would justify a particular outcome. When Frankfurter wished to exercise judicial restraint, the issue of the case was framed in terms of the existence of other remedies, whereas an exercise of judicial intervention would be justified by framing the issue in the case as one of individual rights. Danzig continues:

> Why was it that Frankfurter's questions were frequently loaded? I suggest that contemporary circumstances were very important factors in the case discussed here, and that it was at the point of question framing that these factors were most readily absorbed in the Justice's opinion. In general, I suggest, the technique of loading questions, whether by means of inflation or by differential focusing, permits simultaneous deference to two conflicting but greatly valued imperatives. It gives play to the judge's sense of what is right and necessary in the everyday world, while it preserves the purity of an opinion's legal logic. The judge refrains from smuggling things personal and expedient into the analysis. Instead, they are made part of the premise from which the analysis proceeds.

Id. at 259. Accordingly, Frankfurter's position in *Gobitis* cannot be understood without reference to his zealous concern over the European situation and the need to mobilize the American people for war (Harold Ickes at the time described Frankfurter as "not really rational these days on the European situation").

> [Frankfurter] seemed determined to make the *Gobitis* case—even if it was marginal to the war effort—an occasion for giving a clear signal to legislatures that their attempts to prepare the nation for war would not be hampered as efforts at dealing with past problems had been.

Id. at 266. As will be discussed in chapter 5, one of the major obstacles to a fair determination of a free exercise conflict is societal panic or paranoia which can, to use Danzig's term, "inflate" the context of a free exercise case to a height of abstraction that renders the actual case distorted, even unrecognizable. In chapter 6, I show how the "War on Drugs" obscured the issues and the context of the 1990 Supreme Court case of *Employment Div. v. Smith*.

42. The Court at that point was in retreat from the so-called *Lochner* doctrine, a doctrine under which the judicial power was used to overturn legislative enactments that were felt to encroach upon individual liberty to contract and upon property rights. Lochner v. New York, 198 U.S. 145 (1905). Under *Lochner*, such social reform legislation as minimum wage laws had been declared unconstitutional infringements on the liberty to contract. The *Lochner* doctrine was substantially eroded by 1937 (see West Coast Hotel v. Parrish, 300 U.S. 379 (1937)), but *Lochner* would not be specifically overruled until 1949 (in Lincoln Federal Union v. Northwestern Iron and Metal Co., 335 U.S. 525, 535 (1949)). See Laurence H. Tribe, *American Constitutional Law*, 2d ed. (Mineola, N.Y.: Foundation Press, 1988), 567–86.

As noted by Tribe, the *Lochner* era was characterized by a rigorous judicial scrutiny of "both the ends sought and the means employed in challenged legislation." *Id.* at 568.

Seen in this light, Frankfurter's opinion for the Court in *Gobitis* was an effort to maintain the deference to legislation that hallmarked the Court's break with the *Lochner* era.

43. Minersville v. Gobitis, 310 U.S. at 594.

44. *Id.* at 597–98, 596 (emphasis added). In the 1990 case of *Employment Div. v. Smith*, which will be discussed in detail below, Justice Scalia reiterates the notion that the courts are not competent to decide between competing goods in free exercise claims, citing to Justice Frankfurter's opinion in *Gobitis* for support, but without acknowledging that *Gobitis* was reversed in the *Barnette* case.

45. *Id.* at 597, 599.

46. In a contemporary (1942) analysis, William G. Fennell argues that the *Gobitis* opinions represent a case study of the important difference in approaches between the "liberal democratic jurist" (Frankfurter) and the "liberal constitutionalist jurist" (Justice Stone, dissenting opinion). Frankfurter places trust in the democratic process to correct "foolish legislation," and he only uses strict judicial scrutiny where the democratic process has been hindered in some way, such as interference with the right to vote, to assemble, to spread information. Justice Stone would extend judicial scrutiny to include legislation which interferes with the other enumerated rights protected in the first ten amendments, "especially legislation violating constitutional rights of national, religious, or racial minorities." Otherwise, Fennell notes, the message sent by the Court is that the popular majority has a free hand. The liberal democratic jurist "says in effect to the affected minority: 'Your remedy is at the next election. We will not hold this legislation unconstitutional, even though it comes within the prohibitions of the First Amendment. We will keep you free to assemble, to publish, and to speak; and if we do that you have no cause to complain.'" William G. Fennell, "The 'Reconstructed Court' and Religious Freedom: The Gobitis Case in Retrospect," *Contemporary Law Pamphlets* 1, no. 34 (1940): 3.

47. Minersville v. Gobitis, 310 U.S. at 604. (J. Stone, dissenting). He laid out the Court's obligations of "searching scrutiny" as follows:

> [W]here there are competing demands of the interests of government and of liberty under the Constitution, and where the performance of governmental functions is brought into conflict with specific constitutional restrictions, *there must*, when that is possible, *be reasonable accommodation between them so as to preserve the essentials of both* and that it is the function of courts to determine whether such accommodation is reasonably possible. In the cases [mentioned earlier in the opinion] the Court was of the opinion that there were ways enough to secure the legitimate state end without infringing the asserted immunity, or that the inconvenience caused by the inability to secure that end satisfactorily through other means, did not outweigh freedom of speech or religion.

Id. at 603 (emphasis added).

Precedent for distinguishing between economic legislation (requiring deference) and legislation which interferes with guarantees of procedural fairness or Bill of Rights protections (requiring searching scrutiny) was offered in the (now-famous) footnote four of the opinion in the case of *United States v. Carolene Products*, 304 U.S. 144, 152 (1938). For a defense of the historical legitimacy of the distinction drawn in footnote four, see William E. Nelson, "The Eighteenth Century Constitution As a Basis For Protecting Personal Liberty," in William E. Nelson and Robert C. Palmer, eds., *Liberty and Community: Constitution and Rights in the Early American Republic* (New York: Oceana Publications, 1987), 15–52.

48. Stevens, *Salute!* 41–42; Manwaring, *Render Unto Caesar,* 84.

49. West Virginia Board of Education v. Barnette, 319 U.S. 624 (1943). Justice Jackson, who wrote the opinion of the Court, was appointed to the bench in 1941, after the *Gobitis* opinion. Justices Douglas and Black wrote concurring opinions which explained their change of view since the *Gobitis* case. Justices Roberts and Reed dissented, voting to uphold the opinion expressed in *Gobitis.* Justice Frankfurter also dissented, writing a lengthy opinion defending his analysis in *Gobitis.*

50. *Id.* at 636.

51. *Id.* at 630.

52. *Id.* at 636, 631.

53. *Id.* at 642.

54. *Id.* at 642.

55. *Id.* at 639–40.

56. *Id.* at 638.

57. *Id.* at 639.

58. As noted earlier, the term "Other" (capitalized) is used throughout this book to describe an outsider group which seems to the dominant society to be radically different and radically deviant from the societal norm.

59. John E. Mulder and Marvin Comisky, "Jehovah's Witnesses Mold Constitutional Law," *Bill of Rights Review* 2 (1942): 262, 266 (note that the *Gobitis* opinion was announced on June 3, 1940, and the *Barnette* opinion was announced on June 14, 1943). The magazine references in the text quoted are as follows: *Life* [fn: Life, Aug. 12, 1940, pp. 20–21], *Time* [fn: "Witnesses In Trouble," Time, June 24, 1940, p. 54], *Christian Century* [fn: Christian Century, April 30, 1941, p. 581], and the *Nation* [fn: Southworth, The Nation, Aug. 10, 1940, pp. 110–12]. The article cites further narrative examples of police brutality and mob violence against the Witnesses. Manwaring undertakes a more formalized and statistical analysis of the violence, concluding in part:

> The persecution of Jehovah's Witnesses in the early 1940's was both substantial and serious. The record is a reflection of both the temper of the public during that period and that of the Witnesses. The peaks on the graphs would not have been so high, had not the Witnesses leaped forward so eagerly to be persecuted.

Manwaring, *Render Unto Caesar,* 185; see generally 163–86. His observation is echoed on a larger basis by R. Laurence Moore, who observes that a quintessential tendency among American religious groups is to cultivate the image of Outsiderhood, whether or not the self- perception is factually accurate. R. Laurence Moore, *Religious Outsiders and the Making of Americans* (New York: Oxford Univ. Press, 1986).

60. Manwaring, *Render Unto Caesar,* 187–93. However, Manwaring notes that three state courts refused to follow the *Gobitis* ruling.

61. *Id.* at 625–26.

62. The pledge they offered in lieu of a flag salute is as follows:

> I have pledged my unqualified allegiance and devotion to Jehovah . . . I respect the flag of the United States and acknowledge it as a symbol of freedom and justice to all. I pledge allegiance and obedience to all the laws of the United States that are consistent with God's law, as set forth in the Bible.

Id. at 628, fn 4. The Court further noted that concessions and resulting modifications were made to the resolution as a result of objections by the Girl and Boy Scouts, the Parent and Teacher's Associations, and the Federation of Women's Clubs. As noted, however, no accommodations were offered to the Jehovah's Witnesses. *Id.* at 627–28.

63. *Id.* at 626, fn 2.
64. *Id.* at 640–41.
65. *Id.* at 641.
66. Murdock v. Pennsylvania, 319 U.S. 105 (1943).
67. Jones v. City of Opelika, 316 U.S. 584 (1942) (hereafter, *Jones I*), reversed, 319 U.S. 103 (1943) (hereafter, *Jones II*).
68. *Jones I* at 606–07.
69. Murdock v. Pennsylvania, 319 U.S. at 107 n.2.
70. *Jones I*, 316 U.S. at 592–93.
71. *Id.* at 598.
72. *Id.* at 592.
73. *Id.* at 593.
74. *Id.* at 594.
75. *Id.* at 595.
76. *Id.* at 596.
77. *Id.* at 596.
78. *Id.* at 597–98.
79. *Id.* at 598.
80. *Jones II*, 319 U.S. at 119 (Reed, J., dissenting).
81. *Jones II*, 319 U.S. at 131–32 (Reed, J., dissenting).
82. *Id.* at 122 (Reed, J., dissenting) (emphasis added).
83. *Id.* at 132 (Reed, J., dissenting) (emphasis added).
84. *Id.* at 140 (Frankfurter, J., dissenting).
85. *Id.*
86. *Jones I*, 316 U.S. at 621 (Murphy, J., dissenting).
87. *Id.* at 608 (Stone, C.J., dissenting).
88. As Justice Frank Murphy noted in his dissent in *Jones I*:

Consideration of the taxes [as written, or "on its face"] leads to but one conclusion—that they prohibit or seriously hinder the distribution of petitioners' religious literature. The opinion of the Court [the majority in *Jones I*] admits that all the taxes are "substantial." The $25 quarterly tax of Casa Grande approaches prohibition. The 1940 population of that town was 1,545. With so few potential purchasers, it would take a gifted evangelist, indeed, in view of the antagonism generally encountered by Jehovah's Witnesses, to sell enough tracts at prices ranging from five to twenty-five cents to gross enough to pay the tax. . . . While the amount is actually lower [in the other towns, which also have larger populations] . . . these exactions also place a heavy hand on petitioners' activities. . . . There is the unfairness present in any system of flat fee taxation, bearing no relation to the ability to pay. And there is the cumulative burden of many such taxes throughout the municipalities of the land, as the number of recent cases involving such ordinances abundantly demonstrates.

Jones I, 316 U.S. at 615–18 (Murphy, J., dissenting).
89. *Id.* at 609 (Stone, C.J., dissenting).
90. Murdock v. Pennsylvania 319 U.S. at 113.
91. *Id.* at 111.
92. The nature of the Court's concerns in *Jones II* and *Murdock* can best be illustrated by contrast with the 1990 case of *Jimmy Swaggart Ministries v. Board of Equalization of California*, 439 U.S. 378 (1990). In *Swaggart*, the Court ruled unanimously that religious sales of books and merchandise can constitutionally be subject to generally

applicable sales and income taxes. While such taxes do decrease the amount of income ultimately available to the religious group to carry out its religious activities and mission, the tax is neither a precondition for the activity nor a burdensome "flat fee" imposed regardless of sales.

93. Murdock v. Pennsylvania 319 U.S. at 108–09 (footnotes omitted).

94. *Id.* at 115.

95. Prince v. Massachusetts, 321 U.S. 158 (1944). The adult guardian was in fact the child's aunt.

96. Commonwealth of Massachusetts v. Prince, 46 N.E.2d 755, 757–58 (Mass. 1943).

97. *Id.* at 758.

98. See Appellant's Brief at 18 (the child labor law was meant to prevent commercial exploitation of the child, which was not present in the case), at 23–25 (no proof of harm), *Prince v. Massachusetts* (No. 43-98); Brief On Behalf of the Appellee The Commonwealth of Massachusetts, at 5 (relying upon the state court's decision that the Jehovah's Witnesses "were not engaged in their way of worship and that there was no question of a practice of religion in issue"), 19–20 (state statute should be presumed to be valid and need not be narrowly drawn); Appellant's Reply Brief, at 6 ("The Commonwealth must establish from the particular facts of record an abuse of [parental prerogatives] by showing that some real, substantial and serious injury will be suffered by the child by permitting it to preach the gospel with appellant in the forum of the public streets. . . . The undisputed evidence fails to show any injury real or imaginary, present or future, that might come to the child").

99. Prince v. Massachusetts, 321 U.S. at 170.

100. The coalition put together to reach the outcome in *Prince* presented a dramatic departure from the previous Jehovah's Witnesses cases: Several justices who had previously sided with the Witnesses now voted to deny their free exercise claim, but the reasons set forth for their decision were rejected by the group of justices who had consistently voted against the Jehovah's Witnesses' claims. These justices joined in a separate concurring opinion written by Justice Jackson. But this concurrence in *Prince* is so oddly framed that the official reports of the U.S. Supreme Court made the unusual mistake of placing it *after* Justice Murphy's dissent, and thus out of the usual order.

Justice Jackson in that concurrence states that the difference between the group of justices who provided the "swing" vote against the Jehovah's Witnesses in this case (as represented by the opinion of Justice Rutledge), and the group who dissented consistently in the earlier cases of *Murdock* and *Jones II* and now concur in the *Prince* decision, is "the *method* of establishing limitations which of necessity bound religious freedom." *Id.* at 177 (Jackson, J., concurring in the result) (emphasis added). Justice Jackson describes the analytical method used by his group as follows: "I think the limits [on religious freedom] begin to operate whenever activities begin to affect or collide with the liberties of others or of the public (*Id.*). This framing of the limits on the right of free exercise is (as will be developed in chapter 3) within the paradigmatic conceptions of the relationship between individual conscience and the state. The relevance and applicability of this limit to the facts of the *Prince* case, however, is problematic. What exactly was the public liberty which was being affected by the Jehovah's Witnesses? The limit Justices Jackson and Frankfurter draw in the *Prince* case is a purely physical one: The Jehovah's Witnesses crossed the boundary into the chaotic, lawless wilderness when they failed to confine their activity to their own church and their own members. In this case, the public right which Justice Jackson protects is the right to not be solicited from a religious group other than one's own private church. Furthermore, the justices' definition of "limits" has the potential of according religious liberty a low priority, to the extent that it implies that the mere existence of a conflict of liberties should result in the automatic yielding of the religious adherent. There is no means, using the analytical method of Justice Jackson and Justice Frankfurter, for conducting a searching analysis of the conflicting goods at stake.

The problem is compounded by the telescopic, acontextual view of the religious action at issue. To the concurring justices, the evangelism of the Jehovah's Witnesses is a money-raising activity like "bingo" and "lotteries."

> All such money-raising activities on a public scale are, I think, Caesar's affairs and may be regulated by the state so long as it does not discriminate against one because he is doing them for a religious purpose, and the regulation is not arbitrary and capricious.

Id. at 178 (Jackson, J., concurring in the result). Because the justices considered the activity commercial, any regulation for any rational reason would be sustainable under the free exercise clause. This lax standard of review has also been referred to as the "demonstrable lunacy" test: One (in this case, the religious adherent) has the burden of demonstrating that there is no sane, rational reason whatsoever, no matter how tenuous, to support the regulation. This is the nature of the bright, hard line these justices would draw; it has the virtue of clarity, but nondominant religious groups have argued that the clarity comes at the price of justice.

101. *Id.* at 175 (Murphy, J., dissenting) (emphasis added). Justice Murphy furthermore notes the strong opposition the Jehovah's Witnesses have encountered in society and expresses the fear that the Court's ruling in this case will be another avenue of harassment of the sect:

> From ancient times to the present day, the ingenuity of man has known no limits in its ability to forge weapons of oppression for use against those who dare to express or practice unorthodox religious beliefs. And the Jehovah's Witnesses are living proof of the fact that even in this nation, conceived as it was in the ideals of freedom, the right to practice religion in unconventional ways is still far from secure. Theirs is a militant and unpopular faith, pursued with a fanatical zeal. They have suffered brutal beatings; their property has been destroyed; they have been harassed at every turn by the resurrection and enforcement of little used ordinances and statutes. [citation omitted] . . . We should therefore hesitate before approving the application of a statute that might be used as another instrument of oppression. Religious freedom is too sacred a right to be restricted or prohibited in any degree without convincing proof that a legitimate interest of the state is in grave danger.

Id. at 175–76 (Murphy, J., dissenting).

A short address given by Justice Murphy to the Alumni Association of the New York University Law School in March 1940 offers some insight into the concerns he brought to these cases involving free exercise conflicts:

> [The greatest danger to the American democracy] is the danger that lies dormant in the belief—so often sincere—that our national troubles are attributable to one group or another of the population. It is the danger born of the tendency to seek a scapegoat in a religious or racial or political or economic group. . . . We need to be reminded that when a people turn away from the reign of law, and equal justice under law, to a system of discrimination and persecution, it is not as if they merely discard a worn-out garment. They cast away, instead, the dearly-won gains of centuries of human struggle and anguish.

Frank Murphy, "Lawyers and the Reign of Freedom," *Contemporary Law Pamphlets* I, no. 30 (1940): 2–4.

102. Sherbert v. Verner, 374 U.S. 398 (1963).

103. *Id.* at 403, quoting NAACP v. Button, 371 U.S. 415, 438 (1963).

104. Sherbert v. Verner, 374 U.S. at 407–08 (citations omitted).

105. *Id.* at 404.

106. *Id.* at 406.

107. *Id.* at 407–08.

108. *Id.* at 401, quoting 240 S.C. 286, 303–04, 125 S.E.2d 737, 746.

109. *Id.* at 419 (Harlan, J., dissenting) (emphasis added).

110. *Id.* at 419–20 (Harlan, J., dissenting).

111. Cf. Aesop's fable of "The Dog in the Manger." A hungry dog menacingly keeps equally hungry cattle from eating the hay in a manger, under the rationale that if he, being hungry, couldn't eat the hay, no one else should eat it either. The dissent in *Sherbert* was based upon an equally curious equality principle. Since the single mother of three children could not collect unemployment due to personal reasons, no one else could, either. This ignores the special distinction accorded to religion in the First Amendment; the two situations were not constitutionally comparable.

112. Wisconsin v. Yoder, 406 U.S. 205 (1972).

113. *Id.* at 209–10.

114. *Id.* at 212–13.

115. *Id.* at 214.

116. *Id.* at 213–14.

117. *Id.* at 215.

118. See, for example, Henry S. Richardson, "Specifying Norms as a Way to Resolve Concrete Ethical Problems," *Philosophy and Public Affairs* 19 (1990): 279, 285, and Childress, "Moral Norms in Practical Ethical Reflection," in Lisa Sowle Cahill and James F. Childress, eds., *Christian Ethics: Problems and Prospects* (Cleveland: The Pilgrim Press, 1996), 213, wherein Childress notes that Richardson has "pressed the metaphor of balancing too far" into an abstraction, and that *practical* balancing incorporates discursive rationality in several ways.

119. Wisconsin v. Yoder, 406 U.S. at 219.

120. *Id.* at 219.

121. Recall that these arguments were relied upon by the Court in the *Reynolds, Gobitis,* and *Jones I* cases.

122. Wisconsin v. Yoder, 406 U.S. at 221.

123. *Id.* at 232.

124. *Id.* at 233–34.

125. Prince v. Massachusetts, 321 U.S. 158 (1944).

126. Wisconsin v. Yoder, 406 U.S. at 230.

127. *Id.* at 245, 245 n.2, 247 n.5 (Douglas, J., dissenting in part) (Douglas dissented to the extent that the views of the children on the matter of attending high school were not obtained or considered).

128. The Record on Appeal From the Superior Court, County of Plymouth, State of Massachusetts, *Prince v. Massachusetts,* 321 U.S. 158 (1944) (No. 43–98) (hereafter referred to as "Record") indicates that the trial court ruled: "I do not find that the cause of defendant's arrest was that they, the defendant and Betty M. Simmons [the child], were engaging in their way of worship. I do not so find. Worship in this case, religion in this case, Christianity in this case, are not the questions at issue." *Id.* at 9. The Record also reflects that the defense made several proffers of proof with respect to testimony that the trial

court deemed "irrelevant." The defense tried to introduce testimony from the child that she was "an ordained minister and as such to preach the gospel by the distribution of literature on the streets." Further proffers of proof noted that disallowed testimony would have shown: (1) "that according to this girl's conscience if she does not do this work she will be condemned to everlasting destruction at Armageddon, and she conscientiously and sincerely believes this"; (2) "that [the defendant guardian/aunt] obeys the commandment of God to preach the gospel from house to house, on the street, and it is her conception of her way of worship"; and (3) "that there is no profit and no commercial or pecuniary benefits in the work of Jehovah's Witnesses." *Id.* at 10–13.

The Record reflects that the sole reason the trial court excluded this testimony was that the court agreed with the state's position that the case did *not* involve the free exercise of religion: "I want to make it understood that the State does not care whether this girl is an ordained minister or not. The only position the Commonwealth takes is that she is a minor under 18 years of age." (*Id.* at 10–11, argument by state's prosecutor, Mr. Clark.)

129. Employment Div. v. Smith, 494 U.S. 872 (1990).

130. The case of *Employment Div. v. Smith* will be analyzed in great detail in chapter 6.

131. *Id.* at 883. Parenthetically, this is an odd statement given that *Smith* was an unemployment compensation case.

132. *Id.* at 892 *et seq.* (O'Connor, J., concurring).

133. *Id.* at 908 (Blackmun, J., dissenting).

134. Church of the Lukumi Babalu Aye, Inc. v. City of Hialeah, 508 U.S. 520 (1993).

135. *Id.* at 524.

136. The following did not join in Part II-A-2: Chief Justice William H. Rehnquist, Justice Antonin Scalia, Justice Clarence Thomas, Justice Byron White (as to all of Part II-A), Justice David Souter (as to all of Part II), Justices Harry Blackmun and Sandra O'Connor (concurring in result, only). Justice Blackmun, in a concurring opinion joined by Justice O'Connor, would have applied the compelling state interest test which a majority in *Smith* had rejected in favor of a "neutrality and general applicability" standard. Souter's concurring opinion criticized the "neutrality" standard employed by Kennedy to the extent that it meant "formal" neutrality, which would only prohibit a law that is designed (either literally as written or by its purposes) to discriminate against religion. He argued instead that free exercise protections also require "substantive neutrality," that is, laws must also be neutral in their *effects* upon religion. 508 U.S. at 560–62 (Souter, J., concurring in part and concurring in judgment) (citing to, Douglas Laycock, "Formal, Substantive, and Disaggregated Neutrality Toward Religion," *DePaul Law Review* 39 (1990): 993).

137. Church of the Lukumi Babalu Aye, Inc. v. City of Hialeah, 508 U.S. at 540.

138. *Id.* at 540–42.

139. Douglas Laycock asserts that Justice Kennedy would confine free exercise protection to cases in which "bad motive" is proven, a standard that would be supremely difficult to meet and would severely further narrow the *Smith* standard. Laycock notes that Justice Kennedy also wrote the opinion of the Court in *City of Boerne v. Flores* (discussed below), in which Kennedy "used the phrase 'religious bigotry' as a shorthand for what *Smith* required. . . . [T]his is not an accurate summary of *Smith*." Douglas Laycock, "Conceptual Gulfs in *City of Boerne v. Flores*," *William and Mary Law Review* 39 (1998): 743, 779.

On the other hand, I read Part II-A more optimistically (or perhaps more naively?) as a step toward a more casuistical analysis of free exercise conflicts, and away from a formal neutrality which looks only to the words of the statute itself. Kennedy writes that "mere compliance with the requirement of facial neutrality" is *not* determinative. Getting behind the neutral facade to discover a discriminatory purpose, as Kennedy does in Part II-

A-2, is another step toward answering the general contextual question, "What is going on here?" While it could be interpreted (and Kennedy may indeed mean it) as creating a *standard* to be met (religious bigotry, as Laycock argues), the inquiry into legislative purpose can also be interpreted as simply a process, an additional series of inquiries (beyond the wording of the law itself) aimed at understanding the core concern and paradigmatic harm that led to the law. If bigotry is not found, the case is then not necessarily and automatically over: Other key tools, such as paradigmatic illustrations, analogies, and so on, can also be used to establish the appropriateness of bridging the garden and the wilderness, as reflected in cases going back to *Cantwell*.

140. Church of the Lukumi Babalu Aye, Inc. v. City of Hialeah, 508 U.S. at 526–27.

141. *Id.* at 544, 545 (citations and brackets omitted).

142. *Id.* at 529–30.

143. Justice Blackmun, for example, notes that the result of the case "does not necessarily reflect this Court's views of the strength of a State's interest in preventing cruelty to animals." "A harder case," he writes, "would be presented if petitioners were requesting an exemption from a generally applicable anticruelty law." *Id.* at 580 (Blackmun, J., concurring).

144. Laycock, "Conceptual Gulfs," 778.

145. The Religious Freedom Restoration Act of 1993, Pub. L. No. 103–141, 107 Stat. 1488, codified at 42 U.S.C. Section 2000obb.

146. U.S. Congress, House of Representatives, Committee on the Judiciary, *Religious Freedom Restoration Act: Report 103–88*, 103d Cong., 1st Sess., 11 May 1993, 1.

147. *Id.* at 3, n.4.

148. The details of the *Smith* case will be analyzed in chapter 6. As to the problems with Justice O'Connor's use of the compelling state interest test, see Sanford Levinson, "Identifying the Compelling State Interest: On 'Due Process of Lawmaking' and the Professional Responsibility of the Public Lawyer," *Hastings Law Journal* 45 (1994): 1035.

149. *Boerne v. Flores*, 117 S.Ct. 2517 (1997).

150. Tracy Levy, "Rediscovering Rights: State Courts Reconsider the Free Exercise Clauses of Their Own Constitutions in the Wake of *Employment Division v. Smith*," *Temple Law Review* 67 (1994): 1017–50.

Chapter 2

1. Kenneth E. Kirk, *Conscience and Its Problems: An Introduction To Casuistry*, with an Introduction by David H. Smith (Louisville, Ky.: Westminster John Knox Press, 1999, repr. London: Longmans, Green, 1927), 125.

2. *Id.* at 128.

3. *Id.* at 123. Indeed, Kirk offers the following admonition to those who espouse the virtues of rigorism and absolutism:

> With them [the "high principled"] it is often a matter of conscience to maintain the rigor of the law at all costs; they adhere obstinately to the parrot-cry (— the "slogan," in the pet phrase of modern journalism—) of the original definition. Like Austin Feverel, every rigorist is "morally superstitious"; he makes of his "system of aphorisms" a fetish whose cult he dare not mitigate.

Id.

4. As noted in the preface, at the heart of emotivism is the belief that all discourse concerning values and principles is premised simply upon personal preference and opinion. Differences are incommensurable. Thus, in deciding a conflict of principles or val-

ues, the Court is only competent to review the legal procedures, that is, were the proper legal rules of procedure followed? If so, the Court's inquiry must end. The objective, content-less neutrality of valid legal procedural processes (including the democratic process and the legislative process, as well as the judicial process), is deemed sufficient to legitimize the substantive law.

5. Kirk, *Conscience and Its Problems*, 191–92.

6. Other helpful works explaining and developing casuistry as an analytical process are: Albert R. Jonsen and Stephen Toulmin, *The Abuse of Casuistry: A History of Moral Reasoning* (Berkeley: Univ. of California Press, 1988); John D. Arras, "Principles and Particularity: The Role of Cases in Bioethics," *Indiana Law Review* 69 (1994): 983 (published as part of "Symposium: Emerging Paradigms in Bioethics"); Richard B. Miller, "Narrative and Casuistry: A Response to John Arras," *id.* at 1015; Richard B. Miller, *Casuistry and Modern Ethics: A Poetics of Practical Reasoning* (Chicago: Univ. of Chicago Press, 1996). James F. Childress notes the widespread use of a casuistical type of process in resolving ethical issues (a process, that is, that eschews absolutist principalism), in Childress, "Moral Norms in Practical Ethical Reflection," in Lisa Sowle Cahill and James F. Childress, eds., *Christian Ethics: Problems and Prospects* (Cleveland: The Pilgrim Press, 1996), 196.

7. For example, the same car accident under icy road conditions may be judged under very different tort law precedents depending on the quality of the actions or state of mind of the driver: Was the driver speeding recklessly, was the driver drunk, was the driver proceeding slowly and carefully, or was the driver momentarily negligently distracted as she adjusted the radio? In each case, the mere fact of a car accident does not absolutely indicate liability, regardless of the context. Such absoluteness indeed would enjoy the advantage of clarity and certainty, but it would violate most people's sense of justice. Here, the facts and context do matter, for all of these drivers are intuitively not considered equally culpable for the accident.

8. Jonsen and Toulmin, *The Abuse of Casuistry*, 36 *et seq.*

9. See, for example, Aristotle, *The Nicomachean Ethics*, trans. David Ross (New York: World's Classics, Oxford Univ. Press, 1980), book V.5: "[T]he just action is intermediate between acting unjustly and being unjustly treated . . . proportion may be violated in either direction. In the unjust act to have too little is to be unjustly treated; to have too much is to act unjustly." *Id.* at 121–22.

10. For example, at the very beginning of the *Nicomachean Ethics*, Aristotle explains:

> Now fine and just actions, which political science investigates, exhibit much variety and fluctuation, so that they may be thought to exist only by convention, and not by nature. And goods exhibit a similar fluctuation because they bring harm to many people; for before now men have been undone by reason of their wealth, and others by their courage. We must be content, then, in speaking of such subjects and with such premises to indicate the truth roughly and in outline, and in speaking about things which are only for the most part true, and with premises of the same kind, to reach conclusions that are no better. In the same spirit, therefore, should each type of statement be received; for it is the mark of the educated man to look for precision in each class of things just so far as the nature of the subject admits; it is evidently equally foolish to accept probable reasoning from a mathematician and to demand from a rhetorician demonstrative proofs.

Id. at book I.3, 3.

11. John D. Arras, "Getting Down to Cases: The Revival of Casuistry in Bioethics," *Journal of Medicine and Philosophy* 16 (1991): 29, 31.

12. As Kirk notes: "[T]here are very few moral principles which human language can express at once so absolutely and exactly that no possible exception to them can be imagined." Kirk, *Conscience and Its Problems*, 211. For all of their rigorous attempts to eschew the perceived laxity of the Catholic moral framework, Reformation ethicists also sought to escape the problems inherent when an absolutist moral stance clashes with "the particulars," and they used competing paradigms or moral examples from the Bible to mitigate the harsh results of the application of a moral absolute.

One method by which Luther reconciled a moral absolute, "Thou shalt not kill," with practical contingencies presented by competing goods, was to separate the ethics of civil government from the moral world of the private person. Luther borrowed this tactic from Augustine, who sanctioned as a civic good the government's taking of human life for the punishment of evil, protection of the peace, etc. Indeed, Luther deems it a "Christian act" to "kill, rob, and pillage the enemy" when one's country is in peril. (Martin Luther, "Secular Authority: To What Extent It Should Be Obeyed," in *Martin Luther: Selections From His Writings*, edited and with an introduction by John Dillenberger (New York: Doubleday, 1961), 398.

While Calvin asserts an all-or-nothing ethic which insists that there is no gradation of sinfulness and that there is no distinction between mortal and venial sin, Calvin's ethic also takes into account "the particulars." One vehicle used by Calvin to relax an otherwise strict biblical admonition is the use of *intention* and motive to permit something that would otherwise have been banned (also reminiscent of Augustine and Aquinas). For example, despite St. Paul's prohibition on suits before a court, Calvin reasons that a Christian is permitted to engage in a lawsuit *if* done without bitterness, hate, or any other passion of harm or revenge. If done to seek what is fair and good, lawsuits are permissible. John Calvin, *Institutes of the Christian Religion* (Philadelphia: Westminster Press, 1960), 1506 (book IV, chapter XX, section 18).

Yet another way Calvin evades the harshness of a biblical absolute under compelling circumstances is to use the interpretive principle *in pari materia*. In justifying rebellion against evil rulers, Calvin begins with the interpretive move that the rule, "Vengeance is mine saith the Lord," does not forbid the civil imposition of a death penalty because the magistrate or the prince acts as the sword of God. Hence, the biblical commands, that one owes obedience even to bad kings and that a wicked king is to be endured and obeyed as a judgment upon the people from God, can be reinterpreted in light of the previous notion of a human person acting in the role of the sword of God. In this case, however, the sword is directed back against the evil ruler. God, notes Calvin, "raises up open avengers from among his servants and arms them with his command to punish the wicked government and deliver his people, oppressed in unjust ways. . . ." Calvin, *Institutes* at 1517 (book IV, chapter XX, section 30).

13. Jonsen and Toulmin, *The Abuse of Casuistry*, 257.

14. *Id.* at 253–54.

15. Richard Weisberg similarly argues in the legal arena for the use of "poethics." "Poethics, in its attention to legal communication and to the plight of those who are 'other,' seeks to revitalize the ethical component of law." Narrative, Weisberg argues, can contribute to jurisprudence a much-needed "sensitivity to the needs of the disempowered." Classic literature dealing with legal themes reveals "the tendency of those in authority to avoid seeing those who are 'other.'" These narratives challenge the law to "recognize that each person deserves the caring, fully-involved look that seeks to include, not dismiss." Weisberg distills three lessons that narrative teaches about justice:

1. The law cannot *do* justice without fathoming the inner worlds, aspirations, and values of those who are different from itself;
2. The law cannot *speak* justice unless its practitioners continuously scrutinize their *own* values to strive for what is most fair and least hostile in them;
3. The striving for justice can finally be accomplished only through an act of communication with an audience whose own prejudices and values must be engaged, without sacrificing or even compromising the speaker's informed sense of fairness.

Richard Weisberg, *Poethics and Other Strategies of Law and Literature* (New York: Columbia Univ. Press, 1992), 46, 41, 45 (emphasis in original).

16. Kirk, *Conscience and Its Problems*, 107.
17. Jonsen and Toulmin, *The Abuse of Casuistry*, 35 (emphasis added).
18. *Id.* at 254.
19. *Id.* at 318.
20. Miller, *Casuistry and Modern Ethics*, 4, as well as discussions at 25–26.
21. *Black's Law Dictionary* (6th ed. 1990), s.v. "Presumption."
22. "A conclusive presumption, called also an 'absolute' or 'irrebuttable' presumption, is a rule of law determining the quantity of evidence requisite for the support of a particular averment which is not permitted to be overcome by any proof that the fact is otherwise. [citations omitted] It is an inference which the court will draw from the proof, which no evidence, however strong, will be permitted to overturn." *Black's Law Dictionary* (rev. 4th ed. 1968), s.v. "Presumption. Of Law."

A rebuttable presumption, in turn, is one "that can be overturned upon the showing of sufficient proof. In general, all presumptions other than conclusive presumptions are rebuttable presumptions. Once evidence tending to rebut the presumption is introduced, the force of the presumption is entirely dissipated. . . ." *Black's Law Dictionary* (6th ed. 1990), s.v. "Presumption. *Rebuttable presumption.*"

23. See the discussion in chapter 3 of types and paradigms most appropriate to a free exercise jurisprudence.
24. *McCormick's Handbook of the Law of Evidence*, 2d ed., Edward W. Cleary, gen. ed. (St. Paul: West Publishing Co., 1972), 826 (section 345).
25. *Id.* at 783–84 (section 336).
26. *Id.* at 827 (section 345).
27. I understand that the centrality requirement has the potential of raising a messy issue. Certainly, in all religions there are innumerable splinter groups whose practices and beliefs will differ from the main body of adherents. But, for example, even if there was a splinter Santeria group that had abandoned the practice of animal sacrifice, this should not serve as "proof" that animal sacrifice is not central to the Church of the Lukumi Babalu Aye. What the religious adherent must prove under the centrality requirement is simply what the church did in the *Lukumi* case: explain its core religious tenets and show how the practice is *vital* to the religion. Cross-examination would only test the internal truthfulness, coherence, and consistency of the claim of centrality. I maintain that centrality is a necessary requirement to limit an otherwise litigious and anarchic group from making the proverbial federal case out of every trivial regulatory imposition.
28. Jonsen and Toulmin, *The Abuse of Casuistry*, 257.
29. Albert R. Jonsen, "The Confessor as Experienced Physician," in Paul F. Camenisch, ed., *Religious Methods and Resources in Bioethics* (Dordrecht: Kluwer Academic Publishers, 1994), 169.

30. The crux of Pascal's famous polemic against the Jesuit casuists, for example, was that the ethical system which they advanced was essentially unprincipled, offering "something for everyone." Blaise Pascal, *The Provincial Letters*, trans. and introduction by A. J. Krailsheimer (London: Penguin Books, 1967), 76. Human need and a misplaced kindness drove their theories, and not the laws of God. "[T]hey cloak their human politic prudence under the pretext of divine Christian prudence; as if the faith, and the tradition which maintains it, were not always one and immutable in all times and in all places. . . ." *Id.* at 77. Indeed, Pascal charged that the Jesuit casuist's only guiding principles were accommodating the sinner and the "changing times." *Id.* at 182. The examples which brought down the credibility of casuists were apparently accurately stated but taken out of context and certainly not representative. Regardless, however, of the overall fairness of Pascal's portrayal of casuistry, the examples which he uses as rhetorical weapons do appear morally outrageous, such as justifying as "self-defense" the killing of a person who has merely slapped another, for example.

31. Aristotle, *Nicomachean Ethics*, 133 (book V.10).

32. As noted, free exercise cases are conflicts between competing principles. To characterize a decision in favor of the principle of free exercise as a mere "exemption" from a law is misleading. But even if the tag "exemption" is applied, there is strong legal precedent in many other areas for exceptions in various situations. And the potential for abuse of exemptions and defenses is inherent in every legal interpretation and in every defense or exception (premised upon a competing "good") built into a rule. To this day, lawyers debate the ethics of advising clients on the law, including the particulars of any and all defenses, prior to having the client commit to a version of the events. The fear is that the informed client may favorably alter the story once the legal ramifications become better known. Certainly an "exception" driven by a competing principle, such as self-defense, is open to misuse, but that does not mean that the law should (or could, as a matter of justice) do away with the defense.

33. One example of such explanation is the emphasis in the *Yoder* opinion on several limiting aspects of the Amish situation:

1. the inseparability of the Amish religious faith and their mode of living (i.e., secular, "philosophical" considerations are not protected);
2. the objective, severe, and inescapable impact which the law would have on the Amish religion;
3. the imposition of the legal requirement would mean that the state, and not the parent, would determine the religious future of the child.

Given these facts and circumstances, not only was the exemption clearly explained and defended to the rest of the public who are still bound by the law, but also the hurdles to be met by those who would seek to be exempted were clearly spelled out. The facts of this case create a paradigm by which future claims for exemptions may be assessed, hence limiting any "slippery slope" which might undermine the state's authority over education requirements.

Mary Ann Glendon similarly laments the impoverishment of discourse. She notes that "[u]nfortunately, American political discourse has become vacuous, hard-edged, and inflexible just when it is called upon to encompass . . . problems of unparalleled difficulty and complexity." Mary Ann Glendon, *Rights Talk* (New York: Free Press, 1991), 172. In contrast, Glendon posits several exemplars including the "uncelebrated majority of American judges" who

are engaged in a kind of work that is characterized by careful distinction and discerning accommodation. Practical reason, not abstract theorizing, dominates the day-to-day activity of the typical American judge. Year in and year out, she weaves back and forth between facts and law, the parts and the whole, the situation at hand and similar situations that have arisen in the past or are likely to arise in the future. She attends carefully to context, she explores analogies and distinctions, the scope and the limits of generalizing principles. She recognizes that neither side has a monopoly on truth and justice. She is neither a mere technician nor a tyrant, but something between an artist and an artisan, practicing what the Romans called the "art of the good and equitable."

Id. at 175–76. Although this description seems more like an ideal than the norm, Glendon has in effect described the quintessential casuist.

34. Arras, "Getting Down to Cases," 41 (emphasis in the original).

Chapter 3

1. H. Richard Niebuhr, *Christ and Culture* (New York: Harper & Row, 1951; repr. Harper Torchbook, 1975), 44.

2. For a detailed history of religious freedom in the West, see Henry Kamen, *The Rise of Toleration* (New York: World University Library, 1967), and Leo Pfeffer, *Church State and Freedom*, rev. ed. (Boston: Beacon Press, 1967). Another basic introduction to Christian thought on the separation of church and state (from biblical writings to Pat Robertson) for the general reader is William M. Ramsay, *The Wall of Separation: A Primer on Church and State* (Louisville: Westminster/John Knox Press, 1989).

3. With respect to the levitical worldview, Mary Douglas notes that "this is a universe in which men prosper by conforming to holiness and perish when they deviate from it." "Holiness" is order, a "matter of separating that which should be separated." It is "unity, integrity, perfection of the individual and of the kind." Mary Douglas, *Purity and Danger: An Analysis of the Concepts of Pollution and Taboo* (New York: ARK Paperbacks, 1984; repr. New York: Routledge & Kegan Paul, 1966), 50, 53, 55, and chapter 3, passim. To translate this into the parlance of the levitical type, tolerance mixes what should be separate and hence violates the order of the state. Any such mixing of religions, doctrines, worship, etc., produces a state of unholiness or contamination, which in turn invites punishment (one perishes for deviation).

4. Also Mark 12:17; Luke 20:25.

5. See also John 6:15 (RSV) (Jesus resists efforts by the crowd to make him king). "If you were of the world, the world would love its own; but because you are not of the world, but I chose you out of the world, therefore the world hates you" (John 15:19 (RSV)). "I have given them thy word; and the world has hated them because they are not of the world, even as I am not of the world" (John 17:14 (RSV)).

6. Matt. 13:24–30 (RSV). A few lines later, Jesus explains this parable to his apostles:

He who sows the good seed is the Son of man; the field is the world, and the good seed means the sons of the kingdom; the weeds are the sons of the evil one, and the enemy who sowed them is the devil; the harvest is the close of the age, and the reapers are angels. Just as the weeds are gathered and burned with fire, so will it be at the close of the age. The Son of man will send his angels, and they will gather out of his kingdom all causes of sin and evildoers, and throw them into the furnace of fire; there men will weep and gnash their teeth.

Then the righteous will shine like the sun in the kingdom of their Father. He
who has ears, let him hear.

Matt. 13:37–43 (RSV).

7. G. E. M. de Ste. Croix, "Why Were Early Christians Persecuted?" *Past and Present* 26 (Nov. 1963): 6–38. (My thanks to Craig Wansink for bringing this article to my attention.) The Roman religion was considered the foundation of the state, "an essential part of the whole Roman way of life."

8. Tertullian, *The Apology* (ch. 39), quoted from *The Ante-Nicene Fathers*, vol. 3, ed. Alexander Roberts and James Donaldson (n.d.; repr., Grand Rapids, Mich.: Wm. B. Eerdmans, 1989), 47 (emphasis added) [hereafter referred to as "Tertullian" with the particular title of the individual treatise within volume 3 noted].

9. Tertullian, *Apology*, 43. A text illustrating this priority of conscience is the reply of Peter and the apostles, who continued to preach in the name of Jesus despite being ordered not to: "We must obey God rather than men." Tertullian explained the seemingly contradictory notion that earthly laws and rulers are of God's appointment, and yet laws could be made which are not to be obeyed because of a higher law, as follows: "If your law has gone wrong, it is of human origin, I think; it has not fallen from heaven." *Id.* at 21.

10. *Id.* at 42.

11. *Id.* at 51.

12. *Id.* at 49.

13. According to Paul, for example, Christians are to maintain the strictest of boundaries against fallen "insiders" while recognizing that Christians still must live in the world. Concomitantly, judgment of "outsiders" was not their concern, but, rather, a matter left to God.

> It is actually reported that there is immorality among you. . . . Let him who
> has done this be removed from among you. . . . I wrote you in my letter not
> to associate with immoral men; not at all meaning the immoral of this world, or
> the greedy and robbers, or idolaters, since then you would need to go out of the
> world. But rather I wrote to you not to associate with anyone who bears the
> name of brother if he is guilty of immorality of greed, or is an idolater, reviler,
> drunkard, or robber—not even to eat with such a one. For what have I to do
> with judging outsiders? Is it not those inside the church whom you are to
> judge? God judges those outside. "Drive out the wicked person from among
> you."

1 Corinthians 5:1–2, 9–13 (RSV). In summary, purity of association is a matter of congregational, not civil, enforcement.

14. "In truth, we are not able to give alms both to your human and your heavenly mendicants; nor do we think that we are required to give any but to those who ask for it. Let Jupiter then hold out his hand and get. . . ." Tertullian, *Apology*, 49.

15. Tertullian, *On Idolatry*, 67 (emphasis in original).

16. Locke's definition of "civil privileges due all citizens" included buying and selling, living by a calling, and so on. Tertullian calls for a voluntary restraint of the exercise of some of these privileges of citizenship by Christians where the pall of sin and contagion threatened Christian soul. Tertullian's list of forbidden trades is quite extensive: schoolmasters and all other professors of literature (because of the appearance of commending the gods to the students, and of the necessity of consecrating some part of one's salary to Minerva); any art which makes a "similitude" of any things which are in the

heaven, on earth, or in the sea (i.e., only decorative abstracts/patterns can be the subject of art); no trades which participate in the building or adornment of temples; the (then-considered) science of astrology; any public office (unless that office was in no way connected with taking an oath, temple sacrifice or maintenance, public festivals, killing/capital punishment, etc.—which Tertullian indicates is not likely); and observance of festivals and days connected with idolatry. *Id.* at 61–76, passim.

In the modern parlance of religious freedom, the early Christians' problem of false worship or idolatry required of schoolmasters and public officials, as well as the problem of state-sponsored idolatry as a part of public gatherings and festivals, would be obviated by the establishment clause principle separating church and state. The arena of commerce and "callings," however, is still seen by some as presenting threats to souls, and Tertullian's call for self-selective withdrawal is instructive here. Individual claims to free exercise protection for a religiously compelled action that tends to limit another citizen's participation in an endeavor that is otherwise generally available to the public must be thoroughly scrutinized. By way of example, if one has religious scruples about selling to or dealing with pagans or sinners, the duty and burden should be on that individual to refrain from that commercial activity rather than discriminating against discrete members of the general public. Included within our conception of "civil privileges due all citizens" in the United States is openness of commerce and of opportunity: The "free market" does not allow the selective banning of citizens from otherwise open and public commercial activity for reasons irrelevant to that commercial activity. See, for example, Title VII of the Civil Rights Act of 1964, forbidding employment discrimination on the basis of, for example, race or gender.

17. *Id.* at 69–70 (emphasis in original).

18. *Id.* at 66–68.

19. Cary J. Nederman, "Liberty, Community, and Toleration," in Cary J. Nederman and John Christian Laursen, *Difference and Dissent* (Lanham, Md: Rowman and Littlefield Publishers, 1996), 17, 32.

20. *Id.* at 30.

21. Martin Luther, "Secular Authority: To What Extent It Should Be Obeyed," in John Dillenberger, ed., *Martin Luther: Selections from His Writings* (1523; repr. New York: Doubleday Anchor Books, 1962), 366–67.

22. *Id.* at 371.

23. *Id.* at 382–83.

24. *Id.* at 372.

25. *Id.* at 388.

26. *Id.* at 384.

27. *Id.* at 389.

28. *Id.* at 390.

29. See Kamen, *The Rise of Toleration*, chapter 7, 161, passim, and William R. Estep, *Revolution Within the Revolution: The First Amendment in Historical Context, 1612–1789* (Grand Rapids, Mich.: Wm. B. Eerdmans, 1990), 49, passim (chapter 3).

30. This was an epoch when memories still freshly recalled that the pope not only excommunicated Queen Elizabeth, but also declared that she was to be dethroned. The launching of the Spanish Armada was an attempt by Catholic Spain to carry out this edict by outside force. Catholic priests (Edmund Campion, for example) were put to death, not for their religious beliefs per se, but for what was deemed civil treason against the state (promoting Catholicism). No difference in kind was seen between religious dissidents seeking to overthrow established church authority and political dissidents seeking to overthrow the English monarchy.

When analyzing the English struggles over religious tolerance in this period, care must be taken, therefore, to avoid a modern tendency to assume the separateness of politics and religion. See, for example, Nancy Elnora Scott, *The Limits of Toleration Within the Church of England from 1632 to 1642* (Philadelphia: New Era Printing, 1912) (Ph.D. dissertation, University of Pennsylvania). Scott meticulously compares and contrasts the attitudes toward toleration of influential Anglican prelates William Chillingworth, John Hales, Joseph Hall, William Laud, and Jeremy Taylor (examining their writings during the decade before the Civil War). She determined that "the controlling factor in their religious policy was the conviction that conformity to the one authorized system of worship was vitally necessary to the safety of the State." *Id.* at 1. Scott concluded, however, that their support for governmental intolerance of different worship practices was "founded *wholly* on their *political* conceptions," and "[i]n no case was the danger, feared as the result of separation, *other than political.*" *Id.* at 112, 113 (emphasis added). Considering the emphases within the Christian tradition (see discussion of Augustine and Calvin, below) on the divine "goods" of peace and order, the duty of obedience, and the "parental" duty of the Christian ruler to correct wayward subjects, such a distinction between what is purely political and what is purely religious motivation cannot be so clearly and conclusively drawn for this time period.

31. Kamen, *The Rise of Toleration*, 116–19, 161–90, 201–15. Notably, the religious debate became inseparable from the political debates of these times, for these same parties also aligned themselves along similar positions on the issue of which form of political government should be established to rule England (Anglicans favored the monarchy; Puritans favored the Parliament). It is no accident that the Church of England hierarchy and the political monarchical hierarchy became merged in the minds of friends and foes alike. Similarly, Puritan presbyterian order became merged with the fight for parliamentary dominance in the political realm at this time. Dissenters thus came to merge arguments for religious liberty with arguments for political liberty: "The intolerance of the Presbyterians drove many Englishmen, notably Milton, to take up their pens in defense of both civil and religious liberty, and it became universally accepted by the end of the Protectorate that these two were interdependent." *Id.* at 179.

32. [Note: Throughout this chapter, I have taken the liberty of modernizing the spelling (including translating abbreviations into full words) in order to enhance the readership qualities of the primary texts.] Roger Williams, *The Bloudy Tenent, of Persecution, for cause of Conscience, discussed, in A Conference betweene Truth and Peace* . . . , (n.p., 1644), repr. in *The Complete Writings of Roger Williams*, vol. 3, ed. Samuel L. Caldwell (New York: Russell & Russell, 1963), 3 (preface) (emphasis in original) [hereafter referred to as *The Bloudy Tenent* with a citation to pages of volume 3 in the *Complete Writings* series]. This separation of "law" from "gospel" is common to the two kingdoms type. In a piece attributed to Thomas Helwys, for example, a similar assertion is made: "[The civil magistrates and the kings do not have the same power] that the kings of Israel had. . . . [N]o mortal man, whatsoever he be, can compel any man to offer the sacrifices of the new testament, which are spiritual." [Anon.], *Persecution for Religion Judg'd and Condemn'd* . . . (n.p., 1615; repr. 1662), reprinted in Edward Bean Underhill, ed., *Tracts on Liberty of Conscience and Persecution, 1614–1661* (London: J. Haddon, 1846), 124–25.

33. Williams, *The Bloudy Tenent*, 104 (chap. XXI) (emphasis in original).

34. *Id.* at 125–26 (chap. XXXIII) (emphasis in original).

35. *Id.* at 124 (chap. XXXII) (emphasis in original).

36. *Id.* at 142 (chap. XLII) (emphasis in original).

37. Estep, *Revolution Within the Revolution*. Estep cites to many others within the

same tradition as Williams (such as Thomas Helwys and Mark Leonard Busher) who supported their claims with scriptural arguments echoing the two kingdoms type.

38. H. Wheeler Robinson, "Introduction," in Thomas Helwys, *The Mistery of Iniquity* (1612; repr. London: Baptist Historical Society, 1935), xiii.

39. Helwys, *The Mistery of Iniquity*, 69.

40. Williams, *The Bloudy Tenent*, 171 (chap. LVI) (emphasis in original).

41. *Id.* at 160 (chap. LI) (emphasis in original).

42. [Anon.], *Persecution for Religion Judg'd and Condemn'd*, in Underhill, ed., *Tracts on Liberty of Conscience*, 145.

43. *Id.* at 108, 133.

44. Williams, *The Bloudy Tenent*, 253.

45. William Jeffrey, John Reve, George Hammon, and James Blackmore, "A Free and Faithful Acknowledgment of the King's Authority and Dignity in Civil Things, Over All Manner of Persons, Ecclesiastical and Civil, within His Majesty's Domain, etc." (London: Thomas Smith, 1660) (part of "The Humble Petition and Representation of the Sufferings of Several Peaceable, and Innocent Subjects, Called by the Name of Anabaptists . . .), repr. in Underhill, ed., *Tracts on Liberty of Conscience*, 304.

See also, for example, Thomas Monck et al., "Sion's Groans For Her Distressed, or Sober Endeavors To Prevent Innocent Blood, &c." (n.p., 1661), repr. in Underhill, ed., *Tracts on Liberty of Conscience*, 369, wherein, with respect to the Golden Rule, it is written: "And it is a sure and standing rule, by which all men . . . might measure the justice of their proceedings towards others."

46. This would belie the strong, if not conclusive, presumption in favor of the validity of the exercise of the state power, as seen in the *Reynolds* and the *Smith* cases, for example.

47. Romans 13:1–4 (RSV).

48. Kamen, *The Rise of Toleration*, 12, et seq.

49. Augustin, *Contra Litteras Petiliani*, book II, chap. 10, trans. Rev. J. R. King, repr. in Philip Schaff, ed., *A Select Library of the Nicene and Post-Nicene Fathers of the Christian Church*, vol. 4 (Grand Rapids: Wm. B. Eerdmans, 1956), 535 [hereafter cited as *Contra Litteras Petiliani* with page reference to volume 4 of *A Select Library*]. Note that in all citations Augustine's name will be spelled as indicated on the title page: Augustin.

50. Augustin, Epistle 93: "Letter to Vincentius," trans. J. G. Cunningham, in Philip Schaff, ed., *A Select Library of the Nicene and Post-Nicene Fathers of the Christian Church*, vol. 1 (Grand Rapids: Wm. B. Eerdmans, 1956), 383 [hereafter cited as "Letter to Vincentius"].

51. Augustin, Epistle 185: *De Correctione Donatistarum*, in Schaff, ed., *A Select Library*, vol. 4, 636 [hereafter cited as Epistle 185]; see also Augustin, "Letter to Vincentius," 384–85.

52. P. R. L. Brown's insightful article, "St. Augustine's Attitude To Religious Coercion," *The Journal of Roman Studies* 54 (1964): 107, warns that Augustine's "attitude" (Brown declines to call it a "doctrine") is not merely an ad hoc response to "the social and political necessities of the North African provinces." Rather, Augustine's views on religious coercion are linked to a larger effort at reconciling and resolving the tensions between the Old Testament and the New Testament, in order to come to an "ideal of authority":

[W]hat is common to Augustine's attitude to coercion and his thought in general is the acceptance of moral processes which admit an acute polarity — a polarity of external impingement and inner evolution, of fear and love, of constraint and freedom. . . . [These polarities] approximated to, without ever co-inciding with, the division of the Old and New Testament. They were thought of as the "duae voces" of the Scriptures of the One God.

Id. at 112, 113. External force, fear, and constraint are necessary to break the intractable "force of habit" of the life of the senses; only then can the free will be genuinely free to experience the "grace of the New dispensation." Hence, coercion as envisioned by Augustine is pastoral, not retributive or punitive. It is part of an ideal, of a positive process of corrective punishment which is aimed at "rebuking" and "setting right."

    53. Augustin, Epistle 185, 640.

    54. *Id.* In *Contra Litteras Petiliani*, 583, Augustine writes further of the special duty of Christian rulers:

> For all men ought to serve God,—in one sense, in virtue of the condition common to them all, in that they are men; in another sense, in virtue of their several gifts, whereby this man has one function on the earth, and that man has another. . . . Accordingly, when we take into consideration the social condition of the human race, we find that kings, in the very fact that they are kings, have a service which they can render to the Lord in a manner which is impossible for any who have not the power of kings.

    55. Augustin, Epistle 185, 640–41.

    56. Augustin, "Letter to Vincentius," 392–97. Schism from the church cannot be justified by claiming that the sinful will contaminate the pure, and hence the pure must separate themselves. Augustine noted that those who justify schism with such a claim are "full of self-sufficiency and pride"

> for assuming to themselves that which the Lord did not concede even to the Apostles,—namely, the gathering of the tares before the harvest,—and the attempting to separate the chaff from the wheat, as if to them had been assigned the charge of removing the chaff and cleansing the threshing-floor. . . . [N]o man can be stained with guilt by the sins of others. . . . [I]t is manifest that the righteous are not defiled by the sins of other men when they participate with them in the sacraments. . . .
>
> [N]o man in the unity of Christ can be stained by the guilt of the sins of other men if he be not consenting to the deeds of the wicked, and thus defiled by actual participation in their crimes, but only for the sake of the fellowship of the good, tolerating the wicked, as the chaff which lies until the final purging of the Lord's threshing-floor.

Id. Accordingly, Augustine firmly rejects any sectarian notion of the church as a "pure remnant."

    57. Augustin, *Contra Litteras Petiliani*, 545, 586, 599.

    58 Augustine, *The City of God* (New York: Modern Library, 1950), book 15, ch. 6.

    59. *Id.* at book 19, ch. 13.

    60. *Id.*

    61. *Id.* at book 1, ch. 21.

    62. *Id.* at book 19, ch. 26.

    63. Augustin, "Letter to Vincentius," 400.

    64. Brown, "St. Augustine's Attitude," 111. Brown notes that Augustine "circumvented the previous tradition of thought available to Christians on the subject of coercion":

It had appeared self-evident that freedom of choice—*voluntas* or *liberum arbitrium*—was the essence of religion; that adherence to a religion could be obtained only by such free choice; and that a religious institution which resorted to force must be a *figmentum*, a merely human "artifice", since only an institution resting on human custom could resort to such all-too-human means of securing obedience.

Id.

65. Augustin, "Letter to Vincentius," 389. In *Contra Litteras Petiliani*, 599, Augustine makes this further comparison: "The punishment of chastising therefore is not an evil. . . . For indeed, it is the steel, not of an enemy inflicting a wound, but of a surgeon performing an operation."

66. Calvin declares that the distinction between the kingdom of Christ and the civil government "does not lead us to consider the whole system of civil government as a polluted thing which has nothing to do with Christian men." Calvin, *Institutes*, "On Civil Government," I.

67. *Id.* at V, VI, and IX.

68. Calvin, *Institutes*, "On Christian Liberty," XV.

69. Calvin, *Institutes*, "On Civil Government," I.

70. *Id.* (emphasis added).

71. *Id.* at II.

72. For an extensive discussion of Calvin's concept of a new order, see David Little, *Religion, Order and Law: A Study in Pre-Revolutionary England* (New York: Harper & Row, 1969; repr. Chicago: Univ. of Chicago Press, 1984), chapter 3, passim.

73. *Id.* The dedication of the *Institutes* to Francis I of France also reflects this blurring of the lines between the civil and the spiritual:

For the ungodly have gone to such lengths that the truth of Christ, if not vanquished, dissipated, and entirely destroyed, is buried, as it were, in ignoble obscurity, while the poor, despised church is either destroyed by cruel massacres or driven away into banishment, or menaced and terrified into total silence. . . . If there be any persons desirous of appearing most favorable to the truth, they only venture an opinion that forgiveness should be extended to the error and imprudence of ignorant people. For this is the language of moderate men. . . . Thus all are ashamed of the Gospel. But it shall be yours, Sire, not to turn away your ears or thoughts from so just a defense, especially in a cause of such importance as the maintenance of God's glory unimpaired in the world, the preservation of the honor of divine truth, and the continuance of the kingdom of Christ uninjured among us. This is a cause worthy of your attention, worthy of your cognizance, worthy of your throne. This consideration constitutes true royalty, to acknowledge yourself in the government of your kingdom to be the minister of God. *For where the glory of God is not made the end of a government, it is not a legitimate sovereignty, but a usurpation.*

Calvin, *Institutes* (emphasis added).

74. *Id.* (emphasis added).

75. This reciprocal sense of defilement is not present in Augustine's writings on coercion; indeed, as noted, Augustine rejects any arguments based on contamination or contagion—there is no sense of corporate guilt for individual sin. Rather, Augustine premises the need for coercive measures in religion upon the need to break through "hard walls" of human habit. See Brown, supra, "St. Augustine's Attitude."

76. Calvin, *Institutes*, "On Civil Government," at III.

77. *Id.* at VII.

78. *Id.* at IX.

79. Mark Goldie, "The Theory of Religious Intolerance in Restoration England," in O. P. Grell, J. I. Israel, and N. Tyacke, eds., *From Persecution to Toleration: The Glorious Revolution and Religion in England* (Oxford: Clarendon Press, 1991), chapter 13, passim (especially 335–45).

80. Joseph Hall, "A Common Apology of the Church of England Against the Unjust Challenges of the Over-Just Sect, Commonly Called Brownists . . ." [hereafter referred to as "Apology"], in Philip Wynter, ed., *The Works of the Right Reverend Joseph Hall*, vol. 9 (New York: AMS Press, 1969; repr. of 1863 Oxford edition), 57 (section 29) [hereafter referred to as *Works*].

81. Richard Hooker, *Of the Lawes of Ecclesiasticall Polity*, repr. in W. Speed Hill, gen. ed., *The Folger Library Edition of the Works of Richard Hooker*, vol. 1 (Cambridge, Mass.: Belknap Press of Harvard Univ. Press, 1977) (hereafter cited as *Lawes, Folger vol. 1*), 81 (book 1:7.7) (translation: [book]: [chapter.section]).

82. *Id.* at 17–18 (preface: 3.10–3.11) (emphasis in original).

83. Hall, "Apology," in Wynter, ed., *Works*, vol. 9, 37 (sect. 17).

84. The freedom of belief is exceedingly narrow and restricted. While admitting that no law has the power to command an opinion, Hooker does note that the law can and should, for the sake of public unity, bar speech of contrary opinions. Note, here, the distinction drawn between action and belief: Thoughts unspoken and private are beliefs, but speak them and your utterance is a matter for regulatory action.

> No man doubts but that for matters of action and practice in the affairs of God, for the manner of divine service, for order in Ecclesiastical proceedings about the regiment of the *Church* there may be oftentimes cause very urgent to have laws made. But the reason is not so plain wherefore human laws should appoint men what to believe. Wherefore in this we must note two things. First, that in matter of opinion the law does not make that to be truth which before was not, as in matter of action it causes that to be duty which was not before, but it manifests only and gives men notice of that to be truth, the contrary whereunto they ought not before to have believed. Secondly, that as opinions do cleave to the understanding and are in heart assented unto it is not in the power of any human law to command them, because to prescribe what men shall think belongs only unto God. . . . As opinions are either fit or inconvenient to be professed, so man's law has to determine of them. It may for public unity's sake require men's professed assent or prohibit contradiction to special articles. . . .

Richard Hooker, *Of the Lawes of Ecclesiasticall Politie*, repr. in *The Folger Library Edition of the Works of Richard Hooker*, vol. 3, ed. P. G. Stanwood (Cambridge, Mass.: Belknap Press of Harvard Univ. Press, 1977), 389–90 (book 8:6.5) (hereafter cited as *Lawes, Folger vol. 3*).

85. Hooker, *Lawes, Folger vol. 1*, 206 (book 3:1.14). See also Hall, "Apology," in Wynter, ed., *Works*, vol. 9, 39: "Private profession is one thing; public reformation and injunction is another."

86. Hooker writes,

> [E]arnest challengers you are of trial by some public disputation. Wherein if the thing you crave be no more then only leave to dispute openly about those matters that are in question, the schools in Universities . . . are open unto

you: they have their yearly Acts and Commencements, besides other disputa-
tions both ordinary and upon occasion, wherein the several parts of our own Ecclesiastical discipline are oftentimes offered unto that kind of examination; the
learnedest of you have been of late years noted seldom or never absent from
thence at the time of those greater assemblies; and the favor of proposing there
in convenient sort whatsoever you can object . . . neither hath (as I think) nor
ever will (I presume) be denied you. [But] your suit be to have some great extraordinary confluence, in expectation whereof the laws that already are should
sleep and have no power over you, till . . . some disputer can persuade you to
be obedient. A law is the deed of the whole body politic, whereof if you judge
yourselves to be any part, then is the law even your deed also. . . . Laws that
have been approved may be (no man doubts) again repealed, and to that end
also disputed against, by the authors thereof themselves. But this is when the
whole does deliberate what laws each part shall observe, and not when a part refuses the laws which the whole hath orderly agreed upon.

Hooker, *Lawes, Folger vol. 1*, 27–28 (preface: 5.1–5.2).
  87.

But of this we are right sure, that nature, scripture, and experience itself, have
all taught the world to seek for the ending of contentions by submitting it self
unto some judicial and definitive sentence, whereunto neither part that contends may under any pretense or color refuse to stand. This must needs be
effectual and strong. . . . For if God be not the author of confusion but of
peace, then can he not be the author of our refusal, but of our contentment, to
stand unto some definitive sentence, without which almost impossible it is that
either we should avoid confusion, or ever hope to attain peace.

Id. at 29–32 (preface: 6.1–6.3). Here, the divine good of peace is clearly considered equally
applicable to the civil as well as the religious realm. Peace can only be had when there is
a means of resolving disputes, and all are equally bound to abide by the resolution.
Hooker cites to the Council of Jerusalem (act. 15, controversy over the admission of gentiles) as a precedent for such resolution of dissension within the Christian church.

To small purpose had the Council of Jerusalem been assembled, if once their
determination being set down, men might afterwards have defended their
former opinions. When therefore they had given their definitive sentence, all
controversy was at an end. Things were disputed before they came to be determined; men afterwards were not to dispute any longer, but to obey. The sentence of judgement finished their strife, which their disputes before judgement
could not do. This was ground sufficient for any reasonable man's conscience
to build the duty of obedience upon, whatsoever his own opinion were as
touching the matter before in question.

Id. at 32. Hooker acknowledged the problem of getting the dissidents to agree upon such a
"court" for the determining of all controversies, however.
  88. Later, the church (after decades of bitter turmoil) would lose patience with dissenters who wished to be heard, and it banned and silenced all public debate on "matters
of indifference." As Joseph Hall writes in 1622:

There is no possible redress but in a severe edict of restraint, to charm all
tongues and pens upon the sharpest punishment from passing those moderate
bounds which the church of England, guided by the scriptures, hath expressly

set. . . . If any man herein complain of an usurpation upon the conscience, and an unjust servitude, let him be taught the difference between matters of faith and scholastical disquisitions. Those have God for their author; these, the brains of men. . . . Those do mainly import our salvation; these not at all. In those the heart is tied to believe, the tongue must be free to speak; in these the heart may be free, the tongue may be bound. Of this latter sort are the points we have now in hand . . . how unfit they are for popular ears, and how unworthy to break the peace of the church . . . in the unimportance of the ill raised differences.

Joseph Hall, "Via Media: The Way of Peace" (1622), in Wynter, ed., *Works*, vol. 9, 498 (article 5).

89. Hooker, *Lawes, Folger vol.* 1, 212 (book 3:3.4). By way of further definition:

[W]e teach that whatsoever is unto salvation termed *necessary* by way of excellence, whatsoever it stands all men upon to know or doe that they may be saved, whatsoever there is whereof it may truly be said, *This not to believe is eternal death and damnation*, or *This every soul that will live must duly observe*, of which sort the articles of Christian faith, and the sacraments of the Church of Christ are, all such things. . . . But as for those things that are accessory hereunto, those things that so belong to the way of salvation, as to alter them is no otherwise to change that way, then a path is changed by altering only the uppermost face thereof, which be it laid with gravel, or set with grass, or paved with stone, remains still the same path . . .

Id. at 211 (3:3.3) (emphasis in original).

90. Jeremy Taylor, "Sermon Preached at the Opening of the Parliament of Ireland, May 8, 1661, Before the Right Honourable The Lords Justices, and The Lords Spiritual and Temporal, and the Commons," in Reginald Heber, ed., *The Whole Works of the Right Rev. Jeremy Taylor*, vol. 6 (London: James Moyes, 1839), 332, [335] (preface), [hereafter, *The Whole Works*"].

91. Hooker continues, "And if things or persons be ordered, this does imply that they are distinguished by degrees. For order is a gradual disposition. The whole world consisting of parts so many so different is by this only thing upheld, he which framed them has set them in order" (Hooker, *Lawes, Folger vol.* 3, 331 [book 8:2.1]).

92. Which is not to say, of course, that there were no other elements or groundings to its intolerance. Witness, for example, Bishop Joseph Hall's rants about the rabble among the dissenters:

Alas! My lords, I beseech you to consider what it [the danger from schismatics] is: That there should be in London and the suburbs and liberties no fewer than fourscore congregations of several sectaries, as I have been too credibly informed; instructed by guides fit for them, *cobblers, tailors, feltmakers, and such like trash:* which are all taught to spit in the face of their mother, the Church of England. . . .

Hall, "A Speech in Parliament," in Wynter, ed., *Works*, vol. 8, 277 (emphasis added) (no date indicated; printed in *Works* before two speeches to Parliament in 1640 and 1641, and after a letter to the House of Commons dated 1628).

93. Rhys Isaac describes this type of patriarchal order as it was transplanted to Colonial Virginia in *The Transformation of Virginia: 1740–1790* (New York: W.W. Norton, 1982; repr. 1988), part I, "Traditional Ways of Life," passim. Gordon Wood also aptly de-

scribes this order, notes its pervasiveness among the 13 colonies, and documents the radical transformation which the American Revolution wrought in this patriarchal order, in *The Radicalism of the American Revolution* (New York: Vintage Books, 1991; repr. 1993).

94. As argued by Hooker:

> Yea the very deity itself both keeps and requires forever this to be kept as a law, that wheresoever there is coagmentation of many, the lowest be knit to the highest by that which being interjacent may cause each to cleave unto other and so all to continue one. This order of things and persons in public societies is the work of polity and the proper instrument thereof in every degree is *power*, power being that ability which we have of ourselves or receive from others for performance of any action. . . . And if that power be such as has not any other to overrule it, we term it dominion or power supreme, so far as the bounds thereof do extend. When therefore Christian Kings are said to have spiritual dominion or supreme power in Ecclesiastical affairs and causes, the meaning is, that within their own precincts and territories they have authority and power to command even in matters of *Christian Religion*, and that there is no higher, nor greater, that can in those causes overcommand them, where they are placed to reign as *Kings*. But withall we must likewise note, that their power is termed *supremacy* as being the highest not simply without exception of any thing. For what man is there so brainsick [!] as not to except in such speeches God himself, the king of all the kings of the earth?

Hooker, *Lawes, Folger vol.* 3, 331–32 (book 8:2.1–2.3) (emphasis in original).

95. This is not to say, however, that Hooker and other Anglican theologians of the period hold that God has a direct, interfering hand in who is made king, or even what kind of government a country adopts. God does not, as a general rule, "micromanage":

> First unto me it seems almost out of doubt and controversy that every independent multitude before any certain form of regiment established has under *God's* supreme authority full dominion over it self, even as a man not tied with the bond of subjection as yet unto any other has over himself the like power. God creating mankind did [imbue] it naturally with full power to guide it self in what kinds of societies soever it should choose to live. . . . By which of these means [divine authority—via special appointment as in the Hebrew Bible, or through conquest; or human authority—"according unto mens discretion"] soever it happens, that *Kings* or governors be advanced unto their seats, we must acknowledge both their lawful choice to be approved of God, and themselves for *God's Lieutenants* and confess their power his.

Id. at 334–35 (book 8:2.5) (emphasis in original).

96. Hall, "Apology," in Wynter, ed., *Works*, vol. 9, 102.

97. Hooker writes,

> In a *Church* well ordered that which the supreme Magistrate has is to see that the laws of God touching his worship and touching all matters and orders of the *Church* be executed and duly observed . . . in a word . . . unto the earthly power, which *God* has given him, it does belong to defend the laws of the *Church*, to cause them to be executed and to punish the *Transgressors* of the same.

Hooker, *Lawes, Folger vol.* 3, 410–11 (book 8:6.14) (emphasis in original).

98. Hooker, *Lawes, Folger vol.* 1, 237 (book 3:9.2) (emphasis in original).

99.

But were it so that the Clergy alone might give laws unto all the rest, forasmuch as every estate does desire to enlarge the bounds of their own liberties, is it not easy to see how injurious this might prove unto men of other condition? Peace and justice are maintained by preserving unto every order their rights and by keeping all estates as it were in an even balance. Which thing is no way better done then if the *King* their common parent whose care is presumed to extend most indifferently over all, does bear the chiefest sway in the making of laws which all must be ordered by.

Hooker, *Lawes, Folger vol.* 3, 394 (book 8:6.8) (emphasis in original).

100. Jeremy Taylor, "Epistle Dedicatory, to A Sermon Preached at the Opening of the Parliament of Ireland, May 8, 1661," in Heber, ed., *The Whole Works*, vol. 6, 336–37.

101. Note the resemblance between the duly ordered relationships type and the reasoning of the Court in the cases of *Reynolds, Gobitis, Prince,* and *Smith.* All emphasize stark duality (either anarchy or obedience), as well as the deference and strong favorable presumption to be accorded the state.

102. I am not unmindful of the body of work that depicts the antagonism between Anglicans and Puritans as one of traditional order versus rational-legal order. See Little, *Religion, Order and Law.* Both of our projects trade in religious interpretations of "order" but tread different territories. Little's study, in contrast, focuses on the influence of religious worldviews upon the development of an economic order, and particularly upon the rise of capitalism. The Puritan worldview in particular is a complex, contradictory matter. As Little explains, for example, "the countervailing tendencies within Calvinist Puritanism" produced both "self-initiated economic behavior" and "a religious elite which seeks, to a degree at least, to subordinate the old order to its perception of righteousness." *Id.* at 222, 223.

103. *The Dictionary of National Biography,* vol. VIII (London: Oxford Univ. Press, 1949), 1238.

104 Nathaniel Hardy, "The Arraignment of Licentious Libertie and Oppressing Tyrannie. Sermon, Preached Before the House of Peeres . . . Febr. 24, 1646," p. 10, repr. in Robin Jeffs, gen. ed., *Fast Sermons to Parliament,* vol. 27, The English Revolution series, no. 1 (London: Cornmarket Press, 1971), 65, 80 (emphasis in original).

105. *Id.* at 71.

106. *Id.* at 81–82.

107. Obadiah Sedgwick, "The Nature and Danger of Heresies . . . Sermon before the Honourable House of Commons, January 27, 1646," 16, repr. in Robin Jeffs, gen. ed., *Fast Sermons to Parliament,* vol. 26, The English Revolution series, no. 1 (London: Cornmarket Press, 1971), 352.

108. *Id.* at 355.

109. *Id.* at 353–54.

110. *Id.* at 373–75. For a brief summary of Obadiah Sedgwick's life, see *The Dictionary of National Biography,* vol. XVII (London: Oxford Univ. Press, 1950), 1121.

111. Act of November 4, 1646, *Records of the Governor and Company of the Massachusetts Bay in New England,* pp. 100–03.

112. Act of October 17, 1654, *Records of the Governor and Company of the Massachusetts Bay in New England,* p. 433.

113. Act of November 13, 1644, *Records of the Governor and Company of the Massachusetts Bay in New England,* pp. 66–67.

114. John Cotton, *The Bloudy Tenent, Washed, And Made White in the Bloud*

of the Lambe (London: Matthew Symmons, 1647; repr., New York: Arno Press, 1972), 12, 13.

    115. *Id.* at 18.
    116. *Id.* at 67.
    117. *Id.* at 70.
    118. *Id.* at 151.
    119. *Id.* at 89.
    120. *Id.* at 34–35.
    121. *Id.* at 92–93. Cotton states,

> excommunication of an heretic is no persecution: and therefore by proportion neither is the civil punishment of an Heretic persecution; And the Reason in my words following reaches both: for to persecute is to punish an Innocent; But an Heretic is not an Innocent, but a culpable and damnable person.

Id. at 144. Note the mixing, here, of an Augustinian (duly ordered relationships) argument with a levitical type argument.

    122. Cotton, for example, writes:

> And therefore the Magistrate need not to fear, that he should exceed the bounds of his Office, if he should meddle in the affairs of the Church in Gods way. . . . But if he shall diligently seek after the Lord, and read in the word of the Lord all the days of his life . . . that he may both live as a Christian, and rule as a Christian, if he shall seek to establish and advance the Kingdom of Christ more than his own: If he shall encourage the good in a Christian course, and discourage such as have evil will to Zion: and *punish none for matter of Religion, but such as subvert the Principles of Saving truth (which no good Christian, much less good Magistrate can be ignorant of)* or at least such as disturb the Order of the Gospel in a turbulent way, verily the Lord will build up and establish the House and Kingdom of such princes, as [they] do thus build up his.

Id. at 162 (emphasis added).

    123. The levitical type's concern with contamination and corporate guilt explicitly supported and justified the congressional vendetta against the Mormon practice of polygamy in nineteenth century America. Congressmen popularly used the Bible and the notion of God erupting in history to show his pleasure and displeasure, as support for their arguments. For example, the committee report on the antipolygamy bill stated the issue in unmistakably biblical terms: The Mormons were "false prophets" spreading "damnable heresies" as warned of in the Bible, and the United States would face the same destructive wrath of God as did Sodom and Gomorrah. *House Committee on the Judiciary, Report on Polygamy in the Territories of the United States,* H.R. Rep. No. 83, 36th Cong., 1st Sess., 2, 4 (March 14, 1860).

    The fear of divine retribution was developed further by Representative Nelson in the debates on the House floor. Nelson declared that popular sovereignty (i.e., the fact that by democratic majority, polygamy remained legal in Utah) must defer to national interests in this matter, for the sins of the majority in Utah would bring ruin and destruction upon the entire nation if the Congress were to let the Mormons continue their polygamous ways.

> Who that believes in the truth of revelation, Mr. Speaker, can for a moment doubt that there are national sins, and that war, pestilence, and famine, are scourges which an Almighty Power brings into requisition in order to rebuke

those sins, and to show his abhorrence of them? . . . [W]ho can shut his eyes against the great fact that there are national crimes and delinquencies for which national punishment has been inflicted in times past, and may be in times to come? [Nelson then discussed the examples of Babylon, Nineveh, and Petra.] . . .

Let us, then, beware how we shall provoke the displeasure of the Almighty, by nourishing and cherishing a population whose crimes are undoubtedly hateful in His sight.

Congressional Globe, 36th Cong., 1st Sess., appendix 194–95 (1860) (remarks by Representative Nelson, April 5, 1860).

124. Act of November 4, 1646, *Records of the Governor and Company of the Massachusetts Bay in New England,* 99, states:

Albeit faith be not wrought by the sword, but by the word, & therefore such pagan Indians as have submitted themselves to our government, though we would not neglect any due helps to bring them on to grace, & to the means of it, yet we compel them not to the Xtian faith, nor to the profession of it, either by force of arms or by penal laws . . .

125. *Id.*

126. William McLoughlin, for example, has classified all non-"pietist" support for disestablishment in the Founding Era as "radically rationalist" and "secular pietism." The implication, here, is that arguments for religious freedom premised upon common sense, pragmatism, and reason are outside of the Christian tradition. Furthermore, there is an implication that Revolutionary and Founding Era support for religious freedom was limited to a small "radical fringe" (i.e., radical pietists or radical rationalists). William McLoughlin, "The Role of Religion in the Revolution," in Stephen G. Kurtz and James H. Hutson, eds., *Essays on the American Revolution* (New York: W.W. Norton, 1973), 209–10.

In contrast, I have placed the enlightenment type squarely within the Christian tradition, and furthermore within the mainstream moderates and as a force for moderation and balance, as opposed to a fringe movement force for "radicalness." See Henry May, *The Enlightenment in America* (New York: Oxford Univ. Press, 1976), particularly May's discussion of the "moderate enlightenment."

127. The examination of Tertullian's thought, here, is not necessarily an idiosyncratic academic exercise: American colonists were familiar with Tertullian's writings and his works were quoted in debates over religious freedom. See, for example, Cotton, *The Bloudy Tenent, Washed,* 147; Williams, *The Bloudy Tenent,* chap. LXX, pp. 196 et seq. Isaac Backus, in turn, frequently referred to these debates in his arguments for religious freedom during the Founding Era.

128.

Without ceasing, for all our emperors we offer prayer. We pray for life prolonged; for security to the empire; for protection to the imperial house; for brave armies, a faithful senate, a virtuous people, the world at rest, whatever, as man or Caesar, an emperor would wish. . . . [T]he scripture says, "Pray for kings, and rulers, and powers, that all may be at peace with you."

Tertullian, *Apology,* 42.

129.

But as it was easily seen to be unjust to compel freemen against their will to offer sacrifice (for even in other acts of religious service a willing mind is required), it should be counted quite absurd for one man to compel another to do honor to the gods. . . . "Let Janus meet me with angry looks, with whichever face of his faces he likes; what have you to do with me?" You have been led, no doubt, by these same evil spirits to compel us to offer sacrifice for the well-being of the emperor; and you are under a necessity of using force, just as we are under an obligation to face the dangers of it.

Tertullian, *Apology*, 41.

130.

Yes, and no one considers what the loss is to the common weal,—a loss as great as it is real, no one estimates the injury entailed upon the state, when, men of virtue as we are, we are put to death in such numbers; when so many of the truly good suffer the last penalty.

Tertullian, *Apology*, 49. Note the similarities to the arguments of medieval communal functionalism.

131.

One thing . . . [the Christian church] anxiously desires of earthly rulers—not to be condemned unknown. What harm can it do to the laws, supreme in their domain, to give her a hearing? . . . For what is there more unfair than to hate a thing of which you know nothing . . . ? Hatred is only merited when it is *known* to be merited. But without that knowledge, whence is its justice to be vindicated? [F]or that is to be proved, not from the mere fact that an aversion exists, but from acquaintance with the subject. . . . [Other criminals] have full opportunity of answer and debate; in fact, it is against the law to condemn anybody undefended and unheard. Christians alone are forbidden to say anything in exculpation of themselves, in defense of the truth, to help the judge to a righteous decision; all that is cared about is having what the public hatred demands—the confession of the name, not examination of the charge: while in your ordinary judicial investigations, on a man's confession of the crime . . . you are not content to proceed at once to sentence,—you do not take that step till you thoroughly examine the circumstances of the confession—what is the real character of the deed, how often, where, in what way, when has he done it, who were privy to it, and who actually took part with him in it. . . . But instead of that, we find that even inquiry in regard to our case is forbidden. . . .

For it is neither the number of their years nor the dignity of their maker that commends them [i.e., laws], but simply that they are just; and therefore, when their injustice is recognized, they are deservedly condemned, even though they condemn. Why speak we of them as unjust? Nay, if they punish mere names, we may well call them irrational. But if they punish acts, why in our case do they punish acts solely on the ground of a name, while in others they must have them proved *not from the name but from the wrong done?* . . . It is not enough that a law is just, nor that the judge should be convinced of its justice; *those from whom obedience is expected should have that conviction too.* Nay, a law lies under strong suspicions which does not care to have itself tried and approved; it is a positively wicked law, if, unproved, it tyrannizes over men.

Tertullian, *Apology*, 17, 18, 21 (emphasis added).

132. Luther, "Secular Authority," 393 (emphasis added).

133. *Id.* at 402 (emphasis added).

134. Williams, *The Bloudy Tenent*, 142 (chap. XLII) (emphasis in original).

135. Hooker, *Lawes, Folger vol. 1*, 222, 227 (book 3:8.5, 8.10). "Goodness," he writes, "is seen with the eye of the understanding. And the light of that eye, is reason." *Id.* at 78 (book 1:7.2). "For the laws of well doing are the dictates of right reason." *Id.* at 79 (book 1:7.4).

136. Isaac Backus, "A Door Opened For Equal Christian Liberty, And No Man Can Shut It" (Boston: Philip Freeman, 1783), repr. in William G. McLoughlin, ed., *Isaac Backus On Church, State, and Calvinism* (Cambridge, Mass.: Belknap Press of Harvard Univ. Press, 1968), 438 [this collection hereafter referred to as *Backus*].

137. Henry F. May, *The Enlightenment in America* (New York: Oxford Univ. Press, 1976), xiv. May's book is devoted to identifying and describing the four strains of the Enlightenment: the moderate enlightenment, 1688–1787; the skeptical enlightenment, 1750–1789; the revolutionary enlightenment, 1776–1800; the didactic enlightenment, 1800–1815. Locke, Madison, and the spirit of the 1787 Constitution, for example, are classed within the moderate enlightenment. It is this aspect of the Enlightenment, therefore, that primarily molds the enlightenment type outlined and discussed in this chapter.

138. *Id.* at 13, 11.

139. John Locke, "A Letter Concerning Toleration," in John Horton and Susan Mendus, eds., *John Locke, A Letter Concerning Toleration In Focus* (New York: Routledge, 1991), 14.

140. *Id.*

141. *Id.* at 42.

142. *Id.* at 38–39 (emphasis added).

143. *Id.* at 39.

144. *Id.* at 25.

145. *Id.* at 39.

146. *Id.* at 24–25. "The civil power is the same in every place: nor can that power, in the hands of a Christian prince, confer any greater authority upon the church, than in the hands of a heathen; which is to say, just none at all." *Id.* at 25.

147. *Id.* at 30.

148. *Id.* at 26.

149. *Id.*

150. *Id.* at 26–27. Recall Thomas Hooker's similar disparagement of religious zeal and enthusiasm, under the rubric of the duly ordered relationships type. The two kingdoms type, however, characteristically is respectful of religious enthusiasts. Kamen, for example, notes that Milton's defense of freedom of the press in his 1644 work, *Areopagitica*, includes a nod to freedom of religion for such enthusiasts: "Some have decried enthusiasm among the sects, but, he says: What some lament of, we rather should rejoice at, should rather praise this pious forwardness among men. . . .'" Kamen, *The Rise of Toleration*, 179.

151. Locke, "A Letter Concerning Toleration," 26–27.

152. William Penn, "The Reasonableness of Toleration and the Unreasonableness of Penal Laws and Tests" (London: 1687), title page, 2, 29, 30.

153. *Id.* at 12, 29–[35].

154. Locke, "A Letter Concerning Toleration," 50.

155. *Id.* at 49.

156. *Id.* at 46.

157. *Id.* at 51.

158. Bernard Bailyn's remarks about human frailty are important to keep in mind when examining the inconsistencies between rhetoric/ideals/principles supporting religious freedom and the actual application of them: "The Founding Fathers were mortals,

not gods; they could not overcome their own limitations and the complexities of life that kept them from realizing their ideals." Bernard Bailyn, "Central Themes of the Revolution," in Stephen G. Kurtz and James H. Hutson, eds., *Essays on the American Revolution* (New York: W.W. Norton, 1973), 31. Anti-Catholicism was characteristically rampant in the England of Locke's day, as well as among American attitudes during the colonial period and into the nineteenth century.

159. "Those are not at all to be tolerated who deny the being of God. Promises, covenants, and oaths, which are the bonds of human society, can have no hold upon an atheist. The taking away of God, though but even in thought, dissolves all." Locke, "A Letter Concerning Toleration," 47.

160. *Id.* at 45–47.

161. Williams, *The Bloudy Tenent*, 109 (ch. XXIV).

162. Recall H. Richard Niebuhr's comment, cited in detail at the opening of this chapter, that "[w]hen one returns from the hypothetical scheme to the rich complexity of individual events, it is evident at once that no person or group ever conforms completely to a type." Niebuhr, *Christ and Culture*, 44.

163. Both English and colonial laws often included oaths which, by their very wording, served to exclude Catholics. One example is the following, adopted by Parliament after the Glorious Revolution of 1689: ". . . and I do declare that no foreign prince, person, prelate, state or potentate hath or ought to have any power, jurisdiction, superiority, preeminence or authority, ecclesiastical or spiritual, within this realm, so help me God." "An Act for the Abrogating of the Oaths of Supremacy and Allegiance, and Appointing Other Oaths," 1689, in Francis X. Curran, S. J., *Catholics in Colonial Law* (Chicago: Loyola Univ. Press, 1963), 60.

164. "Toleration Act of William and Mary," May 24, 1689, as excerpted in Curran, *Catholics in Colonial Law*, 61.

165. Penn, "The Reasonableness of Toleration," 26–27, 36.

166. *Id.* at 7.

167. *Id.* at 31–32. Penn is able to find them violative of religion in that he deems "Liberty of Conscience" to be a "Law of God."

168. Locke, "A Letter Concerning Toleration," 44.

169. *Id.* (emphasis added).

170. *Id.* at 36, 37.

171. *Id.* at 37 (emphasis added).

172. *Id.* at 45.

173. *Id.*

174. Bailyn, "Central Themes of the Revolution," 6.

175. *Id.* at 5.

176. Lawrence H. Leder, *Liberty and Authority: Early American Political Ideology, 1689–1763* (Chicago: Quadrangle Books, 1968; repr., New York: W.W. Norton, 1976), 10, 11.

177. Thomas Buckley, for example, attributes the vigorous and extensive efforts by Baptists, Methodists, and Presbyterians in Virginia against Patrick Henry's Bill for Establishing Teachers of the Christian Religion, and for Madison's efforts to enact Jefferson's Bill to Establish Religious Freedom, to pure opportunistic, interest-driven politics.

> Willing to embrace Jefferson's legislation in terms of the freedom it guaranteed their own activities and the coup de grace it administered to what had once been an overbearing established church, they did not accept its author's philosophy on separation of church and state. What the law stated was of much less importance than what it enabled them to do. It served their purposes.

Thomas E. Buckley, S.J., *Church and State in Revolutionary Virginia, 1776–1787* (Charlottesville: Univ. Press of Virginia, 1977), 180. Rather than assuming that Founding Era Dissenters were actually closet duly ordered authority types, there is another explanation for the Dissenters' alliance with Jefferson that does not require public deception on the part of the Dissenters: There is indeed common interests and principles (universal, inclusive religious freedom and lack of government power in matters of religion) between the two kingdoms type and the enlightenment type. The *public arguments* made by the Dissenters in Virginia were premised within the two kingdoms model and were arguments of public currency.

178. John Phillip Reid, *In a Rebellious Spirit: The Argument of Facts, the Liberty Riot, and the Coming of the American Revolution* (University Park, Pa.: The Pennsylvania State Univ. Press, 1979), 1.

179. *Id.*

180. Founding Era political philosophies are commonly divided into three general schools. As Herbert Schneider writes: "In the Revolutionary generation three distinct systems of thought, three historically separate faiths, were flourishing; for want of better terms I shall call them rationalism, pietism, and republicanism." Rationalism stood for "the ideals of the American Enlightenment" or "natural religion." Pietism represented "the emotional enthusiasm of the religious revival," "New Light Evangelicalism," "Calvinistic pietism." Republicanism, in turn, was equated with "moral liberalism," with the "civic or social conception of virtue," with "social progress." Herbert W. Schneider, *A History of American Philosophy*, 2d ed. (New York: Columbia Univ. Press, 1963), 55–57. These descriptive categories, however, are not as useful when the task is to systematize and typologize traditional (up to and including the Founding Era) Western attitudes precisely toward religious freedom and the proper relationship and boundaries between conscience and the authority of the state. Hence, this project has used typologies/paradigms that are definitionally distinct from Schneider's terms which were developed for a different purpose. For example, all persons otherwise philosophically in harmony with the various systems under Schneider's schema would not necessarily also be in agreement on the type most appropriately applied to the relationship between the religiously compelled conscience and the state.

181. Estep, *Revolution Within the Revolution*, 149–50.

182. Thomas Jefferson, "An Act for establishing Religious Freedom [1779], passed in the Assembly of Virginia in the beginning of the year 1786," repr. in Thomas Jefferson, *The Life and Selected Writings of Thomas Jefferson*, eds. Adrienne Koch and William Peden (New York: Modern Library, 1944), 313 (emphasis added). A legal citation for the statute is William Waller Hening, *The Statutes At Large* (1823), XII, 84–86.

Jefferson's language was both more limiting, and more liberal, than language of a similar proposal in 1780 for protecting religious freedom in Massachusetts, offered by "Philanthropos," an anonymous writer described by McLoughlin as a "New Light member of the Standing Order." Philanthropos, in the first of a series of influential letters published in Massachusetts newspapers and arguing against ratification of article 3 of the Massachusetts Constitution, proposed an alternative to article 3 titled, "Bill for the Establishment of Religious Liberty":

All men have a natural and inalienable right to worship Almighty God according to their own conscience and understanding; and no man ought, or of right can be compelled to attend any religious worship, or erect or support any place of worship or maintain any ministry contrary to or against his own free will and consent. Nor can any man who acknowledges the being of God, be justly deprived or abridged of any civil rights as a citizen on account of his religious sentiments or peculiar mode of religious worship. And that no authority can or ought to be vested in or assumed by any power whatever, that shall in any case interfere with or in any manner control [*sic*] the right of conscience in the free exercise of religious worship.

Philanthropos, "Letter," *Independent Chronicle*, 6 April 1780 [n.p.], repr. in William G. McLoughlin, *New England Dissent, 1630–1833: The Baptists and the Separation of Church and State*, vol. 1 (Cambridge, Mass.: Harvard Univ. Press, 1971), 618–19, and n.10. Philanthropos, whom McLoughlin describes as "having no sympathy for deists," denies freedom of conscience to atheists while expanding religious freedom beyond "opinion" to include "exercise."

183. Jefferson, "An Act for establishing Religious Freedom," 312–13.

184. *Id.* at 313.

185. Jefferson, "Notes on the State of Virginia," in *The Life and Selected Writings*, 275 (written 1782) (query XVII) (emphasis added).

186. Jefferson, "Letter to a Committee of the Danbury Baptist Association, dated January 1, 1802," in *The Life and Selected Writings*, 332. In a letter to James Madison, dated July 31, 1788, Jefferson wrote, "The declaration, that religious faith shall be unpunished, does not give impunity to criminal acts, dictated by religious error." *Id.* at 451.

187. Jefferson, "Letter to Peter Carr, dated August 10, 1787," in *The Life and Selected Writings*, 431.

188. Jefferson, "Notes on the State of Virginia," in *The Life and Selected Writings*, 275–76.

189. *Id.* at 276–77.

190. The general assessment bill is described as follows:

Thomas Matthews presented on behalf of a committee for religion a resolution stating that "the people of the Commonwealth, according to their respectful abilities, ought to pay a moderate tax or contribution, annually, for the support of the christian religion, or of some christian church, denomination or communion of christians, or of some form of christian worship." A committee of ten, with Patrick Henry as chairman, was appointed to draw up a bill based on this resolution.

Estep, *Revolution Within the Revolution*, 141–42. The actual wording is reproduced below:

A BILL ESTABLISHING A PROVISION
FOR TEACHERS OF THE CHRISTIAN RELIGION
Patrick Henry, sponsor, 1784

WHEREAS the general diffusion of Christian knowledge hath a natural tendency to correct the morals of men, restrain their vices, and preserve the peace of society, which cannot be effected without a competent provision for learned teachers, who may be thereby enabled to devote their time and attention to their duty of instructing such citizens, as from their circumstances and want of education, cannot otherwise attain such knowledge; and it is judged that such provision may be made by the Legislature, without counteracting the liberal principle heretofore adopted and intended to be preserved by abolishing all distinctions of preeminence amongst the different societies or communities of Christians;

Be it therefore enacted by the General Assembly, That for the support of Christian teachers, _____ per centum on the amount, or _____ in the pound on the amount, or _____ in the pound on the sum payable for tax on the property within this Commonwealth, is hereby assessed, and shall be paid by every person chargeable with the said tax at the time the same shall become due; . . .

And be it enacted, That for every sum so paid, the Sheriff or Collector shall give a receipt, expressing therein to what society of Christians the person from whom he may receive the same shall direct the money to be paid, keeping a distinct account thereof in his books. . . .

And it be further enacted, That the money to be raised by virtue of this act, shall be by the Vestries, Elders, or Directors of each religious society, appropriated to a provision for a Minister or Teacher of the Gospel of their denomination, or the providing places of divine worship, and to none other use whatsoever, except in the denominations of Quakers and Menonists, who may receive what is collected from their members, and place it in their general fund, to be disposed of in a manner which they shall think best calculated to promote their particular mode of worship. . . .

Source: Buckley, S. J., *Church and State in Revolutionary Virginia*, app., 188–89. For a history of the Virginia Baptists' efforts to obtain religious liberty, see generally Robert B. Semple, *A History of the Rise and Progress of the Baptists in Virginia*, rev. and extended by G. W. Beale (Richmond: Pitt and Dickenson, 1894).

191. Estep, *Revolution Within the Revolution*, 145.

192. *Id.* at 148–49.

193. Sanford H. Cobb, *The Rise of Religious Liberty in America* (n.p., 1902; repr. New York: Cooper Square Publishers, 1968), 497. Specifically, Madison's "Memorial and Remonstrance" garnered 1,552 signatures. Estep, as indicated in a previous note, reports that altogether 12,000 signatures were gathered on over one hundred petitions against the bill. Estep, *Revolution Within the Revolution*, 148–49.

194. James Madison, "A Memorial and Remonstrance" (1785), repr. in Edwin S. Gaustad, ed., *A Documentary History of Religion in America to the Civil War* (Grand Rapids, Mich.: William B. Eerdmans, 1982), 262–67. Madison's arguments are included below in greater detail:

> 1. Because we hold it for a fundamental and undeniable truth, "that Religion or the duty which we owe to our Creator *and the manner of discharging it*, can be directed only by reason and conviction, not by force or violence." The religion then of every man must be left to the conviction and conscience of every man; and it is the right of every man to exercise it as these may dictate. This right is in its nature an unalienable right. . . . This duty [to one's Creator] is precedent, both in order of time and in degree of obligation, to the claims of Civil Society. . . . We maintain therefore that in matters of Religion, no mans [sic] right is abridged by the institution of Civil Society and that Religion is wholly exempt from its cognizance.

Id. at 262–63 (emphasis added). Note that the "inalienable" right of conscience clearly includes not simply the right to believe, but also the right to act on one's beliefs in order to discharge the duties imposed by conscience. The rejection of a *de minimis* argument is also included below, in greater detail:

> 3. Because it is proper to take alarm at the first experiment on our liberties. . . . Who does not see that . . . the same authority which can force a citi-

zen to contribute three pence only of his property for the support of any one establishment, may force him to conform to any other establishment in all cases whatsoever?

Id. at 263. (The "Memorial and Remonstrance" is also reprinted in the appendix to the U.S. Supreme Court case of *Everson v. Board of Education*, 330 U.S. 1, 63 (1947), and in the appendix to Semple, *Virginia Baptists*, 500–09. Citations to it, however, will be from the Gaustad text.)

195. Madison, "Memorial and Remonstrance," 262–67.

196. *Id.* at 263 (emphasis in original).

197. *Id.* at 265.

198. *Id.* at 263.

199. *Id.* at 264. There is, furthermore, a sense of resentment (recall Aesop's "Dog in the Manger" fable) at the assumed "better" position in which the exemption places these two sects, giving them a "recruitment" advantage: From Madison's rhetoric it seems as though they are exempt from the taxes to be levied in support of Christian education, but the wording of the Henry bill refers only to a freedom to spend the tax monies in any way they choose. "Ought their Religions be endowed above all others with extraordinary privileges by which proselytes may be enticed from all others?" *Id.* at 264.

200. Paragraph 4 of the "Memorial and Remonstrance" contains the major portions of the equality of rights argument, and it is reproduced below in more detail to give a better sense of the flow of the argument:

> 4. Because the Bill violates that equality which ought to be the basis of every law, and which is more indispensable, in proportion as the validity or expediency of any law is more liable to be impeached. If "all men are by nature equally free and independent," all men are to be considered . . . as relinquishing no more, and therefore retaining no less, one than another, of their natural rights. Above all are they to be considered as retaining an *"equal* [emphasis in original] title to the free exercise of religion according to the dictates of Conscience." Whilst we assert for ourselves a freedom to embrace, to profess and to observe the Religion which we believe to be of divine origin, we cannot deny an equal freedom to those whose minds have not yet yielded to the evidence which has convinced us. . . . As the Bill violates equality by subjecting some to peculiar burdens, so it violates the same principle by granting to others peculiar exemptions. Are the Quakers and the Mennonists the only sects who think a compulsive support of their Religion unnecessary and unwarrantable? Can their piety alone be entrusted with the care of public worship? Ought their Religions to be endowed above all others with extraordinary privileges by which proselytes may be enticed from all others? We think too favorably of the justice and good sense of these denominations to believe that they either covet pre-eminences over their fellow citizens or that they will be seduced by them from the common opposition to the measure.

Id. at 263–64.

201. James Madison was a major contributor to *The Federalist Papers*, a collection of letters to the public that first appeared in New York newspapers in the years 1787–1788. These letters were collected and published together in 1788 in support of ratification of the newly proposed Constitution. See preface by Clinton Rossitor to *The Federalist Papers* (New York: A Mentor Book, New American Library, 1961).

202. Madison wrote:

It could never be more truly said than of the first remedy [promotion of societal conformity through the curbing of liberty] that it was worse than the disease. Liberty is to faction what air is to fire, an aliment without which it instantly expires. But it could not be a less folly to abolish liberty, which is essential to political life, because it nourishes faction than it would be to wish the annihilation of air, which is essential to animal life, because it imparts to fire its destructive agency. . . .

When a majority is included in a faction, the form of popular government, on the other hand, *enables it to sacrifice to its ruling passion* or interest both the public good *and the rights of other citizens.* To secure the public good and private rights against the danger of such a faction, and at the same time to preserve the spirit and the form of popular government, is then the great object to which our inquiries are directed. . . .

James Madison, *The Federalist No. 10,* in Rossitor, ed., *The Federalist Papers,* 78, 80 (emphasis added).

203. *Id.* at 77, 78, 80–84.
204. Madison, *The Federalist No. 51,* 324.
205. *Id.* (emphasis added).
206. Estep writes,

"Dissenting Protestantism," as William Lee Miller has called it, made common cause with rationalism and deism to bring about a revolution within the Revolution. The coalition thus formed functioned effectively despite basic theological and philosophical differences, as William Warren Sweet and Sidney Mead pointed out years ago. If either side in this coalition had been missing, the cause almost surely would have failed—at least until the unbridled religious pluralism of the new nation would have demanded some kind of accommodation. However, as this work has attempted to demonstrate, religious freedom guaranteed by the institutional separation of church and state was not primarily the result of a practical solution to an indissoluble problem but the outworking of a basic theological principle rooted in the gospel of the "twice born," a gospel that had found its earliest expression in the Reformation of the sixteenth century among the Continental evangelical Anabaptists and their English counterparts.

Even though [William Lee] Miller is correct when he attributes the ground swell of religious liberty in the colonies to "dissenting Protestantism" rather than to the French Enlightenment, Edwin Gaustad reminds us that dissenting Protestantism alone could not have "stormed the gates of the establishment." He continues, "More power was required, more troops needed to bring down alliances of church and state, for behind those alliances stood all the force of history, all the authority of received wisdom, all the assurance of axiomatic truth." One need look no further than a simple comparison of Virginia with Massachusetts and Connecticut. The one element missing in Massachusetts and Connecticut that was present in Virginia was statesmen of the stature of Madison and Jefferson committed to religious freedom.

Estep, *Revolution Within the Revolution,* 171–72. Citations to works mentioned in the quote are as follows: William Lee Miller, *The First Liberty: Religion and the American Republic* (New York: Knopf, 1985); William Warren Sweet, *The Story of Religion in America,*

2d rev. ed. (New York: Harper & Row, 1950), 189–95; Sidney E. Mead, *The Lively Experiment* (New York: Harper & Row, 1963), 43; Edwin S. Gaustad, *Faith of Our Fathers: Religion and the New Nation* (San Francisco: Harper & Row, 1987), 34.

207. John Leland, "The Virginia Chronicle" (Virginia: n.p., 1790), repr. in John Leland, *The Writings of Elder John Leland*, ed. L. F. Greene (New York: Arno Press, 1969; repr., New York: G.W. Wood, 1845), 15.

208. Leland, "An Elective Judiciary, with other things, recommended in a Speech pronounced at Cheshire, July 4, 1805," repr. in Leland, *The Writings of Elder John Leland*, 294.

209. William R. Estep notes Leland's friendship with Thomas Jefferson and James Madison, and reprints a copy of Leland's "Objections to the Constitution without a Bill of Rights," sent to Madison dated February 28, 1788, in the appendix to Estep, *Revolution Within the Revolution*, 199–201.

Four years after Leland's death, a Miss L. F. Greene published a collection of Leland's writings, as well as a few biographical notes. Greene writes:

> The great object, (next in importance to his mission as a preacher of Christ,) for which he seems to have been raised up by a special Providence, was to promote the establishment of religious liberty in the United States. His efforts, perhaps, contributed as much as those of any other man, to the overthrow of ecclesiastical tyranny in Virginia, the state of his adoption, and exerted a beneficial influence, though less successful, towards the promotion of that same end in that of his nativity [Leland was born in Massachusetts and returned there to live in 1791]. In the former [i.e., in Virginia], in the years 1786–7–8, we find his name in the doings of the Baptist General Committee, with which he stood connected, as messenger to the [Virginia] General Assembly, appointed to draft and present memorials respecting the *Incorporating* act, the application of *glebe lands* to public use, etc. Though the cause of religious freedom was the common cause of all dissenters, yet the Baptists, as a sect, took the lead in those active, energetic, and persevering measures, which at length prevailed [*sic*] in its establishment.

L. F. Greene, "Further Sketches of the Life of John Leland," in Leland, *The Writings of Elder John Leland*, 52.

210. Leland, "The Virginia Chronicle," in Leland, *The Writings of Elder John Leland*, 107, 108, 118 (emphasis added).

211. Leland, "A Blow At the Root: Being a Fashionable Fast-Day Sermon Delivered at Cheshire [Mass.], April 9, 1801," in Leland, *The Writings of Elder John Leland*, 238.

212. Leland writes,

> As it is not in the province of civil government to establish forms of religion and force a maintenance for the preachers, so it does not belong to that power to establish fixed holy days for divine worship. . . . If Jesus appointed the day to be observed, he did it as the head of the church, and not as the king of nations; or if the apostles enjoined it, they did it in the capacity of Christian teachers, and not as human legislators. As the appointment of such days is no part of human legislation, so the breach of the Sabbath (so called) is no part of civil jurisdiction. . . . [T]hese times should be fixed by the mutual agreement of religious societies, according to the word of God, and not by civil authority. I see no clause in the federal constitution, or the constitution of Virginia, to empower either the federal or Virginia legislature to make any Sabbathical laws.

Leland, "The Virginia Chronicle," repr. in Leland, *The Writings of Elder John Leland*, 118–19.

213. Leland writes,

> Under this head ["The Excess of Civil Power Exploded"], I shall also take notice of one thing, which appears to me unconstitutional, inconsistent with religious liberty, and unnecessary in itself; I mean the paying of the chaplains of the civil and military departments out of the public treasury. . . . If legislatures choose to have a chaplain, for Heaven's sake, let them pay him by contributions and not out of the public chest. . . . For chaplains to go into the army, is about as good economy as it was for Israel to carry the ark of God to battle: instead of reclaiming the people, they generally are corrupted themselves, as the ark fell into the hands of the Philistines. The words of David are applicable here: "Carry back the ark into the city." But what I aim chiefly at, is paying of them by law. . . . Such golden sermons and silver prayers are of no great value.

Id. at 119.

214. In "The Yankee Spy," a pamphlet published in 1794 under the pen name "Jack Nips," John Leland writes:

> What leads legislators into this error [the error of compelling public worship], is confounding *sins* and *crimes* together—making no difference between *moral evil* and *state rebellion:* not considering that a man may be infected with moral evil [note the use of imagery from the levitical type!], and yet be guilty of no crime, punishable by law. If a man worships one God, three Gods, twenty Gods, or no God—if he pays adoration one day in a week, or seven, or no day— wherein does he injure the life, liberty or property of another? Let any or all of these actions [note the use of the term "actions" as opposed to "beliefs"] be supposed to be religious evils of an enormous size, yet they are not crimes to be punished by the laws of state, which extend no further, in justice, than to punish the man who works ill to his neighbor.
>
> When civil rulers undertake to make laws against moral evil, and punish men for heterodoxy in religion, they often run to grand extremes. . . . In short, volumes might be written, and have been written, to show what havoc among men the principle of mixing *sins* and *crimes* together has effected, while men in power have taken their own opinions as infallible tests of right and wrong.

Jack Nips [John Leland], "The Yankee Spy" (n.p., 1794), repr. in Leland, *The Writings of Elder John Leland*, 221.

This concern about mixing moral and civil evils led Leland to also condemn the flip side of this issue, that is, the mixing of justice and mercy. A legislator is solely concerned with dispensing and insuring justice; "mercy" is the work of private individuals. Leland writes:

> Human laws reach no farther than to force a man to be just to his neighbor. The divine law enjoins on men . . . mercies. Mercy is a moral duty not a legal one. No man can perform moral virtue when forced against his will . . . If men are forced to relieve the distressed, it cannot be mercy. To force a man to part with his hard-earned property, to relieve the needs of another, cannot be just. . . . I see no clause in the constitution which authorizes congress to dis-

pose of the money in the treasury for the relief of any sufferers by fire; therefore, such laws must be unjust.

John Leland, "An Elective Judiciary," repr. in Leland, *The Writings of Elder John Leland*, 293.

215. John Leland, "A Blow At the Root," repr. in Leland, *The Writings of Elder John Leland*, 237–38.

216. *Id.* at 239.

217. *Id.* at 236.

218. *Id.* at 250. Leland does not stop at the point where others' interests are directly harmed, but he continues to justify this limitation on religious conscience by indicating that the law, under the proper strict separation of church and state, *cannot* take religious motives into account when judging the criminality of actions: "Whether this lawless sect should plead that they were influenced by their God, or by the devil, or neither of them, it would not alter their case in the least; for the court would not judge of their motives, but of their actions." *Id.* This remark is legally accurate with respect to the paradigmatic setting in which it was made, (i.e., destruction of the property or injury to the person of another). Where the crime does not directly involve such injury or destruction to another person, Leland's assertion that courts should not consider religious motivation becomes more problematic. In crimes where motive is an element, for example, a motive of religious compulsion would be treated differently (i.e., disregarded) from other motives. Where legal "excuses" or exemptions or exceptions are incorporated into a law, religion should be open to equal consideration; to do otherwise is, again, to give religious obligations an *unequal,* "second-class" status. The further away the situation is from the paradigms used by Leland, the less applicable his pronouncement on the inadmissibility of religious motive becomes.

219. Leland, "An Elective Judiciary," repr. in Leland, *The Writings of Elder John Leland*, 295 (emphasis added). Leland broadly, and perhaps with tongue in cheek, suggests that if such unjust and improper laws be imposed by a majority as in accordance with *their* rights of conscience, then at the very least these laws should be written in such a way that they apply only to those with such conscientious scruples:

> [A] man, therefore, who believes in religious incorporation, can joyfully give in his name to be taxed; and he who believes that law has nothing to do about religious worship, can as joyfully stay at home. The last of these have as good grounds to judge that the first plead conscience for cruelty, as the first have to judge that the last plead conscience for covetousness.

Jack Nips [John Leland], "The Yankee Spy," repr. in Leland, *The Writings of Elder John Leland*, 225. See also Isaac Backus's discussion of the third article of the proposed Massachusetts Bill of Rights, in Backus, "Truth is Great And Will Prevail" (Boston: n.p. (Philip Freeman, seller), 1781), repr. in McLoughlin, ed., *Backus*, 402 *et seq.,* esp. 418–25.

220. Backus's sources are heavily premised within the two kingdoms' scriptural authorities. For example, Backus argues that a new covenant governs the New Testament Church:

> The constitution, priesthood, and ordinances of the Jewish church served unto the *example* and *shadow* of heavenly things, but this is a *better* covenant which is established upon *better promises.* That *old* covenant Israel *brake,* and he *regarded them not.* But this *new* covenant is established upon better promises which are, *I will* and *they shall, Heb.* viii, 5–13. I can't imagine that 'tis possible for words to express more plainly than these do that there is an essential differ-

ence between the *materials* as well as the *forms* of the two churches; even the same that there is between shadow and substance, flesh and spirit, type and anti-type.

Isaac Backus, "A Fish Caught in His Own Net" (Boston: Edes & Gill, 1768), repr. in McLoughlin, ed. *Backus*, 181 (emphasis in original). The tract was written in response to sermons published by a Mr. Joseph Fish of Stoningham, in which Fish claims that the "*Standing Churches* in *New England* are built upon the *Rock,* and . . . that *Separates* and *Baptists* are joining with the *Gates of Hell* against them." *Id.* at 171 (emphasis in original). See also, *id.* at 187–88, where Backus discusses the parable of the tares and the wheat. Interestingly, the "public currency" of arguments for religious liberty which were premised within the enlightenment type is evinced by Backus's own resort to such arguments in his public advocacy against the "Standing Order." See, for example, his statement that men who support church establishment argue and act "contrary both to Scripture *and reason.*" *Id.* at 199 (emphasis added).

221. Backus, "An Appeal To the Public For Religious Liberty" (Boston: John Boyle, 1773), repr. in McLoughlin, ed., *Backus,* 312, *et seq.* Backus writes, "God has appointed two kinds of government in the world which are distinct in their nature and ought never to be confounded together, one of which is called civil the other ecclesiastical government." *Id.* at 312.

222. *Id.* at 313–14.

223. *Id.* at 315.

224. *Id.* 314, 316 (emphasis in original). See also Backus's arguments in Isaac Backus, "A Door Opened For Equal Christian Liberty, And No Man Can Shut It" (Boston: Philip Freeman, 1783), repr. in McLoughlin, ed., *Backus,* 436–38. Herein, Backus again rejects the example of ancient Israel, noting: "In Israel God was their only lawgiver, and our fathers run into their error by attempting to form a Christian Commonwealth in imitation of the Theocracy of the Jews." *Id.* at 436. Succinctly, Backus writes that

> no man can become a member of a truly religious society without his own consent and also that no corporation that is not a religious society can have a right to govern in religious matters. Christ said, *who made me a judge, or a divider over you?* And Paul said, *what have I to do to judge them also that are without? Luke* xii, 14; *Cor.* v, 12. Thus our Divine Lord and the great apostle of the Gentiles explicitly renounced any judicial power over the world by virtue of their religion.

Id. at 437 (emphasis in original).

Backus further echoes the two kingdoms type as he asserts that true "Christianity is a voluntary obedience to God's revealed will, and everything of a contrary nature is antichristianism." *Id.* at 438. Backus reasons,

> [T]he highest civil rulers derive their power from the consent of the people and cannot stand without their support. And common people know that nothing is more contrary to the rules of honesty than for some to attempt to convey to others things which they have no right to themselves, and no one has any right to judge for others in religious affairs.

Id. at 436.

225. Isaac Backus, "Government and Liberty Described; and Ecclesiastical Tyranny Exposed" (Boston: Powars and Willis, 1778), repr. in McLoughlin, ed., *Backus,* 353 (quoting Phillips Payson, Election Sermon at Boston, May 27, 1778).

226. *Id.* at 353, 358.

227. Isaac Backus, "An Appeal To The People of the Massachusetts State Against Arbitrary Power" (Boston: Benjamin Edes and Sons, 1780), repr. in McLoughlin, ed., *Backus*, 394 (emphasis added).

228. Isaac Backus, "Policy, As Well As Honesty, Forbids the Use of Secular Force in Religious Affairs" (Boston: Draper and Folsom, 1779), repr. in McLoughlin, ed., *Backus*, 371.

229. *Id.* at 372.

230. Backus writes,

> Now who can hear Christ declare that his kingdom is NOT OF THIS WORLD, and yet believe that this blending of church and state together can be pleasing to him? For though their laws call them "orthodox ministers," yet the grand test of their orthodoxy is the major vote of the people, be they saints or sinners, believers or unbelievers.

Backus, "An Appeal To the Public," in McLoughlin, ed., *Backus*, 318 (emphasis in original). See also *id.* at 321.

231. *Id.* at 323 (emphasis in original).

232. Backus, "A Fish Caught in His Own Net," in McLoughlin, ed., *Backus*, 251 (emphasis in original).

233. *Id.* at 240–41. Backus writes,

> Mr. *Fish* insinuates that 'tis our lusts which move us to deny their way of supporting ministers, and says, "Let the Lord of conscience judge whether 'tis not *covetousness* (accompanied with *wilfulness* and *disobedience*, all founded upon *weakness*) rather than *pure conscience* that enduceth the *Separates* to *forfeit* their honor in breaking their *own* and their *father's* civil covenants to save their money," p. 164.

Id. (emphasis in original). Backus notes that orthodoxy by majority "emboldens them to usurp God's judgment seat, and (according to Dr. Mather's account which we have often seen verified) they daringly give out their sentence that for a *few* to profess a persuasion different from the *majority*, it must be from bad motives. . . ." Backus, "An Appeal To the Public," in McLoughlin, ed., *Backus*, 321 (emphasis in original).

234. *Id.* at 253–57. Such accusations increased Backus's conviction that a person cannot judge another's heart:

> And what I have endured has taught me the vast importance of the divine caution which we have against *judging the counsels of others hearts.* What they say and do we have a warrant to judge upon and to labor to convince them where we think they are in the wrong, but to charge them with being *biased* by corruption if they don't presently yield to our arguments; as it is a violation of the law of God, so no tongue can express all the mischiefs which it has made among God's people in all ages. . . . For wherever this enemy creeps in among any denominations it moves ministers and people to slander those who differ from them. . . .

Id. at 260–61 (emphasis in original).

235. Backus, "A Door Opened," in McLoughlin, ed., *Backus*, 433.

236. Backus, "A Fish Caught in His Own Net," in McLoughlin, ed., *Backus*, 241–42 (emphasis in original).

237. *Id.* at 244–45.

238. *Id.* at 273. Backus notes that whenever God turns persons from darkness to light, inevitably

> a loud noise is soon raised about *disorders, delusions and imprudencies,* and all arts are used to blind peoples' minds, and to settle them back into carnal security again. . . . And the destroyer of souls would persuade them that there is nothing in religion. Or if there is some reality therein, yet that common people can't discern the difference and therefore must be directed by such as know better than they. . . . Nor is the disorder less on the other hand when any under a pretense of *special teachings* and *divine influence* crowd their improvements upon those who are not edified thereby, and plead their right to do so because they see further than others who they say can't discern where they are. . . .

Id. at 280, 281 (emphasis in original).

Hence, it is reasonable to conclude that claims of civil disorder and disturbance of the peace were made against the Separatists, who in turn argued that it was the majority's intolerance and denial of their rights of conscience which breached the civil peace. It is also reasonable to conclude that Backus advocated, according to the two kingdoms type, a free exercise of religion which (1) extends beyond mere freedom of belief and includes *practice* and (2) is premised in the worldview that since all are depraved, government and church leaders have no special insight into truth, and thus every individual including the "common man" must be accorded freedom of conscience in religious matters.

239. Backus, "Policy, As Well As Honesty," in McLouhlin, ed., *Backus,* 373. Backus writes:

> If any inquire how tyranny, simony, and robbery came to be introduced and to be practiced so long, under the Christian name, the answer is plain from the word of truth. It was by *deceitful reasonings* from the *hand-writings* which Christ *blotted* out and *nailed to his cross, Col.* ii, 8, 14. In those writings direction was given to Israel to seize the lands and goods of the heathens, to make slaves of them, and in other respects, to make a visible distinction in their dealing betwixt their own brethren and all others. A high priest was also set up at the head of their worship who, with his family, were to have the whole direction thereof and at whose sentence unclean persons were to be excluded from their camp, unclean houses pulled down and removed, and who had power to turn even a king out of the temple. And who can describe all the superstition, blind-devotion, and church-tyranny that have been brought in by deceitful reasonings from thence!

Id. (emphasis in original) (note the references to "unclean"). Backus gives "two infallible marks" by which a false church ("that mystery Babylon") can be known:

> 1. By not holding the HEAD, even the ONE LAWGIVER, in whom the church is COMPLETE but imposing *ordinances* upon her after the *doctrines and commandments of men* which have a *show* but not the reality of *wisdom, Col.* ii, 10, 19; *James* iv, 12.
>
> 2. By not allowing each believer to act *as he has been taught* but others *puffed up with a fleshly mind,* assume the power to *judge* for them in religious matters, *Col.* ii, 7, 16–18.

Id. at 373–74.(emphasis in original). Backus then concludes that human laws which invade the province of religion all bear the mark of the "beast":

> And can any religious establishment by human laws be found without at least these *marks* of the beast and the *number of his name*, which is the *number of a man*. . . . [T]he whole of the late ecclesiastical laws of this province were commandments of men which empowered the ruling party to judge for the rest in religious affairs and to enforce that judgment with the sword.

Id. (emphasis in original).

240. Backus, "Policy, As Well As Honesty," in McLoughlin, ed., *Backus*, 374–75 (emphasis in original). See also *id.* at 375–76 (further remarks refuting arguments that civil society apply religion "for the good of the state," etc.). McLoughlin interestingly interprets Backus, in this pamphlet, as "insist[ing] that he believed as strongly as the Standing clergy that Massachusetts should be a Christian state." William G. McLoughlin, "Editor's Introduction to Pamphlet 7, Policy, As Well As Honesty," in McLoughlin, ed., *Backus*, 369.

241. Backus, "A Fish Caught in His Own Net," in McLoughlin, ed., *Backus*, 278 (emphasis in original). Backus continues, "And let who will deny others the liberty which they take themselves or *judge* and *set at naught* their brethren for taking such liberty, yet the day is hastening when we must all stand before the *judgment seat* of HIM who has *eyes like a flame of fire.*" *Id.* (emphasis in original).

242. Backus, "Government and Liberty Described," in McLoughlin, ed., *Backus*, 350.

243. Backus, "An Appeal To the Public," in McLoughlin, ed., *Backus*, 309, 310, 311 (emphasis in original).

244. Backus, "Policy, As Well As Honesty," in McLoughlin, ed., Backus, 371.

245. Backus, "A Door Opened," in McLoughlin, ed., *Backus*, 438 (emphasis in original).

246. Note that, under the levitical and the duly ordered relationships types, the government would have the authority and power of the sword to preserve and protect true religion.

247. Backus, "Truth Is Great," in McLoughlin, ed., *Backus*, 422 (emphasis in original).

248. McLoughlin maintains that Backus's inclusiveness did not extend to Roman Catholics, noting that Backus deplored that Roman Catholics could hold positions in the Massachusetts legislature. William G. McLoughlin, *Isaac Backus and the American Pietistic Tradition* (Boston: Little, Brown, 1967), 148–50. In light of Backus's specific referral to Papists in "Truth is Great," quoted above, however, it would seem that Backus's inclusiveness, at least in his public writings, did extend further than John Locke's, and included the (despised) Roman Catholics.

249. William G. McLoughlin, "The Role of Religion in the Revolution," in Kurtz, Hutson, eds., *Essays on the American Revolution*, 212 at n.18.

250. Backus, "Truth is Great," in McLoughlin, ed., *Backus*, 425 (emphasis in original).

251. Michael W. McConnell, "The Origins and Historical Understanding of Free Exercise of Religion," *Harvard Law Review* 103 (1990):1410, 1512–13.

252. The Constitution of Pennsylvania, September 28, 1776, stated:

> II. That all men have a natural and unalienable right to worship Almighty God according to the dictates of their own consciences and understanding; And that no man ought or of right can be compelled to attend any religious worship, or erect or support any place of worship, or maintain any ministry, contrary to, or against, his own free will and consent: Nor can any man, who acknowledges the being of a God, be justly deprived or abridged of any civil right as a citizen, on

account of his religious sentiments or peculiar mode of worship: And that no authority can or ought to be vested in, or assumed by any power whatever, that shall in any case interfere with, or in any manner control, the right of conscience in the free exercise of religious worship.

"Constitution of Pennsylvania" (September 28, 1776), in Francis N. Thorpe, *Federal and State Constitutions, Colonial Charters, and other Organic Laws of the States, Territories, and Colonies Now or Heretofore Forming the United States of America*, vol. 5 (Washington, D.C.: U.S. Government Printing Office, 1909), 3082, repr. in Curran, *Catholics in Colonial Law* 113–14.

253. [Samuel Bryan?], "The Address and Reasons of Dissent of the Minority of the Convention of Pennsylvania to their Constituents," (December 18, 1787), in Ralph Ketcham, ed., *The Anti-Federalist Papers and the Constitutional Convention Debates* (New York: Mentor (Penguin), 1986), 255.

The editor's note indicates that this address was signed by twenty-one of the twenty-three-member minority who voted against the ratification of the Constitution at the Pennsylvania convention. The editor also notes: "The address was subsequently reprinted often in Pennsylvania and other states, becoming in some way a semi-official statement of anti-federalist objections to the new Constitution." *Id.* at 237.

254. Richard K. MacMaster, *Conscience in Crisis: Mennonites and Other Peace Churches in America, 1739–1789*, Studies in Anabaptist and Mennonite History, no. 20 (Scottsdale, Pa.: Herald Press, 1979), 27, 50, and see especially 211 *et seq.* "The nonresistant sects . . . made up no more than a fourth of the population in Pennsylvania and a much smaller proportion of the settlers in the other colonies."

255. MacMaster, *Conscience in Crisis*, 298–300. Mennonite gunsmiths were renowned for their "Pennsylvania rifle" craftsmanship. Making rifles to kill deer for food was quite a different matter from filling an order for the military. MacMaster notes, however, that a few Mennonites continued to make guns to arm Washington's army. *Id.*

256. As noted by MacMaster, Mennonites served in the wagon service during the Revolutionary War. Such items as "cattle, clothing, farm produce, and blankets" were also provided by the peace churches, both voluntarily and also by legal requisition. *Id.* at 297–98, 345–49.

257. As indicated in a petition by conscientious objectors, the fine was "in such a Degree, whereby numbers of Families would be reduced to utter Ruin, and such Fines to be raised by distraint of their Goods, by military force." Untitled petition, Document 135, drafted at a meeting on September 1, 1775, repr. in *id.* at 256–57.

258. *Id.* at 324–25.

259. As MacMaster notes,

Even without the influence of the peace churches, the first large-scale military draft in American history was bound to cause resentment as men were dragged from their homes to fight for a cause that many did not really support and that many more believed could not succeed. Quakers, Mennonites, and Methodists, each a readily identifiable minority, provided an easy excuse for the lack of enthusiasm that spread through every religious, ethnic, and economic group in the newly-independent United States on the first anniversary of the signing of the declaration.

Id. at 288–89.

260. See, for example, U.S. Representative Bob Barr, "Barr Demands End to Taxpayer-Funded Witchcraft on American Military Bases," press release, May 18, 1999. The

U.S. military had simply allowed its members to practice their rituals on base, under the same generally applicable rules of conduct and decorum applied to any faith group. The full text of Barr's press release is as follows:

BARR DEMANDS END TO TAXPAYER-FUNDED WITCHCRAFT
ON AMERICAN MILITARY BASES

WASHINGTON, DC—U.S. Representative Bob Barr (GA-7) has demanded an end to the taxpayer-supported practice of witchcraft on military bases. Barr's request came in response to reports that chaplains at Fort Hood, and other bases, are sanctioning, if not supporting, the practice of witchcraft as a "religion" by soldiers on military bases.

"This move sets a dangerous precedent that could easily result in the practice of all sorts of bizarre practices being supported by the military under the rubric of 'religion.' What's next? Will armored divisions be forced to travel with sacrificial animals for Satanic rituals? Will Rastifarians demand the inclusion of ritualistic marijuana cigarettes in their rations?," said Barr, in letters to military and congressional leaders.

In support of his request, Barr noted the Supreme Court's decision in Goldman v. Weinberger, 475 U.S. 503 (1986), in which Chief Justice Rehnquist wrote, "[t]he military need not encourage debate or tolerate protest to the extent that such tolerance is required of the civilian state by the First Amendment; to accomplish its mission, the military must foster instinctive obedience, unity, commitment, and esprit de corps . . ."

"A print of the painting, "The Prayer At Valley Forge," depicting George Washington on bended knee, praying in the hard snow at Valley Forge, hangs over the desk in my office. If the practice of witchcraft, such as is allowed now at Fort Hood, is permitted to stand, one wonders what paintings will grace the walls of future generations," Barr concluded in his letters.

Barr, a former United States Attorney, serves on the House Judiciary, Government Reform, and Banking committees.

261. H. J. Eckenrode, *Separation of Church and State in Virginia: A Study in the Development of the Revolution* (New York: Da Capo Press, 1971; repr., Richmond: Virginia State Library, 1910), 112.

262. *Id.* at 86. James Madison's notes respecting his debate with Patrick Henry are also reproduced in John T. Noonan, Jr., *The Lustre of Our Country: The American Experience of Religious Freedom* (Berkeley: Univ. of California Press, 1998), 61–64, quoting James Madison, *The Papers of James Madison*, vol. 8, ed. Robert A. Rutland and William M. E. Rachal (Chicago: Univ. of Chicago Press, 1973), 197–99.

263. As already noted, The Virginia Bill for Establishing Religious Freedom was enacted January 16, 1786. Other state constitutions had provided for a broad freedom of religion a bit earlier. Although many states still retained limitations on civil rights for non-Protestants (holding office and/or voting, usually), the following had opened up religious freedom to non-Protestants by eliminating Papist exclusions, etc.: New Jersey (July 2, 1776), Delaware (September 21, 1776), Pennsylvania (September 28, 1776), Maryland (November 11, 1776), North Carolina (December 18, 1776), Georgia (February 5, 1777), New York (April 20, 1777), Vermont (last anti-Catholic oath removed 1793), South Carolina (June 3, 1790). Curran, *Catholics in Colonial Law*, 110–25 (containing excerpts).

As noted, some limitations on civil rights, such as the right to hold public office, remained in spite of state declarations of religious freedom. The Constitution of North Carolina, while broadly declaring that "all men have a natural and unalienable right to worship Almighty God according to the dictates of their own consciences," denied state officeholding to any who "shall deny the being of God, or the truth of the Protestant religion, or the divine authority either of the Old or New Testament, or who shall hold religious principles incompatible with the freedom and safety of the State. . . ." *Constitution of North Carolina,* sections XIX, XXXII (December 18, 1776), repr. in Curran, *Catholics in Colonial Law,* 115.

Vermont, as late as July 8, 1777, had passed a constitution which stated, "nor can any man who professes the Protestant religion, be justly deprived or abridged of any civil right, as a citizen, on account of his religious sentiment, or peculiar mode of worship. . . ." *Constitution of Vermont,* chapter 1, section III (July 8, 1777), repr. in Curran, *Catholics in Colonial Law,* 118. Notably, less than ten years later the subsequent Vermont Constitutions of 1786 and 1793 eliminated the restrictions on religious liberty.

South Carolina is another interesting example of the momentum in the Founding Era for religious liberty. On March 19, 1778, South Carolina adopted a constitution which provided that "The Christian Protestant religion shall be deemed, and is hereby constituted and declared to be, the established religion of this state. That all denominations of Christian Protestants in this State, demeaning themselves peaceably and faithfully, shall enjoy equal civil and religious privileges." *Constitution of South Carolina,* section XII (March 19, 1778), repr. in Curran, *Catholics in Colonial Law,* 119. Two years later, in 1790, South Carolina "produced a new constitution more in agreement with the other states, outside of New England, on the question of religious freedom. The 'Christian Protestant religion' was disestablished, religious tests were abolished, and religious freedom was proclaimed." *Id.* at 120. This revised South Carolina Constitution of 1790 states, "The free exercise and enjoyment of religious profession and worship, without discrimination or preference, shall forever hereafter be allowed in this State to all mankind. . . ." *Id.*

264. Gaustad, ed., *A Documentary History of Religion,* 276–79.

Chapter 4

1. Michael J. Sandel, "Religious Liberty—Freedom of Conscience or Freedom of Choice?" *Utah Law Review* 1989: 598.

2. *Id.* at 609.

3. *Id.* at 611. William Penn, for example, protested against penal laws enforcing religious conformity, arguing that it is a fundamental element of penal law that the forbidden action must be "voluntary" in order for a person to be legitimately punished. Penn (who believed Reason in matters of religion to be God given) accordingly questioned the "voluntariness" of a failure to conform oneself to laws requiring orthodoxy in religion:

> Force is Punishment, and consequently unjust, unless the offense be voluntary: but he that believes according to the evidence of his own Reason, is necessitated to that Belief, and to compel him against it, were to compel him to renounce the most essential part of man, his Reason.

William Penn, "The Reasonableness of Toleration and the Unreasonableness of Penal Laws and Tests" (London, 1687), 11.

4. Charles Taylor, "Cross-Purposes: The Liberal-Communitarian Debate," in Nancy Rosenblum, ed., *Liberalism and the Moral Life* (Cambridge, Mass.: Harvard Univ. Press, 1989), 163.

5. *Id.* at 164–65 (emphasis added).

6. Charles Taylor, *Sources of the Self: The Making of the Modern Identity* (Cambridge, Mass.: Harvard Univ. Press, 1989) 16, 18.

7. *Id.* at 26.

8. *Id.* at 19.

9. *Id.* at 19, 20 (emphasis added).

10. Religious systems in the United States tend to be theistic, and the transcendent Other would be referred to, for example, as God, Spirit, Goddess, etc. There are non-theistic religions such as some types of Buddhism, and this nontheism, while not squarely within Christian assumptions about religion, would certainly be considered within the free exercise paradigm of "religion" if it had a framework constructed upon premises of a transcendent reality which has requirements and obligations perceived as derived from something besides the merely human. The key, here, is that there be Other-than-human requirements which compel the conscience. Humanist-centered philosophies or belief systems would not fall within the traditional paradigms of free exercise of *religion*. This is not the place to discuss issues concerning the scope of the term "religion," but I do note that a free exercise casuistical process would probably tend not to apply an outright conclusive presumption against those who fall outside of the traditional paradigm; it does mean that the further on the continuum one is from the core of the paradigm of "religion" the less probable it is that the free exercise clause would apply.

11. Taylor, *Sources of the Self*, 18. This is sometimes the plight of the religious perfectionist, and such religious perfectionism is not confined only to the realm of the "bizarre" cult. Indeed, many of this country's major internal battles over political and social issues (abolition, temperance, anticontraception, anti-choice/antiabortion, etc.) have been and continue to be fueled by the levitical paradigm's concern with God's retributive wrath and corporate responsibility for sin.

12. *Id.* Interestingly, the California Supreme Court in the case of *Walker v. Superior Court*, 47 Cal.3d 112, 763 P.2d 852, 253 Cal. Rptr. 1 (1988), called attention to what it perceived as a *lack* of *internal* religious consequences under the Christian Science framework when a believer violates that framework and resorts to medical assistance. The assertion certainly exhibited a lack of understanding of Christian Science and was a highly inappropriate application of dominant Protestant norms. What is most interesting to note at this point, however, is the *Walker* court's failure to consider the consequences to a religious community and to its adherents when the religious framework is destroyed by *external* legal persecution.

13. Taylor, *Sources of the Self*, 27.

14. *Congressional Globe*, 36th Cong., 1st Sess. (remarks of Representative L. M. Keitt, April 4, 1860), appendix 198 (emphasis added).

15. Richard K. Sherwin, "Rhetorical Pluralism and the Discourse Ideal: Countering *Employment Division v. Smith*, a Parable of Pagans, Politics, and Majoritarian Rule," *Northwestern Univ. Law Review* 85 (1991), 388, 437–39.

16. The court's opinion in *U.S. v. Myers*, 906 Fed. Supp. 1494 (D. Wyo. 1995), contains a definition of "religion" reached after a lengthy review of the judiciary's attempts at defining the term as used in the Bill of Rights.

Phillip E. Hammond, however, argues for including all "claims of conscience" within the protection of the religion clauses of the Constitution. In response to the point that religion is, after all, specifically mentioned in the Bill of Rights, Hammond offers the following argument, framed in terms of establishment clause considerations.

[T]he religiously plural society that honors religious liberty cannot give privileged status to religion on the basis of the nature and content of its beliefs. To do that is necessarily to establish or favor some religion(s) over others. The solution therefore is to define religion not by content but by function, which is the maner by which conscience becomes, for legal purposes, the equivalent of religion.

Phillip E. Hammond, *With Liberty For All: Freedom of Religion in the United States* (Louisville, Ky.: Westminster John Knox Press, 1998), 85.

17. Parent participation forms for a public school series of sports camps included the following statement of acknowledgment and release:

I/we hereby give consent for my son/daughter to participate in the ____camp. I/we know of and acknowledge that my son/daughter knows of the risks involved in athletic participation, understands that serious injury, and even death, is possible in such participation, and choose to accept any and all responsibility for his/her safety and welfare while participating in this camp. . . .

Similarly, an Indiana gymnastics school has the following statement on its parental release form: "I recognize that my child will be participating in tumbling, gymnastics, cheerleading, and trampoline activities, that my child could possibly be injured very seriously, including permanent paralysis or death." Yet, it is not "child abuse" to send one's child to sports camp or allow her to participate in sports activities such as gymnastics.

18. Walker v. Superior Court, 47 Cal.3d 112, 139; 253 Cal. Rptr. 1, 19 (1988). "Sin" and "divine retribution" were the court's own terms. This case is discussed in some detail in chapter 7.

19. United States v. Ballard, 322 U.S. 78 (1944) (charge of mail fraud).

20. But freedom of speech is not and probably has never been an "absolute" and is generally subjected to "content" testing. For example, speech which slanders or libels a person is unprotected; harmful "prank" speech such as the proverbial yelling of "fire" in a crowded theater is also unprotected; commercial (e.g., business advertisements) speech is not as protected as political speech; speech about a private citizen is less protected than that which is said about a public figure. Additionally, all speech is subject to regulations as to reasonable time, place, noise/volume, parade permits, etc.

21. Employment Div. v. Smith, 494 U.S. 872, 886–87 (1990).

22. *Id.* at 889, n.5 (emphasis added).

23. See, for example, *Thomas v. Review Board*, 450 U.S. 707 (1981), in which the State of Indiana argued that Thomas was not entitled to worker's compensation benefits because his claim that, as a Jehovah's Witness, his religious beliefs would not allow him to participate in the manufacture and production of war materials, was not true for all Jehovah's Witnesses. The state lost. The Court in the *Thomas* case explained:

The Indiana court also appears to have given significant weight to the fact that another Jehovah's Witness had no scruples about working on tank turrets; for that other Witness, at least, such work was "scripturally" acceptable. Intrafaith differences of that kind are not uncommon among followers of a particular creed, and the judicial process is singularly ill equipped to resolve such differences in relation to the Religion Clauses. . . . Courts are not arbiters of scriptural interpretation.

450 U.S. at 715–16.

24. *Reynolds v. United States*, 98 U.S. at 166.

Chapter 5

1. Kenneth E. Kirk, *Conscience and Its Problems: An Introduction to Casuistry*, with an introduction by David H. Smith (Louisville, Ky.: Westminster John Knox Press, 1999; repr., London: Longmans, Green, 1927), 113–14.

2. Jonathan Z. Smith, *Map Is Not Territory* (Leiden, The Netherlands: E. J. Brill, 1978), 134–35.

3. *Id.* at 136.

4. Howard S. Becker, *Outsiders: Studies in the Sociology of Deviance* (New York: Free Press, 1963), 2.

5. Richard Slotkin, *Regeneration Through Violence: The Mythology of the American Frontier, 1600–1860* (Middletown, Conn.: Wesleyan Univ. Press, 1973), 77–78. This discussion was raised in the context of the Puritans' Indian war narratives.

6. Kai T. Erikson, *Wayward Puritans: A Study in the Sociology of Deviance* (New York: John Wiley & Sons, Inc., 1966), 11.

7. *Id.* at 9–11.

8. For a more philosophical description of the distinctions among judicial, legislative, and public knowledge-discourse, see Richard K. Sherwin, "Rhetorical Pluralism and the Discourse Ideal: Countering *Employment Division v. Smith*, a Parable of Pagans, Politics, and Majoritarian Rule," *Northwestern University Law Review* 85 (winter 1991): 388, 400–06.

9. The Court in the case of *City of Boerne v. Flores*, 117 S.Ct. 2157 (1997), invalidated the federal 1993 Religious Freedom Restoration Act to the extent that it applied to actions by state governments. Hence, the extent of Congress's ability to expand upon basic liberties protected in the Constitution is now in question; see Douglas Laycock, "Conceptual Gulfs in *City of Boerne v. Flores*," *William and Mary Law Review* 39 (1998): 743, 758–71.

10. This function of the courts as protectors of individual rights guaranteed under the Constitution has come under fire lately as an elitist threat to the democratic process. See, for example, Robert H. Bork, *The Tempting of America: The Political Seduction of the Law* (New York: Touchstone Book, Simon & Schuster, 1991). Even Judge Bork, however, grants that the power of the courts is not simply to preside over trials that decide issues of fact (i.e., was the law broken?), but also to decide issues of law by "seeing that the powers granted [to the legislature] by the Constitution are not used to invade the freedoms guaranteed by the Bill of Rights." *Id.* at 4.

The powers which Judge Bork would see granted more properly to the democratic majority are sweeping. He limits the scope of the free exercise clause only to laws which explicitly ban a religion or a religious practice. Hence, he criticizes the Court's decision in *Yoder* by noting that the "Wisconsin statute . . . was in no way aimed at religion." *Id.* at 247. The "great expansion of the free exercise clause," Bork continues, "serves to reinforce individual autonomy even against laws that are in no way aimed at religion." *Id.* at 248. Bork instead argues that the only proper thing for the courts to do is uphold the moral sensibilities of the majority as reflected in statutory enactments. Bork in essence has a duly ordered relationships view of the power between the individual conscience and the state (here, the "state" is the democratic majority). Judge Bork accords emotivist deference to the hard objective legitimacy of legislative enactments, and he denounces judicial "searching scrutiny" for what Bork deems soft subjectivity and its grounding in the individual tastes of the judges.

11.

[T]he central fact about deviance . . . [is that] it is created by society. . . .
[S]ocial groups create deviance by making the rules whose infraction constitutes

deviance, and by applying those rules to particular people and labeling them as outsiders. From this point of view, deviance is *not* a quality of the act the person commits, but rather a consequence of the application by others of rules and sanctions to an "offender." The deviant is one to whom that label has success-fully been applied; deviant behavior is behavior that people so label.

Becker, *Outsiders*, 8–9 (author's emphasis). Examining the phenomenon of social de-viance as a series of interactions between society and its outsiders is proposed here as a procedural (i.e., a methodological) tool. As noted, the *Reynolds* Court made the *proce-dural* decision to accept, unchallenged, all legislative pronouncements as to social de-viance, and to apply them without question to the criminal punishment or sanctioning of religiously motivated behavior. The distinction between the investigative *process* (which, for the purposes of this book, can be compared to the judicial function) and the ultimate judgment that some practice is "deviant" is noted by Becker:

> Both sides [the "centrist critics" and the critics on the "Left"] want to see their ethical preconceptions built into scientific work in the form of uninspected fac-tual assertions relying on the implicit use of ethical judgments about which there is a high degree of consensus. Thus, if I say that rape is *really* deviant or imperialism *really* a social problem, I imply that these phenomena have certain empirical characteristics which, we would all agree, make them reprehensible. We might, by our studies, be able to establish just that; but we are very often asked to accept it by definition. Defining something as deviant or a social prob-lem makes the empirical demonstration unnecessary and protects us from dis-covering that our preconception is incorrect (when the world isn't as we imag-ine it). When we protect our ethical judgements from empirical tests by enshrining them in definitions we commit the error of sentimentalism.

Howard S. Becker, "Labelling Theory Reconsidered," in Paul Rock and Mary McIntosh, eds., *Deviance and Social Control* (London: Tavistock Publications, 1974), 58. Similarly, the point here is that the Court must not protect legislative enactments and their particu-lar applications from constitutional scrutiny by "enshrining" them in the *Reynolds* doctrine.

12. Erikson, *Wayward Puritan*, 8.

13. *Id*, at 4.

14. As noted by Smith, in the religious context of the wilderness myth, chaos is at once sacred power and the antithesis of the sacred: Chaos supplies the necessary energy, creativity, motion, life, to the realm of sacred.

> Like the famous myth of the charioteer in Plato's *Phaedrus*, both horses are equally necessary. If one had only the white horse of decorum, temperance, and restraint, he would never reach heaven and the gods. . . . Thus, chaos is never, in myths, finally overcome. It remains as a creative challenge, as a source of possibility and vitality over against, yet inextricably related to, order and the Sacred.

Smith, *Map Is Not Territory*, 97.

15. Stanley Cohen, *Folk Devils and Moral Panics: The Creation of the Mods and the Rockers* (London: MacGibbon & Kee, 1972), 9.

16. The Santeria practice of animal sacrifice in the *Church of the Lukumi* case, for example, was religiously deviant to some Christians of Hialeah and abominable to secu-lar animal welfare groups.

17. For a detailed discussion of the creative measures attempted, with varying success, by overzealous, "vindictive" prosecutors in Utah against the Mormon polygamists, see Edwin B. Firmage, "The Judicial Campaign Against Polygamy and the Enduring Legal Questions," *Brigham Young University Studies* 27 (summer 1987) 96–108, and Edwin B. Firmage and Richard C. Mangrum, *Zion in the Courts: A Legal History of the Church of Jesus Christ of Latter-day Saints, 1830–1900* (Urbana: Univ. of Illinois Press, 1988), chapter 7.

Firmage also notes that the Court, while completely depriving the Mormons of substantive rights of religious practice, did take some measures to curtail the worst of the procedural abuses being inflicted by the combined efforts of federal judges and prosecutors in Utah under the 1882 Edmunds Act. See In re Snow, 120 U.S. 274 (1887), and U.S. v. Bassett, 137 U.S. 496 (1890).

18. In the case of *Church of the Lukumi Babalu Aye v. City of Hialeah*, for example, the Court noted that the city ordinances, ostensibly aimed at animal abuse by banning animal sacrifice, were both overbroad and underinclusive: "The proffered objectives are not pursued with respect to analogous non-religious conduct, and those interests could be achieved by narrower ordinances that burdened religion to a far lesser degree." 508 U.S. at 546.

19. See the brief and the *amicus* briefs submitted on behalf of the respondents, Alfred Smith and Galen Black, as well as the Oregon attorney general's brief, in *Employment Division v. Smith*. These will be discussed, in chapter 6

20. Alexander Hamilton, *The Federalist* No. 78, in Clinton Rossitor, ed., *The Federalist Papers* (New York: A Mentor Book, New American Library, 1961), 467–68.

As the Mormon persecutions escalated to the point where even the right to vote could be stripped from them, Alexander Hamilton's statements should have served as guidance and a warning to the judiciary concerning its proper role in constitutional controversies. Instead, the interpretive guide of legislative history, or "original intent," was selectively manipulated to achieve the desired result. James L. Clayton has further noted that

> the reasoning in *Reynolds* seems excessively eclectic. [Justice] Waite sifted through both Jefferson's writings and Lieber's books to find what was supportive while rejecting equally compelling material from these same authors which supported the Mormons' case. Waite ignored Jefferson when Jefferson wrote that the legitimate powers of government extend only to actions injurious to others. He ignored Professor Lieber's teaching that people had a right to disobey the law for religious reasons. Nor did Waite tell his audience that Jefferson was not a Christian but a Deist, suspicious of all revealed religion, or that Lieber was as blatantly anti-Mormon as he was anti-Catholic—hardly unbiased sources on the duties of the faithful.

James L. Clayton, "The Supreme Court, Polygamy, and the Enforcement of Morals in Nineteenth Century America: An Analysis of Reynolds v. United States," *Dialogue: A Journal of Mormon Thought* 12 (winter 1979): 56.

21. Hamilton, *The Federalist* No. 78, 469–70.

22. Firmage and Mangrum, *Zion in the Courts*, 208, citing *Congressional Record* 19: 9231 (1888). They write, "In retrospect, it is difficult to offer any explanation for this judicial conduct toward Mormon wives besides a spirit of vindictiveness. . . . These prosecutions, which step over the line to become persecution, signal clearly that it was Mormonism itself, not just polygamy, that the federal government wished to eradicate." *Id.* at 209.

23. Hamilton, *The Federalist No. 78*, 470.

24. Clayton, "The Supreme Court," 56.

25. *Congressional Globe*, 36th Cong. 1st Sess. (remarks of Representative Thayer, April 3, 1860), 1520. See also, *Congressional Globe*, 36th Cong., 1st Sess. (remarks of Representative L. M. Keitt, April 4, 1860), appendix 198. Indeed, the boundary-protection function may be seen as not simply a protection of the minority, but also of vital importance to the peace of society as a whole: Sherwin posits that rendering an entire segment of society "outlaw" in the absence of what he terms "principled judicial discourse" encourages that segment to confront the police/enforcing powers in acts of civil disobedience or even of violent rebellion. Sherwin asks whether a religious believer, "thrust beyond the margins of society," has any stake left in that society. Indeed, how can such a person "reasonably be expected to submit to his own demise?" Sherwin,"Rhetorical Pluralism," 437–39.

26. Clayton, "The Supreme Court," 48.

27. Klaus J. Hansen, *Mormonism and the American Experience* (Chicago: Univ. of Chicago Press, 1981), 176. Hansen believes that "modernism" may have been taking its toll internally on the Mormons, many of whom were passively resisting polygamy by the 1870s. *Id.*

28. See Page Smith, *John Adams*, vol. 1 (New York: Doublday, 1962), 120–26.

Chapter 6

1. Kenneth E. Kirk, *Conscience and Its Problems: An Introduction To Casuistry*, With an introduction by David H. Smith (Louisville, Ky.: Westminster John Knox Press, 1999; repr. London: Longmans, Green. 1927), 112.

2. Legal scholars have spilled much ink criticizing the *Smith* opinion. Two of the most respected responses are Douglas Laycock, "The Remnants of Free Exercise," *Supreme Court Review* 1990: 1, and Michael McConnell, "Free Exercise Revisionism and the *Smith* Decision," *University of Chicago Law Review* 57: (1990) 1109.

3. Interestingly, this distinction was actually at the heart of the firing controversy. The claimants' employer followed the prevailing theory that one never recovers from an addiction, but rather is always in a state of "recovering." On the other hand, under the tenets of the Native American Church, one indeed could be freed from one's alcoholic addiction and be made "well" in the sense that one would be cured of the addictive craving for alcohol through spiritual efforts. Under either notion, one would not take another drop of alcohol; the distinction was in one's self-concept: a "sinner" always on the edge of falling back into sin, or a cured (redeemed?) person, free and holy. Such concepts clearly have an underlying religious theme and are not purely and simply "medical."

4. Employment Division v. Smith, U.S. Supreme Court Docket Nos. 86-946, 86-947 (October term, 1986), opinion printed at 485 U.S. 660 (1988), Statement of John Gardin II, joint appendix p. 39 (hereinafter, Docket Nos. 86-946 and 947, including briefs, transcript of oral argument, Court's opinion, etc., shall be referred to as *Smith I*). Abstinence, here, referred not just to alcohol, but to any substance considered to be "addictive," as will be seen.

5. Black v. Employment Division, 75 Or. App. 735, 707 P.2d 1274, 1276 (1985); Smith v. Employment Division, 301 Or. 209, 212, 721 P.2d 445, 446 (1986); *Smith I*, Respondent's Brief at 3.

6. Oregon defined "misconduct connected with work" as

a wilful [*sic*] violation of the standards of behavior which an employer has the right to expect of an employe [*sic*]. An act that amounts to a wilful [sic] disregard of an employer's interest, or recurring negligence which demonstrates wrongful intent is misconduct. Isolated instances of poor judgment, good faith errors, unavoidable accidents, absences due to illness or other physical or mental disabilities, or mere inefficiency resulting from lack of job skills or experience are not misconduct for purposes of denying benefits. . . .

Smith v. Employment Div., 721 P.2d at 448.

7. "Referee" was the term used for Oregon's version of an administrative law judge, who is the person who conducts the fact-finding procedure, makes a finding of fact with respect to all contested issues, and then reaches conclusions of law by applying the facts to the judge's understanding of the law.

8. Oregon Revised Statutes Section 657.176(2)(1985) states:

An individual shall be disqualified from the receipt of benefits until the individual has performed service in employment subject to this chapter, or for an employing unit . . . for which remuneration is received which equals or exceeds four times this individual's weekly benefit amount subsequent to the week in which the act causing the disqualification occurred, if the authorized representative designated by the assistant director finds that the individual:
(a) Has been discharged for misconduct connected with work. . . .

"Misconduct" is defined in Oregon Administrative Rule 471-30-083(3)(1986), quoted above in note 6.

Smith I, Brief for Petitioners, at. 1–2.

9. The Black hearing was held separately from the Smith hearing. Black was not represented at the hearing before the referee or on the appeal before the EAB, and he therefore did not know to raise the religious freedom issue at the agency level. Smith was represented by counsel, and the free exercise issue was addressed during his hearing and on appeal to the EAB. Thus, any reference to the actual proceedings held or decisions reached at the hearing level or by the EAB, with respect to the free exercise issue, is directed to the administrative process in the *Smith* case only. Black did raise the free exercise issue on appeal to the Oregon appellate court, and in that court, as well as in the Oregon Supreme Court, the *Smith* and the *Black* matters were dealt with on equal basis. The matters were consolidated for appeal to the U.S. Supreme Court. *Smith I*, Brief for Petitioners at 3, n.3.

10. Black v. Employment Div. 707 P.2d at 1277; Smith v. Employment Div. 721 P.2d at 446.

11. *Smith I*, Respondents' Brief at p. 11 (Black and Smith were the "Respondents" in the U.S. Supreme Court case).

12. The referee at Black's hearing had determined that the ingestion was an "isolated instance of poor judgment" and granted Black unemployment benefits. The referee's decision was overturned by the EAB. Black v. Employment Div., 707 P.2d at 1276.

13. *Smith I*, Respondents' Brief at 31–32, and cases cited therein.

14. *Id.* at 27, quoting Giese v. Employment Division, 27 Or. App. 929, 557 P.2d 1344 (1976), review den. 277 Or. 491 (1977).

15. *Smith I*, Respondents' Brief at 27.

16. *Id.* at 28, referring to the case of Hoard v. Employment Division, 72 Or. App. 688, 696 P.2d 1168 (1985); 79 Or. App. 62, 717 P.2d 664 (1986).

17. Black v. Employment Div. 707 P.2d at 1278.

18. The Oregon Constitution, Article I, sections 2 and 3, provide:

Section 2. Freedom of worship. All men shall be secure in the Natural right, to worship Almighty God according to the dictates of their own consciences.

   Section 3. Freedom of religious opinion. No law shall in any case whatever control the free exercise, and enjoyment of religeous [*sic*] opinions, or interfere with the rights of conscience.

19. Oregon Revised Statutes Section 657.176(2)(1985); as noted earlier, "misconduct" is defined in Oregon Administrative Rule 471-30-083(3)(1986). *Smith I*, Brief for Petitioners at 1–2.

20. The use of the term "benefits" with respect to unemployment compensation can be misleading. The Oregon statute refers to "benefit *rights*" which are not exactly "free hand-outs" but are "based upon wages earned prior to the date of discharge." ORS 657.176(3), quoted in Smith v. Employment Div., 721 P.2d at 450, n.3.

21. Smith v. Employment Div., 721 P.2d at 448.

22. *Id.* at 448–49 (emphasis added).

23. *Id.* In a footnote, the Oregon Supreme Court quoted from ORS 657.176(3) (disqualification for "commission of a felony or theft in connection with the individual's work"), and it specifically found that "[t]his statute does not apply to claimant herein." *Id.* at 450–51, n.3.

24. Referring to the 1870s Mormon polygamy case of *Reynolds v. United States*, discussed previously in chapters 1 and 5.

25. *Smith I*, Transcript of the Oral Argument before the Supreme Court of the United States, 14: 2–6 (argument of Deputy Attorney General Gray) (hereafter cited as Tr. Oral Arg., page: lines).

26. *Smith I*, Tr. Oral Arg., 9:6–11:11 (argument of Deputy Attorney General Gray).

27. *Smith I*, 485 U.S. at 669.

28. *Smith I*, 485 U.S. at 666.

29. *Smith I*, 485 U.S. at 674 (Brennan, J., dissenting).

30. Smith v. Employment Div., 307 Or. 68, 72–73, 763 P.2d 146, 148, (1988).

31. Smith v. Employment Div., 307 Or. at 72, n.2, 763 P.2d at 148 n.2.

32. Smith v. Employment Div., 307 Or. at 73, n.3, 763 P.2d at 148, n.3.

33. Employment Division v. Smith, 494 U.S. 872 (1990), Brief *Amicus Curiae* of the American Civil Liberties Union (ACLU) and the ACLU of Oregon. The brief noted that if the Court were to uphold "a burden on the exercise of fundamental rights based on a state interest that the state's highest court has declared immaterial[,] [a]ny such result would turn somersaults with traditional notions of federalism." *Id.* at 19. Note: hereafter, the 1990 *Smith* case, docket 88-1213, and including briefs, etc., shall be referred to as *Smith II*.

34. Or, rather, adopted the state attorney general's assertion of what the state's interests were: The U.S. Supreme Court disregarded the obvious conflict between the attorney general's notions of the state interest, on the one hand, and the determinations by the judicial branch (the Oregon Supreme Court's opinion) and the Oregon State Legislature (a conviction for a violation of the criminal law was, in and of itself, not a reason to disqualify someone for unemployment compensation, *unless* there was a conviction for a theft or felony connected with work—not the situation here), on the other.

35. *Smith I*, Brief For Petitioners at 15–16.

36. *Smith I*, Statement of Robert Steiner, Joint Appendix at 27–30.

37. DeSmet writes,

Working in a medical center I have seen time and time again a chemically dependent individual being placed on pain medication or other mood altering drugs for a specific medical reason, and this use resulting in a return to drug dependency and all the dysfunctional behavior that goes along with dependency.

Smith I, Statement of John L. DeSmet, Joint Appendix at 33, 34.

38. My emphasis. Note that DeSmet does not make this statement "within a reasonable degree of medical certainty," the standard usually required for admissibility.

39. *Id.* at 35–36.

40. *Id.* at 36, 37.

41. *Smith I*, Affidavit of Dr. Robert Bergman, Joint Appendix, 18–19.

42. *Smith I*, Affidavit of Omer C. Stewart, Joint Appendix at 20, 21.

43. The "harmful entanglement" test is not used in free exercise cases. It is an establishment clause test used to determine when a state-conferred benefit (such as aid to public schools) may cross over the boundaries between church and state. Establishment clause cases determine the propriety of financial or other governmental assistance to a religious group as voted by a majority-sponsored legislature. Free exercise issues determine when legislative (or other governmental branch's) activities have unconstitutionally curtailed the religious observances of a minority religious group.

Apparently, the religious groups which used sacramental wine survived the "intrusiveness" of Prohibition regulations, although not without complaint. The Prohibition commissioner's regulations included such controls as limitations on amounts of, and proofs of entitlements to, sacramental wine. In the case of *Shapiro v. Lyle*, 30 F.2d 971 (W.D. Wash., 1929), it was noted that under Prohibition regulations, each Jewish family was allotted five gallons of wine per year and had to have an approved permit issued by the rabbi. The *Shapiro* case concerned the padlocking of eighteen gallons of wine in a room of the rabbi's home by Prohibition agents. As was the case in *Smith*, if the government is allowed to ban the religious practice, the religious framework itself could be dealt a devastating blow. It seems specious for the state to protest the intrusiveness of governmental regulation on behalf of the nondominant religious group when the alternative is a complete destruction of the religious practice, if not of the religion itself.

44. 21 U.S.C.A. Section 823(a) (1981).

45. By way of analogy, the environment formerly was an intangible easily overlooked by government administrators and officials. Just as the legislature mandated the use of environmental impact statements to ensure that the environmental repercussions of an action are given full and fair consideration, so, too, (as envisioned by Alexander Hamilton) should the U.S. Supreme Court signal to all governmental officials—legislators, prosecutors, attorneys general, the president, and governors alike—that the constitutional rights of nondominant religious followers must be given full and fair consideration.

46. 21 U.S.C.A. Section 802(20) (1981).

47. 21 U.S.C.A. Section 823 (1981 and West Supp. 1991).

48. See, for example, U.S. v. Rosenberg, 515 F.2d 190 (9th Cir. 1975), cert. denied. 423 U.S. 1031.

49. *Smith II*, Brief for Respondents, 25–31. Smith v. Employment Div., 307 Or. at 72, n.2, 763 P.2d at 148, n.2. The court noted that federal exemption was expressed in 21 C.F.R. Section 1307.31 (1987). The eleven states with express exemptions were listed by the court as Arizona, Colorado, Iowa, Kansas, Minnesota, Nevada, New Mexico, South Dakota, Texas, Wisconsin, Wyoming. The twelve states which simply incorporated the federal exemptions by reference, and thus included the peyote exemption, were indicated

as Alaska, Mississippi, Montana, New Jersey, North Carolina, North Dakota, Rhode Island, Tennessee, Utah, Virginia, Washington, and West Virginia. A state which exempted peyote as a matter of constitutional right to freedom of worship was California in *People v. Woody*, 61 Cal.2d 716, 40 Cal. Rptr. 69, 394 P.2d 813 (1964).

50. *Smith II*, Brief for Respondent, Appendix B, "Texas Drug Laws Including Rules Relating to the Controlled Substances Act and Schedule of Penalties Relating to Controlled Substances."

51. *Smith II*, Brief of Respondents, 37, quoting DEA Final Order of July 19, 1988, in Olsen v. Drug Enforcement Agency, 878 F.2d 1458, 1463 (D.C. Cir. 1989) (distinguishing marijuana use by the Ethiopian Coptic Church from peyote use by the Native American Church). For the same eight-year period, the DEA seized in illegal trafficking and analyzed 15,302,468.7 pounds of marijuana. *Id.*

52. *Id.* at 17.

53. *Id.* at 21.

54. *Smith I*, Tr. Oral Arg., 28:10–17 (December 8, 1987). The transcript does not identify by name which justice has asked a question or made a comment.

55. *Smith I*, Tr. Oral Arg., 31:3–16 (December 8, 1987).

56. See, for example, *Smith II*, Tr. Oral Arg., 16:9–11, 16:18–19, 17:3–7.

57. *Smith II*, Tr. Oral Arg., 41:2–5.

58. Hoffman-LaRoche, Inc. v. Kleindienst, 478 F.2d 1, 11 (3rd Cir. 1973).

59. *Smith II*, Brief Amici Curiae of Association On American Indian Affairs, et al. in Support of Respondents, 52–53; *Smith II*, 494 U.S. at 914, n.7 (Blackmun, J., dissenting).

60. 494 U.S. at 914, n.7 (Blackmun, J., dissenting).

61. Hoffman-LaRoche, Inc. v. Kleindienst, 478 F.2d at 9–11.

62. *Id.* at 9.

63. 21 U.S.C.A. Section 811(c) (1981).

64. 21 U.S.C.A. Section 812(b) (1) (1981).

65. *Smith II*, Petition for Writ of Certiorari to the Supreme Court of the State of Oregon, 13.

66. Toledo v. Nobel-Sysco, Inc., 892 F.2d 1481, 1491–92 (10th Cir. 1989) (Title VII action brought by a member of the Native American Church alleging discrimination on the basis of religion, where trucking company refused to hire him on the basis of his religious use of peyote).

67. National Organization for the Reform of Marijuana Laws v. Bell, 488 F. Supp. 123, 139 (D.D.C. 1980); U.S. v. Middleton, 690 F.2d 820, 823 (11th Cir. 1982) (psychiatrist Dr. Thomas Ungerleider testified that marijuana does not satisfy any of the Schedule I requirements); U.S. v Greene, 892 F.2d 453, 455 (6th Cir. 1989) (testimony of pharmacologist Dr. Lipman that no pharmacological basis exists for the inclusion of marijuana in Schedule I); U.S. v. Fogarty, 692 F.2d 542, 547 (8th Cir. 1982), cert. denied, 103 S.Ct. 1434 (1983) (defendant's allegation that classification of marijuana against the current weight of medical knowledge is of no moment, for the classification survives the minimal rationality test and the judgment was a political one).

68. National Organization for the Reform of Marijuana Laws v. Drug Enforcement Administration, 559 F.2d 735, 749 (D.C. Cir. 1977).

69. *Smith II*, 494 U.S. 872 (1990). Chief Justice Rehnquist and Justices White, Stevens, and Kennedy joined in Justice Scalia's opinion. Justice O'Connor filed a separate opinion in which she concurred in the result, but disagreed with (dissented from) the process by which the result had been achieved (the discarding of the compelling state interest test). Justice Blackmun filed a dissenting opinion, in which Justices Brennan and Marshall joined. These justices also joined in parts I and II, only, of Justice O'Connor's

concurrence. Thus, the case was decided by a 6-3 vote, but Scalia's opinion was supported by a 5-4 margin.

70. *Id.* at 874.

71. *Id.* at 876.

72. *Smith II*, Brief in Opposition To Petition For Certiorari, at 2, and at Appendix A.

73. *Smith I*, 455 U.S. at 674–75, 676–77 (Brennan, J., dissenting).

74. *Smith II*, Tr. Oral Arg., 42:16–21. See also *Smith II*, Brief in Opposition To Petition For Certiorari at 5–7.

75. *Smith I* 455 U.S. at 878, 882.

76. The *Sherbert* case was the first of a line of U.S. Supreme Court cases holding that unemployment benefits could not be denied to persons who were fired or had to resign when the exercise of their religious obligations was not compatible with the employer's requirements. Such a denial of benefits, according to the Court, impermissibly forced a choice between one's livelihood and one's religious obligations. Another way of stating this is that the state could not withhold a societal "safety net" from one who is fired for honoring a duty to God above a duty to an employer. See Thomas v. Review Board of the Indiana Employment Div., 450 U.S. 707 (1981) (a Jehovah's Witness who could not participate in the production of weapons), and Hobbie v. Unemployment Appeals Commission, 480 U.S. 136 (1987) (recent convert to Seventh-day Adventism who could no longer work Saturdays).

77. *Smith II*, 494 U.S. at 881–82.

78. See chapter 3 discussion of the duly ordered relationships typology.

79. *Smith II*, 494 U.S. at 888 (Court's emphasis). Note the presumption which Justice Scalia has attributed to the compelling state interest test: a presumption of invalidity. A proper casuistical analysis specifically rejects this kind of presumption as not appropriate in cases in which there is a clash of principles. Instead, both sides have the burden of coming forward with evidence. See chapter 2.

80. Madison, *The Federalist*, No. 51, 324.

81. The briefs of the Oregon attorney general, and the Court's opinion in the *Smith II* case, place great emphasis on such cases as these. The case of *Leary v. United States*, 383 F.2d 851 (5th Cir. 1967), involved the trial of Dr. Timothy Leary for marijuana possession. Leary testified that he was aware that usage of the drug was against the law, but that he possessed it for religious use and for personal scientific experimental use. The court in the case noted that Leary "believes he has both a moral and a political right to possess marihuana [sic]." *Id.* at 857. An American-born Hindu monk verified the use of marijuana by the Brahmakrishna sect, and other scientific experts testified on Leary's behalf concerning the "religious nature and character of the Millbrook Center [Leary's home, and a religious meditation and spiritual retreat center] in New York." *Id.* at 858. The court was disturbed at the prospect that someone like Leary could escape the charges and continue to lead the youth of America astray.

> It would be difficult to imagine the harm which would result if the criminal statutes were nullified as to those who claim the right to possess and traffic in this drug for religious purposes. For all practical purposes the anti-marihuana laws would be meaningless, and enforcement impossible. The danger is too great, especially to the youth of this nation, at a time when psychedelic experience, "turn on," is the "in" thing to so many, for this court to yield to the argument that the use of marihuana for so-called religious purposes should be permitted under the Free Exercise Clause. We will not, therefore, subscribe to the

dangerous doctrine that the free exercise of religion accords an unlimited freedom to violate the laws of the land relative to marihuana.

Id. at 861. Thus, using the "compelling state interest" test, the 5th Circuit had no trouble
finding that Leary's claim of religious use had to bow to the interests of the government.

The court also had little trouble discerning the fraudulent claims of the "Boo Hoos"
in the case of *United States v. Kuch*, 288 F. Supp. 439 (D.D.C. 1968). The Boo Hoos religion was founded to evade the marijuana laws; its sacred hymns, for example, included
"Row, Row, Row Your Boat." The opinion of District Court Judge Gesell noted resentment at even having to decide such a matter:

> There is abroad among some in the land today a view that the individual is free
> to do anything he wishes. A nihilistic, agnostic and anti-establishment attitude
> exists. These beliefs may be held. They may be expressed but where they are
> antithetical to the interests of others who are not of the same persuasion and
> contravene criminal statutes legitimately designed to protect society as a whole,
> such conduct should not find any constitutional sanctuary in the name of reli-
> gion or otherwise

Id. at 445–46. Gesell mistakenly believed that the founding fathers never intended there
to be any consideration given to religious actions. He bemoaned the "compelling state interest" test and longed for a return to the "pristine view" espoused in *Reynolds*. Judge
Gesell, and the Supreme Court in *Smith II*, believed that the use of the "compelling state
interest" test could only result in a *dilution* of religious protection. They contended that
society will be "helpless to protect itself" from such abusers of the system as the hapless
Boo Hoos and suffer a resulting breakdown of all legal protections. In the name of religious diversity, the Court must sacrifice some marginal believers in order to save all.

82. *Smith II*, Tr. Oral Arg., 43:9–45:6.

83. Or, at least a limited universal proscription, for the drug laws themselves contain
socially acceptable exemptions.

84. Alisdair MacIntyre, *After Virtue*, 2d. ed. (South Bend, Ind.: Univ. of Notre Dame
Press, 1984), 26.

85. *Id.*, at 34.

86, *Id.*, at 26.

87. *Id.*, at 34–35.

88. *Smith II*, 494 U.S. at 890.

89. *Id.*, at 879, quoting Reynolds v. United States, 98 U.S. at 166–67.

90. *Smith II*, 494 U.S. at 885 (citations omitted).

91. *Id.* at 889, n.5.

92. Justice Scalia appears to be putting the same question to those who use a balancing process, as Henry S. Richardson: "how their weightings are to be explained or justified. . . . [T]o the extent that the balancing is genuinely distinct from application it affords no claim to rationality, for to that extent its weightings are purely intuitive, and
therefore lack discursively expressible justification." Richardson, "Specifying Norms as a
Way to Resolve Concrete Ethical Problems," *Philosophy and Public Affairs* 19 (1990):
282–83. The Richardson article was published in the same year as the *Smith II* opinion.
James F. Childress notes that Richardson's concerns over discursive justification are only
supportable in the rare instance of "pure" balancing. Childress shows that the process of
balancing normally incorporates discursive rationality in several ways. Childress, "Moral
Norms in Practical Ethical Reflection," in Lisa Sowie Cahill and James F. Childress,

eds., *Christian Ethics: Problems and Prospects* (Cleveland: The Pilgrim Press, 1996), 213, *et seq.*

93. 494 U.S. at 902 (O'Connor, J., concurring in the judgment).

94. *Id.* at 889, n.5.

Chapter 7

1. Olmstead v. United States, 277 U.S. 438, 479 (1928) (Brandeis, J., dissenting opinion).

2. The *Wagstaffe* case, which will be discussed in thorough detail, was cited in the *Reynolds* case. In *Reynolds*, the Court distinguished *Wagstaffe* from the Mormon polygamy case because the type of coercion involved was different. In *Reynolds*, the law forbade the religiously compelled behavior, whereas in *Wagstaffe*, the law compelled behavior which was against the religious convictions of the parents. The Court in *Reynolds* thought it prudent to draw the line at the action/no action distinction; *compelling* one to act against one's conscience was possibly just too far for the law to go. Ironically, the validity of the distinction fell in the eyes of the courts when religious adherents tried to use it in their favor in faith healing cases brought in the United States.

A far more influential case than *Wagstaffe* was the decision in *People v. Pierson*, a New York case also discussed below at great length. The Jehovah's Witnesses case of *Prince v. Massachusetts* (child with her guardian selling religious literature in the street violated child labor laws), for example, relied primarily upon the opinion of the court in *Pierson*.

3. *The New York Times Index*, 1899–1901 (New York: N.Y. Times Co.), 8. In 1900, 33-1/3 percent (fourteen out of forty-two) editorials on "religious affairs" concerned faith healing.

4. *New York Times*, 19 December 1900, p. 8, col. 4.

5. See, for example, "Christian Science: Is It Infidelity?" *New York Times*, 22 April 1901, p. 5, col. 1 (subheading: Rev. Douglas preaches upon the subject, says that it menaces the morals of the young and the lives of the people); "Faith Healers Denounced: Academy of Medicine Members Discuss Christian Science," *New York Times*, 5 April 1901, p. 2, col. 3.

6. See, for example, *New York Times*, 24 June 1899, p. 2, col. 3 (report on the death of Mrs. Santiago Porcella, and the anticipated prosecution of a faith healer, Mrs. Lee of Cranford); *New York Times*, 15 April 1900, p. 14, col. 6, and 16 April 1900, p. 6, col. 5 (Dean J. Osgood, death "hastened"); *New York Times*, 30 May 1901 p. 1, col. 7 (Mrs. B. Vance dies under faith healing treatment). Indeed, the *New York Times Index* for July 1 to December 31, 1899, included a special subheading for its reportage of faith healing "failures": "Christian Science-Cases" (*Index*, at 159).

The total number of such news reports of death or "injury" cases is listed as follows in the *New York Times Index* for the years designated: 1899: 14 cases; 1900: 6 cases; 1901: 14 cases.

7. See, for example, *New York Times*, 9 May 1899, p. 5, col. 6, 11 May 1899, p. 5, col. 6, and 6 June 1899, p. 14, col. 1 (Lizzie Kranz's illness; faith cure healer M. Miller arrested); *New York Times*, 21 June 1901, p. 1, col. 2 (St. Louis healer named Barrett to be prosecuted).

8. Statutory codifications which had simply enacted the traditional common law crimes did not necessarily cure the legal problem. In the case of *Justice v. State*, 59 L.R.A. 601 (Ga. 1902), for example, defendant Sion Justice had been convicted at trial of a viola-

tion of the criminal code which required parents to furnish their children with "necessary sustenance." The court had premised the criminal conviction upon Justice's refusal to give his child medicine, based upon an unspecified "religious belief." There is no indication in the opinion as to what, if any, physical harm to the child resulted from the lack of medication.

Although the jury had found Justice guilty, the Georgia Supreme Court felt constrained to overturn his conviction. "Sustenance" under the penal code, according to the court, did not reasonably include medicine, and they could find no other provision of the criminal law under which to hold the father criminally culpable. The court noted that Justice was in no other way cruel to his children, nor did he mistreat them. In fact, a witness "testified that the defendant provided for his family in a decent and respectable manner . . . and was kind to his wife and children." *Id.*

9. Thomas McIntyre Cooley, *A Treatise on the Law of Torts or the Wrongs Which Are Independent of Contract* (Chicago: Callaghan, 1880), 84 (emphasis added). "Most conspicuous and inseparable element" means that a wrongful intent is a necessary finding in a criminal action, but such intent is not necessary to a finding of fault in a civil tort action.

10. See, for example, Frederick Pollack, *A Treatise on the Law of Torts*, New American ed., from 3d English ed. (St. Louis: F.H. Thomas Law, 1894), 33–36.

11. In Maine, for example, the common law rule was that "when the death of a human being from disease is caused or hastened by reason of the omission to call in a physician, or to provide medicine, *when such omission proceeds not from any criminal indifference to the needs of the person, but from a conscientious disbelief as to the efficacy of medicine or medical attendance*, it is not criminal negligence, and does not constitute a basis for conviction for manslaughter." State v. Sanford, 59 A. 597, 600 (Me. 1905) (emphasis added).

12. *Mens* is Latin for: "mind; intention; meaning; understanding; will." *Mens rea* is defined as "a guilty mind" or a "criminal intent" or "a guilty or wrongful purpose." *Black's Law Dictionary* (rev. 4th ed. 1968), s.v. "Mens" and "Mens rea."

13. A definition of "voluntary" manslaughter is as follows:

Voluntary manslaughter is where the act causing death is committed in the heat of sudden passion, caused by provocation. (a) The provocation must be such as the law deems adequate to excite uncontrollable passion in the mind of a reasonable man. (b) The act must be committed under and because of the passion.

William Lawrence Clark, *Hand-book of Criminal Law* (St. Paul: West Publishing Co., 1894), 165.

14. *Id.* at 172 (emphasis added).

15. "Case Note," 6 L.R.A. (N.S.) 685, 686 (1906). For authority on this issue, see the case note cited to the 1837 case, *Regina v. Smith*, 8 Car. & P. 153, in which a master who had denied food and adequate shelter to his apprentice was criminally indicted for the death of that apprentice. The case of *Gibson v. Commonwealth*, 106 Ky. 360, 50 S.W. 532 (1899) also provides a more paradigmatic example of criminal child neglect. In *Gibson*, the unwed mother of a two-month-old infant was charged with responsibility for that death, which the prosecutor claimed occurred because of abandonment. "The coroner who held the inquest testifie[d] that the child was greatly emaciated, and probably died either from starvation or exposure." 50 S.W. at 532. The Kentucky Court of Appeals (Kentucky's highest state court) in this case noted: "The law imposed upon defendant the duty of protecting and caring for her offspring to the best of her ability; and when she wilfully

abandoned it on a cold, raw night, and left it to die from exposure, she was guilty of a felony. . . ." *Id.*

16. 10 Cox Crim. Cas. 530 (Cent. Crim. Ct. 1868).

17. *Id.* at 531.

18. *Id.* at 531–32.

19. The text reads: "Is any among you sick? Let him call for the elders of the church, and let them pray over him, anointing him with oil in the name of the Lord; and the prayer of faith will save the sick man and the Lord will raise him up." James 5:14–15 (RSV).

20. Regina v. Wagstaffe, 10 Cox Crim. Cas. at 533–34.

21. *Id.* at 532 (emphasis added).

22. *Id.* at 533. The judge by way of example questioned the use of faith healing to the extent that it would be used to set a broken leg, indicating that this could reach the afore-mentioned absurd point. Judge Willis's charge may appear to the reader to be quite vague and imprecise: How does one determine whether the situation in *Wagstaffe* is more like a "broken leg" and hence an absurdity, or an honest alternative type of care? It is helpful to consider the evidence which Judge Willes allowed the jury to consider on the issues of absurdity and insanity — the surgeon's testimony as well as the parents' and their church's own experiences and "empirical" testimony.

A reader might be tempted to distinguish this case on the basis that the use of an-timonial wine to cure anything was manifestly absurd and thus the Court was lenient be-cause of the state of medical science at the time. I note, again, that a medical expert testi-fied for the prosecution that the child would have gotten better had a doctor attended to it. We should not attribute, anachronistically, our current knowledge of medicine to Judge Willes or to the jury which refused to convict Mr. Wagstaffe.

23. *Id.* at 533 (emphasis added).

24. *Id.* at 530–31, 532–34 (emphasis added). Interestingly, the prosecutor's unsuccess-ful argument in *Wagstaffe* mirrors the free exercise standard accepted and adopted by the U.S. Supreme Court in *Reynolds*. Yet, the Court in *Reynolds* had distinguished the *Wagstaffe* case (which was, of course, favorable to the religious claimant) as not relevant to the Mormon situation.

25. 176 N.Y. 201, 68 N.E. 243 (1903).

26. 68 N.E. at 244.

27. Although the Christian Catholic Church gets barely a mention in general sur-vey texts of American religious history, this group was receiving extraordinary attention at the time the *Pierson* matter was going through the courts. The founder of the church, Alexander Dowie, first attracted attention with his healing services at the 1893 World Par-liament of Religions in Chicago. He soon became embroiled in controversy for his dis-avowal of medicine in favor of faith healing, and he was attacked by the *Chicago Tribune* in 1895 (and subsequently arrested quite frequently) for practicing medicine without a li-cense. Dowie founded the city (Martin Marty calls it a "theocratic empire") of Zion, Illi-nois (north of Chicago), and within two years Zion attracted ten thousand lessees. Within Dowie, however, were the seeds of both the success and the destruction for this religious group. According to Martin Marty, his followers ultimately rejected him as a "paranoid swindler." Martin E. Marty, *Modern American Religion, Volume One: The Irony of it All, 1893–1919* (Chicago: Univ. of Chicago Press, 1986), 243–44.

It is tempting to dismiss and even ridicule this group for the human failings of its founder. But certainly those who followed the tenets of the Christian Catholic Church were sincere and one cannot easily dismiss the power of the numerous testimonies of the adherents as to healings which occurred. As noted in Marty's book, "Buffalo Bill's niece praised [Dowie] for adding three inches to her shortened leg." *Id.* at 243.

28. *People v. Pierson*, 68 N.E. at 244 (emphasis added).

29. *Id.* at 244.

30. *Id.* at 245. The court states, for example, that

[a]t the Lateran Council of the Church, held at the beginning of the thirteenth century, physicians were forbidden, under the pain of expulsion from the church, to undertake medical treatment without calling in a priest; and as late as 250 years thereafter Pope Pius V renewed the command of Pope Innocent by enforcing the penalties. The curing by miracles, or by interposition of Divine power, continued throughout Christian Europe during the entire period of the Middle Ages, and was the mode of treating sickness recognized by the church."

Id. 68 at 245.

31. *Id.* at 245–46 (emphasis on "civilized" added).

32. *Id.* at 244.

33. *Id.* at 246 (emphasis added).

34. *New York Times*, 23 May 1901, p. 8, col. 5.

35. *Id.* p. 2, col. 4.

36. "Faith Curist Convicted," *New York Times*, 22 May 1901, p. 1, col. 3.

37. "Faith Curist's Son Dead Now," *New York Times*, 24 May 1901, p. 6, col. 1.

At Mr. Pierson's trial, the Westchester County corner, Dr. John A. Shaefmaster, testified that the deceased child "had whooping cough which developed into bronchial pneumonia," and that she died (in February 1901) "of bronchial pneumonia or catarrhal pneumonia, both are the same." *Pierson*, Record of Trial on Appeal, pp. 8–9 (transcript of trial testimony). The pneumonia, according to Pierson's testimony, came upon the child the last 36 to 48 hours before her death, when she suddenly worsened, and during that time he and his wife "were both with her night and day." "It was the best I could do. . . . I did not send for a phsician because I believe in prayer and by faith God will save the sick. I believed that my prayer would cure the child and I cannot answer why it did not. That is one of the unexplicable [*sic*] things." In fact, as noted in the text, Pierson believed that if they called in a physician, "instead of the child being saved, it would surely die." Pierson then testified, "No, I did not believe the child was dying. I believed that God would raise her up almost to the last moment and then like a great many other fathers when seeing the dear one turn away from them, I weakened as I felt the little one slip away from my grasp, and it broke my heart." *Id.* at 14–15, 17.

Dr. Charles E. Birch testified that "Catarrhal pneumonia is recognized as curable by medicine and also whooping cough. [Question from the prosecutor:] Whooping cough cures itself? [Birch's response:] Yes; it runs a limited course." Dr. Birch later testified, however, that "whooping cough is not always curable. . . . If the child had had the best medical treatment it is possible then that the child might have died." *Id.* at 12, 13, 14. Indeed, the newspaper account indicated that Pierson's son died in May 1901 of the same illness as his daughter. Keep in mind that it wasn't until 1906 that medical science isolated the B. pertussis organism that causes whooping cough. James Cherry notes that "[i]n the 1930's pertussis vaccines were used both to prevent pertussis and for treatment. During this period, different types of vaccines were experimented with, and some were found to be efficacious." James D. Cherry, "Historical Review of Pertussis and the Classical Vaccine," *The Journal of Infectious Diseases* 174, suppl 3: (1996): S259-63, 60 (emphasis added). Antibiotics, of course, would also not come into use for several decades. What options in the general 1901 time period did medical doctors have in treating whooping cough developing into bronchial pneumonia? A review of the 1916 catalogue-index of the U.S. surgeon general's Medical Library, indexing international medical journal articles from the nineteenth century through 1916, included reports on the use of the following treatments for whooping cough: by abdominal bandage, with antiseptics, with hypnotics and sedatives, with belladonna (and cannabis), with bromoform, with chloroform, with compressed air, with ozone and oxygen, with morphine and opiates, with quinine, by rectal injections of CO_2, by sulphurous acid fumigation, etc. *Index—Catalogue of the Library of the Surgeon General's Office, United States Army,* second series, vol 21 (Washington, D.C.: U.S. Government Printing Office, 1916), 84–103. A medical encyclopedia copyrighted in 1919 gave the following information on whooping cough: "The direct cause of whooping cough is unknown. . . . Statistics show that it is the most fatal of all diseases of children under one year, that sixty-eight per cent of the deaths from whooping cough occur under the age of two. . . ." The following remedies are recommended: quinine sulphate, lemon and honey, and a wrap made up of a pad soaked in a mixture of thymol, sassafras, eucalyptol, turpentine, ether, alcohol, liquid tar, and pepermint oil, among other remedies. J. L. Corish, M.D., ed., *Health Knowledge: A Thorough and Concise Knowledge of the Prevention, Causes, and Treatments of Disease, Simplified for Home Use,* vol. 1 (New York: Medical Book Distributors c. 1919, 1926), 437–441. Bronchial pneumonia, listed as a potentially fatal complication of whooping cough, is recomended to be treated by the use of an emetic of tartar or ipecac, followed by a purgative of Epsom salts. Sweating should be promoted by tincture of aconite or tincture of veratrum viride. *Id.* at 691. It is within this general context that a medical doctor unsuccessfully treated Pierson's son and that Pierson treated his daughter with loving care and prayer and was jailed for her death.

38. Editorial, *New York Times,* 24 May 1901, p. 8, col. 5.

39. See generally Marty, *Modern American Religion, supra.*

40. Sydney E. Ahlstrom, *A Religious History of the American People* (New Haven: Yale Univ. Press, 1972), 731 *et seq.*

41. *New York Times,* 29 July 1899, p. 6, col. 4. One wonders how this controversy reached such a crisis point in mid summer, when school is normally adjourned.

The term "Quimby-Eddyism" refers to Mary Baker Eddy, founder of Christian Science, and to Phineas P. Quimby, a nineteenth-century hypnotherapist who practiced mental/spiritual healing methods. See generally Phineas Parkhurst Quimby, *The Quimby Manuscripts,* ed. Horatio W. Dresser (New York: T.Y. Crowell, 1921).

42. *New York Times,* 5 February 1900, p. 6, col. 4.

43. *New York Times,* 17 December 1900, p. 7, col. 3.

44. Editorial, *New York Times,* 14 October 1900, p. 20, col. 5.

45. Mark Twain, *Christian Science* (New York: Harper, 1907; repr., Buffalo: Prometheus Books, 1986), 43. A footnote by Twain to the above quote indicates that he wrote these estimates in 1899, and believed in 1907, when published in book form, that these estimates were still "not far out." *Id.*

46. V. Doyno, foreword to *Christian Science,* iv.

47. *New York Times,* 12 June 1901, p. 1, col. 2. Note that Pierson was tried and convicted on or about May 21, 1901, and that at this point his appeal was pending before a higher court.

48. *New York Times,* 17 June 1901, p. 1, col. 3.

49. *New York Times,* 1 February 1903, p. 1, col. 3.

50. *New York Times,* 16 February 1903, p. 9, col. 1.

51. *New York Times,* 27 September 1903, p. 31, col. 1.

52. *New York Times,* 14 October 1903, p. 1, col. 3, and p. 1, col. 5. Note that both of these stories headlined the front page of the *Times* that day. Compare these with the court's opinion, as noted in detail above, which castigated Pierson for the "slaying" of his son and criticized religion's historic interference with the progress of science.

53. *New York Times*, 20 October 1903, p. 1, col 7. This headline proclaimed, "HOS-TILE AUDIENCE HOWLS AT DOWIE: Proclamation of Himself as Elijah Nearly causes Riot; 'Restorer' Heaps Abuse on Press and Clergy, Denounces Freemasons, and Raves at Listeners Who Decline To Stay."

54. *New York Times*, 22 October 1903, p. 3, col. 1.

55. Walter I. Wardwell, "Chiropractors: Evolution to Acceptance" in Norman Gevitz, ed., *Other Healers: Unorthodox Medicine in America* (Baltimore: Johns Hopkins Univ. Press, 1988), 157.

56. See, for example, Paul Starr, *The Social Transformation of American Medicine* (New York: Basic Books, 1982); Charles E. Rosenberg and Janet Golden, eds., *Facing Disease: Studies in Cultural History* (New Brunswick, N.J.: Rutgers Univ. Press, 1992); Charles E. Rosenberg, *No Other Gods: On Science and American Social Thought* (Baltimore: Johns Hopkins Press, 1976); Harris Livermore Coulter, *Political and Social Aspects of Nineteenth-century Medicine in the United States: The Formation of the American Medical Association And Its Struggle With Homeopathic and Eclectic Physicians* (Master's Thesis, Columbia University, 1971).

57. Norman Gevitz, "Three Perspectives on Orthodox Medicine" in Gevite, ed., *Other Healers*, 8, 16.

58. *Id.* at 16–17; Norman Gevitz, "Osteopathic Medicine: From Deviance to Difference," in Gevitz, *Other Healers*, 132–33, *et seq.*

59. Walker v. Superior Court, 47 Cal.3d 112, 136, 253 Cal. Rptr. 1, 16–17 (1988). The reference to *"Hines"* was to the English case of *Regina v. Hines*, 80 Cent. Crim. Ct. 309 (1874), which ruled as a matter of law that defendant parent was not criminally negligent for relying on prayer for healing treatment. The modern *Walker* court dismissed the reasoning in this case (which was favorable to the defendant) by declaring the decision an act of prescience by the English court in recognizing the inadequacy of England's then-modern medicine. This interpretation, however, is highly questionable. The court in *Hines* deliberately declined to follow a statute imposing on parents the duty to seek medical attention for their children. This statute was enacted in response to the jury's dismissal, in the aforementioned 1868 English case of *Regina v. Wagstaffe*, of a parent accused of criminal negligence for reliance upon healing by prayer instead of upon the common medical practices of the day. That the court in *Hines*, in the absence of a free exercise constitutional protection, would have disregarded a legislative assessment that one should seek medical attention based upon the court's own superior *knowledge* that prayer would be better than the medical attention of the day, is remote. More likely, the *Hines* court had a sense that one should not be criminally charged for the death of a child because one in faith and sincerity followed one's religious beliefs.

60. Dr. David Eddy, director, Duke University Center For Health Policy Research, in the *San Jose Mercury News*, 18 February 1990, p. 23A, col. 1, quoted in Note, *"Walker v. Superior Court*: Religious Convictions May Bring Felony Convictions," *Pacific Law Journal* 21 (1990): 1069, 1101 n.278.

61. An *amicus curiae* brief was submitted to the court in *Walker* by the First Church of Christ, Scientist. This brief concluded with the following paragraph, which highlights the discordance the church sees when devout parents are criminalized for practicing their religion:

This case admittedly poses troubling and emotional issues for the Court. The death of any child is a tragic loss, and one which is felt by no one more than by parents who loved and cared for their child as best they could. Each day in this State, parents lose children to disease and sickness, most in hospitals or under the care of medical doctors who work unsuccessfully to save them through medical science. Those parents bear quietly the grief of their great loss. In these proceedings [the *amicus* brief was submitted for two cases proceeding about the same time], the tragedies of two children's deaths have been compounded by the prosecution of parents who deeply loved and cared for their child, and who believed sincerely that they were doing what was best for the health and recovery of their child. The actions of those Christian Science parents, taken in good faith and in accordance with deeply-held religious beliefs, is not the sort of conduct to which the manslaughter or felony child abuse statutes of this State were directed.

"*From* Brief of *Amicus Curiae* on Behalf of The First Church of Christ, Scientist," in *Freedom and Responsibility: Christian Science Healing for Children* (Boston: First Church of Christ, Scientist, 1989), 65.

62. Walker v. Superior Court, 47 Cal.3d 112, 139; 253 Cal. Rptr. 1, 19 (1988).

63. Prince v. Massachusetts, 321 U.S. 158, 170 (1944) (denial of free exercise claim of followers of Jehovah's Witnesses that religious beliefs dictated that their children assist them in selling religious literature in the street in violation of child labor laws).

64. 253 Cal. Rptr. at 21.

65. Note, "*Walker v. Superior Court*: Religious Convictions May Bring Felony Convictions," *Pacific Law Journal.* 21 (1990): 1069, 1101–02.

66. *Id.* at 1102, n.279.

67. *Id.*

68. *Id.* at 29.

69. *Id.* at 30.

70. Comment, "Faith-Healing and Religious-Treatment Exemptions To Child Endangerment Laws: Should Parental Religious Practices Excuse the Failure To Provide Necessary Medical Care To Children?" *University of Dayton Law Review.* 13 (1987): 79, 106.

71. *Id.* at 79.

72. Paula A. Monopoli, "Allocating the Costs of Parental Free Exercise: Striking a New Balance Between Sincere Religious Belief and a Child's Right To Medical Treatment," *Pepperdine Law Review.* 18 (1991): 319. Monopoli goes on to describe the Massachusetts Christian Science faith healing case involving the Twitchell family.

73. Charles Taylor, *Sources of the Self: The Making of the Modern Identity* (Cambridge, Mass.: Harvard Univ. Press, 1989), 410.

74. "Numerous writers have noted that Mary Baker Eddy falsified information about her age, her marriages, and a host of other details about her private life." Gevitz, "Three Perspectives on Unorthodox Medicine," in Gevitz, ed., *Other Healers*, 13. Mrs. Eddy was subject to numerous plagiarism charges which also were aimed at branding her method of healing with the label "dishonest":

> Orthodox physicians further argued that these individuals ["unorthodox" medical practitioners] laid claims to theories and practices of others without acknowledgement. . . . Mary Baker Eddy's discovery, despite her protestations to the contrary, was said to be simply a variation of a system developed by her mentor, Phineas Parkhurst Quimby—a magnetic healer.

Id. These charges were either denied or explained by Mrs. Eddy and her supporters.

75. See, for example, Rennie B. Schoepflin, "Christian Science Healing in America" in Gevitz, ed., *Other Healers*, 196 ("to practitioners it [Christian Science] of-

fered the possibility of a profitable vocation"), at 200 (references to "drum[ming] up business," fee charging, and "financial edge" on competitors), and at 205 (the undercutting of the livelihood of practitioners). The chapter article on other forms of faith healing also referred to personal advantages of power and wealth. David Edwin Harrell, Jr., "Divine Healing in Modern American Protestantism," in Gevitz, ed., *Other Healers*, 219 (an imitator of Oral Roberts was motivated by Roberts's power over the audience), 220–22 (references to "slick" publications, the raising of large sums of money, and business talents of preachers).

76. David J. Hufford, "Contemporary Folk Medicine" in Gevitz, ed., *Other Healers*, 248.

77. *Id.*

78. Monopoli, "Allocating the Costs," 333.

Monopoli herself expresses moral outrage at the existence of the faith healing exemptions. She denounces them as "clearly the result of lobbying efforts by a very powerful special interest group, the Christian Science Church." According to Monopoli, such exemptions for nondominant religious practices would be legitimate only if they were the result of "a groundswell of feeling." *Id.* at 334.

79. Note, *"Walker v. Superior Court*: Religious Convictions May Bring Felony Convictions," *Pacific Law Journal* 21 (1990): 1069, 1102.

80. See, for example, James F. Childress, *Who Should Decide? Paternalism in Health Care* (New York: Oxford Univ. Press, 1982), 3–9.

81. William F. May, *The Physician's Covenant: Images of the Healer in Medical Ethics* (Philadelphia: Westminster Press, 1983), 18.

82. *Id.* at 25–26.

83. Prince v. Massachusetts, 321 U.S. 158 (1944) (Jehovah's Witnesses' religiously motivated practice of having their children assist them in distributing their church literature violated child labor laws).

84. See generally Joseph M. Hawes, *The Children's Rights Movement: A History of Advocacy and Protection* (Boston: Twayne Publishers, 1991). Hawes has a generally positive view of the modern developments in the field of children's rights. Cf. Michael King and Christine Piper, *How the Law Thinks About Children* (Brookfield, Vt.: Gower, 1991). King and Piper contend that the law constructs artificial concepts of the child which conflict: for example, "the child as a bundle of needs" or "the child as bearer of rights." "Children, it seems, are to be treated differently . . . depending upon the role they are to play in the legal proceedings. Child victims are different people from child offenders." *Id.* at 56, 59.

85. King and Piper, *How the Law Thinks* 70 (their emphasis). They continue, "For law, the problem is not so much one of designing institutions capable of enforcing children's rights (as some authors would have us believe), but of generating universally accepted concepts which are able to take decision-makers beyond the simplicity of rights discourse." *Id.* at 70 (footnote omitted).

86. Taylor, *Sources of the Self*, 35.

87. *Id.* at 35.

88. Prov. 22:6 (RSV).

89. Taylor, *Sources of the Self*, 35–36.

90. *Id.*, at 36 (emphasis added).

91. Prov. 20:11 (RSV).

92. Twain, *Christian Science*, 39.

93. Regarding the difficulties which arise when one attempts to understand another's worldview without first upturning one's own normative assumptions, see Marilyn

Strathern, *The Gender of the Gift: Problems With Women and Problems With Society in Melanesia* (Berkeley: Univ. of California Press, 1988), especially at 4.

94. Richard A. Nenneman, *The New Birth of Christianity: Why Religion Persists in a Scientific Age* (San Francisco: HarperSanFrancisco, 1992), 153–54.

95. DeWitt John, *The Christian Science Way of Life* (Englewood Cliffs, N.J.: Prentice Hall, 1962), 18.

96. The comparison to mathematical principles is also helpful in explaining the freedom of the Christian Scientist in spiritual healing matters. Prosecutors have made much of the fact that Christian Scientists are not "coerced" (whatever that means) by the church to refrain from using medical doctors to treat illnesses. The prosecutors have used this to argue that Christian Scientists are thus free to use allopathic medicine to cure their illnesses. But the lack of coercion by the church is simply a respect by the church for the autonomy of each individual's spiritual choice; it does *not* mean that allopathic medicine is at all compatible with Christian Science spirituality. A person, for example, is equally free to apply the principles of mathematics incorrectly and arrive at the wrong answer. The point is that if a person wishes to arrive at a correct and useful answer/result, she will correctly apply the principle. And once a person has demonstrated to herself the usefulness of applying the principle correctly, while she is still certainly free to apply it incorrectly or even to abandon it, why would anyone want to do so?

97. Christian Science Publishing Society, *A Century of Christian Science Healing* (Boston: 1966), 241 (hereafter cited as *Century*).

98. At one Wednesday service which I attended several years ago during research for this chapter, I heard testimonials of the healing of pets, as well as a healing of financial affairs, for example.

99. The church has stringent requirements of authentication for these testimonials. Each witness of a healing must be supported by three affidavits from those with personal knowledge of the facts and situation described in the testimonial. One member of the Christian Science Committee on Publication wrote:

> Over the twenty-year period from 1969 to 1988, for example, *The Christian Science Journal* and the *Christian Science Sentinel* published over 7,100 testimonies of physical healings. While these accounts are definitely religious documents rather than clinical histories, some 2,338 of the healings described involved medically diagnosed conditions. In many more cases the testimonies implied that there had been diagnosis but did not specifically state it. Many— literally hundreds—of the diagnoses involved x-rays or were confirmed by second opinions by specialists or other physicians.

David N. Williams, "Viewpoint: Christian Science and the Care of Children: Constitutional Issues," *Church and State* (September 1989): 19.

100. *Id.* at 19–20. Williams readily notes,

> Obviously, these healings represent a body of individual cases rather than controlled experimental results. By its sheer volume and variety, however, this body of cases underscores the fact that healing in Christian Science has been regular and tangible—not the exception—and that it cannot be dismissed as merely "doing nothing" or waiting on natural processes.

Id.

101. *Century*, 240.
102. Williams, "Viewpoint," 19.
103. *Id.* at 20.

104. *Century*, 237, 238.
105.

Thinking of God as Truth helps one to see the logic of calling this religion Science. Laws derived from divine Truth—that is, truths expressing the divine order—can be known, understood and demonstrated. It is this demonstration to which the Scientist devotes his prayer and his energies. Knowing that all the goodness and glories of God's wondrous creation are universally true, and knowing that everything true is essentially demonstrable, he views this demonstration as a practical possibility to be realized progressively through spiritual growth. He views this not only as the most satisfying of all life-goals, but also *as the very essence of salvation.*

Dewitt John, *The Christian Science Way of Life*, 46 (emphasis added).

106. Mary Baker Eddy, *Science and Health With Key to the Scriptures* (Boston: First Church of Christ, Scientist, 1994), 9:32 [page:line] (emphasis added).

107. *Id*. at 40:28–30, 11:29–32 (emphasis added).

108. See, for example, Michael Wald, "State Intervention on Behalf of 'Neglected' Children: A Search For Realistic Standards," *Stanford Law Review* 27 (1975): 985 (values the principle of family autonomy and privacy, and recommends limited intervention according to its potential for actual usefulness); Note, "Choosing For Children: Adjudicating Medical Care Disputes Between Parents and the State," *New York University Law Review* 58. (1983): 157 (authored by Elizabeth Sher) (court should "balance" the interests of the state, the child, and the parent, and impose the least restrictive requirements which protect the child and yet preserve the integrity of the family unit); Recent Decisions, "Medical Dependency In Arizona: The 'Known Medical Danger' Standard of *In Re Cochise County Juvenile Action No. 5666-J*," *Arizona Law Review* 25 (1983): 769 (suggests routine school screening program for health concerns, and temporary custody of the child taken by the state where a medical danger is found to be present); Note, "Parental Failure To Provide Child With Medical Assistance Based on Religious Beliefs Causing Child's Death—Involuntary Manslaughter in Pennsylvania," *Dickinson Law Review* 90 (1986): 861 (authored by Daniel J. Kearney) (proposed spiritual healing amendment which clearly exempts parents who used this treatment in good faith from criminal prosecution, but yet allows for court ordering of medical care where a child's life is in danger or "where there is a threat of harm to the public welfare"); Christine A. Clark, "Religious Accommodation and Criminal Liability," *Florida State University Law Review* 17 (1990): 559 (Florida's statutory exemption for faith healing should be rewritten to provide unambiguous protection).

109. Christian Reichel Van Deusen, "The Best Interest of the Child and the Law," *Pepperdine Law Review* 18 (1991): 417, 445.

110. *Id*. at 445.

111. See, for example, *Family Challenges, Family Healing* (n.p.: Christian Science Publishing Society, 1989), 48–64 (testimonies by children and by adults about their childhood experiences); *Parents, Children, and God's Omnipotent Care* (Boston: Christian Science Publishing Society, 1987), 5–6, 11–13; *What Prayer Does* (Boston: Christian Science Publishing Society, 1991) (testimonies from children); *Children of Light* (Boston: Christian Science Publishing Society, 1945).

112. For example, if a local church which practices faith healing in the form of simple, fatalistic reliance on God's inscrutable will (which may or may not be in favor of a child's healing) has a history of communicable and serious childhood illnesses going untreated with serious health damage to the children, it bears close governmental scrutiny

and civil intervention actions. These actions, as suggested by law review articles mentioned *supra*, should not stigmatize the group and should be undertaken with respect for the families. The distinction between this type of situation and that of a Christian Science community would be the lack of a good "track record" of healings and a lack of a holistically healthy lifestyle. Only in rare circumstances, however, should a criminal action be undertaken against otherwise loving, attentive, and caring parents.

113. Childress, *Who Should Decide?* 102.

114. *Id.*

115. *Id.* at 102–05. Childress notes:

> There should be a moral presumption—parallel to the accepted legal presumption—of an adult's competence to make decisions in health care. Then the burden of proof should fall on those who believe that a particular individual is incompetent. . . . We should presume competence and test for incompetence.

Id. at 104–05.

116. *Id.* at 106 (emphasis added).

117. *Id.* at 164. A notable dissenting voice on this issue is Paul Ramsey, who deems the right to refuse treatment as only a relative right. In essence, Ramsey holds that anyone who refuses "medically indicated treatments" is by definition incompetent. Ramsey's position is explained thus by Childress:

> Paul Ramsey has argued that the right of refusal is only a "relative right": "There are medically indicated treatments (these used to be called 'ordinary') that a competent conscious patient has no moral right to refuse, just as no one has a moral right deliberately to ruin his health." [Footnote to Paul Ramsey, *Ethics at the Edges of Life: Medical and Legal Intersections* (New Haven: Yale Univ. Press, 1978), 156.] Thus, Ramsey would justify strong paternalistic interventions at least under some conditions. For him, the right of refusal is relative to medical indications for treatment of a patient who is not dying. The important medical line is between dying and non-dying. . . . For the non-dying, there is an obligation to use medically indicated treatments to save life. This obligation falls both on the patient and the professional.

Id. at 164–65.

118. Indeed, even the use of the term "paternalism" is fraught with images of a parent deciding for the child. Note Childress's introductory remarks and explanations of the term paternalism and note the metaphoric power behind it:

> In discussions of paternalism in politics or health care, the social role of the father is used as an analogue for the social role of government or health care provider. This familial analogy is used to interpret or to legitimate another social role. . . . When paternalism is used to illuminate or to legitimate the role of the professional or the state in health care, two features of the paternal role are prominent. First, the father's motives, intentions, and actions are assumed to be benevolent; they are aimed at his children's welfare. Second, he makes all or at least some of the decisions regarding their welfare rather than letting them make these decisions. . . . [I]ndeed, the beneficiary of the paternalist's actions may even explicitly oppose those actions.

Id. at 4.

119. *Id.* at 105 (emphasis in original).

120. *Id.* at 111 (emphasis in original), citing to Rosemary Carter, "Justifying Paternalism," *Canadian Journal of Philosophy* 7 (March 1977): 138.

121. Childress, *Who should Decide?* 112.

122. *Id.* at 107–08.

123. *Id.* at 109. Under the conclusive presumption which is typically accorded the state in the criminal child abuse/neglect cases, for example, these matters have been wrongfully ignored in favor of a mythic, paternalistic benevolence attached to the notion of medical science.

124. *Id.* at 111.

125. *Id.* at 166.

126. *Id.* at 113.

127. And, indeed, prosecutors in criminal cases have offered narratives of what the suffering child must have gone through without medical intervention, a distorted focus which many medical treatments and procedures would in turn not survive. (Consider, for example, a narrative of a cancer patient's ordeal during a chemotherapy course which was not successful.)

Chapter 8

1. Kenneth E. Kirk, *Conscience and Its Problems: An Introduction To Casuistry*, with an introduction by David H. Smith (Louisville, Ky.: Westminster John Knox Press, 1999; repr.; London: Longmans, Green, 1927), 128.

2. *Id.* at 123. Indeed, Kirk offers the following admonition to those who espouse the virtues of rigorism and absolutism:

> With them [the "high principled"] it is often a matter of conscience to maintain the rigor of the law at all costs; they adhere obstinately to the parrot-cry (— the "slogan," in the pet phrase of modern journalism—) of the original definition. Like Austin Feverel, every rigorist is "morally superstitious"; he makes of his "system of aphorisms" a fetish whose cult he dare not mitigate.

Id.

Index

analogy, use of, 13, 17, 22–25, 29, 36, 42, 120–121, 122–123, 128–131, 133–135, 157, 179, 183–184

anarchy, threat of, vii, 46, 65–68, 75, 86, 88, 91, 92, 97, 98, 105–106, 142, 143, 145–148, 188

Aristotle, 40–41, 46

Arras, John D., 47

Augustine, 60–63, 76

authoritarianism, vii, 11, 15, 39, 188. *See also* duly ordered relationships type

Backus, Isaac, 75, 87, 89–94

Barnette case. *See* West Virginia Board of Education v. Barnette

bible, uses as authority, 4, 14, 20, 24, 51–54, 56–62, 65, 66, 68–69, 70, 74, 76, 78, 90–94, 153, 158

burden of proof, 42–45, 105, 107. *See also* presumptions

Calvin, John, 63–64

Cantwell v. Connecticut, 12–14, 15, 43, 59, 186

casuistry
  application of, 39–47, 80–82, 98, 118–148, 149–185
  hindrances to, 99–108, 109–117, 168–173
  see also analogy; context; paradigm

centrality of belief, 105–107, 146–147

Chandler v. James, 190 n.12

children and free exercise, 14, 25–28, 30–33, 44, 77, 104, 141, 149–185

Childress, James, 181–184

"Christian country," meanings of the phrase, 96–97

Christian Science, 105, 164–185. *See also* healing, religious; *Walker v. Superior Court*

Church of Christ, Scientist. *See* Christian Science

Church of Jesus Christ of Latter-day Saints. *See* polygamy

Church of the Lukumi Babalu Aye, Inc. v. City of Hialeah, 34–38, 245 n.16, 246 n.18

City of Boerne v. Flores, ix, 37–38, 186

communal functionalism, 53–54, 88

context
  court's examination of, 9–10, 17–18, 24, 28–29, 30–31, 35–36, 41, 46
  of religious healing cases, 149–185
  of the *Smith* case, 118–148

deviance, social, 112–115. *See also* panic, societal

Dowie, Alexander, 162–163

duly ordered relationships type, 49, 56, 59–68, 69, 75, 78, 79, 87, 90, 91, 96–97, 125, 142, 148, 186